LOOKING BACK

LOOKING BACK

On Faith, Philosophy and Friends in Oxford

by

BASIL MITCHELL

The Memoir Club

© Basil Mitchell 2009

First published in 2009 by
The Memoir Club
Arya House
Langley Park
Durham
DH7 9XE
Tel: 0191 373 5660
Email: memoirclub@msn.com

British Library Cataloguing in
Publication Data.
A catalogue record for this book
is available from the
British Library

ISBN: 978-1-84104-203-9

Typeset by TW Typesetting, Plymouth, Devon
Printed by Good News Press Ltd, Ongar, Essex CM5 9RX

To Margy

Contents

List of Illustrations

Preface

This is a memoir in what I take to be the root meaning of the word, an account of my life based on memory. I have not undertaken any serious research, but, whenever I have been able to check it, my memory has proved fairly trustworthy. The work is a product of my old age and may show defects that follow from that. This being so, I am particularly grateful to two people. The first version was typed by Mary Banbury and in the later stages Pam Manix not only provided the electronic manuscript, but undertook organization badly needed. I am also grateful to Clare Richards and Bill Knight who designed the cover.

I was greatly helped by John and Morar Lucas who each read the whole book and gave me comments on it; and by Harriet Harris who encouraged me to continue in the early stages, when I was hesitating about the project.

I have dedicated it to my wife who not only put up with my preoccupation while writing it, but supported me devotedly throughout most of the life described in it.

CHAPTER 1

Childhood

OURS WAS A HAPPY CHILDHOOD. I say 'ours' advisedly, because I
cannot remember a time when I was not accompanied by my
sister Betty. Betty was eighteen months younger, but, of course, my
earliest memories do not go as far back as when she was born. What
are my earliest memories? Here there is a problem which always
affects long term memories. Do I actually remember something or do
I remember some later occasion of remembering it? One way or the
other I remember sharing a bath with my mother, which can only
have been when I was very small. I also remember her singing to me
'Lavenders blue diddle, diddle lavenders green' to get me to sleep
(although neither then nor at any other time have I had difficulty in
sleeping). Sometime early on I remember being struck by the beauty
of flowers, celandines on the bank of our garden in Lyncombe Vale.

We lived in Bath in the parish of Widcombe until I was seven. It
was, and still is, almost in the country. There was a row of
semi-detached houses on one side of the road along the bottom of a
deep valley. Opposite was a steep meadow forming one side of the
valley. The houses were villas built of Bath stone and dating, I
imagine, from the 19th century. We were taken for walks of which
I remember only two. One was down the road to the right which
led under a railway bridge. From there we climbed into a field from
which, if we were lucky, we could watch a train pulled by GWR
engines double-banked up the steep ascent. My present-day map of
Bath shows no such railway but there is one in a map of North
Somerset which refers to 'the late King George V'. The other walk
was up to Widcombe and down Widcombe Hill past the station and
along the Bristol road. There on the right were flour mills where
from time to time sacks of flour were lifted or lowered from hoists
projecting from the gables. This was a source of endless fascination.

At, I suppose, the age of five I was sent to a dame school in
Widcombe about which I remember only two things. One was that
on the way I had to pass Widcombe Church and was so scared by

the gargoyles that I used to shut my eyes and run until they were safely past. The other was the golden ringlets of the hair of the girl I shared my desk with. It seems that I went to and from school on my own.

Our family was firmly rooted in Bath. My grandparents on my father's side lived at Gillingham Terrace below Camden Road off Snow Hill. (My father as a boy used to sing in the choir at Walcot Church.) Theirs was a terrace house with views at the back over Bathampton Down and Sham Castle, a noted landmark which Betty and I had to identify as soon as we arrived to make sure it was still there.

I remember my grandfather as a small old man who, in spite of a generally unimpressive appearance, managed to assume a distinctly patriarchal air. He had been a compositor on the local paper and, in his day, a champion road walker. His chief enthusiasm, shared by my father and three uncles, was Bath Rugby Football Club (not the power then that it was later to become). After the game each Saturday they all met for tea at 4 Gillingham Terrace and revisited the game in a spirit of lively controversy. The problem was that they sat by tradition in different parts of the ground (my father even then sat more grandly than the rest in the West Stand). Hence they saw the game from different angles and there were heated discussions as to whether a score had been from a forward pass or whether an opposing player had really grounded the ball. The whole family (but not, I think, my grandparents) were musical and the only occasion that the front parlour was used was on a Sunday evening when they would gather round the piano and take it in turn to sing their favourite piece.

My grandmother, whom Betty and I were distinctly in awe of and never really took to, was a trained nurse and midwife with an established reputation in the neighbourhood. She had a pursed mouth which she only occasionally relaxed into a smile, but it must have been largely her own doing that the four sons and two daughters were conspicuously hard working and set themselves uniformly high standards. Betty and I always knew that with 'Lambridge Nanny' we had to be on our best behaviour (so-called to distinguish her from 'Kingston Nanny').

My grandparents on my mother's side had also lived in Bath for a while at Frankley Buildings, only a few hundred (very steep) yards from Gillingham Terrace. By now they had been at Kingston, near Corfe Castle, since before the War. My grandfather, whom I scarcely remember, died of cancer in the early nineteen twenties. He and my grandmother were born and brought up in Spaxton, a village in the Quantocks not far from Nether Stowey. Alfred Loxston came of a family of stonemasons and was himself a stonemason and a small builder who specialised in the restoration of churches including that of Spaxton itself. (I have often wondered whether the name Loxston derived from masonry 'lock-stone'.) Eventually he found it necessary to give up his business, which cannot have been financially rewarding, and take up paid employment. He was appointed foreman on the estate of Encombe at Kingston in Purbeck, and was responsible to the steward for the entire workforce, which in those days was considerable. He was a keen musician and for many years was organist at Corfe Castle. I learned from my grandmother that he had taught himself Latin so as to be able to understand the words of the mass. It was not until many years later that I inherited a compact wooden desk which was full of notebooks in which he had painstakingly written out pages and pages of Latin vocabulary. He was, in fact, a *Jude the Obscure* character who, a couple of generations later, would have gone to a university and devoted himself to scholarship. I have always regretted that I did not know him.

My grandmother ('Kingston Nanny') was to go on living in Kingston for many years. She died at the age of ninety-seven in 1957. In the early nineteen fifties my wife remembers her, well into her nineties, on the floor playing with her great grandchildren. She was one of those old people who constantly forget their age and all her movements began swiftly until age slowed them down. Like most village girls when she was young she went into service and became lady's maid to the Lowther family in Northumberland, so she knew how things were done properly. Hence, although full of fun, she still had about her something of the air of a grand lady. Mrs Loxston was a personage of some importance in Kingston.

My parents must have met during the time when the families lived close to one another in Bath. When courting they used to walk together to Charlcombe church, which remains a secluded spot in the hills just outside the city. My father appears on my birth certificate (9 April 1917) as a 'builder's draftsman', from which lowly beginning he worked his way up to being in the 1930s the leading quantity surveyor in Southampton. Having left school at thirteen, as he later never ceased to remind me, he had taken one by one the increasingly rigorous examinations required to become a fully qualified quantity surveyor. Both he and my mother attended the Technical College in Bath and they both always remembered the principal there with great affection. It was a world of strenuous self-improvement and my father, almost to the end of his life, displayed more than ordinary determination and moral courage.

My mother was before her marriage employed as a pupil teacher. Given her parentage and in the light of her later development I am surprised that she did not pursue her education further. She was highly intelligent and imaginative and it may be that she subordinated the cultivation of her own talents to the furtherance of my father's career. They had one dominant interest in common – the theatre, particularly Gilbert and Sullivan opera. They both became members of the Bath Operatic Society and my father was later to become an outstanding performer in the George Grossmith or (as people then spoke of them) Henry Lytton parts. He was a small very active man who could sing, dance and act with the vitality that the roles required.

When I was seven and Betty five we moved to London. My father was employed in the office of the Surveyor to the Vintner's Company and we lived in Honour Oak Park in a Victorian terrace house. No sooner had we arrived than I contracted scarlet fever and had to spend six or seven weeks in an Isolation Hospital. The greatest hardship by far was separation from Betty and I longed to see her, which was the occasion of a sad misunderstanding. One morning a nurse said to me brightly, as I thought, 'Today your sister is coming to see you', and I spent the whole day in eager anticipation. By the end of the day I said to the nurse, in tears, 'But I thought you said my sister was coming today!' She replied, 'Bless you, child, what I said was "*Sister* is coming to see you today".' I had not paid any particular attention to the slightly older and smarter nurse who had stopped to ask me a few questions. When at last my mother fetched me to take me home, a small incident occurred which was the first time I noticed any disagreement between my parents. As we passed a toy shop on the way back from the hospital, I saw in the window a little toy windmill which attracted my attention and my mother bought it for me as a sort of compensation for my long stay in hospital. When we got home my father upbraided her for wasting money, which, of course, spoiled my enjoyment of it.

Betty and I were sent to Stillness Road Elementary School which was just round the corner. I have only three memories of it, one mildly to my credit, the second very much to my discredit, the third, I suppose, marking a stage in my development. The first was when in class I made a raffia basket which was deemed to be of such merit that I was sent across the playground to show to the Headmistress of the big girls' school – the first and only instance of my displaying a practical skill. The second, which is remembered by Betty as well as me, was when a bully approached us both and said, 'Which of you shall I hit first?', and I replied, 'Hit her!' The third was that I fell in love for the first time with a girl called Vera Hall who had violet eyes. I don't suppose I ever declared my love, but it is significant that I remember her name and those violet eyes.

My father must have been prospering somewhat because for the first time we had a live-in maid. Dolly was a plump good-natured girl whom Betty and I became very fond of. As a treat I was sometimes allowed to sleep in her bed which was delightfully warm and comfortable. I don't know if my parents knew about this.

An indication of my father's advancement was his becoming a Mason. He was initiated into the South Norwood Lodge of which he remained a faithful member for the rest of his life. He continued his operatic activities and we have a coloured cartoon of him as Wilkins in *Merry England*. This was performed out of doors at Eltham Palace. My mother at this time had a rather elaborate hair-do which she wore on special occasions. I particularly remember her coming back from the theatre where she and my father had been enormously impressed by the performance of Edith Evans.

I cannot remember now what occasioned our move to Bournemouth. I must have been showing some promise at school because the question arose whether I should stay on to take a scholarship examination for Dulwich, St Dunstans and two or three other schools. My headmaster offered to put me up if I stayed, but my parents offered me the choice and I elected to go with them to Bournemouth. On the whole I disliked Bournemouth and I still have an aversion to gravel and magenta rhododendrons. We lived in the suburb of Winton in a typical row of 'by-pass variegated' houses surrounded by a maze of similar streets. Betty and I had a novel way of exploring the neighbourhood. Each day we would strike out in some direction or other and try to get lost. When we no longer knew where we were the fun consisted in finding our way back by trying to retrace our footsteps until we saw something we recognised. It is a pastime children of nine or ten would not be encouraged to engage in today, but it never occurred to us or to our parents that we might come to any harm. Nor did we.

Bournemouth brought a decisive change in my life. I was sent to a preparatory school which, on the whole, I hated. It had two lasting effects, one negative the other positive. It implanted in me a total incapacity for mathematics and it grounded me so firmly in Latin grammar and syntax that I could never forget it. The maths teacher was the only sadistic schoolmaster I ever encountered. He would summon one to his desk and if one failed to answer a question he would jab his fingers into one's stomach with considerable force. On one occasion to the delight of all of us a wretched boy vomited all over him. The Latin was taught to a high standard, as is indicated by the only particular memory I have. On one occasion for some reason I was left to do work on my own at the back of a class which was doing Livy, book XXI, the boys taking it in turn to construe passages. I listened entranced to the story of Hannibal crossing the Alps with his elephants, to the battle of Lake Trasimene and the defeat of the Romans at Cannae. It is an intensely dramatic narrative but even so it is remarkable that I was able to follow the story as rendered in translation by a group of twelve-year-olds.

At this point I need to introduce another individual who was a decisive influence on my upbringing, my Godmother, Miss Fairless, always known to us as Godmama. It was Godmama who paid my fees at St Wulfram's and subsequently at King Edward VI School, Southampton. She was a tiny delicate old lady with beautiful piled-up white hair, blue eyes and a pink and white complexion. Her father, Michael Fairless, had been an art publisher and had made a fortune from the work of Gustav Doré. She lived in a large Victorian house in Addison Road, Kensington, where she had had an organ installed which occupied two storeys. She was a devout evangelical and a regular worshipper at St Barnabas Church, almost opposite her house.

Her connection with our family was through her coachman and later chauffeur who was married to my great aunt Nell, the elder sister of Kingston Nanny. Her relationship with Miss Fairless was a strange one, particularly for that time. Aunt Nell was a tall slim woman of impressive demeanour and obvious intelligence. Although plainly of a different class from Miss Fairless and effectively a servant she was in many ways more of a companion to her. Aunt Nell had no children, though Betty and I were frequent visitors to their mews house, 14a Addison Crescent, just round the corner from Godmama. So we became the objects of Miss Fairless' benevolent interest and as her godson I was the chief beneficiary. She kept watch over my education and, as will be seen later, was prepared to intervene if she thought it was her duty to do so.

Miss Fairless travelled a good deal, almost always to Switzerland (though once to Egypt where we had a photograph of her seated on a camel). We became familiar with the Eiger, the Mönch and the Jungfrau as well as with views of the lake of Lucerne. In spite of this she had very little experience of the wider world. One of her next door neighbours was Charles Kennedy Scott the musician and his son, C W A Scott, the intrepid aviator, was also a godson. My parents heard (probably from Aunt Nell) that he called on her after one of his record-breaking flights to Australia and recounted, among other experiences, how he had been forced down in a jungle in Borneo and how alarmed he had been by the calls of wild animals which were utterly strange to him. 'How tiresome', Godmama remarked. Her unworldliness, combined with her exacting conscience, could cause embarrassment. She was a lifelong member of the RSPCA and, after she had been to stay with us in Bournemouth, we would be visited by RSPCA inspectors investigating complaints made from our address. On one occasion she had reported a cat as having been cruelly treated by one of our neighbours. It turned out that the cat had fallen into a lime pit and lost much of its coat. Far from being ill-treated it had been taken regularly to the vet and carefully nursed by its owners.

Uncle Bill was a quiet and, as it seemed to us, rather characterless man, who was clearly ruled by Aunt Nell. But he was kind to us and took us for walks to Holland Park and Kensington Gardens. At the round pond there occurred one of those tragic incidents which in childhood leave one utterly inconsolable. I had been given a small toy yacht, in no way to be compared with the magnificent facsimile models which grown men used to sail across the pond with their sails expertly set to maintain their course to the other side. Uncle Bill had equipped my boat with a colourful burgee which was too large for the size of the yacht with the result that it capsised in the middle of the pond too far out to be retrieved. I never knew whether it sank or whether eventually it drifted to the edge of the pond. But it was lost to me forever.

It was in Bournemouth that my father purchased his first car. It was a bull-nosed Morris Cowley open two-seater with a 'dicky' in which Betty and I would sit. We used it mainly for visits to Kingston, where the hill up from Corfe Castle was a severe challenge. Near the top were a series of bends with a gradient of 1 in 4 and I seem to remember occasions when all except my father got out and walked so that the car, thus lightened, could complete the journey to the top. We never had to resort, as was not infrequent in those days, to going up in reverse. There was one stretch of road to which Betty and I always looked forward, where the road ran straight past an ordnance dump at Holton Heath and we regularly achieved a speed of fifty-five miles an hour. Betty and I, and, I suspect, my mother, were sometimes embarrassed by my father's habit from time to time of leaning out of the car and reprimanding other drivers for what he took as their misconduct. In due course we progressed to a Morris Cowley four-seater, then a Morris Oxford and finally a Morris Oxford saloon, but we didn't reach this stage until we were established in Southampton.

It was not until we moved to Southampton in 1928 that, so to speak, our 'modern history' began and, so far as I am concerned, went on continuously until the present day. My father was approaching the pinnacle of his career as a partner in a firm of quantity surveyors. There was one other partner, an older man who was to retire within a few years. Our first home was a capacious flat over Barclays Bank in London Road opposite what were then the headquarters of the Ordnance Survey. The place was run by the Royal Engineers and we got used to Reveille in the morning and the Last Post at night. I was sent to King Edward VI School and Betty to the Convent High School, both within easy walking distance.

But by far the most momentous change was my mother's sudden and, as it happened, irreversible attack of rheumatoid arthritis in a particularly severe form, which was to keep her bedridden and helpless for the last twenty years of her life. She suffered very severe pain and her legs were drawn up and her arms and hands useless for any but the simplest movements. Eventually she had to be fed and it was all she could do to turn over the pages of a book. I have forgotten to mention that for some years Betty and I had been joined by a sister, six years younger than Betty who had been born while we were in London. She was so much younger that she was never felt to be a rival by me and Betty, and we continued to be very close to one another. This absence of rivalry was assisted by Myrtle's sunny disposition. She was a beautiful child with curly fair hair and blue eyes and a most affectionate nature.

My mother's incapacity meant that from this time on we needed a full-time housekeeper and a live-in maid. In both we were most fortunate. Sarah Harker was an ample, very motherly widow who was, I think, thoroughly representative of her native Lancashire. She was sensible and good-natured if, perhaps, a little simple, but she grew very fond of the family, and we of her, without her ever threatening to take the place of my mother. The maid, Gladys, came from the Norham area, the most deprived part of Southampton, but she was fresh-faced and smartly dressed and, on Saturdays, would appear in the uniform of a Tawny Owl in the Girl Guides.

When it became apparent that she was not going to recover, we moved my mother into the main room of the flat which had a bay window overlooking the street. I rigged up a mirror so angled that she could see the passers-by. It was at this period that there occurred a very odd episode which illustrates the extent to which perception is influenced by antecedent expectations. One night I was woken by Betty, who at that time used to sleep in my mother's room. My mother had been woken by what she took to be the loud snoring of a tramp in the street below. Could I dress and go downstairs and see if I could find someone sleeping rough below Mummy's window. I duly went down and searched diligently the immediate neighbourhood but could find nothing. Nevertheless all three of us continued to hear the persistent snoring. It was not until a night or two later, after I had observed from my schoolroom window the work going on for the construction of the new Western docks, that, as we again listened intently to the sound, we at last recognised what it was – the sound of dredgers in Southampton water. But as soon as we knew what it was it became impossible to make it sound again like the snoring of a drunken man.

It is significant that my sister did not think of waking my father. He was not to be disturbed. I am afraid that I at no time then or later thought of the impact upon my father of being suddenly deprived of a lively, active and attractive wife. Without her assistance it is my impression that increasingly he began to see his parental role as that of the breadwinner alone. He devoted himself with characteristic energy to building up his professional practice and establishing his position in the town, so that later he became readily persuaded that he had done everything a husband and father could do and the rest of us were insufficiently grateful.

It has always been a matter for wonder to Betty and me how my mother managed not only to cope with her physical disability but to transform her room into a centre of lively conversation and laughter. She had first to accept the likely irreversibility of the change in her condition. She used to date her acceptance of that change to a visit early on from a good friend, Mrs Allen. Mrs Allen was a placid middle-aged lady whose kind intentions were not matched by what nowadays would be called 'interpersonal skills'. My mother, when she asked how things were going, confessed to her that, since the first onset of her illness she had not dared to look at herself in the mirror. 'Well, my dear,' Mrs Allen replied, 'I should get used to it gradually if I were you!' Such was the manifest absurdity of this remark that my mother burst into laughter and discovered that what had indeed been for her a traumatic concern ceased to matter anymore.

So far our family had never lived for more than a few years in a single place. After Bath, neither London nor Bournemouth felt like 'home'. So continuity was provided by where we spent our holidays. In those days family holidays were not the rule and children went to stay with uncles and aunts or grandparents. Betty and I were fortunate in that we were sent either to 'Kingston Nanny' in the Isle of Purbeck or 'Uncle Ern' in Tavistock on the edge of Dartmoor. Uncle Ern was the second brother in my father's family and the only member of the family who was totally without ambition. He was a postman in Tavistock and was content to remain one. He was thoroughly familiar with the western part of Darmoor and loved to take us for long walks on the moor on his days off. Sometimes, against all the rules, he took us with him in his post office van as he did the rounds of the neighbouring villages. At other times we would go off to Whitchurch Down on the edge of the moor and play games of our own devising. As Ern was a bachelor and had no house of his own we were accommodated by a succession of motherly landladies. One of them provided Cornish pasties to take with us on our wanderings. On one of our visits, which proved to be the last, we found that our walks with Uncle Ern ended in the neighbouring town of Horrabridge and he would put us on a bus to Tavistock to find our own way back. Shortly afterwards at the age of forty he married Amy who lived in Horrabridge and our Dartmoor holidays came to an end.

Uncle Ern as a postman was well known in Tavistock and knew everyone but we never ourselves felt part of a community there. Uncle Ern's familiarity with the place came home to me on one occasion when I arrived back at his lodgings in tears. I had taken myself for a walk in a small park by the river Tavy wearing my school cap. This was a conspicuous affair quartered in navy and saxe-blue. I was small for my age and far from 'street-wise' (though that term had yet to gain currency). I was attacked by two louts who seized my cap and played a game with it of 'pig-in-the-middle'. They tired eventually and ran off with the cap. I was desolate at losing it. When I told the story to Uncle Ern he asked me to describe the boys. The larger and, I presumed, older of them was an ill-favoured brute whom I had no difficulty in remembering. 'Come with me', said Uncle Ern, and we proceeded down town and through the park to a terrace house not far from it. He knocked on the door and when a woman came to the door said 'Good evening, Mrs _____, is Tom in?' Tom was fetched and it was indeed the boy I remembered. 'Give back this young man's cap,' said Uncle Ern, which he immediately did. Whereupon Uncle Ern slapped him hard in the face and said 'Don't do it again!' Such summary justice was not unusual at the time and was accepted without protest by both mother and boy.

Things were very different at Kingston, compared with which Tavistock was a metropolis. Kingston was an estate village of a type scarcely to be found any longer. The estate belonged to the Scott family, heirs of the great Lord Chancellor Eldon, and all the houses were occupied by people who worked on the estate. It was, and is, extremely attractive, built entirely of Purbeck stone with roofs of stone slate. It was dominated by the church built by the third Earl Eldon and designed by G E Street in a pure Early English style. From it the street through the Village cascaded downhill to a crossroads where the road from Corfe Castle took a sharp left turn in the direction of Langton Matravers and Swanage. At the bottom of the hill in one of the angles created by the crossroads was the Eldon Arms (now the Scott Arms). In the angle diagonally opposite was the school with the schoolhouse attached and directly opposite it the cottage where my grandmother and my uncle lived. As foreman of the estate my Uncle Gerald was, below the gentry, the leading personage in the village and his mother, 'Kingston Nanny', a person of consequence. She was not only the mother of the foreman, but the widow of the last foreman but one, my grandfather having settled in Kingston some years before the First World War. When he died of cancer in his sixties (when I was about five) he was replaced by a qualified surveyor from London whose remit was to bring the estate up to date. But he could not understand or communicate with the workforce and lasted only a year, after which brief interval the job was offered to my uncle who had been trained as a carpenter but had the decisive advantage of knowing the village and possessing a clear inherited authority.

One important feature of life in Kingston was cricket played against teams in the rest of Purbeck. The pitch was in a superb situation high up between the village and the sea. The opening batsmen were Gerald and Mr Candy. (Did this reflect their position in the village hierarchy?) My uncle did not make many runs but he had a very straight bat and was hard to dismiss. When he was available my uncle George, who was an all-round athlete, could be relied upon for a quick fifty. Betty and I regularly attended the games, attracted mainly by the splendid teas which the village ladies regularly prepared.

It is fascinating to recall the social structure of the village. There was a clear unquestioned hierarchy. Unchallenged at the top was the Earl of Eldon (and his successor, Sir Ernest Scott). Next came the

Vicar (who when we first knew the village was a member of the Scott family); then the Steward, Walter Candy, who occupied a large new house just outside the village. These exhausted the gentry. Next, on the estate, came my uncle and my grandmother and other workmen according to the accepted order of their jobs. There were, in addition, persons of some consequence who were part of the village but not strictly speaking of the estate. They included a number of tenant farmers, the schoolmistress, the blacksmith, the publican and the postmaster.

I am glad to have had the experience of being attached, albeit as a child, to this hierarchical society. People are often tempted to assume that in any such society, the worth of individuals is determined by their status in the hierarchy (it was an age of 'deference') but the situation was more complex than that. My impression is, on looking back (but how much did I recognise it at the time?) that individuals were assessed in three different ways:

1. Obviously, was by their position in the hierarchy. People were keenly aware of that and accepted it without question;
2. But they were also judged by their personal worth as characters. Mr Candy, for example, though accorded the respect due to his position, was reckoned to be rather inconsiderable as a person, not to be equated in this respect with my uncle who was his social inferior;
3. There was also an underlying sense of equality, a conviction that all were equal in the sight of God, whatever their social position or their individual worth.

Although, in principle, these distinctions are clear enough there were odd uncertainties about how they were to be applied in practice. My uncle used to recount with pleasure an argument that took place on the occasion of a pageant at Corfe Castle. The men of Kingston were to provide the Saxon invaders and the question arose who should lead them. It was maintained that my uncle should assume the role. My uncle demurred. He pointed out that (like me in adult life) he was not a particularly impressive figure of a man. He was skinny and had knobbly knees and would not look well cross-gartered. These arguments availed nothing so Uncle Gerald countered with a positive suggestion. The man for the job was Harry Samson. He was a fine upstanding figure of a man and what's more he had been a sergeant in the army whereas he (Gerald) had been a mere lance-corporal. The reply came back at once, ''Arry Samson may have been a sergeant in the Army but he 'aint nobody in this 'ere village.'

Uncle Gerald was normally a silent man but he was expansive on the subject of the pageant. It was an important local occasion and efforts were made to include everyone in the very considerable cast. A 'simple' young man was given the task of throwing a body from the battlements at a crucial moment. The body was a sack full of sand and he kept on mistaking the cue and from time to time the action was punctuated by the thud of a falling corpse. The individual chosen to play Edward King and Martyr, poisoned by his evil stepmother after a hunt at Corfe Castle, was not a horseman, so a particularly stolid mare had to be found for him. As he slumped over the saddle having swallowed the contents of the fatal goblet he was to spur the horse into a gallop which, according to legend, would carry him halfway to Wareham. But the horse refused to stir and the corpse had to continue spurring it urgently until it finally moved off. The charge of the Saxon invaders was somewhat blunted by a sharp shower which curled the sharp points of their spears, made of cardboard.

My grandmother was not able to get out much with advancing age and was curious to get news of the village. Uncle Gerald was not forthcoming. 'Where have you been, Gerald?' 'Nowhere'. 'Who did you see?' 'No one'. 'What did they say?' 'Nothing.' Uncle Gerald had been chosen for his ability to communicate with the men of the estate. He would sometimes take Betty and me with him and I well remember him meeting one of the workmen halfway up the village street. They stopped. 'Oh-ay,' said Gerald; 'Oh-ay,' said the workman. And then after a decent interval they both said 'Oh-ay' again and moved on. But, like all the Loxstons, he was a thoughtful man and a great reader, especially of history. He had a pale complexion and a lean, somewhat ascetic face.

My grandmother got us to help with the housework by the simple device of deeming us housemaids. I was 'Sarah' and Betty was 'Jane'. We dusted, swept floors and helped with the washing up. The heavy work was done by 'Ma Travers', a cheerful, sturdy middle-aged woman who to some extent compensated Nanny for Uncle Gerald's taciturnity by bringing her the latest village gossip. 'Ma Travers' was an expansive personality and Betty and I were convinced that she had given her name to the neighbouring villages of Langton Matravers and Worth Matravers.

Nanny required us to be well behaved and would say from time to time, 'Remember, dears, we have to *live* here.' This was especially so when we paid calls in the village. Mrs Joyce, the wife of the blacksmith, was a very proper lady, dignified and thin with a black choker at her throat. She was somewhat alarming but Mr Joyce was large and affable and on our departure always gave us a half-crown. With this, or part of it, we could buy sweets at the village shop annexed to the Eldon Arms and run by Mrs Bartlett, an acidulated old lady with her grey hair screwed up in a bun. We did not like her sharp tongue and severe expression and, whenever possible, would go instead to 'Aunt Fan' who ran a small sweet shop at the very top of the village who with her ample bosom and ready smile always made a fuss of us.

A less ceremonious visit than to the Joyce's would be to Mr Gale, the gamekeeper whose cottage was a bit out of the village on the edge of the woods. From there Uncle Gerald would return with a couple of rabbits or a brace of pheasants.

But what over the years kept us deeply attached to Kingston was its superb situation on the Purbeck Hills. It was only two miles from the sea at Freshwater or Chapman's Pool and we could walk for miles to Swire Head and beyond or in the other direction to Hounstout and St Aldhelm's Head (known to us and people locally as St Alban's Head). From Swire on a clear day one could see from the Needles in the east to Portland Bill in the west and the geological strata produced an extraordinarily variegated coastline, stone at St Alban's head, black shale at Kimmeridge, chalk at Worbarrow and stone again at Portland. It has always been for me the characteristic, paradigmatic English coastline. Inland was what must surely be one of the finest views in Europe of Corfe Castle bisecting the long line of the Purbeck Hills and behind it an expanse of heath and the extensive waters of Poole harbour. The combination for us of the secure, enclosed world of the village and the openness of the downs and the sea gave our stays at Kingston an impression of permanence, which has never left me. In our subsequent moves Kingston remained an assurance of continuity.

During our time in Southampton we moved twice, first to Archer's Mansions, a large rather Jerry-built block of flats next door to the Dell, home of Southampton football club, then to Northlands Gardens, a cul-de-sac off Hill Lane very close to the Common. All of them were within easy walking distance of my school which was then between the Marlands and the main railway line. It was a brick building with stone facings built in the 1890s to accommodate 250 boys but now filled to overflowing with 450. During my time it must have been the noisiest school in the country. On the one side across the road was being built the new Civic Centre with the sound of constant riveting; on the other the railway which had just issued from a tunnel where trains regularly whistled on their approach, and a few hundred yards down the line the central station in the process of being re-built. Beyond the railway the new Western docks were under construction with the incessant thudding of pile drivers; and beyond that again were the dredgers whose sound my mother had mistaken for a snoring drunk. It was the worst possible site for a school but it quickly became apparent that, in spite of these drawbacks, it had the one thing needful, a talented and dedicated staff.

My first morning at school I remember sitting with others in my classroom while a small group of gowned schoolmasters chatted round the masters' desk. It looked likely that one of them would be my form-master. There was one in particular whom I hoped to avoid, with a black beard, a particularly ragged gown and a no-nonsense air about him. When the group dissolved this one remained and was indeed my form-master. Worse still he turned out to be the Maths master and would be teaching me what I knew would be my worst subject. As things turned out this was a great blessing. T K Slade was a schoolmaster of genius, to whom to a large extent I owe my subsequent career. My performance in Maths was as I feared and I regularly appeared at the bottom of the form order in arithmetic, algebra and geometry, while occupying the first place in Latin, History and English. Moreover I quite often forgot to do my Maths homework.

While we were still at Bank House, TKS (as we came to know him) came to call on my mother and, as it happened, I know what transpired. My mother depended a good deal on the wireless and the aerial was led up into the roof space through a tube in the ceiling of her room which was below my bedroom. The temptation to listen to their conversation by means of this tube was too strong to resist. TKS said that he was puzzled by my poor performance in Maths and my forgetfulness in relation to it. I was, he thought, intelligent and hardworking in general and my problem was specific to Maths. He suspected some psychological blockage.

He then went on to say that something must be done about it. Although my interests obviously lay elsewhere, if I had any hopes of going to Oxford I would need a credit in Maths to obtain matriculation exemption which was needed for entry. (I cannot be sure that Oxford was mentioned at this stage but the Southampton Exhibition at Queen's was the natural target for anyone at KES who wanted to go to university.) His proposed solution was that he should coach me in Maths for School Certificate and that I should pay him out of my pocket money, so that I should take it seriously.

My mother afterwards gave me a carefully edited version of this conversation in which there was less emphasis on my ability and more on the need for hard work on Maths. But I am glad I heard the whole thing. It provided encouragement from a direction in which I least expected it and it opened up possibilities of which I had never dreamed but which increasingly defined my hope for the future. In line with this, a year later the new Headmaster H K Luce persuaded my parents that I ought to switch from German to Greek.

From now on TKS became a family friend and was known to us as 'the oracle'. He lived with his mother in Southview Road on the other side of Hill Lane where I was a constant visitor. He had a 'den' at the back of the house where he had a forge and engaged in all sorts of metalwork and woodwork. Among other artefacts he made jewellery. His mother had difficulty in sleeping and, when she woke up in the night could never find her watch. TKS made a miniature epidiascope which he placed her watch in with a device which projected the time onto the ceiling. She would often wake him up and tell him to go downstairs to make sure the front door was locked, so he perfected a device which would signal if the door was locked and lock it if it wasn't. The den was an untidy clutter of objects but not a disorderly one. TKS could always find what he wanted. He made strenuous efforts to get me to learn a practical skill, but like many adolescents I was reluctant to do anything I wasn't good at. Instead we talked incessantly.

He had a more than desultory interest in psychology and, in 1923, had had a book published by Kegan Paul entitled *Our Phantastic Emotions*, with a foreword by S K Ferenczi, a disciple of Freud. When, years later, I was reading Greats at Oxford and was searching in *Mind 1925* for an article by R G Collingwood, I discovered an article on some aspect of psychoanalysis by T K Slade. I have wondered since why he had not pursued an academic career in Psychology. I think the answer is that after he had taken his degree at Hartley College (which later became University College, Southampton and later still the University of Southampton) his father died suddenly and he took up school teaching in order to provide for his mother. On one occasion he astonished us still further by bringing to our house in Northlands Gardens a number of love songs which he had composed and sang for my mother to his own accompaniment.

When I first went to the school in 1928 the headmaster was The Revd C K Russell, a, to me, remote figure. He was tall with, as I remember, a pale, shiny clerical face and a habit of gliding around the school and appearing in one's vicinity unexpectedly. After my first year he went on to Merchant Taylors, Crosby, where one of his pupils was Robert Runcie, according to whom he was known to the boys as 'creepy Jesus'. It seems that he showed great kindness to Runcie who remembered him with gratitude.

He was succeeded at KES by an even taller clergyman, The Revd H K Luce, who had been Master of the King's Scholars at Eton. He it was who persuaded my parents that I ought to learn Greek. He was an ardent pacifist and one of his first acts was to disband the Cadet Corps. He was also a modernist in theology which may explain why his career got no further than Durham School to which he went after three years with us.

This provoked Godmama into one of her rare interventions into my education, for which she was paying. Once when she was staying with us I came back from school bursting with excitement about a new Divinity teacher who was systematically explaining away the biblical miracles by producing entirely naturalistic explanations. Godmama was outraged and immediately wrote to Luce saying she would like to come and see him about the threat to my religious education. Luce replied courteously saying that he would not for a moment contemplate her coming to visit him and that he would call upon her. This he did. I would love to have seen and heard this encounter. Luce would have towered over Miss Fairless, but she was not the woman to allow herself to be intimidated. I gathered that an accord had been reached, assisted no doubt by Luce's gentlemanly conduct.

Shortly after this I came home one day to find my mother in conversation with a plainly dressed little woman who made lively conversation in a very precise cultivated English accent. She was introduced as Mrs Sandeman. I left them to talk and when I came back later, my mother said, 'Basil, Mrs Sandeman has invited you to stay with her in the New Forest'. She had apparently noticed that I was pale and slight and felt that I needed a taste of a more out-door life. When I eventually went to Godshill that summer I found myself in a remarkable environment, an extraordinary amalgam of high culture and the simple life. The Sandeman's house was a large log hut consisting of three rooms: a very large living room, in which everything happened and on either side of it a bedroom, one for the parents and one for the three boys, Roland, Peter and David. I was to share the latter, it being no problem to add a fourth wooden bed. George Sandeman was a tall imposing figure some years older than his wife. All the time I was there I found him a rather remote presence of who I was in awe. The running of the place was plainly in the hands of Mrs Sandeman, known by the boys as 'Madam' and later as 'Fra'. The boys had been educated at home by their parents. George had been a professor of zoology at the College des Ecossais at Montpellier. Fra had been one of the first women to take a degree in English at Oxford where she was a pupil of Helen Darbyshire at Somerville. So there was no doubt about their academic competence. They all played musical instruments and from time to time would hold impromptu concerts in the living room. Their resources were on occasion augmented by an enormously tall Czech who lived on a smallholding at the other end of the village and played the violin in a passionate bohemian fashion.

I myself was entirely unversed musically, my parents having decided at an early stage that Betty was the musical one. But the ethos

of the place would not permit anyone to be a non-participant and I
was made to play the triangle. As I soon discovered, this was not a
sinecure because if one got it right it contributed little to the total
ensemble, while if one got it wrong, the mistake was conspicuous.

Sandy Balls Wood at Godshill was home to *The Order of Woodcraft
Chivalry*, a collection of people dedicated to the simple life and
alternative life-styles. Members saluted one another by raising the
right arm and saying 'Blue Sky'. This gesture had yet to gather its
sinister associations and struck me as just faintly ridiculous. But I
enjoyed the country dancing. Among those who had been drawn to
Godshill were two girls, Elaine and Vera Faithful, who camped in the
Sandeman's garden. Their father, I understood, was a psychiatrist
who ran an experimental school at King's Lynn roughly on the lines
of Summerhill. Vera, the younger of the two, was the same age as me
and she was the occasion of my falling in love for the second time. I
remember clearly the onset of it. A party of us were walking along a
path on the edge of the wood which was wide enough only for two
at a time. I was aware of this girl at my side and, after walking a little
way in silence, I turned towards her and looked at her. A blush,
starting at her throat, spread upwards over her face. I fancy I replied
by blushing too. That created a bond which was confirmed a few
days later, when she celebrated her thirteenth birthday and seated me
on her right hand. We continued thereafter to walk together when
parties of us went for rambles in the New Forest. Given her
progressive education it was, perhaps, not surprising that she on one
occasion invited me to spend the night with her in her tent. This,
however, was firmly squashed by 'Madam'.

My only other memory of Vera was when we all went swimming
in the river Avon. At the bottom of Sandy Balls Wood was an inlet
of the river, known as 'the creek' and there the Sandemans managed
to teach me to swim. As we were changing, her breasts were revealed
for a moment and I was amazed at their beauty as earlier I had been
by the little girl's golden ringlets at Widcombe. On both occasions
my response was purely aesthetic, or so it seemed.

This holiday at Godshill was in effect the first time I had ever been
away from home. Tavistock and Kingston didn't count because I was
always with Betty. I have wondered in retrospect why I never tried
to keep in touch with Vera Faithful, especially since she had lent me

a romance by Jeffery Farnol, which I never returned. The Sandemans remained lasting friends, but I rather think that after it I came to regard this first holiday at Godshill as a magical interlude out of phase with my ordinary life and Vera as having existence only as part of it.

I was at King Edward's School from 1928 to 1935. During that time I progressed from Form 4^1A via 5^2A and 5^1A to the Sixth Form. The latter transition was all important. It had several major effects. One was that for the first time I was not indebted to Godmama. I won a Foundation Scholarship which exempted me from school fees, and then a £30 p.a. Bursary from Queen's College, designed by the College to encourage bright boys to stay on in the Sixth Form and, no doubt, in due course to try for the Southampton Exhibition at Queen's. The second effect was that I was for the first time freed from the continuous strain of Mathematics. By a miracle, aided by the efforts of TKS, I had got the needed credit in School Certificate which freed me, to set my sights as I increasingly did, on Oxford. But above all I now found myself in the company of people who enjoyed academic work and delighted in intellectual pursuits. I was now enormously at home in the school, although thanks to TKS I had always felt secure there. One of the great things about the school was the extent to which masters encouraged and took part in 'out of school' activities.

I enjoyed debating and given my parents' theatrical interests I was inevitably drawn to the dramatic society. A.S. Arnold (known to everyone as 'Micky' Arnold) had the inspired idea of putting on a succession of Elizabethan comedies, *Ralph Royster Doyster*, *Gammer Gurton's Needle*, and *The Shoemaker's Holiday*. These did not call for subtlety or social poise which would have been beyond us but gave plenty of scope for robust humour and simple gusto. They also offered me the opportunity of regularly playing the leading lady, fortified by the knowledge that in Shakespeare's time this would have been the norm. With my rather delicate features and somewhat flexible voice I think I made a personable girl, the more so as I have always felt that I would rather have liked to be a girl.

Micky Arnold had the gift which the art of a good teacher consists in of mixing encouragement and criticism in due proportion (when criticism was needed he could voice it incisively. The only school report I can remember was one of his for my performance in Chemistry: 'is out of his depth and makes no attempt to swim').

Entry to the Sixth Form meant that I now concentrated on the subjects I was to take in Higher School Certificate, Latin, Greek and Ancient History. There were only three of us in the Classical Sixth and we were taught by another remarkable schoolmaster, A C Jardine. He was a small bitter man with a sallow complexion and pale steely-grey eyes. With him criticism preponderated and encouragement of any kind so rare as to be very highly prized. He was an impeccable scholar who set rigorous standards and was severe on any failure, no matter what the excuse. He was an atheist of the kind who rebelled against God rather than simply denied his existence. Housman's 'Whatever brute and blackguard made the world' was what he railed against. How much this was owing to a sense of being a failure I do not know. By rights he ought to have been a don and not a schoolmaster. But his inexorable insistence on the highest possible standards, if it did not totally discourage me, could not fail to inculcate a reasonably accurate knowledge of the classical languages and in addition he instilled in me a love of Latin poetry, of Virgil and, above all, of Lucretius. I shall never forget his intoning with the most intense fervour:

> O genus infelix humanum, talia divis
> cum tribuit facta atque iras adjunxit acerbas.
> Quantos tum gemitus ipsi sibi, quantaque nobis
> vulnera, quas lacrimas peperere minoribus nostris.
> Nec pietas ull'est velatum saepe videri
> Vertier ad lapidem atque omnes accedere ad aras . . .
> Sed mage pacata posse omnia mente tueri.

Sadly he never achieved Lucretius' peace of mind, and some years later took his own life.

I remember two occasions when he made a more personal approach. On the first he encountered me in the street and invited me to accompany him to a Turkish bath. It was the first and only time I had been to such an establishment and I did not much enjoy it. Jardine was his usual withdrawn self and I had no idea why he had asked me to go with him, unless it was sheer loneliness. The second occasion was when I was about to go up to Oxford and he invited me to dine with him in an exclusive restaurant below the Bar. As we walked back he said that life was a sad affair and then added 'but I think perhaps that you have a chance of being happy and I hope you will be'. I cannot remember what I said and hope that I thanked him for all he had done for me.

At about this time the Headmaster, who succeeded Luce, Clifford Harper, asked me in confidence whether I thought Jardine imposed his atheism on his pupils. I said that he made no secret of it but did not attempt to impose it on us. As it happens all three of the then Classical Sixth became active members of the Church of England. Two were ordained and I was to become Professor of the Philosophy of the Christian Religion. Moreover, two of his later pupils became distinguished churchmen, Dennis Nineham who after two theology professorships became Warden of Keble and Tom Baker who became Dean of Worcester. Was this sheer coincidence or did Jardine's heart-felt anti-theism help to generate a concern with ultimate problems?

Shortly after our move to Southampton we, as a family, encountered the Sufi Movement. I do not know how it happened, but since it became evident that orthodox scientific medicine could do nothing for my mother, she received increasingly offers of help from devotees of alternative therapies and the world views that went with them. Christian scientists and theosophists among others came to visit her. Among them the most personally impressive was E A Mitchell (always knows as 'Mike'). He was a senior journalist on the *Southern Daily Echo*. Among other things he was their drama critic and ran a weekly column as 'Townsman' in which in a lively and entertaining fashion he commented on the affairs of Southampton and delved into curious by-ways of its history. He was a mine of curious and recondite information. We learned that many years earlier he had been reduced to poverty by drink and was utterly down and out. One day when sitting on a bench in one of the parks he was joined by an Indian, an impressive figure in a full and flowing beard. As a result of their conversation he underwent a conversion, recovered hope and set out on a new life. This charismatic figure was Hazrat Inayat Khan, leader of the Sufi Movement in Europe and America. Mike gathered together a number of other disciples in Southampton and initiated a 'service of Universal Worship' on Sunday evenings in the Adyar Hall, headquarters of the Theosophical Society. A key feature of the service was the reading of excerpts from six world religions: Judaism, Christianity, Hinduism, Islam, Buddhism and Zoroastrianism. The intention was to illustrate the extent to which they all conveyed the same essential truth, Sufism having been originally a mystical offshoot of Islam. This truth was fundamentally mystical. It appealed to me strongly as an adolescent and reinforced the Wordsworthian moments I experienced from time to time under the influence of *Lines above Tintern Abbey* and *Ode to Immortality*. (I was a voracious reader of poetry at that time.)

The Bhagavad Gita and the Dhammapada proved the easiest texts in which to find the essential mystical truths we were looking for. The Koran yielded, as I remember, only one or two suitable passages, which were for that reason constantly repeated. Both the Old and New Testaments were fruitful enough if one was highly selective, but there was one difficulty which always worried me. Both are distinctly particularistic with their stress on the action of God in historical events and, taken in their straightforward sense, seemed to claim an exclusive access to truth which was hard to reconcile with the Sufi message. In spite of this Betty and I were confirmed in St Mark's Church. The vicar, Mr Brummit, was a big, breezy man, a Cambridge rowing blue, who did his best for us, but he was a muscular Christian and not the man to confide my intellectual anxieties to. So they remained unresolved and I made my confirmation promises with largely unacknowledged mental reservations.

Meanwhile there was, in the background to our lives, and for one week a year, the centre of them, the annual Gilbert and Sullivan opera performed by the Southampton Operatic Society. Under my father's direction they regularly achieved something like a professional standard and his own performances were as good as anything to be found in D'Oyly Carte. Every year they were warmly and justly applauded by Mike Mitchell in his capacity of drama critic for the Echo and they rapidly established my father as a well-known figure in the town. The cast of the opera, together with the orchestra, involved quite a large number of performers whose families and friends guaranteed a considerable core audience. The Watts Hall in High Street was rapidly found to be inadequate and the show moved to the Royal Pier whose situation and décor added considerably to its atmosphere. Betty and I could soon recite the various operas by heart. It was not until we moved to Northlands Gardens that it became practicable to take my mother to the current opera, which we regularly did in her spinal carriage. It gave us considerable pleasure and amusement to see her holding court in the interval with the dignitaries of Southampton taking turns to talk with her. But before this move to Northlands Garden, members of the cast, who had become family friends, would visit us in our top floor flat in Archers Mansions and sing for her.

The culmination of this was when all the principals of *Iolanthe* performed the entire opera in our flat for her benefit. It was necessary, of course, to warn our neighbours that this was going to happen and give them the opportunity of objecting. We were particularly worried about the young couple in the flat below who were Plymouth Brethren and, as such, opposed to theatrical perform-ances of any kind. They were asked up to tea so that my mother could explain. The husband made plain his objection in principle but felt that, given the circumstances, he could scarcely forbid my mother's entertainment. My mother became aware that the wife, though loyally supporting her husband, responded rather wistfully to the idea of such an occasion and felt that her life was sadly diminished by being denied the theatre. My mother, therefore, set herself to persuade the husband to let the girl come to what was, after all, not an actual theatrical performance, but a purely private entertainment undertaken in a spirit of charity towards one who was denied by circumstances even the most legitimate enjoyments. The wife came and to my mother's delight she was totally entranced.

Our mother's illness might have been expected to curtail our friendships with others of our own age or to ensure that our activities with them took place entirely outside the home. Instead such was the interest she showed in them and her capacity to engage them in lively and entertaining conversation that they began increasingly to congre-gate in her room and to make it a sort of informal salon. I remember that, if I met someone interesting, I would say to them, 'You must come and meet my mother' without finding it necessary to warn them that they would find her bedridden. It would be true, I suppose, that denied any active life of her own, she lived her life through the lives of her children and her children's friends, but the remarkable thing is that she was, so far as we could tell, entirely unpossessive of Betty and me. She had the gift of generating an intellectual excitement of which she was the undoubted source but which did not centre on herself or her own individual ideas. She was, that is to say, a genuine catalyst.

With one exception those who frequented our house were young men, chiefly but not exclusively from the Sixth Form of King Edward's. They included Jack Shipwright who went on for most of his career to teach modern languages at the school and was a talented musician; Robert Vile, the son of police constable, whose promising career in the Colonial Service was cut short after the war by an untimely death; Leonard Lamerton, a physicist who was to become a leading pioneer of radiotherapy in the treatment of cancer; Glyn Seager Thomas who went into the Navy and ended up in command of the Naval Air Station at Yeovilton; Ronald Bailey (always known as 'Bill' Bailey) who spent most of his time in the Diplomatic Service in the Middle East; and, at a later stage, Trev Gardner (then called 'Cod') who, after serving in the Colonial Service in Zambia, became Treasurer of Cambridge University. There was also Rory Jenkins. He was an eccentric youth who with Jack Shipwright was an authority on the ritual practices of the Anglo-Catholic churches in Southampton.

The fact that (with the one exception) they were all male may have something to do with the presence of Betty. At any rate it seems that they almost all fell in love with her and one by one (according to her own account) proposed to her. It is not, in retrospect, difficult to understand this, although it puzzled me greatly at the time. Betty was a constant presence in quiet and demure attendance upon my mother, beautiful in an unemphatic way, a sort of image of self-sacrifice. But when her gentleness was at all presumed upon she had a deflationary wit which was disconcerting and made her something of a puzzle. She had, moreover, her own field of activity in which she remained unchallenged. Coached by Miss Adams who taught English and elocution at the Convent High she regularly won first prize for elocution at the annual Southampton Music Festival; and her gift as an actress was already becoming apparent.

The one exception was Peggy Pope. Peggy was in the form above Betty's at the Convent High. She was undoubtedly the brightest girl there and she was also their star athlete. She was bouncy, ebullient, energetic and effervescent and at the same time intelligent and imaginative, as different temperamentally from me as could be imagined, a to me fascinating compound of extravert and introvert. She was short of stature with a figure which, if had it been less robust and muscular, would have been voluptuous. She had fair hair and surprisingly delicate features with clear and penetrating grey eyes. I cannot now remember how we met, whether through Betty or through one of the societies in the town we both belonged to. Before long we were writing poems to one another which we exchanged regularly at another Southampton institution, the dances organised for teenagers (not then so called) by a body called, unbelievably, the Fairy Ring. What the Fairy Ring was or whether it had any other function than to organise the dances I do not know. The dances were held weekly or fortnightly at the Avenue Hall at the bottom of the Avenue where it leaves the Common and enters the town. Most of us had lessons in ballroom dancing with two maiden ladies of uncertain age and asexual aspect. One was tall and one was short and both could have been chosen to protect adolescent boys and girls from any tendency to associate dancing with sexual desire. (In the summer they taught us all to play tennis.) The dances were decorous affairs. It was not done to stay the whole evening with one partner but, as well as making sure that we danced the last waltz together, Peggy and I would seek an opportunity to dance together early on and in the course of the dance, as unobtrusively as possible, we would exchange the poems we had written for one another. It was then necessary to retire to the cloakroom to read the latest offering.

We were both voracious readers, especially of poetry and not surprisingly our poems were imitative, hers, I think, of Shelley, mine of Wordsworth. We called one another semi-seriously L'Allegro and Il Penseroso and it was natural to us to try to understand our situation in terms of what we were reading. On one occasion I received a letter which began:

> Being your slave, what should I do but tend
> upon the hours and times of your desire?

It was not until much later that I read Virginia Woolf's delightful essay on the poverty of our language to describe pain, in which she

says: 'The merest schoolgirl has the language of Shakespeare to
express her feelings.' I have the impression in retrospect that it was
Peggy who was the moving force in our relationship, but that may
be because I have only her letters to go on. We were both struggling
to find ourselves and determine what we were to be and do, while
painfully conscious of how ill equipped we were for the tasks ahead.

Peggy's interpretation of what was going on comes out in a letter
I received while on holiday in Kingston at Easter 1935:

> Since your departure on Thursday my existence has consisted of three
> recurrent occupations: first, and least important, doing things; second,
> reading the letter you gave me last Tuesday; and third and most
> important, thinking of you – not in the sentimental sense, but in the
> finest and highest sense possible for a vivacious and irresponsible
> schoolgirl. You said you could not change your nature or your
> temperament – but neither can I change mine and why should we?
> Surely these natures of ours cannot be so very bad since they are only
> just beginning to develop consciously . . . We cannot remain as we
> are, but at the same time there is no necessity for us to drift along . . .
> But obviously if we are not to drift along, we must have not only the
> force and impulse, but also some stars by which to steer our course.
> These stars are, I think, ideals which we can imagine and strive to
> attain and are guiding lights to something far greater beyond them
> which we cannot even imagine fully in our own minds, still less hope
> to attain directly. Now you seem to consider our natures or
> temperaments very different from one another – it may be true – but,
> Basil, I feel that if you think as I do that the purpose of life is much
> more important than life itself then temperament is only a trivial
> matter compared to the question?

Peggy's idealism was to be sorely tested later in the company of
another man, but her letter brings out the extent to which we felt
our love to be incomplete, but still genuine. It must be almost wholly
incomprehensible to a later generation that our love never reached
greater physical expression than our being in one another's arms
during the last waltz or a chaste kiss on the way to her home in
Shaftesbury Avenue as we parted at the far end of Westwood Road.
By this time I had read most of Havelock Ellis, lent me by TKS, but
it never occurred to me that the practices there described bore any
relation to my feelings for Peggy. I wonder now whether, if we had

engaged in sexual exploration, we should have had time or inclination for the endless conversations about psychology, politics, religion and other topics which we shared with our group of friends in my mother's room.

The idealism which we shared was much influenced by the addresses which Mike gave at the weekly services of Universal Worship. He would start awkwardly and hesitatingly, seeking painfully for words. Then after a few minutes he was suddenly in full flow as if possessed by some overmastering spirit. The moment of inspiration could be timed precisely. In spite of the impression these talks made on me I cannot now remember the precise content of any of them. But they represented life as a spiritual quest in which one sought to realise one's true self which was at the same time the divine spark within oneself. The hindrances to this quest were ignorance and self-centredness. The stress on ignorance was a version of the 'Avidya' of the *Vedanta*; and the moral emphasis on active love was straightforwardly Christian. Buddhism could be incorporated into this spiritual philosophy so long as, in the manner of Mrs Rhys David, one interpreted what seemed to be its atheism and its denial of the substantial self by taking the self denied to be the phenomenal self, the object of self-love and the atheism as a repudiation of crude attempts to conceive of God through personal analogies.

Mike's impressiveness as a preacher was enhanced by the way he clearly lived his message. He was a sort of provincial Dr Johnson without the great doctor's acerbity, a large ungainly man with a smile of pure benevolence. He was an exemplar of Gabriel Marcel's 'disponibilité' and was always ready to engage with the young in serious conversation on entirely equal terms. On Sunday mornings he used to take a stroll on the Common to prepare his talk that evening and, from time to time, I used to waylay him and put to him some problem of my own. I do not remember him ever trying to put me off – or was I too self-absorbed to notice it?

Meanwhile we were all very hard at work. We were none of us of that class which was able to take going to a university for granted. As soon as I indicated my desire to go to Oxford my father said that I should have to pay for myself. Neither at that time nor later (until I was plainly a 'success') did he regard what I was doing as constituting work. It has to be admitted that I was a grave disappointment to him. He would have like me to succeed him in his job as a quantity surveyor but I had no aptitude for mathematics. Not I but Betty had inherited his acting ability; and I never showed any sign of becoming the Rugby footballer he would like to have been himself. As it happened, in fact, I have never in my life worked so hard as in the years when I was studying for Higher School Certificate (the then equivalent to A levels). I used to suffer from headaches which have never troubled me since. I had discovered that the Southampton Exhibition at Queen's – the financial equivalent of a Scholarship – at £100 a year would cover just under a half of what was reckoned at the time to be needed to keep someone at Oxford. Assuming I could get that, I must also win a State Scholarship, of which in those days 75 were awarded in the whole country. For that I needed two distinctions in Higher School Certificate.

Jardine was not the man to provide sustained encouragement but the school was generally supportive. Moreover, we were all in the same boat and, happily, not in direct competition with one another. Ronald Vile and Bill Bailey were doing French and Spanish; Jack Shipwright French and German; Leonard Lamerton, of course, Physics and Chemistry. It was my mother's room which provided a sort of junior common room for us all.

This account of our time in Southampton would not be complete without some mention of ships. As a family we had no connection with the shipping which was the town's raison d'être, but it was impossible not to be aware of it. When the Western docks were completed, I would see from my school room window a succession of ocean liners entering and leaving the quays and, before the completion of the King George V Graving Dock, we would see from our top floor flat in Archers Mansions the *Berengaria* or the *Majestic* raised in the Floating Dock over the roofs of the town. My favourite line was the White Star Line, although Cunard was not far behind. I could name all of them, although the fact that mine was only a distant acquaintance is shown by my regularly mispronouncing 'Homeric' as I had only seen it in writing. My sole direct encounter with a sea captain was with Peggy's father, an officer in the Royal Mail Line, who opened the door one night when I brought her home and rebuked me severely (though I felt not too seriously) for bringing her home so late. He looked the part eminently and I saw where those clear grey eyes came from. I happened to be in town some years later when the *Mauretania* left on her final voyage to the breakers' yard among salutes from all the sirens in the port. She was quite the most beautiful of all the ships which sailed from Southampton and there were people weeping in the street. There are, of course, family reasons why I no longer feel strongly attached to Southampton, but one reason undoubtedly is that since the war and the demise of the Atlantic liner the place seems to have lost its soul.

During my last years at school everything was concentrated upon the examination for the Southampton Exhibition at Queen's which was to take place in November 1934. When the time came, although I could have stayed in College, it was decided that I should spend the two nights with my Uncle George and Aunt Hilda who had a bungalow at Forest Hill, five miles from Oxford just off the London Road. With the other candidates for scholarships I sat the papers in the College hall. By an unhappy mischance I had a boil on the left cheek of my bottom which reacted badly to the benches on which we sat. As we left the hall my neighbour turned to me and said, 'Ee but that Greek prose did get my goat'. He subsequently got a Hastings Scholarship open to boys from the North of England which was the main regional attachment of the College whose founder Robert de Eglesfield, who came from Cumberland, was chaplain to Queen Philippa, wife of Edward III. Nevertheless, as I later discovered, the Southampton connection went back to the foundation of the College and it was rumoured that much of the wealth came from areas of the docks which it owned.

An important part of the examination was the interview of particular interest to the Greats tutors for whom the candidate's performance in classics did not of itself provide sufficient evidence of how well he might do later in Philosophy. My interview was to take place on the evening of the final day. My instructions were to go to the Upper Senior Common Room and wait my turn. On enquiring at the Lodge as to where the Upper Senior Common Room was to be found I was told to follow the signs in the Front Quad and I would find it at the top of the staircase. Unfortunately the porter must have forgotten that there were two staircases marked 'Upper Senior Common Room' and I took the first. When I reached the top I was confronted by a door with no notice at all on it. I heard voices on the other side and assumed that was where I was supposed to be. I knocked and, receiving no reply, went into a panelled room where three dons were interviewing another candidate. One of the dons, a very tall man whom I later recognised as Guy Chilver, the Ancient History tutor, got up and ushered me through a further door into a long gallery where a number of other candidates were waiting. They were plainly surprised to see a boy coming out who was not the one they had seen go in. I took a seat and was covered in confusion. As it happened I was the last candidate to be interviewed that night so I had a long time in which to meditate upon my faux pas. I was still embarrassed when I at last sat before the three examiners. I do not remember any of the questions I was asked. My later impression was that I had coped well with some and made rather a mess of others. All I remember is that when eventually the chairman (who, as I later discovered, was Oliver Franks) had looked briefly at each of his two colleagues to see if they had anything more to say duly terminated the interview, what he said was, 'And now Mr Mitchell which way would you like to go out?' I replied, 'Well, I came in that way; perhaps I had better go out that way.'

When I went out of the College into the High it was raining and the time was around eleven o'clock. I had missed the last bus and I had somehow to get back to Forest Hill. It never occurred to me to take a taxi which in those days we should have regarded as an unpardonable extravagance. My aunt and uncle were not among the minority of people who then had a telephone. So I had no alternative but to walk, which I did, getting steadily wetter over Magdalen Bridge, along St Clements up Headington Hill, through the whole extent of Headington and out into the open country and the turn to Forest Hill where I arrived soaked to the skin and so disturbed at the trouble I was causing to my aunt and uncle that I almost forgot my anxieties over the interview.

I have conducted innumerable such interviews since and have always tried to make sure that the candidates knew exactly where to go and were not kept late at night. Franks left the College after my first year for a career of ever increasing distinction. Such was his astonishing competence that he was often thought to be a little inhuman, but I have two pieces of evidence to the contrary. One was from the time years later when my niece Libby Stokes was his secretary at Worcester. She said that whenever he dictated a rather difficult letter to her he would take care to explain to her what the relevant issue was so that she shouldn't feel that her role was purely instrumental. The other was that final remark at my entrance interview which was nicely calculated to tell me I needn't worry about my initial gaffe.

When I returned to school and discussed my papers with Jardine and told him about the interview I was far from confident and he characteristically said nothing to relieve my anxiety. Nevertheless, as TKS told me later, after our talk Jardine marched into the staff room and announced 'Mitchell has got the Queen's'.

I had made an arrangement with an old Edwardian at St Edmund Hall, Jack Quinn, that he would look in next door at Queen's, read the notice of the results and send me a telegram. This he did in Greek: XAIPE NIKAIS. The natural translation was 'Hail, thou conquerest', but in my uncertain frame of mind, I couldn't help thinking that it might also mean 'Farewell to Victories', so that I did not fully believe in my success until I received the formal letter from the Provost. To have got the Southampton Exhibition was undoubtedly the first and essential step to my achieving my hopes of Oxford, but I still had to secure the State Scholarship and that meant two more terms of hard work for Higher School Certificate.

CHAPTER 2

Oxford: The Queen's College 1935–40

THE NEXT FOUR YEARS saw a regular alternation of Term and Vacation in the course of which I discovered a curious fact. In the eight weeks of term time it was hard to believe that 6 Northlands Gardens continued to exist at all, and although I wrote and received letters it was as if to and from a remote foreign country. Similarly once I was at home during the vacation I was hard put to it to believe in the reality of Queen's and my life there. This was the case even though my Oxford friends came to stay with me from time to time in Southampton, and even though some of my most significant experiences were home-based rather than Oxford-based.

Many have written about the sense of liberation in their Oxford years. I had been so free at home and at school to do the things I wanted to do that I never had that particular experience. It would, indeed, take time to recreate the easy friendships I had taken for granted in Southampton. We were all scattered with the exception of Jack Shipwright who was reading Modern Languages at St Edmund Hall. Bill Bailey and Robert Vile were at Cambridge, Leonard Lamerton was at Hartley College, soon to be University College, Southampton and Peggy was at LSE. It would not be until a year later that Trev Gardner came up to Queen's on a Stirling Scholarship.

Like most of those who have been 'clever' at school I encountered initial disappointments. I auditioned unsuccessfully at OUDS and gave up all ambitions at the Union after a disastrous attempt to hold a declining audience late at night. Most of my contemporaries seemed more self-confident than I was and I remember that, initially, I decided that 'I loved the place but hated the people'. These disappointments made me ever more determined to do well at work. The first target was Honour Mods (Honour Moderations in Greek and Latin Literature) to be taken after the first five terms in Hilary Term 1937. My tutor, T E Wright, was reckoned in the University to be something of a slave driver, but it would be hard to imagine a gentler one. He was a quiet, comfortable bachelor, small and old for his age who bore an uncanny resemblance to the portrait of the Founder, Robert de Eglesfield, to be seen in the College Hall, especially when he raised one limp hand in greeting. As he corrected one's proses or unseens he would circle a mistake in red ink and say 'Oh laddy, laddy'. A more serious mistake would earn two circles and an 'Oh laddy, laddy, laddy', and a really grave error three circles and 'Oh laddy, laddy, laddy, laddy!' He was, even for the time, an old-fashioned Mods don whose interest lay in the grammar and syntax of what we were reading and the authenticity of the text rather than its literary value. We were required to read an enormous amount, including the whole of the Iliad and the Odyssey (but even then, less than our predecessors). Wright himself lectured on Horace and I decided not to choose that for my set book. For some reason he vetoed my own preference, which was for Lucretius, lectured on by Cyril Bailey. We compromised with Juvenal, which led to a curious misunderstanding. The lecturer, Henderson, had a somewhat Teutonic accent and referred constantly to Hausmann's edition of Manilius. Eventually, as the lectures went on, it became apparent that this German Scholar was of such importance that I must consult the introduction to his edition of Manilius. After searching in vain for Hausmann in the College library, I discovered that he was no other than the poet A E Housman, whose reputation as a scholar I knew nothing about.

Quite early in the term – it may even have been in the first week – I was sitting in hall at the end of dinner when I was approached by a tall strikingly handsome man with a ravishing smile who said he wanted to make my acquaintance. He introduced himself as Christopher Rieu who came from Highgate School and was also reading classics. He shared my disillusion with the way we were being taught and in due course decided not to go on to Greats but to transfer to English. To be picked out by such a person did a great deal for my self-confidence and Christopher became a lifelong friend notwithstanding certain temperamental difference between us and a tendency on his part to be somewhat proprietorial in respect of me. Among other things he taught me to ride a bicycle, patiently putting me through my paces on the road from Wood Eaton to Marston, then an almost entirely unfrequented track. (There had been an earlier unsuccessful attempt to teach me by the Sandemans on a grassy hill outside Lyndhurst, where they then lived. They put me on the bicycle at the top of the hill and pointed it towards the bottom, reckoning correctly that the gradient and the speed of my descent would keep the bicycle upright and me on it. They had not noticed – or had they perhaps? – that at the foot of the hill there was a narrow stream which cut across it. I noticed it early in my descent but decided that any attempt to swerve to right or to left would throw me violently off the bicycle. I therefore gritted my teeth and held on in the desperate hope that I should somehow sail over the obstacle. I crashed spectacularly and was unwilling to repeat the experiment.)

At a fairly early stage I was thrown together with Theo Cadoux, also a classicist and one of Wright's best pupils. He lived in Oxford, his father being Vice-Principal of Mansfield College and a noted Congregational divine. Theo was at the time in revolt against the puritanical ethos of the parental home and was aided in this by a friend, Harold Herzmark, a modern linguist and a lively talker, who affected a Nietzschian 'transvaluation of values'. He was far more sophisticated than any of us. Harold had a friend, Jean Fuller, who had a room in a house off the Iffley Road where she had moved in order to be close to Harold. She was a year or two older than us, beautiful with a perfect oval face, fair hair and a shapely mouth. She had trained as an actress and had a small private income which was enough for her to live simply without having to work for a living. In my innocence (and I was astonishingly innocent) I had no idea what their relationship was and it was not until a year or two later, when we met in Paris, that Harold felt it necessary to explain to me that if I called on them too early I should be likely to find them in bed together.

My friendship with Christopher was self-standing and he never became part of the group of Theo, Harold, Jean and I. He similarly had his own little set of friends, of whom I was not one. But I now clearly remember that my whole outlook on Oxford and my place in it was transformed as soon as I had this happy nucleus of friendship. One small thing is perhaps worth mentioning. Christopher was from Highgate, Theo from King's School, Taunton, Harold from St Paul's, Jean largely self-educated. Neither then nor at any time later did I encounter the divide between 'public school' and 'grammar school' which is said to have been prevalent at the time. It is true that Queen's had a relatively high proportion of scholarship boys, many from North Country grammar schools, and an ethos of hard work which set it apart from some other colleges, like Christ Church and Trinity, but in a lifetime's career at Oxford involving membership of three other colleges, including Christ Church, I have never suffered any such disparagement on account of my schooling.

There were, of course, people from King Edward's at Oxford with whom I was in touch and who helped one feel at home. A F Wells, by this time a Fellow of University College and the model set before me by Jardine, was now out of reach, but Ted Abraham at the outset of his enormously distinguished career was a friendly presence at Queen's and Jack Quinn and Jack Shipwright were next door at St Edmund Hall. Gordon Merifield became well known as cox of the Oxford crews who first defeated Cambridge after an unbroken series of Cambridge victories in the 20s and 30s.

I learnt at an early stage of another school connection which was to be a precious resource throughout my time at Oxford. The annual concert of the Eglesfield Music Society was held in Queen's in the Michaelmas Term and it was indicated to me by Ted Abraham that as the most junior old Edwardian present it was my job to act as host to the Aunts. The Aunts were two maiden ladies, Aunt Ada and Auntie Lett, the Misses Lindsey, who lived in Summertown and whose nephew John ran Lindsey's butcher's shop in the Covered Market. The Aunts had befriended an earlier generation of old Edwardians, the first of whom was I think David Davis, who in my time was a household name as 'Uncle David' on the Children's Hour. The Miss Lindseys had continued to act as 'aunts' to succeeding 'nephews' ever since. They held open house for tea on Sunday afternoons. It was a pleasant interlude of 'Town' when the pressures of 'Gown' were becoming oppressive. Aunt Ada was tall and stately, Auntie Lett small and energetic, and the two of them refuted any notion that lifelong spinsters lacked anything to live for. The entire family were pillars of the Congregational Church in Summertown. From time to time in summer they would take a picnic to a meadow on the outskirts of Yarnton, belonging to the family, which had an open barn in a corner of it. This was for them a veritable expedition. My other link with 'Town' was my uncle George whom I would meet at summer eights when he drove the Thames Conservancy Launch.

One thing which could not easily carry over from Southampton to Oxford was my relationship with Peggy. We met, of course, regularly during vacations and corresponded quite a lot about matters of common interest but it became steadily apparent that something was missing. The obvious explanation was that we were growing apart and the difference between 'allegro' and 'penseroso' was making itself felt. Peggy was becoming more active politically and travelled quite a bit. I was by no means reconciled to this change in our relationship and wanted to hold onto and reanimate the old strong sentiment for one another. I think, in retrospect, that we were not so much growing apart as growing up and she was growing up faster than I was. She was no longer content with the old romantic friendship and did not want any intensification of it. She wrote to me in the summer of 1936 and assured me that our friendship was unchanged and that I was losing only something further which I had hoped would eventually come about, but which had never actually existed between us. There was some sexual attraction but not enough, and not of the same kind; I felt it in my imagination, she in her senses. All this was undeniably true and, for good measure, she added another factor that made a difference between us. She said that she was hungry for experiences, while I could make do with very little. It was 'l'Allegro' and 'Il Penseroso' again. I suppose I realised by now that, although a great deal of sympathy and understanding remained, there was little likelihood of my longer term hopes being realised. In the middle of Michaelmas Term 1936 I decided to make one further attempt to overcome the growing separation and arranged to visit her at Ashridge where she was on a course. I do not remember at all the tenor of our conversation, but only the misery of my journey back to Oxford in the rain. I missed my bus connection at Berkhampstead and had to ring the College to tell them of my late arrival. I remember the next few months as being deeply depressed.

Peggy became more and more active in the pacifist cause in the next few years and in 1938 she wrote to tell me that she and a friend, Hugh Bingham, who was also a dedicated pacifist, were going together to Palestine on a mission to do what they could to heal the breach between Jews and Arabs in that increasingly divided country.

It meant leaving college without taking her degree but she had persuaded her teachers that this was the right thing for her to do. They arrived in Palestine in December 1938 and had some initial success in mediating between influential people in both communities. But in February 1939 Hugh was shot and seriously wounded by two Israeli policemen and lay severely paralysed in hospital until his death in April. Peggy had tended him devotedly during that time.

I wondered later whether the break with Peggy was in any degree responsible for my subsequent failure in Mods. I had worked hard for a First but in the event I got a Second. With thirteen papers, all of which counted, it was the toughest examination I ever took. To get a First one needed 'A's in a majority of papers. I had calculated in advance that if I got 'A's in all the prepared books I should be home and dry. So I decided to concentrate on them and did in fact work very hard at them. The unprepared papers I would have to leave to chance. As it happened I obtained 'A's in all the unprepared papers, six of them, and high 'B's in the seven prepared papers. This result was distinctly odd and I came to the conclusion that I had simply worked too hard on the prepared books endeavouring to make sure that I covered everything and leaving nothing to inspiration on the day. In the unprepared papers I had had to live on my wits and they had risen to the occasion.

I was now determined that, come what may, I should get a First in Greats, when I was examined in June 1939. But this presented an obvious problem. I must not repeat my mistake and work too hard, but clearly I must work effectively. Here I had the benefit of a piece of research I had undertaken in the Long Vacation of 1936 when I had to read the whole of Homer. It occurred to me that this was a golden opportunity to discover the best hours of the day for academic work. Each day I worked from 10 to 1, 2 to 4, and 5 to 7, until I had completed the Iliad and the Odyssey. At the end of each hour on each day I noted the number of lines of Homer read. It was to be expected that my rate would improve as time went on, but this would not affect the comparative performance in the course of a single day. When I had finished the whole of Homer I analysed the notes and they were definitive for the remainder of my life. From 10 to 11 I averaged 350 lines, from 11 to 12 400 and from 12 to 1 350 again. From 2 to 4 the score was 200 lines an hour; and from 5 to 7 it was back to 300/350. The verdict was clear: the afternoons were a dead loss and the best times for working were the forenoon and the evenings before dinner. I did not try the after dinner hours because I knew that I was a lark and not an owl and that as night approached my intellectual powers declined. (This was to be a considerable handicap in my academic career; most philosophical meetings take place after dinner and this gives a distinct advantage to those who, like, notoriously, Dick Hare, are at their best late at night or in the early hours of the morning.) So I reckoned that I had good statistical evidence for the traditional university day in which the forenoon and the early evening were devoted to academic work, while the afternoon was given over to athletic pursuits or other forms of exercise, unless you were unlucky enough to have to attend committees which, presumably, were not thought to require much in the way of intellectual exertion.

So in the Trinity Term of 1937 I began Greats. So far as I was concerned Mods was a prolegomenon. I had never reckoned myself to be more than a competent classicist and the second in Mods was a disappointment rather than a disaster. Greats were different. I don't think that at the time I was hoping to teach Philosophy, but to study it was what I had come to Oxford for and would equip me, as I earnestly believed, to answer the great problems of life. It was a severe blow to me to discover that these were systematically avoided. We were started by way of Descartes, Locke, Berkeley and Hume on the problems of perception and I became acquainted with sense-data and the challenge of phenomenalism. Initially we were required to read Bradley's *Appearance and Reality* and *Principles of Logic*, but only, it became apparent, in order to appreciate better the force of Russell and Moore's destructive criticism of them. Our tutor, A D Woozley, was severely Socratic in his methods and patiently demolished my arguments without at all indicating what his view of the matter might be. There was to begin with plenty to demolish, because I persisted in reading the works of Bergson, whose heady speculations and attractive style presented a beguiling alternative to our staple diet. I was unwise enough occasionally to introduce some of the ideas and much of the style into my essays until I learned better. Tony Woozley who, as I discovered later, was only five years older than I was, did his best without undue discouragement, to initiate me into the spare style and disciplined habits of thought characteristic of analytical philosophy. All the same, for one of my temperament, Stuart Hampshire, who taught us subsequently, was a more effective tutor. He always had a line of his own on the matter in dispute and, by arguing for this, challenged one to develop one's own alternative point of view. With Woozley I always felt constricted and constrained; with Hampshire I could begin to get my bearings and form some inkling of how a coherent philosophical position might be developed which would illuminate a range of problems and not just the one being currently dealt with. This process did not, of course, extend to the questions I longed to explore of how or why the world existed, what was one's place in it and how one ought to live, but, as time went on, the exclusion of these came to seem to me more and more arbitrary and artificial. Nevertheless Tony Woozley was always friendly and considerate. On one occasion he remarked with an air of resignation 'the trouble with you Basil is that you are interested in the great rolling themes of philosophy'.

Ancient History, I was surprised to discover, I enjoyed rather more. Guy Chilver, who taught us both Greek and Roman History, was an enthusiast whose interest in his subject was infectious. Theo and I shared tutorials and this was very good for me. He had a ready grasp of detail which I lacked but was challenged to acquire and we made an effective pair, my contribution being a capacity to think up alternative scenarios of what *might* have happened. Since, unlike Theo, I had no ambitions to become an Ancient Historian, I could revel in the sheer intellectual pleasure of the subject as I could not in Philosophy where the outcome mattered too much.

It was in this summer term of 1937 that an encounter occurred which was to become the centre of my life for the next ten years. I was introduced by Christopher to Phoebe Llewellyn Smith who was also reading Greats at St Hugh's. Christopher had invited her along with Elizabeth Marshall to tea. Elizabeth was tall and graceful with soft brown eyes and it was clear at once that Christopher was attracted to her and would leave Phoebe to me. The first impression she made on me was of intelligence, the next of an exceedingly sharp sensibility. It was only after I had received these impressions that I took notice of her features which were highly expressive of these qualities. In repose they had something of the character of an Italian

Renaissance drawing – a matter of line rather than colour as she was
distinctly pale. Her eyes were her most distinctive feature, clear and
pale blue, with the curious habit of deepening in intensity when she
was laughing or concentrating hard, so that at times they seemed to
be almost black. In the following weeks we met again and walked
often in the Oxfordshire countryside. She came and stayed with us
in Southampton and the walks continued in the New Forest. I
learned that she was the youngest daughter of a distinguished civil
servant Sir Hubert Llewellyn Smith of whom, I discovered later, Roy
Jenkins in his biography of Churchill wrote 'Churchill also had the
good luck to have as his permanent secretary Sir Hubert Llewellyn
Smith, one of the greatest constructive civil servants of his day'.

For a short period of time, ending some four months later, early
in the Michaelmas Term, I was happier than at any time before or
since in my early life. It was the sort of confident carefree happiness
in which present enjoyment is intensified by being seen against a
receding background of taken-for-granted hope. Each of us had the
experience of finding for the first time someone else who was
sufficiently alike to understand one's thought intuitively and sufficiently different to extend one's imaginings indefinitely into hitherto
unknown territories. It was not long before I found myself to be
hopelessly in love. It began when she invited me to a dance at St
Hugh's and appeared with her abundant straw-coloured hair un-
bound instead of turned up in a sort of snood as she usually wore it,
and was confirmed when she with her friend, Elizabeth Marshall,
Christopher and I spent a week rowing in a skiff on the river up to
Lechlade and back in early July. This was a magical interlude and I
was entranced and fascinated by the liveliness of her imagination and
the sharpness of her intellect. I think it true to say that I was so
absorbed in these mental and spiritual qualities and in the changing
expressions of her face which so accurately reflected them that I did
not at the time think about any more physical relationship or feel the
need of it. That I confidently felt could come later and I saw no need
to accelerate it. This was a mistake as I was to discover early in
Michaelmas Term when I saw her one evening in the Banbury Road
hanging on the arm of another young man in the light of a street
lamp. So ended my brief experience of unclouded happiness, but it
did not end our friendship which was destined to continue until her

death sixteen years later. What happened to Philip I never knew but it was plain that he did not play as important a part in her life as I did. I never met him, but, given the manifest impossibility of our parting forever, Phoebe and I were constantly in one another's company and talked insatiably and continued to go for long walks together. We were in our third year now and I was living in a college annexe in the Iffley Road opposite the OURFC ground. My room had a magnificent bay window which overlooked the ground over to Hinksey Hill, much frequented by Matthew Arnold, and I have a vivid memory of standing in the darkened room listening to the slow movement of Beethoven's seventh symphony and watching a star-like light flickering on the hillside opposite; a fit symbol of my not yet entirely extinguished hope. It remains something of a mystery why the two of us over the years grew into an ever closer friendship, albeit a one-sided one in that I never ceased to be in love with her. In retrospect I think that she felt that she needed the sort of undemanding unconditional affection that I represented. It was not until much later that I discovered that she had a somewhat strained relationship with her family to which she was devoted but who were all older than herself – her parents old enough to have been her grandparents. It is just possible that I provided her with the kind of steady background to her life which she could not, would not, let her family be, but only, of course, so long as I did not erupt into anything more demanding. However that may be, there came a time when, in writing to me, she began to use the formula 'with love from', saying that I mustn't misunderstand it, but she always used it to her girl-friends who meant less to her than I did. It will seem strange to anyone at home in today's world that a man and a woman should share so much and yet have so little physical contact, let alone not sleep with one another, but the likelihood is that, if it had been otherwise, we should not have spent so much time exploring spiritual and intellectual byways. As it happened Phoebe became, as a matter of course, part of the group of friends formed by Theo, Harold, Jean and myself who, with Christopher as a sort of out-flyer, were at the centre of my remaining time as an undergraduate.

One virtue of Greats as it used to be was that there were very few options, with the result that people in one's own and other colleges were studying the same books at the same time. And, in our first year of Greats, after the brief introduction to logic and epistemology, Theo, Phoebe and I found ourselves reading Plato's *Republic*, attending the same lectures and, for the most part, writing the same essays. I discovered then for myself, what later as a tutor I tried to bring about, that discussions among ourselves were even more educative than tutorials and lectures. In Plato I encountered philosophy on a grand scale. In the *Republic* the questions I had always wanted to explore were not only ventilated, they were explicitly raised and answered. It is true that our teachers were, as a rule, not interested in these aspects of the work which they tended to regard as peripheral to the contributions to logic and epistemology which were the proper topics of philosophy and which we were invited to criticise by the use of superior modern analysis. Nevertheless, to our minds, the Parable of the Cave and the Myth of Er were superb imaginative creations which hinted at profound truths in, arguably, the only way in which such truths can be expressed. It would be wrong to suppose that I did not benefit from Woozley's careful instruction. Although I was always to feel, with H H Price, that clarity was not enough, I badly needed to develop standards of clarity and rigour in all cases where these were applicable and the results of Woozley's ministrations were, I think, reasonably apparent. One consequence was that, although I always remained attached to Christopher, I grew impatient with what appeared to me to be his tendency to uncritical, sentimental, if not sententious, generalisation; and I think he found me increasingly lacking in proper profundity. My own innate inclination to theory and unwillingness to rest until I had discovered some all-encompassing explanation was constantly checked by Phoebe who had a lively sense of the particular, so that, while still liable to Wordsworthian moments when walking in the countryside, I also had my attention called to seasonal changes of colour and texture that I had never noticed before. One that I specially remember was the way that in autumn elms changed colour in patches – something which I always continued to notice until, sadly, there were no more elms.

The effect of philosophy tutorials, at any rate in Woozley's hands, was they tended to atomise philosophy. We learned to detect errors, particularly our own, but there was little positive encouragement to develop an alternative solution to the problem under discussion, let alone a comprehensive solution to a range of such problems. An antidote to this, to which Phoebe and I both resorted, was provided by the lectures of H H Price, then Wykeham Professor of Logic. These were exemplary lectures, carefully worked out and delivered with immense clarity. They could be heard without difficulty in any part of the imposing medieval hall of New College. Price, a notably shy man, kept his eyes fixed on one corner of the roof. This helped to give the lectures an essential element of eccentricity together with the humour which was introduced chiefly by way of the examples. Such as, in the case of universals, Chimaerahood and Seaserpentitude. Price was the soul of courtesy and this informed his lectures and, as I later discovered, his informal classes. It was a principle of his, when criticising a position he did not hold, to reformulate it in what he thought its strongest form and only then to expound his own preferred alternative. In this way one was taught how actually to philosophise; and, in the informal classes, where his starting point had to be a stumbling assertion of one's own, he would take it up, however muddled it was, and say, 'I wonder whether something like this is what you want to say?' and there would follow a sentence with the following characteristics: it was clear; it was, so far as one could tell, true; and it was recognisably what one was trying to say.

I think that for me this was a turning point in my development as a philosopher or, rather, into a philosopher. It gave me confidence, hitherto lacking, that where I felt dissatisfaction with a philosophical position, I could hope, if I thought hard enough, to arrive at a defensible alternative. This would in itself have represented a considerable debt to Price, but he later increased it by inviting me to walk with him in and around Oxford. I cannot now remember when these walks started but it was well before the end of my undergraduate career. In the course of them I disclosed to him my interest in Eastern religions and my Sufi background and my consequent disappointment at the severely analytic character of philosophy as I was being taught it. To my surprise he confessed to similar dissatisfaction and expressed his conviction that there was a spiritual reality beyond the perceived material world. At that stage his main hopes were placed in psychical research and he was a leading figure in the Society for Psychical Research. I found, then and later, that I shared his interest in psychical research, but I was never able to give it the spiritual importance it had for him. I thought it was intellectually intriguing and I relished oddities which called in question the dominant materialistic conception of the world. Price valued it as providing a decisive refutation of materialism which opened the way for serious metaphysical speculation.

When I met him again after the war he had become, he told me, 'a non-denominational theist' and, on further consideration, be became a communicant member of the Church of England. With characteristic humility he demonstrated his new-found faith, not by attendance at the imposing services of New College Chapel, but by becoming churchwarden at the unpretentious hall church at the foot of Jack Straw's Lane. Sadly in his later years he became a victim of Alzheimer's disease and when I met him once at an Encaenia garden party in the company of his sister, and tried to say how much I owed to him, it became apparent that he did not understand a word I was saying and simply stood there smiling ineffably.

At his memorial service in New College Chapel I was sitting next to Don MacNabb, who had known him well. As we left the chapel MacNabb said 'In his last few years he was nothing but a shell', and then he added 'a shell of courtesy'. Some years before that Henry Chadwick and I sought to persuade him to deliver the Sarum Lectures. He was very reluctant to undertake them, protesting that he was unsure if he was still capable of it. In the event he did deliver them and they were published under the title *Essays in the Philosophy of Religion*. There was one lecture in which he endeavoured to apply the findings of psychical research to the Witch of Endor and Walls of Jericho. I was afraid that, if published, it would invite ridicule on account of its total ignorance of critical Old Testament scholarship, an indication that his judgement was beginning to fail. I succeeded in persuading him and I am glad I did because the rest of the book is a worthwhile contribution to the philosophy of religion. In particular, it contains the best account I know of what heaven may be like. If, as I confidently believe, he now knows, he will be finding it a remarkably interesting experience. Phoebe was not involved in my relationship with Price, who was not at ease with women, but he was regarded as a resource equally by both of us and when we encountered an intractable difficulty, we would say 'we must ask Price'.

It was expected that one would occupy the afternoons in some form of athletic pursuit. Christopher was Captain of College athletics and also of Soccer. Harold, somewhat incongruously, appeared on the wing for the Second Rugby XV. I decided in my second term to take up rowing and went down daily to the College barge, which unlike the ornate wooden ones, was an all metal affair with a conspicuous red eagle as figure head. My light weight proved a handicap – I never, until after the war, exceeded 9st 13lb – and after a spell at bow in the Second Eight, I was transferred to the other end of the boat as cox. For this I had a good carrying voice and I proved quite expert at estimating the currents of the Isis and controlling the boat as we, from time to time, negotiated the locks on the way to Port Meadow where we could train unencumbered by other craft.

After Mods I dropped rowing and from there on transferred my interest to the Cherwell. In the course of time, I became an expert punter who viewed with scorn the majority who trailed the pole in order to avoid ramming the bank or collision with other punts, while I maintained a steady momentum by gentle alterations of course achieved by planting the pole at the correct angle. I like to think that I presented an elegant figure, apt to impress whoever was lying at my feet – whenever possible, Phoebe. Quite often in the Summer Term, with or without a companion, I would take a punt upstream, moor it in the reeds among the willows and read Plato or Aristotle or some book not among those prescribed; or more often enjoy vacancy. There must have been many such afternoons as I do not pick up physical skills quickly. This means that quite often the weather must have been fine, unlike in recent years when May and June have been miserable months.

Meanwhile in the summer of 1938 momentous events occurred at home. Our family was deeply involved in the Sufi Movement and, I do not remember how, it was arranged that Betty and I should take my mother to stay at the Sufi Headquarters at Suresnes, a suburb of Paris bordering on the Bois de Boulogne. It was by no means a straightforward journey. Invalids were not expected to travel much in those days and my mother's spinal carriage, although light and manoeuvrable – she herself weighed almost nothing – could not be got into a ship's cabin or saloon or in a railway carriage. Fortunately my father knew the Manager of the Southern Railway who ran the steam packets to Le Havre and had contacts with the SNCF, so everything was done that could be done to expedite her journey. My mother was placed on a platform under the bridge which provided some degree of shelter and Betty and I sat with her. At one point we ran into fog and the Captain sent a sailor down from the bridge to warn her whenever he was about to sound the foghorn. In the train from Le Havre to Paris we travelled in the luggage van, my mother's carriage secured by wedges to prevent her accidentally sliding through the one side of the van which was entirely open to the French countryside. On arrival at the Gard du Nord I cannot remember how we got to Suresnes. Probably we took turns to push her, as we did later, when we took her to the great Paris Exhibition. What I do remember is that she was an object of great interest in the streets of Paris, where an invalid carriage was an unusual sight. Betty and I used to be embarrassed at the way people stared at her with uninhibited curiosity whenever we stopped, but she did not seem to mind and they just went on staring.

The house, Fazal Manzil, at Suresnes had a large park-like garden, which was home to a sort of ashram. There was a large one-storey hall and a number of other low buildings providing accommodation. The whole had a pleasantly relaxed atmosphere with people wandering in quiet conversation along the paths. They turned out to be mainly northern European, predominantly Dutch and Scandinavian and all English-speaking. My memory is of a distinctly upper class, mainly middle-aged, set of people. Betty and I were very much the youngest and we naturally gravitated to the members of the Inayat Khan family living in the house itself. Inayat Khan had died some while ago, leaving his American widow and four children. The eldest, Hidayat, a professional viola player, was not resident, but Vilayat was there together with his two sisters Noorunnissa and Chairunnissa (Babulie and Mamulie, pronounced Bubbly and Mummly). All three were very attractive with an innate dignity as befitted a royal family, which is what they were. Vilayat, it was generally assumed, would in due course become the leader of the movement and was treated by the middle-aged ladies with a veneration which he affected to scorn, but which, Betty and I thought, he secretly enjoyed. His was, in fact, a difficult assignment. He was a cultivated, liberal young Frenchman, more cosmopolitan that most, but endowed with a spiritual persona which was not just assumed. He ran a Triumph sports car. Noorunnissa was quiet and gentle and content to remain in the background with a haunting sing-song voice. The youngest, Chairunnissa, had evidently decided to adopt the European side of her inheritance. She used make-up to bring out and emphasise the paleness of her complexion and she had auburn hair which may or may not have been tinted. All three were musical. Vilayat played the cello, Noor the violin and Chairunnissa the piano. She also composed piano sonatas in the manner of Mozart. Their mother was fair with a rather faded beauty and gave the impression of having been overwhelmed and overawed by her husband, whose personality could still be felt; indeed there was a palpable distinction among the devotees between those who had known him and those who had not.

Of the same generation as him were two older members of the family, Maheboob Khan and Ali Khan. Mabeboob Khan was provisionally leader of the movement until Vilayat was ready to take over. He was an unimpressive little man who was scarcely adequate to his role. Ali Khan, on the other hand, was a formidable figure. He was of average height, but he weighed, we were told, twenty stone and had been at different times a champion wrestler and an opera singer. No musical occasion was complete without his rendering in a fine tenor voice with a distinctly Italian style the aria from Mendelssohn's *Elijah*, 'If with all your heart ye truly seek me'. He was also said to have powers as a healer. There was at Fazal Manzil an atmosphere of gentle spirituality, which we found congenial, and my mother became, as always, a centre of attention. One person who became particularly attracted to her and the only one of those present to become a lifelong friend, was Hayat Bouman. She was christened Leny, and Hayat was her Sufi name, which she always used. She was a tall handsome woman who only just failed of being beautiful, although with plucked eyebrows and careful make-up she made the very best of her looks. She came from Rotterdam and was in love with two countries besides her own, England and India. She had learned English and gained her love of the language from regular attendance at prayer book services in the Anglican Church at Rotterdam. Her English was well nigh perfect except that she could not manage her 'th's which became 'd's. It has always seemed to me that one of the virtues of the English language, as distinct say from French, is that it sounds attractive when spoken by foreigners, and it was certainly so in the case of Hayat. One thing which endeared Hayat to us was that she had acquired a very English sense of humour (though quite how the Book of Common Prayer had imparted this, I never understood). So while she remained a lifelong Sufi and ended her days at the Sufi Centre in Delhi, she shared with us our amusement at the more absurd manifestations of belief at Suresnes (which were in fact more theosophical than distinctively Sufi, since the two often overlapped in individuals, especially women) as when an earnest middle-aged female lecturer asked someone to shut the window because there was risk of her aura blowing out of it.

When we arrived in Paris I knew that Harold and Jean and Theo were to be there and we duly met. I made no attempt to involve them with our life at Suresnes and we met little. When we arrived we learned that Theo was in hospital with some not very serious complaint and I determined to call on him. I thought that a suitable gift for an invalid would be a packet of dates. I looked up 'date' in the dictionary and found 'millésime'. So I went into a fruitier and asked for 'un paquet de millésimes'. Not surprisingly the assistant was baffled until I saw a box of dates and pointed to it. 'Ah, dattes', she exclaimed. So I took them to Theo and doubtless my story hastened his recovery.

Our main Paris expedition was to the Grand Exposition which was being held that year. Betty and I determined to take my mother to it, which meant pushing her all the way from Suresnes to the exhibition site and all the way back again. I dare say Hayat helped us but it was an enormous distance to walk, let alone push her carriage, in a city we did not know, negotiating the crowds and the traffic. Moreover we stayed for the fireworks which were a dramatic spectacle over the Seine. We were disappointed with the British pavilion whose half-hearted understatement compared unfavourably with the brutal monumentality of the German and Soviet pavilions (captured so brilliantly by Osbert Lancaster in *From Pillar to Post*).

While we were at Suresnes, Hayat had some stomach trouble and also some problem with her eyes. She decided to avail herself of Ali Khan's powers as a healer. According to her own account he dealt with the former by getting her to lie on her back on the ground and walking on her tummy and the latter by pulling her eyes from their sockets and letting them spring back into place. She did not go back for further treatment and reckoned she now understood the basis of Ali Khan's reputation as a healer. All his patients avoided any repetition of the treatment by declaring that they were miraculously healed.

At the end of our time at Suresnes Hayat suggested that I might come and spend a fortnight with her family in Rotterdam. This I did and it was a curious mixture of carefree enjoyment and incipient terror. Hayat's family lived in a terraced brick house on Spangensche Kade, which did not survive the German bombing of May 1940. Her family were warmly welcoming. Her father, a tall man with a grey crew-cut, was in charge of the joinery work at Wilton's shipyard and, as an instance of Dutch courtesy, I remember being taken by him to buy timber at Dordrecht. We inspected the vast tree trunks which lay floating alongside a quay, having been towed down river, and when he and his opposite number repaired to the latter's office on the quay they plied me with schnapps and insisted on carrying on their business in English. Most of the time Hayat and I explored Rotterdam and the surrounding countryside on bicycles which were evidently for most people the chosen means of transport. The whole area was not the maze of motorways it is now and my memory is of flat straight roads alongside canals with windmills at intervals and astonishingly clear views of distant churches under huge skies with marvellous cloud-scapes. We went for one longer expedition to stay with her married sister near Utrecht. On the way we visited Gouda, famous for cheeses, but interesting to us on account of its equally famous 16th century stained glass. This journey gave me some problems with the bicycle. Dutch bicycles did not have handbrakes. You broke by putting backward pressure on the pedals which was easy to master except on hills. How, whether uphill or downhill, could you start riding while at the same time using the pedals to stop yourself sliding downhill?

Hayat was very good company. She was ten years older than me and I enjoyed being seen in the company of a good-looking older woman. The idea of falling in love with her did not occur to me, but we were companionable in a way that owed something to sexual attraction. Hayat had confessed to Betty that she wished she was ten years younger and I did sometimes later wonder whether I had too much taken her for granted, but all in all these were for both of us days of unworried pleasure. The fun I had had in Suresnes at her expense on account of her imperfect pronunciation of English was matched by her amusement at my attempts to speak Dutch, especially the 'sch' sound, as in 'schiedam' and 'scheveningen'.

I do not think it was simply my ignorance of Dutch which made the morning service she took me to at the Oude Kerke in Rotterdam the most tedious I have ever had to endure. As I remember it the sermon lasted one and a half hours, punctuated at half hour intervals by the passing round of the collection bag. I have always found it difficult to reconcile myself to Protestantism in its Calvinistic form and my reaction is partly aesthetic. The interiors of those splendid Dutch Gothic churches, designed to concentrate the eyes of the worshippers on the elevation of host at the altar at the east end, are ruined by the enormous pulpit half way down the nave with the seating very often arranged to centre on it.

The obvious way to get from Rotterdam to Southampton was by one of the transatlantic liners which called in at Southampton and I was able to book a passage on the Holland Amerika Line's *Statendam*. Before I left for home Holland was beginning to be overshadowed by the increasingly threatening noises from across the border in Germany – literal noises. Wherever Hayat and I walked round Rotterdam there were little knots of people gathered round radios listening to broadcasts of the Nuremberg rallies, Hitler's staccato speeches and the answering 'Sieg Heil, sieg Heil'. Throughout my undergraduate days we had always realised that in the background of our lives was the threat of war, but we never seriously expected it to become actual. While I was in Holland the Munich agreement was signed which afforded some relief, but it was an unhappy state of mind, because we most of us felt that we should have gone to war to save Czechoslovakia. I don't think I was at the time clear-headed enough to admit that it was only a reprieve. As I have recounted elsewhere, the gravity of the situation only hit me on the short voyage home when on the first morning at sea we passed through the straights of Dover and saw the white cliffs glistening in the sun. And then it was not a matter of rational conviction, but of an uncontrollable bursting into tears.

Back at Oxford for my final year I was able to live in College again by sharing rooms with Trev Gardner. Trev had been brought up in

Southampton too but attended the rival school, Taunton's. He was a shade taller than me and had a round face with fair hair, so fine and short as to approximate to baldness. He had got to meet our family in Southampton and fell under my mother's spell. Like all my friends he fell in love with Betty, but in his case it became an obsession and on more than one occasion he threatened suicide. Once, indeed, he disappeared entirely from Oxford and I was sufficiently alarmed when he did not occupy his bed, to alert the College authorities. My worry was his threat of suicide. In the event he was found to have gone to Southampton to see Betty and she and my mother between them managed to calm him down and persuade him to return to Oxford. It was not surprising that Trev was somewhat unbalanced. His mother, a widow, had gone off to India with a lover and left Trev in late adolescence to look after himself and two brothers. The eldest of the three, Stafford, was a brilliant student who, while at Christ Church on a scholarship, had a severe breakdown which was diagnosed as schizophrenia. Stafford was a long stay patient in the Littlemore Hospital. It fell to Trev to visit him regularly and sometimes I went with him. He would find Stafford deep in a book or sunk in lethargy and, in order to attract his attention, it was necessary to strike a match and wave it in front of him. It was plain to all of us that Trev was afraid that he would experience a similar breakdown himself, but with enormous courage he managed to suppress these fears most of the time and was an amusing and engaging companion. Trev and I occupied a double room on the ground floor of the Front Quad in Queen's. It was a splendid panelled room, its sole drawback being that it was rather dark, facing over Queen's Lane to St Peter in the East. It was a convenient place for people to drop in and dump things and was a regular meeting place for our friends, Theo, Phoebe, Jean and Harold and, more occasionally, Christopher.

We were all in our final year and by now thoroughly at home in Oxford. We knew how to ration attendance at lectures. We had mastered the art of writing essays for tutorials. Theo and I went together both to Hampshire and to Chilver and I had learnt, as most bright undergraduates do, not to put my own convictions on the line, but to consider philosophy as an elaborate game, whose rules one was becoming familiar with. My reports at the end of term were consistently good and there were hints that 'he should justify himself in Schools'. The custom on these occasions was for one's tutor to read a brief report on the term's work and for the Provost to comment on it. I remember only two of these occasions. On one of them Woozley had read a distinctly congratulatory report on my progress, when Provost Hodgkin wheeled round, glared at me and said 'This will not do at all. You must pull your socks up.' I was beginning to think that he was a bit hard to please, when Woozley intervened. 'This is Mr Mitchell, Provost'. Hodgkin beamed and said, 'Well done, Mitchell'. Another was when Woozley read a report from Hampshire, who, of course, as a Fellow of All Souls, was not himself present, which began 'Although not a brilliant student, Mr Mitchell has done an excellent term's work'. It was the negative not the positive element in this report which stayed with me and led me to wonder whether I was foolish to want to become a philosopher.

Phoebe meanwhile had been discovered to be anaemic and had been ordered by her doctor not to do more than five hours work a day. This was a blessing and saved her from the overwork which is the regular temptation of women students. It was a good time for Phoebe. She was enjoying her work now that the pressure was off and she was doing bits of painting and writing poetry. At the St Hugh's Christmas concert the choir sang a carol of which she had composed both the words and the music. She had two would-be lovers, neither of whom was unduly demanding.

I do not remember that we were particularly oppressed by the international situation. There had been so much said and written about the horrors of aerial bombardment that, however, imminent it might be, war was not really thinkable. Meanwhile we had Schools to prepare for and, unlike war, this was a matter we could do something about. Our regular course work was over by Christmas and the Hilary Term and the first part of the Trinity Term were given over to revision. Much has been said over the years about the disadvantages of a final examination and the strains it imposed upon candidates, but it had one signal advantage. These terms of revision enabled one to gather together the philosophical and historical themes we had been pursuing in the last two years and weave them into a coherent pattern. In philosophy this had the further advantage that by now we had developed some understanding of philosophical method and could apply this to work we had done earlier as we could not have done if it had been examined piece by piece at earlier stages of the course. Almost more important, it meant that our tutors were not our examiners and we did not need to impress them; they had a common interest with us in conspiring against the examiners.

Theo and I badly needed to get a First. For Phoebe it did not matter except to the extent that she did not want to let down her family. In any case her doctor's orders prevented her working too hard and provided her with an excuse. The weather was fine and hot when we took the papers in the Examination Schools and we were allowed to remove our jackets, so long as we retained our gowns. It was customary at the time to give every candidate a Viva. Even those whose class was clearly determined by their papers appeared before the examiners for three to five minutes, and it was, as I later discovered, a point of honour among examiners to frame questions which would make the formality an educational opportunity. Theo and I both had formal Vivas which left us wondering what our class could be. It was too much to expect that we had achieved formal Firsts. Phoebe had a longish Viva which left no indication what class she was being viva'd for.

The results were not expected until early August. While we were waiting for them, Phoebe came to stay with us in Southampton. We had arranged with Theo that he would go down to the Schools to read the list and telegraph the results to us. On the day itself Phoebe and I took a bus to Romsey and we spent the day at Mottisfont, where we walked and talked alongside the river Test. By tea time we were back in Romsey and we said 'the results must have come by now' so we rang home and my mother read us Theo's telegram 'Phoebe, yourself, myself all Firsts!' We rode on the top of the bus back to Southampton and for us it was the top of the world.

CHAPTER 3

Adjustment to war: 1939–1940

IT WAS A MERE TWO MONTHS after the exultation of our schools
results that war was declared. Its effect was a complete closing down
of horizons. On the one hand for Phoebe, Theo and me there was
no prospect of the careers which we were now qualified to pursue,
Phoebe in painting, Theo and I in academic research. The path to
these was reasonably clear for the immediate future but destined
shortly to be blocked for an indefinite period and perhaps forever.
The alternative was an almost complete blank, some form of war
service the nature of which we could not envisage. Theo was the best
placed. There was a strong tradition of pacifism in his family and he
would volunteer for the Friends' Ambulance Unit, although, of
course, he had no idea where it would take him or what the work
would actually involve.

One consequence of this uncertainty was that our group of Oxford
friends, who might otherwise have been expected to drift apart, were
determined to keep in close contact with one another so far as the
circumstances of the time allowed. Travel became more difficult and
money was short, but we met as often as possible not knowing where
we should be going next and exchanging long 'stream of consciousness' letters.

This was particularly true of Phoebe and me. Was I still in love
with her? Two years ago she had made it clear that she was not in
love with me and I had settled for a friendship which had become
increasingly close, and it became evident in the present crisis that it
meant as much to her as it did to me. I didn't want to threaten this
by declarations of love which I feared would be unwelcome and she,
I think, was very happy to leave things as they were.

As it happened, I spent most of the first year of the war in a
desperately unhappy state of mind about the issue of conscientious
objection. I had always inclined to a vague pacifism (although,
inconsistently, insistent that we should have resisted Mussolini and
Hitler at an earlier stage). It was now a matter of urgency that I

should decide whether to allow myself to be called up or whether to apply to a conscientious objection tribunal. I found myself in a state of confusion about the matter. I could see the case for fighting clearly enough, but I experienced a deep reluctance to be myself involved in the taking of human life. There were plenty of obvious reasons why I should not relish the prospect of spending, and perhaps losing, my life in the armed services and these, I realised, I must put resolutely on one side. But there was one consideration, which weighed with me and which at least appeared to have some moral force. I had just reached the point at which I could begin to develop as a philosopher and make whatever contribution I was capable of to the sum of human good. Was I to abandon all this in order to engage in activities which anyone could undertake and most much better than me?

As I wrestled with this problem and wrote to Phoebe about it at excessive length, I received from her a letter which, once and for all, settled this particular issue for me. She pointed out that it was natural and, within its sphere, reasonable for me to feel as I did, but was it relevant? There must be many people, among, for example, the defenders of Warsaw, who could say the same. And then, with her gift for the particular, she added:

> It is impossible to estimate the precise value of what we have to give to the world, but we must keep a sense of proportion. Supposing you became as distinguished a philosopher as, say, Bradley and I as distinguished a painter as Dame Laura Knight (I choose these two because they are well above average, yet certainly nothing like in the top class) how can we estimate how much that depth of competence justifies us in setting ourselves apart?

And then she went on to point out that both art and philosophy require a world in which truth and beauty are recognised.

But that consideration also having been put aside, I still felt the pull of the pacifist case. The trouble was that I could not formulate a clear and defensible argument for it.

At this time I was greatly helped by David Rafilovich, to whom I had been introduced by Phoebe. He had got his First a year before us and was now embarked on a D.Phil as Robinson Senior Scholar at Oriel. He had worked out his position as a conscientious objector

more fully than I had and I was helped greatly throughout the
following year by his friendship and his example. He was at that time
a convinced intuitionist and took his stand on the absolute wrongness
of taking human life. I could not share this view but admired the
clarity with which he maintained it as contrasted with my own
muddle-headedness.

I was deeply ashamed of myself. I should have seen this coming
and thought it through earlier. Who was I, in any case, to think that
my decision was of such significance at a time when other people all
over the world had their own problems and often much more serious
ones? Yet the decision in this case had to be mine and I couldn't and
shouldn't escape it. The resulting preoccupation was intensely
self-centred, yet I could see no way of avoiding it.

I did indeed appreciate that there were many other young men in
the same predicament as me and that sometimes induced a sort of
generalised self-pity. How unfair it was that we should be required
to make the decision at a time of life when we had not yet reached
the degree of maturity which would enable us to make it responsibly!

If only I could see more clearly I could act decisively – or, for that
matter, if I could see *less* clearly the merits of opposing points of view.
So I wrote to Phoebe, with a hint of melodrama: 'we poor people
who would be stronger, if we could be blinder, but cannot be blind
enough or strong enough, are in danger of complete ineffectiveness.'

When I saw the Universities Conscientious Objectors Tribunal I
was still in this confused and uncertain state of mind and did apply
for non-combatant service in the Friends Ambulance Service. A D
Lindsay, Master of Balliol, was chairman of the Board and heard me
sympathetically. In a gesture which has always commanded my
profound admiration he sent me a note afterwards saying that he
sensed that I was in two minds about the question and adding that he
would be glad to see me in Balliol if I cared to call on him. I did this
and, although I do not remember that our conversation was
particularly helpful, it was enormously reassuring to be taken
seriously and I have remembered his action ever since as an example
of the disinterested concern for the young which characterises the
best sort of don.

Meanwhile life in the present and immediate future had to be seen
to. On the day war broke out I was on the Central Station at

Southampton helping to shepherd boys from my school who were being evacuated, as it happened for the length of the war, to Poole in Dorset. That afternoon my sister Betty and I took my mother and our younger sister Myrtle, then aged fourteen, to Kingston where they would be well out of danger, Southampton being an obvious target for air raids. At Kingston normality reigned, as Betty and I discovered as soon as we arrived. The train could take us as far as Corfe Castle, from where Betty and I had to push my mother in her spinal carriage the one and a half miles to Kingston. The last half mile or so was a steep hill with a gradient of 1 in 4, which in earlier days had been a stiff challenge to a succession of Morris cars. When we reached the top at the bottom end of the village, with Betty and me not a little tired, a friendly village lady addressed my mother and said, 'Oh, Mrs Mitchell, have you come all the way up that hill? You must be exhausted!'

From then on until Term started I was of no fixed address, dividing my time between our house in Southampton, 6 Northlands Gardens, and Theo's parents' house in Oxford, 179 Woodstock Road, and Kingston. Phoebe meanwhile had an altogether more challenging time. As soon as war was inevitable she had volunteered for war work and was put in charge of ambulances at Waltham Abbey as a branch of ARP. I have a letter from her dated 3rd September 1939 in which she tells the story of that day. Her sister's wedding had been brought forward and she was to be married at Upshire on that day with Phoebe as sole bridesmaid. At 11.15, Phoebe having just changed into her blue bridesmaid's dress, they could hear faintly the notorious air raid siren from Waltham Abbey, which turned out to be a false alarm. She had arranged to have the day off, on the understanding that she would be telephoned if they needed her. They had not telephoned, but nothing had been said about an air raid siren. So she changed out of her bridesmaid's dress and cycled into Waltham Abbey. By the time she returned the wedding was over.

As soon as term started and Oxford had as yet changed little I found I had nothing to complain of. I had notice of my Taberdarship (Senior Scholarship) to the value of £200 a year and embarked upon the work which one day might become a D.Phil thesis on Indian Philosophy. I needed to learn Sanskrit first and here I was extraordinarily fortunate. Formally my supervisor was Radhakrishan, then Spalding Professor of Eastern Religion and Ethics, undoubtedly the best living exponent of Hindu philosophy and destined eventually to a career in public life which was to lead him to the Presidency of India. He took a benign but rather remote interest in me and on the rare occasions when we met and I asked him questions about philosophy, I was somewhat frustrated by his tendency to give a complex answer to a question other than the one I had asked. I tried to ascribe this habit charitably to the policy of the Indian sage to answer not the question one had formulated on the surface of one's mind, but a deeper one which he had intuited that one really at a profounder level of one's being wanted to ask.

For regular instruction in Sanskrit I was entrusted to the then Boden Professor of Sanskrit, E H Johnston. He had been a member of the Indian Civil Service, one of that now almost forgotten band of servants of the Raj who had learned to love the language and culture of India. He had assembled a collection of Indian sculpture, and then exhibited in the Indian Institute, which later became part of the holdings in the Oriental Department of the Ashmolean. And he was himself working on Samkhya Yoga. He was a born teacher and, quickly realising the nature of my interest in the language, started me on the *Bhagavad Gita*, a masterpiece of religious reflection which I am glad to have been able to read in the original, although I have now, sadly, forgotten the language and can no longer even read the Devanagari script. He did not neglect the pastoral side of his job and I have vivid memories of an occasion when he and his wife entertained us all to supper before Christmas, the highlight of the evening being a performance of a play in Latin by their two young Dragon sons.

The other feature of this period, which I remember with warm affection, is my lodging for the first half of the year with the Aunts in 11 South Parade. I had a lovely light room on the first floor looking south down Stratfield Road and was given one main meal a day besides bed and breakfast. There must also have been tea, because I remember that when they discovered that I like ginger cake, there was always a succession of ginger cakes. When one was exhausted, Auntie Lett would march in with another, announcing 'The King is dead, long live the King!' The only source of friction was the rare event of my arriving back late at night. On one occasion, to avoid waking them up, I managed to climb into the drawing room window. They said that they would much rather that I rang the bell so that they could come down and open for me. Next time on a bitterly cold winter night with snow on the ground I could not contemplate this and crept into a garden shed where I froze till morning. Needless to say they were not happy with this either. They did not, however, offer me a key.

By the end of the year we all at least had settled addresses. My mother and sisters were at Kingston where they remained until the following September. I was at 11 South Parade and Phoebe had taken a room at 1 Belsize Square which she always referred to as 'the hen-house'. It appeared to be a sort of boarding house for respectable ladies which afforded a base for the one or two nights a week when she could get to the Central School for her painting lessons.

She and I continued to correspond regularly and met occasionally in Oxford or in London. The letters enabled me to keep in touch with her and she to keep in touch not only with me but with the old Oxford life of free and open discussion between equals which I represented. Her family were kind but 'so old' and her ARP associates often objectionable and, even at their best, from an uncongenial world.

Early in the New Year Phoebe met, I do not know how, a charming and very cultivated couple, Roger and Anne Ormrod. He was later to have a distinguished career on the borders between law and medicine. In their circle was a rising barrister, John Copleston Boughey, whom Anne Ormrod regarded as a sort of protegé of hers. Often in John's company, and in the face of Anne's proprietary disapproval, with the background of general misery and at odds with her family, she threw herself into an affair with John, which lasted for four years.

I knew nothing of this and culpably failed to read the signs which in retrospect seem clear enough. When two years later, on the eve of my setting out on naval service in the southern hemisphere, I confessed that I still loved her deeply, she told me that she was sleeping with John and said that she hadn't told me before 'because it hadn't seemed relevant'. She meant, I suppose, that I didn't need to know because I was not at that time a declared rival for her affections. She must have had some inkling what my long-term hopes were, but I imagine that she did not want to further complicate an already complicated situation by admitting this to full consciousness. I blamed myself later for not having presented any kind of alternative to John, but there was in truth little that I could have done. He was already in an established position as a barrister, five years older and presented a fresh challenge to a woman who always relished new experiences. With John she would be venturing into uncharted waters which were well beyond my imaginative reach at the time. However I was someone whose affection and trust she could always take for granted with whom she could share the greater part of her conflicting thoughts and feelings. I was also independent of her family and uninvolved in the confusions of her present situation. From any objective standpoint I was of more use to her as a close and dependable friend than as another would-be lover, especially as I was of greater competence in the one role than I was likely to be in the other. But she came very near to telling me. She wrote me a long letter in the course of which she confessed:

> I have been very much down in hell trying as usual to see everything from all points of view and to a certain extent succeeding, but completely losing sight of what I might think right or wrong in the process; because when one's seen at least three different (but each internally consistent) ways of looking at one thing, one gets a bit dizzy.

And then she went on to tell me about the misunderstandings between herself, Anne and John, which she admits 'is all very funny'. Then she goes on 'but what isn't funny is my own uncertainty'. There follow five lines scratched out (with apologies for the scratching out). Her instinct plainly was to go on and share this predicament with me as she was used to sharing most things. But it struck her at this point that here was something she couldn't or, at least, shouldn't share. My failing to discern what was going on was plainly due to my intense preoccupation at that time with my own problems of conscience.

It was the time of the 'phoney war' and life settled into some kind of routine. By the spring our circle of friends diminished as one by one its members disappeared into military training establishments all over the country, Theo into a series of FAU camps. This increased the number of letters from each inquiring where the others were.

One sign of returning normality was that at Queen's Mrs Hodgkin resumed formal entertaining. Hodgkin was a dry old stick but his wife was beautiful, lively and the best hostess I have ever encountered. She was one of the three attractive and intelligent daughters of A L Smith, sometime Master of Balliol, who all married dons who duly became heads of houses more, we all thought, because of the talents of their wives than of their own. I was invited to a dinner party of mainly senior people to provide a partner of roughly her own age for a German refugee girl whom the Hodgkin's were looking after at the time. I sat next to Liselott Zierer who was attractive and easy to converse with. We arranged to meet again and we got into the habit of exploring Oxford and the surrounding countryside until the time came when she joined the Land Army and was sent to work on a farm at Ducklington near Witney, where I would cycle over to see her on her days off. Mrs Hodgkin, who noticed such things, stopped me one day in the quad and said how grateful she was to me for helping to entertain Liselott. I got the message that I was not to take advantage of her. She need not have worried. Instead of tumbling her in the hay, which she might have preferred, I recited to her passages of German poetry which I had been learning including the whole of *Du bist wie eine Blume*. If my accent in German was as attractive as hers in English this might have had precisely the effect I had, as I thought, been cautioned to avoid.

The Aunts were not able to have me in the summer term which, instead, I spent with a refugee family, the Cassirers, in Carlton Road beyond Summertown. I had met Heinz Cassirer at a bus stop in Summertown. I was carrying an armful of books in Sanskrit and he interrogated me on what I was doing with them. There followed an invitation to his house and when it became apparent that I was looking for lodgings, the suggestion that I should stay with them. The family consisted of Heinz himself, his wife Eva and his daughter Irene, aged ten. Heinz himself was a striking figure with a large leonine head and a deliberately aggressive manner. I later came to think that this was a defence mechanism adopted to parry any suggestion that he, as a refugee, was somehow inferior. Eva, by contrast, was quiet and undemonstrative with delicate features and a gently attractive voice. But the central character in the family was undoubtedly Irene. Her father clearly doted on her and conversed with her as if she was an adult. Whenever a visitor departed she was called upon to give an assessment of his or her character and intellect. As a result of this treatment she was dreadfully precocious. In spite of this she was extremely good company as I discovered when she was instructed to teach me German. Our textbooks were *Zäppfel Kern*, a rather awful children's book and *Mozart auf der Reise nach Prag* by Edward Möricke, a minor classic. Although Irene's standards were severe and her manner condescending, I enjoyed her instruction and, I think, benefited from it. When asked by her father how Basil was doing in his German, she replied, 'His pronunciation is excellent. I wish I could say the same of his vocabulary.'

One morning at breakfast, a quite astonishing event occurred, in that severely atheistic household. Irene declared that she had not slept the night before, but instead lay awake thinking. 'Finally,' she said, 'I came to the conclusion that there is a God'. 'Don't be absurd,' said her father. 'Can you prove it?' 'You're a philosopher', replied Irene, 'and you know that there are all sorts of important truths which can't be proved.' At this Heinz shifted his ground and said, 'Well, what did you do about it?' She replied, 'I went downstairs and searched the bookcase until I found a prayer book and then I said the longest prayer I could find in it.'

Thereafter Irene took to attending Sunday School at St Michael's Church, where, as I learned afterwards, she posed a problem with her questions to the Vicar, Father Burrough, who was a good and godly man, but no intellectual. I was told later, I think it was by the Walshes, that in due course Irene converted first her mother and then her father. Eva had died prematurely, but Heinz continued to lecture in philosophy at Glasgow University where he succumbed to a kind of religious mania. Late in his career he published a book on St Paul which is a vigorous apologetic for Pauline doctrine, taken very much *au pied de la lettre* with no acknowledgement of biblical scholarship.

In due course Heinz was interned in the Isle of Man. Much has been written since then of the enormity of this action, given that most of the internees were determined anti-Nazis, but Heinz was delighted. I remember him saying when he first read the notice, 'This shows that this country really is taking the war seriously.'

So the household now contained only the three of us. Then an incident occurred which showed just how extraordinarily innocent I then was. One afternoon Eva came up to me, placed her hands on my shoulder and planted a firm kiss on my mouth. She then thrust her tongue between my teeth and explored the inside of my mouth thoroughly before withdrawing it. I was totally taken aback by this and did not know how to respond. I stammered, 'I'm afraid I'm not very experienced,' to which she replied, 'that's obvious.' I was so alarmed by this incident and what it might presage that I wrote at once to Jean Fuller, as the only experienced woman of my acquaintance, to ask her advice. Her reply came by return. Her advice, very sensibly, was to do nothing. She was not likely to try again and I must do my best to disguise my embarrassment.

This I was able to do and life continued as if nothing had occurred. Eva, who doubtless shared with Heinz an 'enlightened' attitude to these matters, had concluded without animosity that I was not a suitable candidate for seduction. When my residence at Carlton Road came to an end I did not see the Cassirers until two years later when I visited them on leave from the Navy, as a sub-lieutenant RNVR. Eva left me to converse with Irene a while until her bed-time. When she rejoined me after seeing Irene to bed, there was a smile on her face and she told me that Irene had remarked that 'Basil had grown up a lot since she had last seen him.'

Heinz did not, of course, approve of my conscientious objection but what most puzzled him was my inability to make up my mind. As a strict Kantian who had edited Kant's *Critique of Judgement*, he asserted roundly that 'there is no difficulty in deciding what one's duty is; the difficulty lies only in doing it.'

As I continued to struggle with the problem I began to see it, as I thought, more clearly, helped by the *Bhagavad Gita*. Arjuna at the head of an army preparing to fight a battle with an opposing force which contained many of his relatives, was reluctant to fight, and entered into dialogue on the matter with his charioteer who was the god Krishna in disguise. Krishna endeavoured to change his mind and his clinching argument was that Arjuna was a member of the Kshatriya caste, whose only dharma was to fight. This had no immediate application to my own situation, indeed the clear assumption that it was not of ultimate importance whether one fought or not I found I could not accept; indeed this lead me to give up my Sufi conviction that the same truth was to be found in all religions. But it suggested the possibility that different individuals might have different roles to perform in their lives and that there were some whose vocation it was to stand for an ideal of non-violence even at a time when for the majority it was right to fight. The question then became, was I one of those individuals? However, in the early summer, when the German tanks rolled through France and my beloved Rotterdam was bombed almost to complete destruction, I found that I could not find adequate justification for standing aside and not doing whatever I could to resist this undoubted evil. So I gave up my status as a conscientious objector and prepared to be called up in due course.

I learned subsequently that David had come to the same conclusion and had renounced his pacifism. He was found medically unfit for combatant service in the Army and after a number of unsuitable postings in the Pioneer Corps, he was transferred to the Ministry of Labour where he remained for the rest of the war. This happened through the intervention of William Beveridge, who was engaged in preparing his famous Plan. Beveridge had complained about the misuse in the Forces of talented individuals and was challenged to prepare a list. Beveridge was Master of University College where David had been an undergraduate and put David on his list. It was, apparently, because Bevin would not like someone with a Russian name that David abandoned 'Rafilovich' and became D Daiches Raphael, the name under which after the war he pursued his distinguished academic career. He was ready to drop his apparent foreignness but not in any way to compromise his Jewishness.

At about the same time Phoebe also entered the Civil Service. She was posted to the Air Ministry and shortly afterwards transferred to the Private Office, where she was assistant private secretary to the Air Minister, Sir Archibald Sinclair. From time to time during the war my mother tried to engineer my own transfer to the Civil Service, but I am glad she failed. It is true that I should have been in closer contact with Phoebe, but, with her affair with John in full swing and so much of her life out of bounds to me, it could not have profited me much. And for her it was much more satisfactory to receive affectionate letters from a distant would-be lover and to be able to continue, as far as the separation permitted, the curiously free and close exchange which characterised our correspondence.

Meanwhile my mother and sisters were still in Kingston where they remained isolated from all their friends and I could make only rare and expensive visits. Return to Southampton was still not advisable, so I undertook to find them lodgings in Oxford. My first attempt at 222 Banbury Road was too noisy and uncomfortable but within a week I had found the ideal solution in 18 Osberton Road, which was to be our family home for the rest of the war. It was a quiet street of late 19th century villas close to the Summertown shops and only one block north of South Parade. Mrs Curtis was an elderly widow who was very happy to let the greater part of her house to an invalid and her quiet, attractive daughters. It became in a very short time the lively centre for a group of friends, old and new, which my mother's presence always guaranteed.

Shortly after we moved in, an incident occurred which caused my family no little amusement. Guiltily conscious that I was doing nothing to forward the war effort, I replied to an advertisement in the *Oxford Times* from the Oxfordshire War Agricultural Executive Committee, appealing for unskilled labour to help farmers in the county. The farmer was to provide accommodation and the county would afford a modest payment. I was duly enrolled to assist a farmer near Bicester and I packed my oldest clothes in a suitcase and set off on my bicycle in the direction of Bicester expecting to be away for an indefinite period. When I arrived at the farm and presented myself as having come from the War Agricultural Committee, he eyed me up and down and asked me what agricultural experience I had. I had to confess to none and pointed out that the scheme explicitly mentioned 'unskilled labour', which was what I was. He did his best to disguise his disappointment, but said in explanation that, willing as I might be, he would have to show me how to do things and in the time it took to do that, he could as well do the job himself. This was entirely reasonable and the only thing I could do was to repeat that he *had* accepted an offer of *unskilled* labour. By way of compensation he gave me an excellent lunch, during which he went into the passage and rang the Committee in Oxford. I knew the explanation he would get, but he continued to remonstrate, 'but I thought you were sending me a proper *man*.'

So I arrived back in Osberton Road in time for tea with no other explanation than that I was not a proper man.

CHAPTER 4

The war years

The Navy 1940–6

HAVING DECIDED TO give up my status as a conscientious objector and to allow myself to be called up in due course for military service, I opted to join the Royal Navy. I have always maintained since that it was because I prefer water unmixed with soil. It is true that I dislike mud but I think it was because, having been brought up in Southampton and done a little sailing, I felt some affinity with the sea.

I had two contacts with the Navy before being actually called up. Charis Fry, a daughter of C B Fry and one of my father's operatic principals, introduced me to her sister, Faith, a WRNS officer who kindly invited me to lunch and told me something about the training establishment, HMS *Collingwood* at Fareham, where she was OC WRNS. I hoped to see more of her, though I could scarcely, as an Ordinary Seaman, expect to consort regularly with a WRNS Officer. Tragically, before I got to *Collingwood*, a bomb fell on the parade ground and killed Faith Fry, along with the party of Wrens she was drilling at the time.

The other contact was pure comedy. Harold Herzmark had hitched a lift with a Capt Coombs RN. In conversation he mentioned that a friend of his was shortly joining the Navy and Capt Coombs said, 'Tell him to get in touch with me, if he is ever in London, at the Admiralty, Rex House, Lower Regent Street.' Harold passed on the message to me and one Saturday morning I found myself at Piccadilly Circus and thought there could be no harm in my trying to ring him as invited. An operator put me through and a voice replied 'Moss-Blundell here'. When I asked for Capt Coombs he replied that Capt Coombs was no longer there, having been posted as a Commodore of convoys. Why did I want him? By this time I was extremely embarrassed and anxious to get out of the whole thing. I said, 'Oh, it's not at all important.' He said 'But you must have had *some* reason for phoning him.' I then explained how Capt

Coombs had told me to ring as I was about to go into the Navy and wanted to know what the order of events would be. Moss–Blundell replied, 'We *are* the Admiralty and are supposed to know these things. Come along to Rex House and ask for me.'

When I arrived at Rex House I was immediately sent up to a spacious room on the first floor. There was a very large desk on one side of which was, I presumed, Moss–Blundell himself and on the other side a Naval Commander in uniform. Moss–Blundell rose to greet me and said, 'this is Commander Fox who is about to leave us to be gunnery officer of the KGV' (the newly commissioned battleship *King George V*). Then he said, 'Well, what do you want to know?' I said, 'Well, I should be interested to know what sort of training I shall get and where it will happen.' Moss–Blundell said 'I'm afraid I really don't know what the training programme is for hostilities-only ratings, do you Fox?' Fox being equally ignorant, M-B said 'There must be *someone* in this building who can tell us. Who shall we ask?' Fox suggested that the man to consult was the Secretary to the Admiral Commanding Reserves. So M-B rang him up and said 'we have a young man here just down from Oxford who is about to be called up in the Navy and wants to know what will happen to him. Can you tell us?' He said he would come along at once and duly did so. He explained that, on the assumption that I would be in the running for a commission, I should go first to an initial training establishment such as HMS *Collingwood* for a period of three months. I should then have to spend a further three months as a rating on a sea-going ship, after which, all being well, I should spend another three months of officer training at HMS *King Alfred*, the training establishment for RNVR Officers.

There was general agreement that this was a good arrangement, especially the three months sea-time, since an officer needed to know what life on the lower deck was like. Polite questions were then asked about my career at Oxford and, when it came out that I had a First in Greats, M-B exclaimed that there must be other options for someone with my academic qualifications. Could I not be commissioned in the Instructor Branch straight away? By now it was clear that my genial hosts wanted to know the answers for themselves and they decided to consult the Director of the Education Department, Rear Admiral Hall himself. He said 'bring him along' and M-B took me along to the Education Department to see Admiral Hall. He told us what I expected to hear, that the Instructor Branch recruited only people with scientific qualifications and that someone like me could only be an executive officer. So as not to make the occasion a complete waste of time, I asked him whether there was anything I could read in advance by way of preparation. He mentioned *Admiralty Manuals of Navigation* Vols I & II, which I should have no difficulty with; Vol III might prove more difficult!

Having thanked him for sparing the time, we went back to the original office. I had been in the Admiralty for an hour and a half or so during which time I had been treated with the greatest courtesy. Still embarrassed, I thanked M-B and Fox for having expended so much time on me and M-B insisted that it was by no means a waste of time for them. They really should have known what the programme of training was for all the young men who were being drafted into the Navy for the duration of the war.

Finding myself once more out on the pavement in Lower Regent Street in the sunshine, I marvelled at the reception I had had during that unexpected interlude. I think that they had really enjoyed meeting an actual specimen of the raw material of the Navy they were administering.

A month or two later, sometime in November 1940 I found myself at HMS *Collingwood* in Fareham. It was physically a collection of wooden huts, each of which housed some thirty-five sailors grouped together as a 'class' under the supervision of a retired petty officer. These were variations of one basic model, small round men with red faces and blue or brown eyes. They were fatherly figures who had the gift, which I later noticed in regular naval officers, of exercising authority without exerting it. Hence there was none of the harsh military discipline which I had anticipated, but rather an orderliness which was entirely taken for granted. My ambition was to escape notice as far as possible by quietly and inconspicuously doing what was required of me. But this ambition was frustrated from the start when I learnt that I was to be 'Class Leader', presumably because of my superior education and because I was to be under observation as a potential officer.

I ran up at once against problems of communication. Thirty-five men from all over the country spoke varieties of English, some of which I found entirely unintelligible. Quite impenetrable were the speech of a Glaswegian, a Liverpudlian and a fisherman from Grimsby. Early on I discovered that the difficulty was reciprocal. I arrived late one night off leave and climbed quietly into my bunk in the darkness. A conversation was in progress and I heard one man saying, 'He's a right enough bloke. The trouble is you can't understand a word that he's saying.' My query 'who are you talking about?' was met with an embarrassed silence.

As I didn't have superior rank to buttress my authority and neither did I possess the physical presence or force of personality that was required in its absence, I was at a loss how to proceed. Fortunately, as deputy class leader I had a splendid man who had both these attributes. His name was Tulloch; a huge man of rugged countenance who had been at different times a cattle rancher in America, a pearl diver in Australia and a sheep farmer in Yorkshire. He and I got on very well and whenever someone looked like ignoring an order of mine, he would be a threatening presence at my side. Eventually, with his agreement, I suggested to our Petty Officer that the true situation should be recognised and Tulloch was made Class Leader with me as his deputy.

On the whole I enjoyed the training, much of which involved learning practical skills which were of obvious use – signalling by Morse and semaphore, elementary seamanship, knots and splices, the use of a compass, handling boats. Although ammunition being in short supply there was little time for this, I discovered that I was quite a good shot. What I hated, as I had at school, was PE, and I never learnt to climb a rope or a rope ladder. But, to my surprise, I enjoyed drill where one could be truly anonymous and my heart swelled with pride while marching round the parade ground to the strains of Hearts of Oak and Old Tom Bowling played by the Royal Marine Band. To the amusement of my mother and sisters, I learned how to crease my bell-bottoms and how to wash my collar in cold water to prevent the blue dye running into the white stripes.

Portsmouth was being heavily bombed at this time and we spent frequent nights in the air raid shelter. It was a very cold winter and the concrete benches rapidly defeated all attempts at keeping warm.

Fareham itself was not a primary target and my first experience of an air raid was on a visit one Saturday to Southampton to see my father. I arrived at the entrance to Northlands Gardens, which was a cul-de-sac off Hill Lane, to find a small crowd assembled with a policeman on duty. Idiotically, I said to the policeman 'Has anything happened?' and he replied 'Has anything happened! Only a landmine which has destroyed several houses.' I explained that I lived there and he allowed me through. The major damage was right at the end of the cul-de-sac, but I could see that our house, though basically intact, had sustained some damage. Fortunately my father and his business partner Margaret Playle had escaped injury. It was a measure of my basic naivety that I did not think to question the relationship between my father and Margaret at that time. In any case, it became clear that another air raid was impending and I needed to make sure of getting back to Collingwood that night. As I walked through Bedford Place towards the centre of town much of it was already on fire and I noticed something which I was often to experience later. Although I was, at one level, distinctly scared, my predominant emotion was an aesthetic one of wonder at the sheer splendour of the scene. The burning fiery furnace was unimaginably beautiful.

My three months' training at *Collingwood* ended, I was transferred to Royal Naval Barracks, Portsmouth, to await drafting to a sea-going ship. The buildings had been badly bombed and the orderliness I had admired in *Collingwood* was no longer in evidence. Most of the people there represented a mass of individuals in constant transition and those in more permanent positions were either individuals who, for one reason or another, were unfit for sea service or others who had learned to work the system and, while drafting others, took care not to be drafted themselves. The result was something not far from Hobbes' state of nature, a war of every man against every man.

My only concern was to get out of this as soon as possible, the more so as air raids were a nightly occurrence. Not surprisingly as I lacked the desire or the means to avoid being drafted, I was within a week duly drafted to the battleship HMS *Queen Elizabeth*, which had recently been refitted and was for the time being based at Rosyth. When our draft arrived at the quayside we found the *QE* lying just ahead of the *Hood* which was also in the process of being re-commissioned. I was reassured at once to discover that we were back in the orderly Navy that I had come to admire at *Collingwood*. While we were waiting on the quay to board the ship a working party came off to collect our kitbags and take them to our messes, to which we ourselves were shown in due course. The senior rating of my mess was a three-badge able seaman, who was also captain of the gun which was to be my action station – a 4.5″ anti-aircraft gun which was part of the additional armament given to the QE on her refit.

The additional armament meant additional manpower to work it and, at the same time, less room to accommodate the extra men. Normally the members of a mess would have slung their hammocks from the deck-head above their mess decks, but there were too many of us for that. I slung mine in one of the 'flats' or corridors that led from one part of the ship to another. Hammocks had two great advantages. They were remarkably comfortable and beautifully private. Once there one would not be disturbed until a petty officer would come along next morning, twang the hammocks strings and shout 'Wakey, wakey, rise and shine! Show a leg there, show a leg,' and sometimes for good measure 'show both legs'. In case this was not enough a bugler would blow 'reveille', a most offensive ditty which seemed to affect a forced cheerfulness. In the hammock one was comparatively quiet (although never entirely so: even in harbour there were always mechanised hums and throbs). It was, therefore, a good place to read and the deck head above provided crevices in which the book could be left until needed again. However, books were regarded as common property, so it was important to choose a book that one's messmates would not want to pinch. My choice was *War and Peace* which was ideal from this standpoint and also had the advantage that it did not suffer from being read in small snatches.

After a few days in Rosyth *Hood* and QE proceeded to Scapa Flow to continue their working-up programme, more than ever necessary because the large majority of their crews were, like me, hostilities-only ratings.

I have to confess that when I saw the two ships lying moored in Scapa Flow I was envious of those who had been drafted to *Hood*. She was a beautiful ship with graceful lines. A First World War battle-cruiser, she had been designed for speed and looked like it, whereas the QE was, by contrast, stubby and dumpy and entirely lacking in aesthetic appeal.

I don't remember much about the training we underwent except that it was physically demanding and I think that at that time I was fitter and stronger than at any time before or since. The two things that I remember best were both by way of respite from all that. When we went ashore on Lyness there was nothing but the NAAFI canteen with sailors consuming as much beer as they had time or cash for. It was incredibly noisy and the one thing I craved was silence. Fortunately one had only to walk a short distance along the narrow island to find oneself in a bleak landscape with no trees; only the sea and the wind and a complete absence of noise. At the end of the path was a wooden hut where two comfortable middle-aged ladies served coffee and cakes at a modest price. This was a Church of Scotland mini-mission to seamen and an absolute godsend to people like me.

The other was also a source of quietness, which at that time I thought of as the supreme good. The chaplain of the *QE* was Launcelot Fleming, a Cambridge don, who took advantage of the licence the Navy gave to chaplains to wear civilian clothes. This was an appropriate symbol of the principle that the chaplain had no rank but assumed the status of whomever he was talking to at the time. Launcelot Fleming was able to be 'all things to all men' while remaining, without any attempt to disguise it, a learned, cultivated, gentle clergyman. There was no doubt that the ship's company esteemed and even loved him. Sensing that what I needed above all else was solitude he invited me to use his cabin when he didn't need it and read books from his library. I am not sure that I ever did this but the knowledge that I could do so was a great help.

There were divisions and prayers on the quarterdeck every Sunday morning. Although it was winter I remember the sun was shining on these occasions with a gentle breeze rustling the chaplain's surplice. My lifelong devotion to the Book of Common Prayer dates from that time and I was then and later in my naval service deeply moved by the prayer for use at sea which, as it seemed to me then and still does, expresses in language as splendid as it is memorable, the sentiments and hopes of those who are serving at sea.

> O Eternal Lord God,
> who alone spreadest out the heavens, and rulest the raging of the sea;
> who hast compassed the waters with bounds until day and night come
>   to an end;
> be pleased to receive into thy almighty and gracious protection

the persons of us thy servants, and the Fleet in which we serve.
Preserve us from the dangers of the sea, and from the violence of the
   enemy;
that we may be a safeguard unto our most sovereign Lord, King
   George, and his Dominions, and a security for such as pass on the
   seas upon their lawful occasions; that the inhabitants of our island
   may in peace and quietness serve thee our God; and that we may
   return in safety to enjoy the blessings of the land, with the fruits of
   our labours;
and with a thankful remembrance of thy mercies
to praise and glorify thy holy name,
through Jesus Christ our Lord. Amen.

After a month or so of regular routine *Hood* and *QE* were suddenly
ordered to sea. We proceeded in line ahead on a southerly course at
full speed and it was obvious that this was a serious emergency. The
explanation was given in exemplary fashion by Commander Gotto
who summoned half the ship's company in turn to the Hangar for a
lecture. He illustrated his talk on a large blackboard. The Admiralty
had learned that the *Scharnhorst* and *Gneisenau*, German battle cruisers,
which had been raiding British shipping in the South Atlantic, were
returning to harbour. It was assumed that they would make for Brest
and all units within reach were being ordered to intercept them. We
were the nearest and might expect to engage them at about 1830.
Meanwhile Force H, consisting of *Ark Royal* and *Renown*, were
coming up from Gibraltar, and the submarine *Echo* was lying in wait
off Brest.

   The ship's company were at Defence Stations, the next degree of
readiness to Action Stations. Two out of the four watches were at
action stations, my watch being one of them. No sooner had we got
our gun in readiness that the Captain himself (Capt Barry) addressed
the ship's company over the Tannoy. What follows is a sort of
Thucydidean version of what he actually said but I am satisfied that
it is reasonably close to the original.

   'You have now, I think, all heard from the Commander what our
mission is. We are to intercept the *Scharnhorst* and the *Gneisenau*,
which are seeking to return to harbour after wreaking havoc on our
shipping in the South Atlantic. It will, I am sure, be as great a
satisfaction to you as it is to me that their Lords of the Admiralty

should have seen fit to send us out, although our gunnery working up programme is not yet complete, to engage these redoubtable warships.' At this point the leading hand of our mess, and captain of our gun murmured 'Christ, where's my lifebelt!?' which expressed the feelings of all of us.

At 1630, two hours before the expected encounter, the ships did a 180° turn and set course for Scapa Flow at reduced speed. The Commander broadcast to say that a signal had been received to the effect that the two warships had entered Brest.

There is no doubt that my dominant emotion was enormous relief, which would have been even greater if we had known what was to happen to the *Hood* later in her encounter with the *Bismarck*. But I have to admit to a very slight disappointment. It would have been one of the major engagements of the war and, in the unlikely event of my surviving, would have been a tale to tell my grandchildren.

After this I naturally expected to serve out the remainder of my statutory three months in *QE*. But then a very odd thing occurred which was to have even odder consequences. A signal was received requiring three ratings, of which I was one, to proceed with all dispatch to HMS *St Vincent*, Portsmouth. It was a complete mystery. I was genuinely sorry to say goodbye to the leading hand of our mess, who had done all he could to help me cope with a way of life to which I was plainly not suited. When we parted he said something which I mention because it gave me great pride. 'I am sorry you are going – you are the rightest bloke we have had!' meaning, I suppose, of those going through for commissions.

What follows will resonate with all who have experience of the forces in wartime. The three of us went by ferry to Thurso and then trundled down by train through wartime Britain until eventually we reached Portsmouth, where we hoped to have the mystery explained. It became apparent at once that nobody at *St Vincent* had any idea why we were there. So we just had to wait for, I think, three weeks during which a large number of other ratings arrived for what was evidently the same purpose, though no one seemed to know what this might be. As we talked among ourselves we discovered that the one thing we had in common was that we all had university degrees or equivalent qualifications. I was, I think, the only classical scholar but there were plenty of men with degrees in arts subjects in addition to a large number of scientists.

Eventually the purpose of this gathering was made known. There was to be a selection board with the object of finding potential officers in electrical engineering, meteorology and bomb disposal. It had been alleged in the House that the Services were not making use of a large number of qualified people who were being wasted in ordinary humdrum jobs, and the Fleet was being combed for suitable persons for these specialisms.

The day of the Board arrived and I have a vivid memory of my own interview. The Chairman was an Admiral and he was assisted by two Captains. On my entry the Admiral, after consulting the papers in front of him, said: 'Know anything about electrical engineering? Nothing elaborate. Wireless sets, that sort of thing. Take them to pieces, put them together again?' 'No Sir,' I said, 'that has never been one of my hobbies'. 'Got a University degree, eh? What in?' was the next question. 'Philosophy and Ancient History,' I replied. 'Philosophy includes the study of dynamics, doesn't it?' was the next question. 'It used to do, Sir, in the Seventeenth Century, but not since,' was my reply. 'Oh is that so,' he said and we went on to meteorology. By this time I was looking ahead, beyond meteorology to bomb disposal. Philosophy might well be a good preparation for that, but I was determined in no circumstances to land up in bomb disposal. I am extremely unhandy and should be a danger to myself and others. So I decided to go all out for meteorology. I said I had always been interested in the weather and should like the opportunity to learn more. The Admiral mentioned my lack of scientific qualifications and I said it was doubtful if meteorology could yet be reckoned a science. But by now he had seen through me and terminated the interview.

That evening as he left the room, he was heard to remark to his Flag Lieutenant, 'Damn fine body of men. Never seen such a damn fine body of men with the wrong qualifications in all my life!'

As I had not completed my three months on a sea–going ship there was nothing for it but to rejoin the QE at Scapa. I think I managed to beg a few days leave, but then I trundled all the way back to Scapa. When I arrived at last the QE was nowhere to be seen and I was sent to the base ship Dunluce Castle where I spent three weeks or so going ashore daily and filling sandbags.

By now there were a number of us destined for the *QE* and, at short notice, we were all transferred to Greenock. Still no sign of the *QE* but the *Repulse* was moored in midstream and after some signalling between ship and shore we were sent out to the *Repulse*. In due course we found ourselves as part of the escort of a convoy bound for Gibraltar. The voyage was memorable as the nearest I ever got to being seasick. In the Bay of Biscay I was sent to paint the deck-head of the bosun's store. It was right forward and what with the foc's'le crashing up and down in the Atlantic swell and the smell of paint mixed with the underlying smell of tarred hemp it was all I could do to prevent myself succumbing.

Before we were landed at Gibraltar there occurred one of those small happenings which helped to sustain the spirit of the Navy. There were by now about thirty of us in transit to the *QE* and other ships. The Master at Arms had us drawn up on the quarterdeck ready to disembark, when he announced that the Captain of the *Repulse*, Captain Tennant, wished to address us. The Captain duly arrived, we were stood at ease and he said: 'I didn't want you to leave the ship without my having the opportunity to thank you for the work you have done while you have been with us and, to wish you God speed for the remainder of your journey'. We then went ashore and I and some others were transferred to the destroyer *Fury*.

I woke up to find that we were already under way and when I got on deck was confronted by an impressive sight. We were on the destroyer screen of what, from the size of the escort, was an important convoy to Malta. Apart from some ten destroyers there were, in addition to the *QE*, the aircraft carrier *Ark Royal*, the battle cruisers *Repulse* and *Renown* and the cruiser *Sheffield*. There were, I seem to remember, five heavily laden merchant ships. From my shipmates in *Fury* it was clear that the question was not whether but when we should be attacked by torpedo bombers. When the attack duly came, I did not see them because my action station was in the after magazine. All we knew, apart from the noise of the anti-aircraft guns, was the sudden throbbing of the engines at full speed and the tilting of the ship as she zigzagged, or altered course to avoid torpedoes. Fortunately only one of the merchant ships was lost and four were able to enter harbour at Valetta. By this time *Ark Royal* and *Renown* had turned back for Gib and the *QE*, *Repulse* and *Sheffield* with a number of destroyers continued on to Alexandria. Four destroyers including *Fury* were sent into Malta. I remember the entry into the harbour at Valetta as more frightening than any other of my wartime experiences. Enemy aircraft had dropped mines in the approaches to the harbour. Although minesweepers had been out to clear a swept channel it was necessary to proceed with great caution. The four ships proceeded in line ahead. All ratings that were not needed to work the ship were ordered to stand in line on the upper deck wearing their life-belts to give them the best chance of survival if the ship did strike a mine. The ships moved at slow speed as a precaution against acoustic mines. One after another they turned as they reached the same spot, following what was obviously not a straight channel. The sea was dead calm and in the sunlight the walls of the harbour were clearly visible at no great distance. In the unnatural quiet and with nothing whatever to do and no conception of what the risk might be, it was impossible not to be overcome by fear.

The grand harbour of Valetta was a most impressive sight in spite of evident signs of damage. We were lodged in St Angelo, a massive fortress which occupied a commanding position in the harbour. We slept in a grand vaulted space which was where the Knights of St John kept their horses.

During the three weeks I remained at Malta I had two jobs. At night I was a mine lookout on the battlements, charged with estimating the range and distance of any land mines dropped by parachute in the harbour. By day, being of above average height I was a regular pall–bearer. A ship had been sunk by a mine a few days before our arrival and bodies were being washed ashore daily. The burial party every morning went up to the mortuary to collect a body bag and went on from there to the military cemetery for a burial service conducted with due ceremony. In a site overlooking the sea, with a sea breeze carrying the words of the service and ruffling the chaplain's surplice and a bugler ending with the Last Post, I found it always deeply moving and tried as best I could to represent the absent family and friends of the man we were burying.

This was my first visit to the Mediterranean and I was struck by the beauty of the place. I did my best to explore it and vowed to return in peacetime (which I did twelve years later).

I can remember only two instance of exploration. On one occasion when wandering in the old city of Valetta, I ventured into a street in which there were a number of gaudily dressed women who took a more than usual interest in me to an extent that was positively embarrassing. I hastily withdrew on realising that this must be the notorious Strata Streta, the red light district of the city. On another occasion with a companion I decided to explore the *hypogeum*, a network of caves, tunnelled in the soft stone, which was presumed to be a prehistoric burial place. We were taken round by a janitor, a very old man with a wispy white beard who gave us each, and had himself, a short stub of candle, there being no other light. As we wandered round the maze of stone corridors, he told us in a quavering voice about the unknown extent of the passages which, it was believed, extended as far as the coast. On one occasion, he averred, some pigs had been driven down there as an experiment to see how far they would go, and they had finally emerged at the seaside. As he recited his spine-chilling tales, my companion and I were looking at the candles and wondering how long their flickering light could possibly last and at the old man who looked as if he himself would flicker out at any moment, and pondering what our chances were of reaching daylight and the world above. We were heartily relived when eventually we emerged to find a dogfight in progress in the sky above us.

We stayed some three weeks in Malta. We were still theoretically in transit to the QE but there was no traffic between Malta and Alexandria and we were simply marking time. It was not until years later that I heard what ended this period of waiting. We had dining with us at Keble the then Bursar of Magdalen, a retired Naval Paymaster Captain. I mentioned to him my time in Malta and my fears that we might be there indefinitely, and he said, 'As it happens I was responsible for your return to the UK. I was secretary to Vice-Admiral, Malta, and on seeing the names of these extra ratings to be paid, I enquired what you were doing there. As soon as I was told that you were bound for QE I said to the Admiral, "But this is absurd. Some of these men are in the running for commissions and the Service needs all the officers it can get."'

We were sent in the destroyer, *Forester*, at full speed to Gibraltar where we arrived in time to see *Ark Royal* and *Renown* return from the sinking of the *Bismarck* (which dates my arrival in Gib to late May 1941).

After two weeks of further sandbag filling we were embarked on the old aircraft carrier, *Argus*, then employed as a troopship, for passage to the UK. Among the passengers was a young Belgian civilian, who was cold-shouldered by the sailors. He knew almost no English, so I engaged him in conversation in my barely adequate French. He was on the way to join the Free Belgian Forces in Britain after a hazardous journey through France into Spain. It was risky for him and also for the members of the network who had assisted him and others on his way. I tried to explain all this to my messmates but to no effect. As far as they were concerned he was a foreigner and therefore a 'fifth-columnist'!

Fortunately the powers that be were prepared to regard my Mediterranean excursions as completing the required three months' sea time and I embarked on the final three months of officer training at HMS *King Alfred*, first at Lancing College, then at the one-time marina at Hove.

By and large I enjoyed this. Although I had for the most part got on well with my companions on the lower deck, it was a relief to get away from the constant swearing which I never got used to. I quickly discovered that it either meant nothing or was totally unconscious (like today's 'y-know') or was used to give emphasis, and as such was often remarkably effective. While appreciating the latter I was never reconciled to its routine use. It was also a relief to be able to take part in rational discussion once more. There were fierce arguments on the lower deck but they were always about matters of fact. Who won the cup final in 1932? Was the *Ark Royal* a Portsmouth or a Devonport ship? My suggestion that we look up the answer in some reference book was treated with contumely as betraying a total failure to understand the point of the game.

I was, of course, well used to preparing for examinations and my histrionic gifts made me quite good at putting on a show of keenness and enthusiasm. Two things in particular surprised me. Having a strong voice and used to performing in public, I developed a good 'power of command' and, in spite of my earlier weakness in mathematics, I took very readily to navigation. In the event I passed out first in the final examination out of seventy-five and was rated number two in the overall assessment, conceding first place, quite rightly, to a New Zealander who was obviously cut out to be a first-rate Naval Officer, as I knew very well I was not.

Sadly the passing-out parade coincided with my sister's wedding in Oxford, which was not held to justify compassionate leave (as, I suppose, her funeral would have done) and I arrived in Oxford only after all the festivities were over.

I was duly commissioned as a Sub-Lieutenant RNVR on the 18th September 1941 and learned that, after a period of leave, I was to be drafted to the Flower class corvette, HMS *Genista* which was building at Harland and Wolff, Belfast.

Flower class corvettes were being built in large numbers to help combat the menace of U-boats which in 1942 threatened to deprive the country of its essential imports. They were designed on the model of whalers to ride the Atlantic swell, which they did most effectively but without regard to the comfort of their crews. It was said that they would 'roll on wet grass'. They had a complement of six to eight officers and sixty men and were armed with depth charges, their main anti-submarine weapons, a four inch gun, a pom-pom, and two rapid fire oerlikon guns, one on each side of the bridge. They were the smallest ships to count as 'major war vessels'.

I was able to spend Christmas at home in Oxford before *Genista* was commissioned at Belfast, after which we proceeded at once to Tobermory on the Isle of Mull. I was the junior officer and the only one who was totally inexperienced. The Commanding Officer Lieut Cdr R M Pattinson RNR was a New Zealander who had been a merchant navy officer in peace time, an older man, who was well accustomed to the sea and set lightly to the routines of the Navy. The First Lieutenant, Roger Leigh-Wood, was a banker who had been a keen yachtsman in peacetime and was a tall, distinctly good-looking man, the pattern in fact of an upper class Englishman. Then there were two Canadians, one of whom was navigating officer and the other gunnery officer. The former, whose name was Nicholls, came from the East Coast and the other, Ken Winsby, from Winnipeg. They were both seconded from the Royal Canadian Navy and hence paid twice as much as the rest of us, a fact which in no way affected our very friendly relations.

Tobermory has one of the most beautiful harbours on the west coast of Scotland, lined with terraced houses, painted in bright colours, with a small waterfall cascading gently into it. When one revisits it in peacetime it is impossible to re-create in imagination its character in wartime. It was the working-up base for anti-submarine vessels other than destroyers. In a fortnight of frenzied activity newly commissioned ships like *Genista* had to be brought to a state of fighting efficiency sufficient to enable them to take their part in the Battle of the Atlantic. Charged with this well-nigh impossible task was a remarkable man who had been brought out of retirement in his sixties for the purpose with the rank of Commodore, Sir Gilbert Stephenson. Always known as 'Monkey Stephenson', he was a small man with ginger hair (what was left of it) and bright blue eyes. Not for nothing was he known as 'the Terror of Tobermory' (excellently portrayed in Richard Baker's book of that title). It was not until later in the more exposed position of First Lieutenant of another corvette that I had closer dealings with him, but I actually met him on the first morning *Genista* arrived in Tobermory. As we approached from the south in the early hours of the morning we became aware of sounds of warlike activity in the darkness ahead and Pattinson as a precaution called the ship to action stations. It was, of course an exercise in night fighting. It was dawn by the time we entered harbour and we were ordered to moor ship near the waterfall. No sooner had this been done with me left as officer of the watch than a launch came alongside and the Commodore sprang on board (before I had time to pipe him aboard as I should have done). 'Where is the Commanding Officer?' 'He is down below shaving, Sir,' I said. 'The First Lieutenant?' 'He is also down below, shaving, Sir.' 'Is *everyone* shaving on this ship?' In due course Pattinson appeared and I don't know what then passed between them, but Monkey Stephenson had made his point. At no time of the day or night could one be sure that he would not appear without warning.

The following fortnight was spent in intensive training in every aspect of marine warfare. In retrospect, I think Stephenson had a dual rationale for making life such a hell for us (whether he had worked it out or not). It was, of course, essential to prepare the ships with largely untrained crews and inexperienced officers, to cope with the challenges of the war in the Atlantic, where our fortunes were at their lowest ebb. But we left Tobermory with the feeling that nothing could ever be worse than this and, if we had survived it, we could survive anything the enemy had in store for us.

From Tobermory we proceeded to Greenock and there occurred two things which confirmed my faith in Pattinson. Our course from Tobermory took us down the Sound of Mull and I was Officer of the Watch. It was the first time I had been in charge of a ship at sea and I was highly nervous. Pattinson set a course and remained with me for a while. Then he left the bridge and retired to his cabin. I noticed a dim light straight ahead (all lights were dimmed in wartime) and went into the chartroom to study the chart. The light was on an island in the middle of the Sound at a point where the Sound took a bend. Clearly we would have to alter course, so I laid out a new course on the chart and shouted the new course down the voice pipe to the quartermaster on the wheel, wondering at what had emboldened me to do this. Shortly afterwards, Pattinson came back onto the bridge and said 'I think we had better alter course' and when I said 'I have already done it, Sir', I felt I had successfully passed a test.

The next incident was less to my credit. We came alongside at Greenock and I was in charge of the quarterdeck. At *King Alfred* we had been told to make fast as quickly as possible, and as soon as the ship came to a stop I had my men over the side and made fast to the nearest bollard. I did not know that at that moment the Captain was saying to the First Lieutenant 'I think we should move up a little further' and being surprised that, although he went from 'dead slow ahead' to 'slow ahead' the ship made no progress through the water. Then he noticed that the stern rope was too taut and the first thing I was aware of was Pattinson, who had come down aft from the bridge, murmuring into my ear 'Mitchell, Mitchell, why persecutest thou me'. In this way he saved my feelings and, more importantly, my standing with the ship's company.

We were then given 'foreign service leave' and issued with tropical clothing. It was at that time, as I have told elsewhere, that, realising that I should not see her for a long time, if ever again, I told Phoebe that I was still deeply in love with her and received the news that she was regularly sleeping with John Boughey.

Towards the end of January 1942 we left Greenock to join a convoy headed for Gibraltar. On the first or second night (I cannot remember which) we ran into a violent storm which made

station-keeping difficult both for us in the escort and for the
merchant ships in the convoy. Our station was astern of the convoy
and, in the weather conditions, all we could do was keep in touch
with the last three vessels in the convoy. When dawn broke and we
could at last see them more or less clearly it was evident that they had
broken off from their station in the convoy, which made them
particularly vulnerable to U-boats which often attacked at dawn.
Warships regularly had action stations at dawn and dusk and *Genista*
was accordingly at action stations. With heavy seas and low clouds
scudding across the sky, we were struggling to be vigilant when a
large aircraft, flying low, loomed up astern of us, and apparently not
seeing us, made to bomb the most laggard of the merchant ships.
Genista opened fire with her three available anti-aircraft weapons. I
was amidships in nominal charge of the pom-pom, which jammed
after two rounds. One of the oerliken gunners on the port side of the
bridge managed, in the brief time available, to pour a stream of tracer
shells into the aircraft which with one engine on fire wheeled away
from the merchant ship and crashed into the sea about a quarter of a
mile away and exploded. It was a Focke Wolff bomber of the type
the Germans were increasingly using to reinforce their U-boat
campaign.

A signal was sent to the Admiralty which prompted a message of
congratulation from the Commodore HMS *Western Isles* at Tobermory. It was gratifying to discover that he bothered to follow the
careers of ships which he had trained.

The war at the beginning of 1942 was going badly and, as I learned
in my next letter from Phoebe, our exploit was mentioned on the
BBC News and in *The Times*. The family was listening to the news
that evening and one of them said 'Isn't that Basil's ship?'

We reached Gibraltar without further incident, dropped our
convoy and proceeded independently, as it happened, to Freetown,
Sierra Leone, but I don't think we knew this. Here we donned our
tropical clothing and spent a little while in rather desultory activity.
One incident remains clearly and still painfully in my mind. One of
the chores I had to undertake as junior officer was that of
Confidential Books Officer. These consisted of a massive naval cipher
together with supplements which changed weekly. They were kept
in a safe to which I had the keys. This was a responsibility which I

loathed. I have always had a propensity to mislay physical objects and this was bound to happen with these keys. The day came when I duly lost them and after a frantic and unavailing search I had no alternative but to report their loss to the Captain. Pattinson said that, strictly speaking, he should report the matter at once to the Admiralty and institute Court Martial proceedings. But they were bound to turn up somewhere and he would give me three days grace. On the third day I found them. Every other day there was an inspection of the magazine and the hatch just outside the Wardroom was removed. I was stepping over the opening on the third day when I thought I saw something glistening on the floor below and it was the missing keys. I duly took them to the Captain and he advised me to prevent it happening again by putting the keys on a lanyard round my waist. I made myself a lanyard and duly attached the keys to it, but there was one drawback. When I went to the heads (the lavatory) the dangling keys got in the way. So I removed them and hung them up on a hook on the back of the door. Shortly afterwards I realised with horror that I no longer had them and went back to heads and found them no longer there. There was no alternative but to go back again to the Captain and explain the embarrassing circumstance in which I had lost them once more. With a very severe expression he lectured me again on the enormity of the offence. Here we were at Freetown, entirely cut off and unable to communicate with higher authority or receive orders from it. Then with a smile he went to his safe and took out the keys. 'Fortunately,' he said, 'I was the next person to go to the heads.'

For the first two or three hours of the morning Freetown was entrancing, nestling amid fresh green hills. After that it was so humid that one sweated even when sitting still. At sea, in the doldrums, it was totally calm except when a squall blew up. These one could see, four or five at a time, and it was possible to set course so as to avoid them. When, however, despite this we actually ran into one, there was a problem what to wear. Normally we were all stripped to the waist and a sharp shower should have been refreshing, but the rain was icily cold. In spite of the sweltering temperature most of the time, one had to have oilskins at hand for protection against it.

Eventually it became known that we were to serve on the South African station and we set off for Cape Town by way of St Helena where, sadly, we did not go ashore, but simply took on fuel.

I can remember only one incident on that voyage in the South Atlantic. I was asleep in my cabin one afternoon having kept the middle watch (12.00–4.00 a.m.) when a knock came at my door and a message from the Bosun's Mate to say the Captain wanted to see me on the bridge. My first thought was 'What have I done or not done now?' as I hastened up the ladder to the bridge. Pattinson smiled genially at me and said, 'You wanted to see an albatross. There is one.' And pointed to an enormous bird, which, like any ordinary seagull was flying in the wake of the ship, keeping station not many yards from the bridge. Poised in the slipstream it had no need to move its wings but hung there as if motionless, looking down on us with a cold contemptuous stare as if to say 'I don't have to do this, but I happen to find it convenient just now.' They are only found well out to sea in the Southern Ocean and I could well understand the superstitious awe with which sailors viewed them. During the next eighteen months when we were always in the South Atlantic or the Indian Ocean they often accompanied us. Sailing independently as we then were they served to accentuate the sense of our being entirely alone with nothing to be seen between us and the horizon in any direction.

After days of continuous sunshine we plunged suddenly into a thick cotton wool fog, which continued to envelope us for the next two or three days as we proceeded down the coast of South West Africa towards the tip of Africa. The fog is caused by the hot wind blowing off the desert encountering the freezing Benguela current which comes up from the Antarctic. On the third day our dead-reckoning indicated that we were off the swept channel to Cape Town. Because of the fog it had been impossible to take any sun sights or star sights and we could only go by our course and speed, while making some allowance for the strength of the current. We altered course in what we hoped was the direction of Cape Town and proceeded at moderate speed. We had a lookout posted at the masthead and another in the bows to avoid the risk of collision. As always with fog, it was very quiet and we instinctively kept our voices low. At about eleven o'clock the lookout in the bow reported a ship to starboard pointed in the same direction as us, and a moment later another ship to port. The fog was rising and there straight ahead of us was the magnificent panorama of Table Mountain, Devil's Peak and Lion Head and Cape Town spread out glistening at their feet in brilliant sunshine. We were to see it often again but never in such dramatic fashion, as if a stage curtain had been raised upon a scene which beggared expectation. I have often thought I should like to repeat the experience, but it could not be done. We would have to approach by sea and in fine weather and, to ensure that we saw it at optimum distance, there would have to be a fog which came to an end precisely at the right place.

Genista was to be on the South African station for some eighteen months, based either at Cape Town or at Durban. When at Cape Town I had a permanent home ashore with Fra Sandeman and David, who lived at Sea Point on the slopes of Lion Head. David had by now become a professional musician and was first flute in the Cape Town Municipal Orchestra, whose concerts I attended whenever they coincided with my leave. Fra was as always lively and opinionated and it was enormously refreshing to be able to engage in uninhibited conversation on any topic and in this way to confirm my attachment to the Sandeman family.

Our routine task was to escort convoys between Cape Town and Durban and sometimes a little further in either direction, as to Lourenço Marques or Beira, or Walvis Bay. Some of the traffic was local between South African ports and some of it was destined for the Western Desert.

This pattern was scarcely established, however, when *Genista* was ordered to take part in a combined operation to seize the port of Diego Suarez in the northern tip of Madagascar. The combined operation to capture Diego Suarez was one of a series of tragic episodes arising from what we saw as the intransigence of the Vichy French and they saw as a requirement of honour. By May 1942 the Japanese had reached the limits of their westward expansion and their submarines were threatening the Cape route to the Middle East. They were hampered, however, by the limits of their supply lines and it was obvious that these could be shortened drastically if they occupied Diego Suarez with its magnificent harbour which was in the hands of the French. The allies hoped that the French would agree to some arrangement by which allied forces would reinforce the garrison sufficiently to deter the Japanese from any attack. The French declined absolutely on the ground of their neutrality and declared that they would, of course, themselves resist the Japanese if they launched an attack.

The allies decided that the risk of a Japanese attack was too great and the consequences too serious to leave Diego Suarez in the hands of the French. A combined operation must, therefore, be launched in order to capture the harbour, and it must be large enough to be sure of success. The task was formidable. There was only one entrance to the harbour, which was some two hundred metres across and defended by heavy guns, making a frontal assault impossible. The only alternative was to try to land troops at the foot of the isthmus which formed one side of the harbour and capture the ridge which dominated the town on that side. But this meant taking a convoy of ocean liners full of troops and their supplies through an archipelago which was very poorly charted and which the French themselves regarded as unnavigable and had, therefore, not fortified. Since surprise was essential, this had to be done at night.

The convoy which assembled off Durban was escorted by the battleship *Ramillies* and a screen of destroyers and corvettes. The role of the corvettes, which were of comparatively shallow draft, was to discover and mark out the most suitable channels to the chosen landing places. This phase of the operation was a complete success and it was not until the invading force reached the ridge that the French were aware of the danger. From that point onwards, however, their resistance was fierce and for some considerable time little progress could be made. It began to look as if the defending forces could not be dislodged unless they were taken in the rear.

What happened then we in *Genista* only learnt afterwards. The destroyer *Anthony* was despatched with a party of Royal Marines to create a diversion. After dark she proceeded against heavy seas on a northerly course which brought her before dawn off the heavily defended harbour entrance. At full speed she raced through the narrow gap and was in the harbour itself before those manning the guns were aware of what had happened. The marines were landed on the jetty by the town and their presence created such confusion that resistance crumbled in a comparatively short time, whereupon the convoy and the attendant warships sailed into the harbour.

The tragic nature of the whole episode was brought home to me when *Genista* was called on to ferry prisoners from the shore to the

Cunard liner, *Ausonia*, which would take them to South Africa. They were utterly exhausted and when I had to ask them to move off the ropes so that we could manoeuvre the ship, they could scarcely find strength to change their position. It was impossible for us to regard them as enemies and desperately sad that they had felt bound to be loyal to a French government which had no longer any genuine independence.

From this time onwards my own reminiscences of the time at Diego Suarez are pure comedy. It started while we were ferrying the prisoners. Pattinson was in peacetime a merchant seaman, and, as he frequently explained, did not feel happy when in close contact with the land or with other ships. Naval officers, he maintained, were brought up to enjoy close manoeuvres and, if they did any damage, the government paid. In the merchant service you kept as far away from other vessels as possible and any damage you did was paid for by the company. Hence, as he freely admitted, he was nervous and over-cautious when handling the ship at close quarters. He was not helped by the fact that corvettes were single screw vessels which made them much harder to manoeuvre than the twin screw destroyers. We were still ferrying prisoners after dark, and each time we had to come alongside the liner on our starboard side to transfer them. On one such occasion, Pattinson did what was required and swung the stern to starboard as he came in; but too slowly with the result that, when he put the engines into reverse to stop the ship, the torque of the propeller, as the ship gathered sternway, pushed the stern out again and she approached the ship at an angle of some forty-five degrees, still going forward. All he could do was order full speed astern, but this only intensified the action of the propeller so that the ship now approached the liner at right angles. There was a dreadful inevitability about what happened next. *Genista*'s bow penetrated the thin skin of the liner's side, until she at last began to move astern and she withdrew leaving a brightly illuminated triangle, on either side of which surprised faces were to be seen. It must have been a disconcerting experience as sailors relaxed in their mess to have the bows of a corvette suddenly appear among them.

The garrison having been reinforced, the ships of the convoy dispersed leaving only the *Ramillies* and two corvettes in occupation of the harbour. The job of the corvettes was to maintain anti-submarine watch at the harbour entrance and this each did for twenty-four hours at a time. One evening *Genista* was off duty, moored off the small port at the inner end of the harbour. We were in the wardroom having a drink before dinner, when there was a muffled sound which led the Captain to say, 'Sounds as if Eccles (the Steward) has dropped his false teeth'. A moment later the Bosun's Mate appeared to say that there had been an explosion in the harbour. Action stations were sounded and we prepared to slip our moorings and make for the open harbour. There was, however, one slight problem: the ship's boat (a five-oared 'trawler boat') was in the water and there wasn't time to hoist her. The solution was to man her with two ratings with orders to take her ashore and await further instructions. The two men chosen were ordinary seamen Smith and Dalby who, it was thought, could well be spared, being notoriously the two most incompetent sailors on board.

I didn't hear the full story of Smith and Dalby until the next morning when, after a night's ineffectual depth-charging around the harbour, *Genista* went alongside the *Ramillies*, which was somewhat down by the bows having been torpedoed by a Japanese midget submarine which had evaded the asdic of our sister corvette. As we paced the quarterdeck together, *Ramillies'* officer of the watch told me what had happened and then said 'Was it your sailors that we nearly shot last night?'

It appeared that, after we had slipped our moorings the night before, Smith and Dalby had duly made for the jetty only to find the Port Officer running up and down shouting 'The *Ramillies* has been torpedoed. All boats away to rescue survivors!' So they turned round and began to pull their craft in the direction of *Ramillies* which they could scarcely see. Meanwhile an oerlikon gunner on the quarterdeck of the battleship saw on his starboard quarter a blob with two dots on it which he took for a midget submarine. He opened fire with tracer bullets and Smith and Dalby became aware that these were splintering the woodwork and ricocheting off the water around them. Neither could swim but they both reacted to the emergency with remarkable presence of mind. Smith dived overboard and learnt to swim there and then. Dalby stood up, waved his arms and sang 'Land of Hope and Glory' at the top of his voice, which as he intended persuaded the gunner on the *Ramillies* that he was not a Japanese submariner. The *Ramillies* then sent a boat to pick them up.

Many years later at a party one Sunday morning at Wootton I was introduced to a brother of one of the guests who had been an Engineer Officer in the Navy. He had spent some time during the war on the *Ramillies* and it transpired that he was with her in Diego Suarez. He confirmed the rumour that we had heard in *Genista* that the midget submarine had been launched outside the harbour by a larger submarine and that the two crew members had beached their craft and made off inland to be subsequently captured by Royal Marines. To my delight he also knew the story of Smith and Dalby, which I had begun to fear I had invented.

Shortly after this the *Ramillies* left to undergo repairs and was replaced by the cruiser *Dauntless*. Otherwise only the two corvettes remained. There was nothing to do ashore. The port was a run–down French colonial town with little but the smell of drains to remind one of metropolitan France. But the harbour was idyllic and, having enough to read, I was entirely content to remain there indefinitely. There was still a threat from enemy submarines and it was necessary to keep watches at the harbour entrance. These were enlivened by conversation with the two signalmen. Leading Signalman Boxall had in peacetime been a Metropolitan policeman and his prose style reflected that. He was a natural malapropist and I remember leaning over the bridge rail together on a particularly splendid day watching the sharks basking around the ship. I remarked on how peaceful and beautiful they looked. 'Yes,' he replied, 'that's as may be; but if you fell into the water, them there sharks would have no punctuation whatever about eating you.' (Later on, back home, when I consulted the text of *The Rivals* I was delighted to discover that Leading Signalman Boxall had spontaneously invented one of Mrs Malaprop's original malapropisms.) On another occasion, he complained about the ship's dog and its habit of 'emasculating upon the upper deck'. He was, I think, a little surprised when I replied, 'Yes, he almost emasculated me the other day'. The other signalman was also a Londoner. He was an orphan brought up in a Dr Barnardo's home and a splendid advertisement for that institution. He explained that they were all taught to be self-sufficient if need arose. He was equipped with a range of basic skills, including cooking, cobbling, sewing and knitting. He used to darn my socks so beautifully that they were almost an improvement on the original.

The powers that be – I am not sure at that stage who they were – evidently felt that it was not good for us to be so happily idle, so they began to devise ways in which we might be usefully employed. The first was a plan to carry out a surprise attack from the sea upon the port of Majunga a little way down the coast, in which I was to lead the landing party. I was glad that this was abandoned.

The second plan actually went ahead. There was in the port a Greek sea captain whose ship had been commandeered by the French authorities and was now moored behind a barrier reef off the island of Mayotta in the Comoro Islands between Madagascar and the mainland. He wished to regain his ship and the allies needed any merchant shipping they could get hold of. So a 'cutting out expedition' was decided upon.

The plan was as follows. HMS *Genista* was to proceed to Mayotta in company with an Admiralty trawler: a warship built on the lines of a trawler and somewhat smaller than a corvette, commanded by a peacetime trawler skipper. *Genista* would carry a party of twenty-five Royal Marines together with a Marine Officer, the whole operation to be commanded by a Lieutenant Commander RN. In order to achieve surprise and avoid close manoeuvring with the larger ships, the boarding party was to be transferred before dawn from *Genista* to a large motor boat, called an R–Boat, which until that point would be towed behind *Genista*. The main entrance to the harbour was well marked and would, of course, be watched. It would, therefore, be necessary for the ships to penetrate the reef by one or other of the narrower passes which were discernible on the charts. Once within the harbour the transfer would take place. The R–Boat was stocked with rope ladders, grappling irons and other devices to enable the boarding party to scale the vessel's sides.

We agreed beforehand which of the passes in the reef we should use and a time when we should meet there. The only worry was that the charts were out of date and uncorrected and, moreover, French, but nothing could be done about that. I should add that the Greek sea captain came with us to take command of his vessel and navigate it back to Diego Suarez. I had with me a copy of the Odyssey and he was delighted when I suggested that we read it together.

Unfortunately when he read it was unrecognisable to me and vice versa. The trouble was not so much the pronunciation as his use of stressed syllables and mine of quantities.

Things started badly. Pattinson ordered the trawler to keep station one mile on our starboard beam, although he ought to have known that trawler skippers dislike station keeping. In no time he had disappeared, but he knew the rendezvous, so that did not matter unduly.

It was dark when we encountered the reef and began to sail along it. It was a magnificent sight with a heavy swell of phosphorescent breakers marking its course so far as we could see ahead. We had not expected to come across any other traffic but not far from our destination we almost ran down an outrigger canoe with two fishermen in it. Pattinson decided that it was too risky to let them go as they might give our presence away, so we had to take them, loudly protesting, in tow.

The crisis came when we reached the pass through the reef. It was not all that easy to pick it out and it looked narrower than we had expected. The Captain's old vice of going too slowly probably was our undoing, for there was a noticeable current setting across the pass and, before we realised what was happening, we were carried by it onto the reef on the port side. Assisted by the considerable swell it rapidly took us a whole ship's length, or some three hundred feet on to the reef and there we stuck.

As dawn was approaching it was imperative to proceed as rapidly as possible with the rest of the plan. The trawler had now arrived and we saw it safely through the reef. The boarding party and the Greek captain were transferred to the R-Boat and it set out at full speed in what we took to be the direction of the merchant ship. It was not until later, when we were all back in Diego Suarez that we learnt what happened next to that part of the expedition. It was pure farce. As the sky lightened, the merchant ship became visible. To everyone's astonishment she was moored head and stern and had steam up. A gangway was in place and there were figures on the upper deck. Clearly there was no question of achieving surprise. The boarding party would simply have to rush the gangway.

As the R-Boat approached the vessel it became apparent that something had gone wrong with its steering and the boat began to go round in ever-increasing circles. There was just time, as it went past the gangway, for the gallant Lieutenant Commander to leap onto the bottom of it, although not for his marines to follow. Without hesitation he ran up the gangway, brandishing his revolver, and said, 'I am an officer of the Royal Navy. I call upon you to surrender. Resistance is hopeless. I have two naval vessels in attendance', not mentioning that one of them was stuck on the barrier reef. The men whom he addressed appeared unimpressed but friendly. It transpired that some days before the Greek crew had overpowered the French officers who were now in custody below and were anxious to leave Mayotta as soon as they could find someone to navigate the ship. The R-Boat was repaired and the Greek captain returned to his vessel. Later that day we in *Genista* had the mortification of seeing her steam out of the harbour through the official entrance. I learned later that the British party had been fascinated by the Greek captain's methods of navigation. He seemed to make no use of charts, but would come onto the bridge from time to time, sniff the air, and point in the direction he wanted the helmsman to steer.

Meanwhile in *Genista* there was the problem of how to get off the coral. It was a matter of some urgency since, apart from U-boats, Japanese submarines armed with twin 5.25″ guns were believed to be in the vicinity. If one of them appeared we should simply provide target practice. Had that not been the case, we could scarcely have been in more delectable surroundings. The ship was now solidly on the reef with only a slight list and a little movement at high tide. There was a distant view of the town of Mayotta nestling beneath a perfectly shaped mountain which changed as the day wore on through various shades of blue and purple. The sea between varied in colour with its depth and the amount of coral beneath it, while the reef itself teemed with brightly coloured fish. It was astoundingly beautiful and, not for the first time, I noticed how one's response to beauty is almost entirely unaffected by the presence of fear.

The orthodox procedure in our situation was to lay out a kedge anchor astern of the ship, and this we attempted to do. The object is to drop the anchor onto the sea bed where the holding is good, make fast to a wire cable, and to use a winch to haul in the cable. Since the anchor is fast the result should be to draw the ship towards it – unless, of course, the ship itself is as fast as the anchor. The problem was to convey the anchor to a point beyond the reef where it could be dropped to good effect. The only means available to us was the trawler boat. So I was sent out with a crew of five, the cable coiled in the bottom of the boat in front of me and the kedge anchor hung over the stern after me. The idea was to pay out the cable as we got further from the ship. The attempt failed utterly. In face of the swell breaking onto the reef, and with the weight of the anchor hanging over the stern, it was impossible for the boat to make any headway.

Two other possibilities remained. One was to exert sternwards pressure on the ship by some other means. The other was to find some way of destroying the coral, which held the ship captive. A combination of the two seemed promising and eventually a threefold scheme was devised:

1. We would lead wire hawsers from two winches aft and make them fast to the two bower anchors. We would then ease out the anchor cables at the same time hauling in on these wires. In this way we would get the bower anchors as far aft as we could, letting them rest on the coral. We should then hoist in the anchors using the capstans in the ordinary way.
2. At the same time we should go astern on the engines in the hope that the propeller would also exert sternward pressure.
3. We would break up the coral so far as we could with explosives. This was risky because any explosives strong enough to demolish the coral might well damage the ship. Nevertheless the gunnery officer, Winsby, set to work to find means of demolishing the coral. He set an able seaman to work with a wooden fid on excavating some of the TNT from a depth charge until what was left would be not too destructive. He also had two high explosive shells lashed together with a depth charge primer and detonator, to be cast overboard astern of the ship. Both of these devices were to be reserved as a last resort, if it became apparent that the only choice was between the risk of using them and the ship's breaking up.

At this point the *Dauntless* came to our assistance and the use of her motor launch enabled us to lay out our kedge anchor. High tide was imminent and with it the opportunity to use all the methods we had assembled. At a pre-concerted moment, we hauled in on the bower anchors and the kedge anchor and set the engines full speed astern. Slowly but surely the ship moved astern and slid off the coral reef. Was there a cheer? I expect so – and certainly there would have been in a film – but all I can remember is enormous relief and a sense that the ship was alive again. Alive but wounded, *Genista* had a twelve degree list to port and a loss of three or four knots in top speed. There were one or two leaks which were quickly repaired.

Back in Diego Suarez, a signal was received from C-in-C Eastern Fleet which said 'Proceed to Mombasa for repairs'. Pattinson had other ideas and replied 'Suggest better facilities available in Durban'. To our astonishment C-in-C agreed and we set course for Durban.

So ended the Madagascar campaign for one of the ships involved in it. I do not suppose there is any record of the cutting out operation still extant, unless the proceedings of the Board of Inquiry are retained somewhere. *Genista*'s escape from the coral reef was a considerable feat of seamanship and was, as I remember, a corporate effort. Although Pattinson and Leigh-Wood, the First Lieutenant, were the prime movers, we all sat round the ward room table and discussed the problem. Winsby's contribution caused a moment of alarm when the ship was already on course for Diego Suarez. I had the forenoon watch and, as the ship rolled in the slight swell, I became aware of something sliding heavily from one side to the other of the gun platform below the bridge. It was Winsby's explosive device of two high explosive shells, a depth charge primer and detonator which had been overlooked in the excitement. Not knowing what arrangements he had made for making it safe, I had pleasure in ordering the gunnery officer to dismantle it.

The authorities were less impressed by our skill in getting off the reef than by our negligence in getting on it in the first place and a Board of Inquiry was held into the incident on our arrival in Durban. Our defence was that the attempt to take a vessel of *Genista*'s size through the reef under cover of darkness, using out of date charts, was inherently risky and justified only as part of a military operation. We had taken every reasonable precaution. Nevertheless we were held to have been negligent and the Captain and the Officer of the Watch (myself) were reprimanded.

When *Genista* went into dry dock in Durban, it was possible to inspect the damage. A number of rivets had been started and some plates dislodged. The keel had been corrugated along its whole length and the blades of the phosphor-bronze propeller had been ground down by the coral to two-thirds of their normal size. It was the inspecting engineer's judgement that, with the plates replaced and a new propeller, she would be even stronger than before. Remarkably she saw out the war on convoy escort duties and for some years afterwards served under the name *Weather Recorder* as a weather ship in the North Atlantic. The makers, Harland and Wolff, had plainly done a good job.

For the next year or so, we were part of the South African Defence Force, escorting convoys from Cape Town to Durban and back or occasionally as far as Walvis Bay or Beira.

After Madagascar Nicholls left *Genista* to return to Canada and his departure left a vacancy for navigating officer. At *King Alfred* I had enjoyed navigation and was anxious to take on the job, although I had had little practice. So I went to see Pattinson in his cabin and rather hesitantly put the suggestion to him. He enjoyed teasing me and said, 'It is one thing to lose the keys of the confidential books, quite another to lose the ship. Are you sure you won't do that?' He agreed and suggested in the nicest possible way that, to begin with, he might take sun sights and star sights as well, just to keep his hand in, and we could compare notes. I was much relieved that Nicholl's replacement as junior officer would now be responsible for confidential books. Before long I became quite a confident and reliable navigating officer. My apprenticeship effectively came to an end on a day when the convoy had to change course on reaching a certain point and we had three positions to choose from, distinct although not wildly discrepant: Pattinson's, the Commodore of the convoy's and mine. I asked which position I was to take as the basis for our change of course. 'Yours, of course', he said.

For the most part the weather was superb – day after day of assured sunshine, until I sometimes longed for a damp, overcast English sky. Usually the convoys were routed close to land, some five to ten miles out, and we became familiar with the magnificent coastline of the Eastern Cape. On one occasion, as I remember, we were sent to rescue survivors from a merchant ship that had been torpedoed well out to sea. It was uncertain whether any of the crew would have survived or how accurate was the position the ship had given, and the strong currents meant that in a few days any raft would have drifted for many miles. Added to this, we should be going to the limits of our range of fuel. We simply had to make the best estimate we could of where we were most likely to find them and turn back when there was just enough fuel for our return to Durban. The Captain had decided to turn 180° at noon and by that time we had sighted nothing. Then he said, 'Let's give them another couple of hours', and very shortly afterwards the masthead lookout sighted a rudimentary sail and we found a wooden raft with five men on it in the last stages of exhaustion and badly sunburned. We carried no medical officer, but only a Sick Berth Attendant, who cared for them well enough to bring them safely back to Durban.

I was to spend a year in the North Atlantic later in HMS *Oxford Castle* but I never encountered storms of such sustained ferocity as those off the southern tip of Africa, Cape Agulhas, in the winter months. Keeping a convoy intact in such weather was difficult, but at least it reduced the danger of U-boat attack.

Particularly in the prevailing fine weather, it was hard to believe in the existence of U-boats, although the German Navy gave high priority to disrupting convoys to the Middle East. The days were to all appearance so calm and peaceful. Nevertheless it was necessary to take every precaution against betraying our position to an enemy whose presence had to be presumed. This would often require an exchange of signals and these were subject to certain conventions. On one occasion we had as part of the escort an Admiralty trawler which was too slow to maintain the pace of the convoy and was unable to zigzag. Accordingly it was stationed ahead of the convoy where it made in daylight an unacceptable amount of smoke and a flurry of sparks at night. The senior officer of the convoy sent a signal which read simply 'Exodus 13–21'. When we looked it up, the message ran 'And the Lord went before them by day in a pillar of a cloud . . . and by night in a pillar of fire . . .'

References were not only to the Bible. On another occasion we were escorting a single merchant ship whose polished brass taffrail was reflecting the rays of the setting sun. The Captain sent a signal to the merchantman pointing this out and received the reply, 'I am Restonji Bomanji'. We thought in *Genista* that we were a reasonably well-read lot, but this defeated us and we sought explication. The reply came,

'The reference is to Kipling "Restonji Bomanji – a parsee the scales of whose hat reflected the rays of the sun with more than oriental splendour"'.

We were on special escort duty on another occasion which very nearly ended in tragedy but had eventually a series of comic consequences. Our task was to escort a large Dutch repair ship which had been undergoing an overhaul in the port of East London for a matter of months. On leaving East London we took station ahead to provide what anti-submarine protection we could. We had only been at sea for three hours or so when, around noon, as we were changing watches, there was a loud explosion and our charge heeled over and sank within minutes. There was no need to pick up survivors since the crew seemed to be taking to the boats without difficulty and, in any case, our first duty was to seek and destroy the U-boat. We therefore carried out the appropriate search procedure to hunt for a submarine. It was my job as Navigating Officer to attend in the chart house and make a track chart on which I should plot the ship's course and any asdic bearings we might get of the U-boat. I had been doing this for some twenty minutes with the assistance of the bosun's mate when the Captain asked me to come out on the bridge and take a sun sight to fix the ship's position as we were now out of sight of land. I told the Bosun's mate to go on jotting down all alterations of course and speed and spent a further twenty minutes fixing our position. When I went back to the chart house I found, to my disgust, that the Bosun's mate had not thought it necessary to carry on with his notes, since I had apparently abandoned the track chart. So I told him to start again and went on with the plotting, leaving a gap to be filled in later.

Eventually we gave up the search and returned to harbour. I never discovered how the sinking occurred. There were no casualties, which may have been because the watches were changing, almost as if it had been planned that way. This suggested the possibility of sabotage. *Genista* had picked up no evidence of a U-boat and had received no warning of a U-boat in the area. I have since learnt that it was indeed a U-Boat.

On our arrival back in Cape Town we were told that there would in due course be a Board of Inquiry and I was asked to send my track chart ashore. This posed a problem because, of course, the chart was incomplete. All I could do was make a copy of that part of the chart which was based on a record of courses and speeds and fill in the gap with an estimate of the ship's track during the time I was taking my sun sight. I got what information I could from the Captain, the quartermaster and the engine room. I sent this in to the naval office with a pecked line to indicate how much of it had been estimated and a note of explanation to that effect.

It was a month or so before the Board of Inquiry was summoned. To my annoyance the naval office had by this time mislaid my track chart and I was asked to provide another one. This request posed an obvious difficulty – how was I to fill in the gap, given that the people I had asked for information originally had forgotten what they said? The best I could do was to sketch in a pecked line which looked so far as possible like the one I had drawn before. So I did this, with another explanatory note.

The Board consisted of two captains RN and a Commander. Pattinson was, of course, present throughout. He declared he was not worried about the outcome – he would get promotion in any case – and, indeed, it was plain to me that he had been drinking. (He was scrupulous about not drinking at sea, but he drank a great deal in harbour and, like many habitual drinkers, showed no obvious effects.)

I remember the course of my own interrogation, for I have used it as a philosophical example ever since:

President: (after the usual formalities) Is this your original track chart?
Me: No, Sir, my original track chart was lost in the naval offices.
President: Ah, quite. Would you mind telling us if there is any difference between this one and the original?
Me: That is not an easy question to answer. That part of the track chart which is in a continuous line is an exact copy. But, owing to a regrettable lapse, for which I take full responsibility (and here I explained what had happened), there is part of the chart drawn in a pecked line which was originally based upon estimation. It is unlikely that, on the second occasion, relying on memory alone I managed to repeat the same line exactly.
President: You haven't answered my question. Is there or is there not a difference?
Me: In the nature of the case, I can't know, but if pressed to give an answer, it is so unlikely that I managed to draw exactly the same line the second time that I am bound to say there *is* a difference.
President: What is the difference?

I took a deep breath and endeavoured to explain. In order to be sure what the difference was I should need to be able to compare the original track chart with the later one, but in the nature of the case I did not have access to the original one. If I was able to presume that my memory was entirely accurate, I should have seen to it that the second line was an exact copy of the first and no question of the difference between them would have arisen. I failed to make myself understood and was reduced to saying simply that I didn't know what the difference was.

I was called back later and asked to confirm some small details. I thought I noticed that the members of the Board were somewhat less peremptory in their attitude on this occasion and Pattinson told me at the lunch break that he had told them that I was a Doctor of Philosophy!

During the lunch interval I was confronted by an awkward dilemma. There was no doubt in my mind that Pattinson was drunk, not having any reason to believe that we should be going to sea. But a message came from the harbour master requesting *Genista* to shift her berth into another dock and it would be his job to do it. To make things more difficult I was officer of the day and, if anyone was to draw attention to his condition, it would have to be me. I decided we should have to chance it. He was a good seaman and it would be a very serious matter for both of us, especially for me, a junior officer, to question his competence.

As soon as we got onto the bridge it was apparent that my fears were justified. His habitual caution was not in evidence and he ordered half speed astern before he had slipped the bow rope and when, at my prompting, he did so, it required full speed ahead and hard a starboard, again at my prompting, to prevent *Genista*'s stern ramming the dockside opposite and get her out of the narrow channel in which she was berthed. The next challenge was to make our way through the harbour entrance and into a neighbouring basin to our new berth between two large merchant ships. The first part of it should have been straightforward except that a sister corvette was already approaching the opening where she had right of way. It was clear that Pattinson had no intention of giving way and all I could do was dance around behind him waving to the bridge party on the other ship to stand clear, which, mercifully, they did. The worst, I feared, was yet to come. Once inside the new basin, he would have to take a full turn and bring *Genista* in starboard side between the two merchant ships. What was required was a particularly neat bit of parking, involving the same manoeuvre as when he rammed the Cunarder at Diego Suarez. But this time his inhibitions were altogether removed by drink and he executed it brilliantly.

After our return from Madagascar *Genista* was in dry dock for some six weeks for repairs to her hull, the finding and fitting of a new propeller and, at the same time, a boiler clean and the fitting for the first time of radar. We were granted a fortnight's leave which brought me into contact with some new friends, the Coppacks. The parents had emigrated from Wales during the depression and they had prospered in South Africa where, as whites, they were automatically middle class although basically Welsh working class. The grown-up children, one boy and one girl, had had their formative years in South Africa, but it saddened me to discover that the parents too regarded the native blacks as an inferior race. There was in the naval offices in Durban a black office boy who, I learned in talking to him, had a degree from Makerere University. I happened to remark to the Coppack parents what a shame it was that a highly educated man should not be given more responsible employment. 'Serve him right' was the reply 'for getting himself a degree.'

I became acquainted with the race problem through some other friends, whom I could not mention to the Coppacks. I cannot now remember how I met them. One was a middle-aged woman, Florence Beyman, who was a columnist on the local newspaper *The Natal Mercury*; the other was a young man of my own age, an Indian freelance journalist called Yusuf. Through them I learned a bit about the problems of the Indian community in Durban which were to the fore at the time. The Indians had been introduced to Natal as indentured labourers in the cotton plantations. Their descendants had prospered in trade, which they virtually monopolised, and some of them were very wealthy. Their growing affluence was felt to be a threat by the whites and the Government had just passed the Group Areas act which drew boundaries for residence along racial lines and was fiercely contested by the Indians. I was introduced by Florence Beyman to Mrs Ballinger who had energetically campaigned against the Act and who took me with her and showed me the striking difference in conditions between the roads and public areas on either side of the boundary. The whites were determined to keep the Indians out of the better served areas into which the richer of them would like to have moved. Yusuf took me to lunch at the Orient Club in Durban, which was the Indian equivalent of the Rand Club in Johannesburg, and I remember disliking intensely the tasteless ostentation to be found there. The Indians in Natal, like the Jews for centuries in Europe, were not allowed to own land and had no alternative left to them but to make money. In both cases the effects were not always attractive and one could see how the prejudice against them, in so far as it was justified, was based upon the inevitable consequences of that very prejudice. Nor were all the effects of their ill-treatment bad: there were splendid schools and crocodiles of well-behaved boys and girls attending them.

We had in *Genista* one happy experience of more enlightened racial policies. We were lying alongside on one occasion when a sloop of the Royal Indian Navy made fast outside us. The wardroom officers crossed over *Genista* in order to go ashore and have dinner together. There was a Sikh in command, a British First Lieutenant, an Indian Gunnery Officer, and a British Navigating Officer, and so on through the ten or so officers on board. Half an hour later they came back to return to their ship. At the Royal Hotel they had been informed that the white officers could enter the restaurant, the others not. So they declared that either all of them would enter or none of them would, and we were able modestly to entertain them ourselves for the rest of the evening.

At some point in this period ashore at Durban, I cannot remember exactly when, I had a surprise meeting with Christopher Rieu. He had fought in Eritrea and been wounded in the leg (in an engagement for which he was awarded the Military Cross). He had been sent to Oribi Military Hospital in Pietermaritzburg and while there had got engaged to a girl from Pretoria. Christabel Cramb was from one of the leading families there and Christopher gave me an eloquent description of her, tall, slim, fair with brown eyes and a seductively deep voice. By his account it was not surprising that Christopher had fallen in love with her and it was no surprise at all to me that she had fallen for him. Christopher had always been astonishingly handsome and gifted with that ravishing smile. In uniform and with crutches he must have been irresistible.

As it happened, I myself was to spend a short stay in Oribi Hospital. Someone in authority decided that a longish spell in harbour was bad for morale and the Captain arranged for two officers with a party of sailors to go to the military camp at Pietermaritzburg for a fortnight's field training. Philip Hall, Nicholl's successor and I were to be in charge.

For some while – ever since I joined the Navy in fact – I had suffered from a skin complaint which at that time chiefly affected my scalp. On arrival in Pietermaritzburg I went at once to Oribi Hospital to see if anything could be done about it. The receptionist said I was in luck as one of their doctors was a specialist in dermatology. He saw me and said he could certainly treat it but needed to keep me in hospital for a fortnight. He would send a signal to my commanding officer to seek his consent. This was duly given and to the understandable disgust of Philip Hall I went into hospital. I was told I had psoriasis which was an inherited condition for which there was no cure but which could be benefited by various treatments, most of them involving tar. He also said it was known as a healthy man's disease: if I was seriously ill it would disappear and it was rarely seen on a corpse. It is now recognised as an 'auto-immune' disease, like rheumatoid arthritis, and I have suffered from it all my life with varying degrees of severity. The treatment at Oribi consisted in my scalp being anointed every night with coal tar ointment which was washed off by a nurse in the morning, after which I was free to leave hospital for the day so long as I returned in time for the evening's anointing which I could do myself.

This liberal regime allowed me to go to a dance with one or other of the nurses, whilst still technically in hospital. At these dances I would sometimes meet my colleague after his day's field training, but he was philosophically content to regard this as the luck of the draw.

Philip was a Cambridge man who liked to tell of his encounter with a well-known beggar in Durban who used to accost British servicemen off the troop convoys and for a shilling tell them what part of the home country they came from. In return for his shilling, this Henry Higgins character listened to Philip and said, 'Sussex followed by Cambridge and then, I think, several years in South Africa', all of which was correct.

While I was still in Durban on leave I was invited by the Coppacks to go with them to stay with friends in Pretoria for a long weekend. On the Saturday night they took me to a ball and there I saw a tall willowy girl in a pale blue dress which set off her fair hair and who was very much a centre of attention. She conformed so well to Christopher's description that, after a moment's hesitation, I asked her for a dance and said, 'I think you must be Christabel. I am a friend of Christopher's'. Thus I was the first of Christopher's friends or family to meet his future wife.

Not long afterwards when we were at sea again I was able to verify the information given me by the dermatologist at Oribi. On one of our longer voyages I suffered from a severe fever which was accompanied by a discharge from my right ear. All traces of psoriasis disappeared. Unfortunately by the time I was able to see a doctor nothing could be done to prevent my losing the hearing of that ear, and I have had to make do with one ear ever since. The doctor, having satisfied himself that the ear was no longer diseased, did not notice the deafness, which I soon got used to.

From the time that our refit was completed in mid 1942 until August 1943 *Genista* was steadily employed escorting convoys up and down the coast of South Africa with occasional forays such as I have already mentioned. There must have been danger of attack from U-boats but none in our immediate vicinity. The Japanese threat had receded. We had a regular routine of Action Stations at dawn and dusk. At both times I, as navigating officer, was busy taking star sights, by which I was able to fix the ship's position and calculate how much our speed had been slowed down or accelerated by the strong Agulhas current which ran all the way down that coast from the equator until, off Cape Agulhas itself, it mingled with the cold Benguela current from the Antarctic to produce the confused seas which, whatever the weather, but particularly in storm force winds, made corvettes more than usually uncomfortable. They were renowned for their seaworthiness so that one was not in danger and one got used to their varying patterns of response to different sorts of seas — so well used, in fact, that I did not feel at all alarmed until I noticed the behaviour of fellow ships. In heavy seas they would disappear out of sight altogether until one would see them emerge from a trough with bows or stern entirely out of the water, and I would realise that this was how *Genista* was behaving too. This responsiveness to the pattern of the seas had one useful consequence. When I was asleep in my bunk – then and later I have always slept very soundly – I would wake up when the ship altered course and go off to sleep again when I realised that we had reached a position where we were due to alter course.

Most of the time now we were too close to land to be accompanied by albatrosses, but there were plenty of other seabirds. We were frequently followed by porpoises which often came so close to the ship that they seemed to collide with her. Pattinson maintained that they did this in order to de-louse themselves. From time to time when one was on watch at night one would see a steady phosphorescent track coming straight towards the ship. It could be a torpedo and, if it was, the correct response was to alter course towards it, so as to minimise the risk of its hitting the ship. It was a text book case of risk avoidance. That it was a porpoise was much more probable; but if it was a torpedo, the consequences would be disastrous. So all three of us, the signalman, the Bosun's mate on the lookout and the officer of the watch would examine the track carefully for the hoped-for wobble, knowing that a sudden change of course, if it proved to be unnecessary, would alarm the whole ship's company from the captain down. There were other marine phenomena from time to time, whales blowing and even flying fish, some of them landing on the foc'sle and providing a welcome change of menu for breakfast next morning. Sometimes the natural phenomena were atmospheric. Normally the skies at night were unimaginably clear and with no lights showing from our own or other ships, the heavenly bodies were displayed in their various constellations with absolute clarity. In the course of a single watch one would be aware of their motion round the Southern Cross. In this way, just as I came to know the eastern coast of South Africa from the sea better than any British coastline, so I became more familiar with the southern sky at night than ever I did with that of the northern hemisphere, which was often cloudy. Moreover, for the only time in my life I could identify the heavenly bodies, the planets, the principal stars and their constellations, as I had a star globe to help me with my navigation.

There were also frequent fogs when cold moist air encountered the warm Agulhas current, and I vividly remember an occasion when the ship at night was moving silently in a cocoon of thick white fog, the whole illuminated by small balls of fire running up and down the rigging. It cast a supernatural light: could it have been St Elmo's fire?

I remember this whole period with warm affection. The wardroom was most agreeable and the ship was without doubt a happy one. I was doing a job which I enjoyed and, I know, was increasingly good at. When ashore, with the Coppacks at one port and the Sandeman's at the other, and increasingly with other friends as well, and with all the comforts of South Africa which, apart from her military contribution, was barely at war, it was an ideal existence. When my mother wrote to say that she was conspiring with David Rafilovich (then at the Ministry of Labour) to get me a civil service job, I discouraged her. Of course, I badly missed my family at home and Phoebe and my other friends but this was incident upon the state of war, wherever I was. My mother and Betty (my mother through Betty) wrote regularly and so did Phoebe, in terms which made it clear that she was missing me almost as much as I was missing her. If I returned home, so far as Phoebe was concerned, I would still be the particularly close friend which was all I seemed destined to be always in her life. I had with me a photograph of her – a poly photo taken in 1940 – and, in any case, a vivid image of her could be summoned at any time, especially in the night watches. I did from time to time wonder if there was anything I could do to better my chances whenever we did meet again. She had in her first letter after my leaving told me not to think of myself as a 'wimp who failed to make hay while the sun shone', but inevitably I blamed my sexual inexperience for having precipitated her affair with John. Thus I did wonder from time to time if I ought not to take steps to remedy that inexperience. It should not have been too difficult for a young and reasonably attractive naval officer. But I was effectively restrained by three things, timidity, fastidiousness and moral principle. Whether, if the opportunity had arisen, the last of these would have prevailed on me if the other two could have been overcome I do not know, but in the event all three stopped me seeking an opportunity. From time to time my colleagues would have a party on board to which Wren officers were invited. The drink would flow freely and the Wrens were encouraged to play uninhibited games until the early hours. I did not enjoy these occasions and would wait until the others were drunk enough not to notice and quietly retire to my cabin.

In September 1942 I received my second ring as Lieutenant RNVR and the ship was becoming over weighted with senior officers. Pattinson was the first to go and was replaced by Leigh-Wood, who in turn was replaced as First Lieutenant by Leonard Thompson who was transferred to *Genista* from *Thyme*, our long-term sister ship. These changes made the company for me even more congenial, although I was sorry to say goodbye to Pattinson, who had nurtured me from the beginning with so much tact and wry forbearance. Leonard Thompson had been a Rhodes Scholar at New College and had a wife and child in Oxford. When I found that she was living in Warnborough Road within easy walking distance of Osberton Road, where my mother and sisters lived, I asked them to visit her, which they did.

With all these changes taking place, it could not be long before my own increasing seniority attracted the attention of the Admiral Commanding Reserves at the Admiralty. At one stage *Genista* had two lieutenant commanders, four lieutenants and one sub-lieutenant. In August 1943 I received instructions to leave *Genista* and return to the UK for a further appointment.

While waiting ashore for a passage home I fell in with *Genista's* leading Radar operator and we had a drink together. He was an older, educated man and had posed us on one occasion an awkward problem. For obvious reasons it was not customary to have regular divisions and prayers on Sundays as it had been in the *Queen Elizabeth*. But Leigh-Wood in command thought we ought to have them once in a while. When this was announced the leading Radar operator put in a request through his divisional officer, me, to the captain to be excused attendance at divine service. He was duly seen and it was explained to him that non-Anglicans were in any case permitted to fall out after Divisions, as they were not required to attend an Anglican service. 'Under what command' the request man asked, 'am I to fall out?' He was told that the customary order was 'Fall out Roman Catholics' but this was understood to cover not only Roman Catholics but any member of the ship's company who was not Anglican. Most politely but firmly the request man replied 'I am sorry to be difficult, but I am an atheist and I cannot conscientiously fall out under the command "Fall out Roman Catholics". Then with the suggestion of twinkle in the eye, he added 'If the command were to be "fall out Roman Catholics and atheists" I should of course have no difficulty in complying.' Leigh-Wood and I could see at once that any such command was out of the question. Not only would it be an unheard of breach of custom but a dangerous one which would be taken by an unpredictable proportion of the ship's company as an invitation to fall out. So a decision was deferred and, in the end, it was a timid compromise. Whenever divisions and prayers were to be held, there would be urgent repairs needed in the Radar cabinet.

I was glad to have an opportunity to talk with a born philosopher and in the course of our conversation he came out with a remark which I have always treasured. I said how sorry I was to be leaving *Genista* and he said 'they will miss you too. They would have done anything for you!'

The only other occasion when we had divine service on board was also memorable. We were taking a naval chaplain on passage from Cape Town to Durban. The weather was rough as usual off Cape Agulhas and the poor man spent most of his time in his cabin. But, heroically, on Sunday he prepared to take Morning Service on the Lower Mess deck, where he and all of us had great difficulty in remaining upright. He announced the first hymn, which was 'Stand up, stand up for Jesus' which the congregation managed to do, if at all, only by hanging onto stanchions, fixed tables, the deck-head and anything immovable.

In the Navy transitions always involved delay and I spent some days in Durban employed in censoring mail, together with other officers awaiting return to the UK. Among them was Charles Kuper who had been an intelligence officer in the Middle East and was on his way back, like me, to discover his next job. He was a big man, somewhat older than me, an entertaining conversationalist, well read with an apt quotation for every occasion. He had been a history master at Wellington and hoped to return there after the war. It was good to know that I was assured of congenial company on the journey back however long that was to be.

It was to be longer and less direct than either of us had expected. On arrival at Cape Town, after a spectacular railway journey through the Karoo and down into Cape Province through the Hex River Valley, we were transferred to the Royal Mail Liner, *Highland Chieftain*, now a troop ship. On board were five hundred RAF officers who had been undergoing training in what was then Southern Rhodesia, twenty army officers and twenty naval officers. As soon as we were at sea we were informed that the ship would be calling in at Buenos Aires to collect a cargo of meat for transit to the UK. We were to be unescorted, in the belief that the ship's speed was sufficient to evade U-boats.

There followed one of those odd interludes which seem to attend naval service in wartime. Having crossed the South Atlantic and arrived in the River Plate, where the fighting top of the *Graf Spee* could still be seen protruding from the water, we were all put ashore at Montevideo. Argentina was an unfriendly neutral which, though happy to sell meat to Britain, was not prepared to entertain a contingent of British servicemen. So we were to spend a fortnight in the care of the friendly Uruguayan Government. And friendly they were. They had seen no British servicemen since the battle of the River Plate and they set out to welcome us. We were lodged in the best hotel in town, given a free ride on all public transport and invited free to all public entertainments. The first of these was a concert to be given in the courtyard of the hotel. An announcement was made at the beginning of the programme that the first item was to be the Uruguayan national anthem, which we were to receive with customary respect. As soon as the first piece started we all stood at attention and saluted. It turned out to be longer than expected and we began to suspect that we had misunderstood the announcement and that what we were listening to was just an operatic overture to begin the normal programme. This impression was supported by the fact that the Uruguayan members of the hotel staff listening on the balcony did not appear to be showing particular respect. We, or at least I, (and I had the sense that my feeling was shared) was just wondering whether we should resume our seats when the piece finished; there was a roll of drums and the band played 'God Save the King'. So it had indeed been the national anthem!

Among the special treats prepared for us was an excursion into the country. We were taken in a fleet of buses for a long and attractive ride out of Montevideo to what at first appeared to be a large country house, but turned out in fact to be a brewery. Not far from the building was a large glade in which trestle tables were set out laden with enormous meat sandwiches. Between the tables were standpipes. When the taps were turned these flowed not, as I had expected, with fresh water but with beer in unrestricted quantities.

It was, apparently, the racing season and all British servicemen were invited to attend the races. The chief event was re-named the 'HM Britannic Forces Cup'. Not being interested in racing, Charles Kuper and I did not go but we heard afterwards what transpired. The President of the Republic expressed the wish that the British forces present should march past. None of them were at all used to formal drill, let alone on ceremonial occasions, but there could be no question of declining the President's invitation. So the mixed company of sailors, soldiers and airmen present were hastily assembled and arranged in some sort of order. Clearly the senior naval officer present had to lead the parade and he, a Lieutenant Commander of the Fleet Air Arm, was probably less experienced than any. My informant told me that all went reasonably well until the column approached the President at the saluting base, at which point the band struck up 'God Save the King'. The proper thing to do was to call the parade to attention and salute, but clearly this was not what was expected, but rather that they should keep on marching and salute the President as they passed. The Lieutenant Commander took what was unquestionably the right decision and committed the column to marching past in three-four time. It was, inevitably, a shambles, but nevertheless greatly appreciated.

Charles and I used to go regularly to the Anglo-Uruguayan Institute, run most effectively by the British Council. There was a great demand for English books and for lessons in English, and teatime in particular offered a good opportunity to meet Uruguayans who could speak English and particularly Uruguayan girls. I was befriended by one Mabel Macgregor who in spite of her name was a Uruguayan of several generations with nothing in her appearance to suggest Scottish ancestry. Her ancestors were part of the Scottish diaspora which had made such a great contribution to the Americas.

It was at tea one afternoon at the British Council that Charles and I were given an unexpected assignment. A woman came along to our table and said to us 'I don't know what I am going to do. I have an

English class of 14–16 year olds at five o'clock and I have lost my voice!' There was nothing for it but for Charles and me to offer our services. 'We are English,' we said, 'and we should be able to keep them interested for while. How long does the period last?' She said 'three-quarters of an hour. The bell will sound at the end of it.' So Charles and I presented ourselves to this mixed class of boys and girls and said 'Your teacher has lost her voice and cannot be with you, so we are taking her place and will talk to you in English for the next three-quarters of an hour. What would you like us to talk about?' They replied, as with one voice, 'The History and Traditions of the Royal Navy'. Charles was an experienced teacher and had some acquaintance with naval history. Between us we could remember, or invent, a reasonable collection of traditions. I was able to supplement these with pictures of naval ships in coloured chalk on the blackboard from the middle ages through the great ages of sail to the present day. There is no doubt that the occasion was a great success. The bell was entirely ignored and the session went on for well over an hour.

We spent a fortnight at Montevideo in this musical comedy world and it was almost Christmas by the time we arrived at Liverpool. After South Africa and South America the contrast with England after four years of war with blackouts and rationing and the Russians calling for a second front was depressing, and family and friends were visibly under strain. Back in Oxford, Betty and Myrtle and my mother were lodging in a small terraced house in Summertown at 18 Osberton Road. My mother was no better and no worse but showing her usual indomitable spirit in spite of constant disputes with my father about the allowance he was giving her. Betty and Myrtle were both working with Norman Heatley at the Blood Transfusion Service as also was Chairunnissa (Mamulie, the younger Inayat Khan daughter; Noorunnissa – Babulie – had enrolled in FANY and no one knew where she was. Vilayat was in the Navy). The most striking difference was in Myrtle, now nineteen, whose sunny disposition had become that of a settled beauty. Betty's husband, George Stokes, had enrolled as an Army chaplain and was serving in the Faeroe Islands. It was good to see Phoebe again, but she too was constantly overworked in the private office of the Air Minister, Sir Archibald Sinclair, and her health was under considerable strain. It became apparent that things were not easy between her and John, although my position remained unchanged. There was nothing I could do but be a friendly presence on the rare occasions that we could meet.

I made the usual visit to the Admiralty at St Anne's Mansions to discuss my future employment. (I am proud to say that, except for the *Repulse*, the nearest I got to seasickness in the Navy was in the antiquated lift at St Anne's Mansions.) I learnt that I was to be First Lieutenant of a new and larger corvette, *Oxford Castle*, now under construction at Harland and Wolff in Belfast. I was not happy at the news. I had hoped that, perhaps, I might be sent for an advanced course in navigation and appointed as navigating officer to a larger ship. The job of First Lieutenant was the one I felt least well equipped to undertake. 'Number One' was responsible, under the captain, for the entire organisation and running of the ship. Ideally he would be able himself to do everything he ordered other people to do and I was very far from being such a person. In *Genista* I had managed to do what I was required to do as officer in charge of the quarterdeck, but there was always someone else to fall back on if I made mistakes. In *Oxford Castle* I should have to ensure that no mistakes were made, least of all by me. I have never been particularly handy and I am bound to say I found myself seriously miscast.

For the second time I had to stand by a ship building in Belfast, but this time it was up to me to keep an eye on the dockyard workers and make sure that nothing was missed. I was given digs with a very nice family in North Belfast where the only room warm enough to work in was the living room in which the family listened to the radio continuously, not excluding the news in Welsh. There it fell to me to write the 'First Lieutenant's Standing Orders' for *Oxford Castle*. Here at least was something that I could make sure of doing properly and, by dint of collating the standing orders of *Genista* and other ships of my acquaintance, I was able to put together a set of standing orders which in the event worked very well and even my new commanding officer could find nothing to complain about.

Lieutenant Holden RNR DSC was a far cry from the genial Pattinson. He himself was in command for the first time, having distinguished himself as First Lieutenant of the sloop *Lagan* when she had her quarterdeck blown off by one of the new and devastating acoustic torpedoes (hence the DSC). He was, so far as I could tell, utterly humourless, and I got the impression that he did not like me personally and was unhappy to have me as his Number One – not unreasonably indeed, but whereas Pattinson had done everything he could to support and encourage me, Holden was inclined to do my job for me. I wished he would concentrate on his own job as captain and leave me to learn my job as best I could, if not with his encouragement, at least without his interference.

It is perhaps significant that I cannot now remember who the officers were in *Oxford Castle* with the exception of one senior lieutenant, Lodge, a quiet reliable man who also had been a peacetime schoolmaster. This is a pity because *Oxford Castle* was a fine ship. The Castle class corvettes were a distinct improvement on the Flower class – larger, more commodious, better equipped and better looking; eight officers and a hundred crew as against six officers and sixty crew. The difference can be seen in the film *The Cruel Sea*, which gives a remarkably accurate impression of what life was like in corvettes. I thought we ought to have a ship's badge prominently displayed and asked Phoebe to prepare a design. She produced an image of the ox in the Oxford City coat of arms, only full face with a heraldic version of the sea underneath. It was up to me then to find a motto to go with it and I thought this should have some connection with the University. I was inspired to look first to the University's own motto 'Dominus illuminatio mea'. 'The Lord is my light and my salvation'. The next line is 'Whom then shall I fear – Quem timebo?' So this line from Psalm 27 became our motto and it was one I thought entirely suitable for a warship.

The ship having been duly put through her trials and commissioned at Belfast, the next item was to be a return visit to Tobermory. This was bound to be an even more alarming experience than the first one, two years before, with *Genista*. I was in a very much more exposed position as First Lieutenant, responsible under the commanding officer for the entire organisation and fighting efficiency of the ship which was to be tested to breaking point on the final day. I was far from sure of my competence. It was generally known that Stephenson had the power to remove any officer from his ship and keep him for as long as he chose for further training in his base ship, *Western Isles*.

As it happened the fortnight passed without serious incident and it remained only to face the Commodore's final inspection. No sooner was he over the side than he announced 'Enemy aircraft bearing green 30'. By the time he reached the bridge there was a fire in the galley and, as soon as the upper deck was strewn with hose pipes, a submarine in sight on the starboard side. The commodore viewed the mounting chaos with every sign of intense satisfaction. Finally he announced that fifteen feet had been blown off the quarterdeck by an acoustic torpedo. I knew that the after damage control party was in the charge of a not very bright and rather slow-moving petty officer from Northern Ireland and I hastened aft to make sure that everything was under control. The critical location was the after magazine and I made straight for that. I was halfway down the ladder into the dim interior when an outraged bellow came up from beneath me, 'You're on my finger, damme boy, you're on my finger'. The Commodore had beaten me to it and a spell in *Western Isles* now seemed inevitable.

The inspection ended with the ship in total chaos. The Commodore then addressed the ship's company in terms I cannot now remember, but probably telling them that the treatment he had given them was only intended as a preparation for what might come later. Finally he shook hands with the officers one by one. To my surprise and relief he seemed gratified by my performance. It was a rather staccato utterance but it contained expressions like 'inexperience – keenness – the right spirit – Nelson, that sort of thing.' I could only suppose that my gaffe in treading on his finger had been interpreted by him charitably as eagerness in the discharge of duty.

The period at Tobermory was attended by one great blessing. I discovered that Charles Kuper had been sent for sea training to *Western Isles*. He told me that the plan was to put him for three months as an additional officer in one or other of the ships that were going through Tobermory. I had no difficulty in persuading him that he should join *Oxford Castle* and to this the Commodore and Holden readily agreed.

Charles had found life in *Western Isles* less alarming than we all had feared. Monkey Stephenson had his human side. On one occasion two French frigates had come into Tobermory. One, the *Escarmouche* was Free French, the other, the *Aventure* Vichy French. The Commodore had been advised of their visit by the Admiralty, whose instructions were to be correct with the Vichy French Captain, but to be affable with the Free Frenchman. He was also warned that the

1. *My mother and I, 1917*

2. *My Father as the Duke of Plaza-Toro in*
The Gondoliers

3. *The Foreman's Cottage at Kingston, Corfe Castle*

4. Phoebe Llewellyn-Smith in 1940

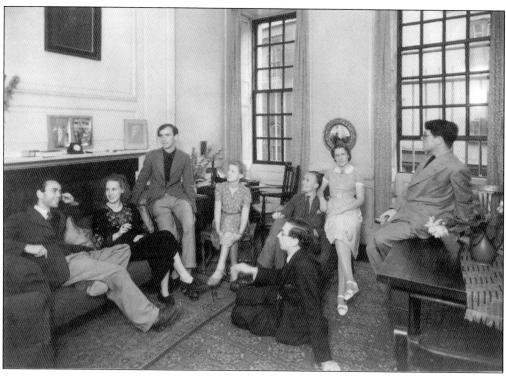

5. A group of friends in our room in Queens 1939. Harold Herzmark, Jean Fuller, Myself, Phoebe Llewellyn-Smith, Trev Gardner, my sister Betty, Jack Shipwright and in front, Theo Cadoux

6. Myself in 1958

7. HMS Genista *in a heavy sea*

8. HMS Genista *off Durban, 1942*

9. HMS Oxford Castle *in Belfast Lough, 1944*

10. Christopher and Christabel Rieu at their wedding

11. In the courtyard of the hotel in Montevideo, 1943

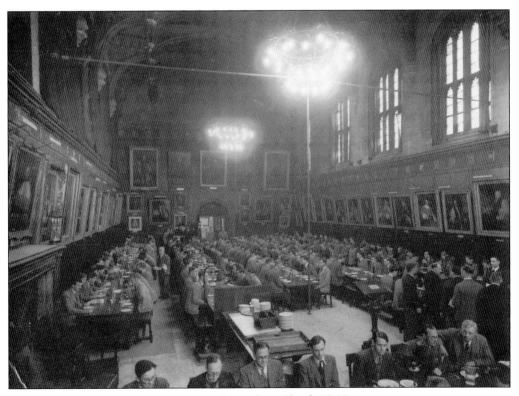

12. Lunch in Christ Church 1946

13. *Our wedding, 18 March 1950*

14. *Margy on our Honeymoon, 1950*

15. *Myrtle aged 21*

16. *The White Cottage, Clifton, Deddington*

17. *Bridge House, Wootton*

18. Nell and Dido in the Garden

19. Ma with Matthew

20. 'Finite and Infinite' Kate aged 3

latter had very little English. Accordingly he sent a formal greeting to the *Aventure* and invited the Captain of the *Escarmouche* to lunch. Having no French himself he invited a Wren officer to act as interpreter. It fell to Charles Kuper as officer of the day to receive the Frenchman on board and conduct him to the Commodore's cabin. As he came over the side the Frenchman remarked 'It is very good of your Commodore to invite me to lunch like this. I do appreciate it very much.' And he continued in this vein as Charles conducted him to the Commodore's cabin. 'Not bad,' thought Charles, 'for a Frenchman supposed to have little English.' Not long afterwards an embarrassed Commodore came trotting along the deck: 'Wrong Frenchman, m'boy, wrong Frenchman. I suppose I shall have to go through with it now.' It transpired that the signalman, for whom one French ship was much the same as another, had transposed the signals.

Oxford Castle then proceeded to Liverpool where she was to be based in Gladstone Dock. By this stage in the war the advantage in the Battle of the Atlantic had swung towards the allies. With increasing air cover and more sophisticated anti-submarine weapons the need for convoy escorts became less and the strategy was shifted to hunting U-boats. My impression is that of our being exposed more to the raging of the sea than to the violence of the enemy. Although we made a number of attacks on suspected U-boats, we had no evidence of damage or destruction during the whole of 1944. As always there were occasional interludes. Once in the spring we had been hunting U-boats off the north west coast of Ireland where they were suspected of using supposedly neutral Irish harbours as temporary bases, when after two or three weeks of ineffectual searching in those stormy waters, *Oxford Castle* was ordered into Lough Foyle, and a day or two later up the river Foyle to Londonderry. This short trip provided a quite magical moment. We proceeded at slow speed up the winding river which was like nothing so much as a country road with beech trees just coming into leaf down to the water's edge. The ship's engines at that slow speed were quiet and the only sound was that of birdsong. In wartime and after a still wintry Atlantic it was an anticipation, even an instalment, of heaven.

An interlude of a different sort occurred on Sunday afternoon in Gladstone Dock. Half the ship's company, including the Captain, were on leave and half the remainder as befitted a quiet Sunday afternoon, were getting their heads down. A signal was received from Captain D, Liverpool, which ran 'A party of girl sea-rangers will be visiting Gladstone Dock this afternoon. *Oxford Castle* will receive them and show them over the ship.' We had only an hour or two to prepare for this invasion. I broadcast the news over the ship's Tannoy and warned those who were planning to get their heads down to ensure that they were decently dressed, as I could not guarantee that the girls would keep away from the mess decks, although I would endeavour to interest them in the working parts of the vessel. Then I summoned the wardroom steward and ordered him to produce the most sumptuous tea he could manage at short notice. I was fairly confident that, if the prospect of this tea was offered early on, the girls would migrate to the wardroom after a merely peremptory inspection of the rest of the ship. In this I was totally mistaken. As soon as they got on board the girls dispersed into every part of the ship, not only those where I had sailors posted to explain what went on there. I remained on the bridge to tell them about the use of the compass and other navigational equipment, the signalling lamps, binoculars for lookouts and so on. It was, in fact, all most rewarding and, so far as I could see, other members of the ship's company were busy explaining the details of anchor work or the winches for hawsers and so on. Then one of my party on the bridge sighted the four-inch gun just below us. She and the others wanted to see gun drill demonstrated. We did not, of course, have a complete gun's crew on board but I managed to assemble a scratch crew who duly went through the motions. While there on the gun platform, one particularly inquisitive girl saw the ship's bell which was hung just below the bridge. 'Why is that bell so dirty?' she enquired. With what I thought was commendable presence of mind, and remembering Restonji Bomanyi, I replied, 'We cannot have it polished in wartime because it might reflect the rays of the sun and give the ship's position away to the enemy.' 'I see,' said she, 'but that's no excuse for having it dirty in harbour.' No doubt it gave great satisfaction to the scratch gun crew to hear Number One thus admonished.

By this time there was no part of the ship that the girls had not penetrated. There were girls in the crow's nest, girls in the engine room and girls in the rudder flat and also, needless to say, on the lower mess deck. Mention of the tea had had no effect and it took some time to shepherd them all into the wardroom to partake of it. Altogether the afternoon must be judged a great success and a triumph for *Oxford Castle*, though what Holden would have thought if he had come on board in the middle of it does not bear thinking about.

I did not have the opportunity in Liverpool to make friends as I did in Cape Town and Durban, but I did benefit indirectly from the well-known friendliness of Liverpudlians. When in harbour I always tried to go to the concerts of the Liverpool Philharmonic, then conducted by Malcolm Sargent. He was not only a very lively, some would say flashy, conductor but he knew how to compile pro-grammes of wide appeal and he used to preface each item with a brief introduction, and these were quite masterly. Unfortunately, never knowing when *Oxford Castle* would be in port, I could not book in advance and the concerts were always fully booked. But I discovered that if I turned up on the day I could almost always get a seat. Either someone had not appeared or, fairly regularly, someone had bought extra tickets for any member of the services who, like me, just turned up.

Meanwhile I had to master, as best I could, the art of running the ship and, with it, the art of getting on with Holden, the one task closely related to the other. A crisis occurred early on of the sort I had feared. We were lowering a boat, which I had never done before, but had learnt from the Seamanship Manual. In trying to remember the correct routine, I got one of the orders wrong and, to prevent disaster, the Chief Bosun's Mate immediately counter-manded it and all was well. I was grateful to him but realised that I could not let the incident pass. The Chief Bosun's Mate was responsible under me for everything that took place on the upper deck and I could not allow my authority to be undermined. Chief Petty Officer Jones was a splendid man, a first-rate specimen of what I had come to recognise as the model of a naval petty officer, short, muscular and energetic with, in this case, dark hair and brown eyes. If I was to succeed in my job at all I must get on with this man and, if possible, earn his respect.

As soon as possible after this incident, I summoned him to my cabin and addressed him somewhat as follows: 'This morning, Chief

Petty Officer Jones, you countermanded one of my orders. You were quite right to do so as I was making a silly mistake, which could have had serious consequences. But I want you to understand that you must not make a habit of doing this. However,' I continued, 'I hope you will not hesitate to do so in similar circumstances. You have been in the Navy a lot longer than I have and you know more seamanship than I shall ever do. It would be absurd for us not to recognise this. But, as you will understand better than anyone, it is essential that my authority as Number One in maintained, so if you see me going wrong again, do not, if you can avoid it, correct me there and then, but I shall be grateful if you will let me know afterwards.'

This concordat lasted very well for the remainder of my time in *Oxford Castle* and I was immensely heartened by the knowledge that, in doing a job which I knew all too well I was unsuited for, I had such a reliable and competent assistant, for whom, as he must have known, I had enormous respect. My chief worry in this trying job was that, being by nature impractical, I was not going to be good at coping with an emergency. I did my best, therefore, to prevent emergencies happening. Whenever there was an elaborate and tricky manoeuvre like oiling at sea or coming to a buoy, I would draw myself diagrams and work it all out in detail beforehand, endeavouring at the same time to anticipate anything that might go wrong. In this way and with the help of my agreement with the Chief Bosun's Mate we had no disasters, and relations with Holden, although never easy, remained tolerable. Indeed, I was greatly relieved when his first quarterly report on my performance read 'A capable officer'.

It turned out that we were to be less fortunate with the other senior rating, the Coxswain, Chief Petty Officer Ham. He was of considerable seniority and had come to us from a destroyer (which ought to have aroused our suspicions). In the hectic weeks of commissioning and working up the ship he put it to us that there was no need to have an officer present at getting the rum up since he was well able to see to it himself.

It was not until six weeks or so had passed that the ship's routine became settled enough for me to measure the rum in the barrel and verify that all was as it should be. It immediately became apparent that it was significantly short and the only possible explanation was that Ham had been putting some aside for the use of himself and other members of the petty officers' mess. This was a serious offence and provoked a crisis. If the Coxswain were put on charge he would lose seniority and perhaps be dis-rated and this would affect his pension. We were reluctant to take this extreme step. On the other hand, if we overlooked it our authority would be gravely weakened. And both the Captain and I had, of course, been negligent.

At this point a miracle occurred. Chief Petty Officer Ham came out all over in spots. We immediately discharged him to hospital and signalled for a replacement who arrived just before we were due to sail.

There remained, of course, the problem of accounting for the missing rum to the Naval Stores officer ashore. There was nothing for it but for me to go to see him and make a clean breast of it. He was extremely helpful. 'Well, he said, 'there are various allowances we are permitted to make. Perhaps if we invoke all of them with a reasonably generous margin for error we can just about account for the loss of rum.' And then he mentioned ullage, corkage, seepage, leakage, drainage and other such factors which he was prepared to allow for, and which together did the trick.

Some six months later we received Ham's papers with full details of his career. He had been dismissed from his last ship, a destroyer, and the Captain had written and had underlined in red ink: 'a competent rating within his known limitations. Under no circumstances should he be sent to a ship with inexperienced officers.'

Ten years later Margy and I and the children were staying on holiday in Fowey with an old friend of hers, Betty King, whose father was the local doctor. She kept a boat moored by the surgery and I was rowing it one day across the harbour when I saw a figure I thought I recognised clad in a peaked cap and a blue guernsey rowing another boat towards the quay. I thought it better to avoid him and altered course. On getting back to the house I described this man to Betty and asked her who it was. 'Oh,' she said, 'that would be John Ham. He is boatman to the Customs and Excise!'

After three months or so it was judged that Charles Kuper had completed his training and to my great distress he left us. He fully understood my difficulties with Holden, 'young omnicompetent' as he called him, and I could always share my problems with him. The strain was noticeably greater after his departure.

Towards the end of 1944 I became increasingly restive. For the first time in my naval career I began to wonder if I was usefully employed. I was doing a job which required considerable effort not to fall down on in company that was not particularly congenial. The war was obviously coming to an end soon and we were engaged in what were no more than mopping up operations. At this juncture, whether by intention or by accident, I cannot now remember, I came to realise that the remedy was entirely in my own hands. One night I slept through an alarm and failed to attend upon the bridge until I was woken by the Bosun's mate. I explained to the Captain that I had failed to hear the alarm and suggested that, when we reached Liverpool, I should have my hearing examined, knowing all the time what the verdict would be. It was duly discovered that I had entirely lost the hearing of my right ear and was, consequently, declared unfit for sea service.

So ended my wartime sea service and I left *Oxford Castle* with none of the regret I had felt on saying goodbye to *Genista*.

I was able to spend Christmas at home and there is no doubt that my enforced release from sea service was a great relief to my mother and sisters. When I went to see Phoebe I found her in considerable distress. Her father had died recently and her affair with John had finally come to an end. The effect of these two blows was to precipitate a severe nervous breakdown from which she was to recover only slowly. From that time on she was in the care of a psychotherapist, Lovell Barnes, whom she saw regularly but did not wholly trust. There was nothing I could do but do my best to comfort her and distract her, especially as she had intimated to me in respect of John that 'that particular niche is not vacant.'

I paid my usual visit to St Anne's Mansions and saw a very agreeable commander. 'Well,' he said, 'with your educational qualifications there are really only two options available. One is intelligence, the other education. There is not much point in intelligence as, once you have been trained, the war will be over. That leaves education. As it happens there is a rather suitable vacancy.' And he went on to explain that all the services had been told to prepare the troops for demobilisation by giving them sessions in World Affairs, usually by way of discussion groups. These were pioneered by the Army in its ABCA scheme. To train newly commissioned RNVR officers to undertake the task of running these, HMS *King Alfred* had added to its usual courses a 'World Affairs Course' to be taken immediately after being commissioned. Its chief purpose was to give them experience of discussion groups, but there were ancillary lectures on matters of current interest.

I protested that I had no knowledge of world affairs. 'That's alright,' he said, 'all you need is some knowledge of modern history which a man of your education should have no difficulty with.' 'But,' I said, 'my study of history ended with the death of Nero in AD 68.' This set him back a bit, but then he brightened and said 'Not to worry. We'll give you a fortnight's leave to work it up.'

Thus began what was, in effect, an extended interlude between my proper sea-going naval career and my discharge into civilian life, eighteen months or so later.

In many ways it was more like my later university life than like my previous experience of the Navy. The young officers under instruction were remarkably like undergraduates and I met some of them later in Oxford. My colleagues were like dons and two of them actually were – Alec Myers, later Professor of History at Liverpool, and John Land, soon to be Principal of the College of St Mark and St John, Chelsea. Mark Littman was to end up as QC and a judge, and John North was to be Director of Education for Buckinghamshire. We were all Lieutenants RNVR except for North who was a Lieutenant Commander. The only indication that we were in a naval establishment was that we attended Divisions and Prayers every morning, where I became familiar once more with the Prayer for Those at Sea and the final verse of Eternal Father, Strong to Save, which was sung at the end of every service. Also there was displayed on the wall of one room a vast map of Europe on which an accurate record was kept of allied and Russian progress in the final months of the war.

Naval discipline meant that our audiences had no alternative but to attend our lectures, which in practice meant that we had no alternative but to be entertaining. In this we were helped by the fact that they were for the most part highly intelligent and were happy to enjoy a week's intellectual stimulation which they were not to be examined on.

It turned out to be an ideal preparation for university teaching. I began by giving what was billed as an introductory lecture on 'Clear

Thinking' in which I made what use I could of Greats philosophy, relying shamelessly on L Susan Stebbing's 'Thinking to Some Purpose', though I like to think my treatment was more lively than hers. Later my repertoire was extended to include 'The American Political System'; 'The Constitutional Problem in India'; and 'Problems of Eastern Europe'. This spread of subjects was to some extent occasioned by the demobilisation in time of my more senior colleagues. One task I inherited from Alec Myers was a set of lectures given by him to the WRNS cooks and stewards on the History of the Royal Navy. For these I relied on the notes he left me together with Callender's 'The Naval Side of British History'. This was quite the most demanding teaching assignment I have ever had. They were totally ignorant of British history, let alone the naval side of it. As at Montevideo, with a more appreciative audience, I illustrated my lectures with drawings of ships in coloured chalk on the blackboard, which attracted some interest. I remember one occasion on which, following Myers, I gave a list from a contemporary source of the officers of a medieval ship, the captain, the lieutenant, the master, the shipwright, the cook and so on. A girl at the back put her hand up said eagerly, 'and the electrician, sir?' I said, 'well of course they hadn't discovered electricity in the Middle Ages, but you have got entirely the right idea. The officer at that time was any one who performed an office, that is who did a distinct job on board, so if they had had an electrician, he would have ranked as an officer.' At other times I had to engage them in discussion and it was well nigh impossible to get them to open their mouths. But, it seems, I had more success than I thought, because sometimes afterwards a departmental officer would ask me 'What on earth did you get these girls to talk about?' I would reply 'I'm afraid I couldn't get them to talk at all.' 'Well,' he would say, 'they haven't stopped talking about it ever since!'

On one such occasion I managed to do some useful sociological research. One of the subjects prescribed by ABCA for discussion was 'the population problem', the problem being that not enough babies were being born to replace the population. So I proposed this subject for discussion. Failing as usual to provoke any discussion I went round the class asking each girl how many children she would like to have. The average number was four and I was able to confound the experts by anticipating the post-war baby boom.

I lodged with a very agreeable family called Marriott in Hove with a large sunny room where I could read or write. On one occasion they invited me to join them at a dance in Hove and offered to put up my partner. Phoebe was still recovering, so I asked my sister Myrtle if she could come. She was then nineteen and I was not the only one to be entranced by her beauty and her sky-blue temperament. Until now I had scarcely had time to know her and I had never seen her in evening dress. The son of the house, an army major who was home on leave, fell for her at once.

On VE Day everyone in Brighton danced in the streets. I went out with a plump pretty Wren called Phyllis Jones who was a pleasant enough companion, but it was a time when what we all wanted was to be with our families and with the friends we started the war with. So far as I was concerned it was a day when I felt that rejoicing was called for rather than actually rejoiced.

Meanwhile at *King Alfred* the collegiate atmosphere was enhanced by a production of *Maria Martin in the Red Barn* in which all the resources of melodrama were splendidly exploited. At the beginning of the performance the audience was exhorted to express its feelings without constraint. Whenever the hero came on we were to cheer and we were to boo the villain. A sigh was to greet the heroine and, as far as the heroine's old mother was concerned, we must do our best to convey our sympathy. Cheers, boos and sighs duly followed as required and, when the old mother came on there was a slight pause and then the audience shouted 'sympathy, sympathy' with one voice. I can only remember one instance otherwise of audience participation though there was plenty of it. The villain in his attempt to seduce the heroine, was painting a vivid picture of the life she would lead if she followed him: 'Come with me and together you and I will tread the primrose path of pleasure and sample all the delights that life has to offer'. A voice cried from the back of the hall 'Join the Navy!'

Towards the end of 1945, the war in Japan having ended, there appeared in the *Oxford University Gazette*, for the first time since the war, an advertisement for Fellowships at All Souls, and Radhakrishnan drew my attention to it. I could lose nothing by attempting it. I was, of course, totally unprepared but then, I reflected, this would be true of most of the candidates. So I applied: I understood that there were forty-five candidates for three Fellowships. Two of these, an army major and myself, were still in the services and, to accommodate us, it was arranged that the two of us should be interviewed and dined on the same day. Before dinner I was to go for sherry at the Warden's lodgings where I would meet the other candidate. He was already there when I was ushered in to the Warden's study. To my alarm and astonishment it was John Boughey. We had only met once at a time when I did not know what his relationship to Phoebe was to be. It was evident that he did not recognise me and I thought it best not to remind him of it.

I did not expect to gain a Fellowship but my earnest prayer was that he should not get one either. In the event neither of us did.

With the war over it was clear that *King Alfred* was going to be run down, but those who were currently going through for commissions would not be due for early demobilisation and it would be some time before it could be wound up altogether. The not inconsiderable rump was transferred to Exbury on the Beaulieu River below Buckler's Hard for what transpired to be another eight months until August 1946. The house was set in a large estate, which had been extensively planted with rhododendrons and azaleas by the owner, Edmund de Rothschild. They were cleverly sited among forest trees, predominantly pines and down through gentle valleys were footpaths that led eventually to the Beaulieu River just short of the Solent. The spring of 1946 was a fine one and we were able to watch the season develop into early summer when the colours were at their best. In February when the gardens were largely quiescent one would walk in the unfrequented country roads outside the gates which were lined with hazels bearing catkins shining in the sunlight.

The wardroom had a sailing dinghy which I used to take out from time to time on the river and, if weather permitted, into the Solent. It was not always possible while in the river to tell to what extent the weather permitted sailing in the Solent. On one occasion I was badly, and could have been fatally, caught out. I had taken a willing cadet with me and what, in the river, had seemed to be a rather gentle wind, turned out in the mouth of the river to be too strong for us to venture into the open sea. I therefore decided to return to our jetty, but by now there was quite a sharp sea and I found I could not go about. When I turned the boat's bow into the sea, the combination of wind and sea kept pushing her back. Reluctant to gybe for fear of capsise I had no alternative but to continue across the Solent. By this time I was distinctly scared, the more so as I was not sure of making Cowes. There was an appreciable risk of our being carried right past into Spithead and to avoid this I had to sail as close to the wind as possible, which made for an uncomfortable ride. Fortunately we got into Cowes all right and were spared the return journey by being offered a tow by a motor boat going back to Buckler's Hard. With little sailing experience and my knowledge taken mainly from books it was irresponsible of me to subject the cadet to that degree of risk. I had learnt my lesson and the rest of my sailing was in a whaler with a crew of five and an experienced skipper. We raced a number of times against a crew from a neighbouring RAF station and they always won.

By the time we got to Exbury, the World Affairs staff was reduced to two, myself and Eric Robinson. Eric had taken a First in Modern History, Part 1, at Jesus College Cambridge and, after his return to Cambridge would get a starred First in English. He had experienced the worst that the Navy had to undergo in the war – convoys to Russia in appalling conditions and with little gratitude from the Russians. He was and has remained a man of great integrity, a gritty and sometimes prickly individual. We shared the curriculum between us and, being in many ways complementary, I think we did a good job together. Not, however, without occasional friction. I cannot remember what it was about, but quite early on we had a row and for the first and only time in my naval career, I pulled rank. 'I am your senior officer,' I said, 'and you will do what I say.' From then on and, as it transpired, for a lifetime we were firm friends.

The Commanding Officer at this stage was Captain Cuthbert Coppinger RN. I learned later that he played a signal part in the sinking of the *Bismarck*, but now he was in semi-retirement. He was a fine looking man with the accent and bearing of an English gentleman of the old school. He clearly had been a considerable athlete and even now turned out on the left wing for the officers against the rest at soccer, and, when the Captain's secretary, himself a competent tennis player, offered him a game, he surprised him by winning comfortably.

What endeared him to Eric and me was his remarkable capacity for saying the wrong thing. The best example we did not ourselves witness but had from his secretary who was there at the time. *King Alfred*, even in its reduced state, was from time to time chosen for official visits from high-ups of one sort or another. On this occasion it was a party of senior WRNS officers. Coppinger had in his possession a collection of plates which had been with Nelson in the Victory. When entertaining official guests he liked to hand them round. He did so on this occasion and, as his guests admired them, remarked, 'Yes, they are very interesting and I find them very useful too. Whenever I have a particularly sticky party, all I have to do is to hand round the plates.'

Another instance I can vouch for. I was conducting a discussion on one of the ABCA topics 'Should society tolerate parasites?' When the Captain came into the room we leapt to attention, but he told us to resume our seats and said he would like to stay and hear the discussion. 'By the way, what are you discussing?' he asked. 'Should society tolerate parasites?' I told him. 'Very interesting,' he said. 'Only the other day I was reading in the paper an article on some stuff they have discovered – DDT I think it was – which wipes the bastards out!'

Every now and then we would have an outside lecturer to address the whole ship's company. Once we had a Mr England to talk to us about the state of Britain. Inevitably Coppinger introduced him as Mr Britain who was to talk to us about the state of England.

On the last day of an intake he would address the young officers and give them advice about their time in the Navy. His main theme was the importance of exercise. It would run as follows: 'You want, whenever you can, to go ashore and get some exercise. It doesn't matter what form it takes so long as you get up a good sweat. I have got up a good sweat at Gibraltar, Malta, Singapore, Portsmouth, even Liverpool. Most places you visit will have at least a squash court. That is as good as anything for getting up a good sweat . . .' and so on.

In the discussion groups one of the things we were supposed to do was involve everyone in the discussion and remain ourselves impartial. There was one occasion when I signally failed to do this. The topic was education and the role of grammar schools. The group was composed predominantly of ex-public schoolboys and they came out with stereotyped views on the inferiority of day schools to boarding schools. The former were purely academic while the latter formed character and, because of their variety of out of school activities, produced rounded individuals. In no time the discussion became a heated debate between the supposedly impartial chairman and the rest of the class. I told them how in my grammar school the premises were occupied every night by societies of every kind and the staff took it for granted that this was part of their job.

Our immediate superior officer, an Instructor Lieutenant Commander RN was a cultivated man who sensibly let Eric and me get on with our job. He had a sizeable collection of gramophone records and once a week would hold a gramophone recital. At a time when classical music was hard to come by and Southampton itself had no regular orchestra, this was well attended and helped to extend my own repertoire, built up slowly on the foundations of the Cape Town Municipal Orchestra and the Liverpool Philharmonic. The one work which I particularly associate with these recitals is the Brahms First Symphony and the splendid theme of the third movement which, following the notes on the sleeve, we knew as 'the Broad and Healthy'.

Altogether this was a quiet and slightly unreal period of my naval service, a betwixt-and-between condition with the naval life fading gently away and my future in civilian life as yet wholly indeterminate. It is not surprising that I retain occasional incidents, which remain in my memory as a sort of cameo. One such occurred on the platform of Southampton station. I used to like to have some flowers in my room and I had bought some to take back with me to Exbury. On the platform was a Wren who used to wait on us at table. She had rich auburn hair and an 'English rose' pink and white complexion. I had danced with her once or twice in our local hops and had learned that she came from South Petherton in Somerset, which gave us a tenuous connection. I asked her where she was going and she said she had just been demobilised and was going home to South Petherton. On impulse I thrust the flowers into her hands and said, 'take this with you as a departure present', and I was rewarded by a deep blush on that delicate complexion.

I was naturally at this time very much concerned about my own demobilisation. I was anxious to get back to Oxford in time for Michaelmas Term and unsure whether I could resume my Taberdarship at Queen's. In any case I was now twenty-nine and it was time to seek a senior position. Just then I was asked if I would be willing to transfer to the Instructor branch RN. I was suspicious at first but was told that it was largely a matter of administrative convenience and would not affect my time of release. Thus I ended my naval career as Instructor Lieutenant RN.

One of the people working with my sisters at the Blood Transfusion Clinic was Ilse Cooke whose husband Arthur was a physicist at New College. Arthur Cooke drew my attention to lectureships at Christ Church which were to be awarded for the coming academic year. Having failed All Souls I was not very confident but, after an extremely friendly interview at Christ Church at which Michael Foster presided, I was duly elected.

HMS *King Alfred* was finally decommissioned in August and I was then demobilised, after just under six years of naval service.

CHAPTER 5

Christ Church 1946–7 and Myrtle

HAVING LEFT QUEEN'S IN MICHAELMAS 1940, I returned to Oxford in Michaelmas Term 1946 as a Lecturer at Christ Church and thus a senior member of the University. A lecturer of my sort, sometimes called a research lecturer, was what at any other college would be called a Junior Research Fellow. I was entirely free to follow my own course of study; other duties were entirely optional and did not include lecturing. I could, and did, do up to six hours tutorial teaching and also assisted with internal examining ('collections').

Christ Church more than any other college was a world of its own. Its constitution was unique and anomalous. The Dean was head of the college and also of the cathedral. The Dean and Chapter were in charge of the cathedral and had at one time formed the governing body of the college, until eventually the tutors, still known as Students, became, with the Canons, the governing body, as in any other college. There were five Divinity professors who were, as such, canons of the cathedral and members of the Governing Body of Christ Church. There was, traditionally, some animosity between the Students and the Canons although, not being a member of the Governing Body, I was not in a position to notice it. When I enquired how this constitution had survived the secularising movement in the University of the late 19th and early 20th century, I was told that the endowments of the cathedral and the college were so bound up with one another that it would be virtually impossible to separate them. Moreover it was suspected that the cathedral would turn out to be, if anything, the major partner. However, whatever internal tensions there might be – and I was not aware of any – Christ Church remained firmly united against any suggestion of interference from outside. All this is summed up in the custom of referring to the college as 'The House', and to this day I always gain entrance freely by saying to the porter 'I am a member of the House'.

My predominant impression of Christ Church was of a combination of grandeur with friendliness. The grandeur was splendidly apparent on two occasions. The first was a visit from the King and Queen to celebrate the 4th centenary of the re-foundation of the college by King Henry VIII in 1546. These were the sort of proceedings which Cardinal Wolsey would have had in mind in designing a hall of such magnificence. The other in its way even more impressive occasion was a performance in the hall of Shakespeare's *King Henry the Eighth*, with Michael Howard appearing in the role of Wolsey. I do not think that Wolsey's famous speech could have been better delivered and I was not surprised when he later told me (as Regius Professor of Modern History and a colleague at Oriel) that, on going down, he had had to decide between history and a career on the stage. The lines about those 'twins of learning . . . Ipswich and Oxford' were greeted with a predictable roar of applause.

The friendliness was not only personal but institutional. By now I was in effect the head of the family. During the war my father's business partner, a very stong minded woman, who had been the first woman to become a chartered surveyor, had moved in with him in Northlands Gardens and by now they had one son. Meanwhile my mother found his allowance to her inadequate and, after taking legal advice, decided to start divorce proceedings as the only way of getting a reasonable financial settlement. In desperation my father suggested that my mother should move in with him and his partner which would have benefited him financially but was otherwise out of the question. So I enquired of the Treasurer, C C C Bosanquet, whether the college had anything to rent that I could afford. He said that they had a very odd house in the country, sixteen miles from Oxford, which they didn't know what to do with. Would I like to consider it? And so I rented the White Cottage, Clifton, near Deddington, at a peppercorn rent of £52 p.a. on the understanding that I did my best to pull the garden around. Bosanquet knew my circumstances and plainly took them into account. My mother and sister duly moved there, and I continued to rent it until 1950. The college then sold it, which is what they would have done earlier if I had not appeared when I did.

It was not until Trinity Term that I actually lived in college. For my first term I was in digs in Regent Street off the Iffley Road. My landlady, Mrs Tubb, was a splendid specimen of that now extinct species. Her husband was a scout at Balliol and she looked after us with motherly care. We regularly had a cooked breakfast, usually bacon and eggs, but I remember as a variant enjoying splendid fried fish. My fellow lodger was a chemist, Morrin Acheson, who ended up as a Fellow of Queen's. He was, as I remember, a small energetic individual of rapid breathless speech and abrupt movement, whose favourite occupation, outside chemistry, was ballroom dancing. So I found myself walking into Oxford over Magdalen Bridge as I had done in my third year at Queen's. It is by far the finest entry to the city and I found myself humming the slow movement from Beethoven's seventh symphony, as I had done at that earlier time.

For my second term, fortunately, I was just opposite the college in a room in Brewer Street. Fortunately, because I did not have far to walk, and my room was of modest height and kept such warmth as was provided by the small electric fire. That term coincided with the great freeze of 1946/7. It was of shorter duration than the one of 1962/3, but it felt more severe and was harder to cope with because fuel and food were scarce and people were tired after the war. Christ Church was a good place to be in those conditions, because dinner in hall, especially at High Table, was comparatively generous and the hall was heated by two heaped up log fires, one on either side, where we could warm our hands when we entered. Dinner itself was fortified every night by tankards of mulled claret. My third term was spent in Tom Quad itself in a room which was carved out of Eric Mascall's set and commanded a view over the quad towards Mercury. It was an ideal situation and I should gladly have stayed there for the full period of my lectureship. This was three years in the first instance with possible renewal for a further two years.

My plan had been to continue my Sanskrit studies with a view to research in Indian Philosophy. As I had already discovered, Sanskrit is to Greek as Greek is to Latin, a highly complex grammar combined with a relatively simple syntax. Before the end of the year I had mastered the grammar and was well placed to read Sanskrit texts with reasonable fluency. I had written two reviews. One was a comparative study of Radhakrishnan's *Indian Philosophy* and Das Gupta's two volume *History of Indian Philosophy*. Neither was wholly satisfactory for the English reader. Das Gupta's was a solid and, I presumed, accurate exposition, with little attempt at interpretation and comparison. Radhakrishan went to the opposite extreme and, with his customary facility and brilliance, interpreted the varieties of Vedanta in terms of the idealist philosophy of Bradley and Bosanquet.

The other was a front page review of F S C Northrop's *The Meeting of East and West* which I was invited to do, surprisingly, by the editor of *The Times Literary Supplement*. The volume, I believe, had a considerable vogue at the time, but I thought it pompous and pretentious and made gentle fun of it in my review. I was paid £25, had lunch with the editor and was never asked to review anything for *The Times Literary Supplement* again.

I had meanwhile to revisit 'Greats philosophy' which I had not kept up with since the end of my undergraduate career. I undertook to take Greats men in Plato's *Republic* and to mark 'collections' for PPE men on Locke, Berkeley and Hume. The *Republic* tutorials were the first I had ever conducted and I remember approaching the very first with considerable trepidation. It was in the event a most agreeable occasion, helped by the fact that this first pupil was Roger Young whom I continued to meet on friendly terms for some years after he left Oxford until he went north to pursue a distinguished career in Scotland as Principal of George Watson's College, Edinburgh.

In fact, although I am not sure how clear I was about it at the time, I was at the point of decision. Was I to continue with my original plan and hope at the end of three or five years to find some appointment in Indian Philosophy; or was I to look for a teaching post in philosophy and go on with the Indian studies, if at all, as a sideline? I sought Price's advice which was to apply for the first Oxford fellowship to come up. This I eventually did and applied for the Philosophy fellowship at Keble, which had fallen vacant when Donald Mackinnon left for a professorship at Aberdeen. When I attempt to analyze my motives for this decision, I find they are several. One was, of course, that I had not only myself to think about; I had responsibility for my mother, and I needed an assured income and a permanent career. Another was that I had steadily been losing faith in the conviction which had inspired my interest in Indian thought in the first place, that essentially the same truth is to be found in all religions. This had been badly shaken by the irrelevance, as it seemed to me, of the *Bhagavad Gita* to my agonisings about conscientious objection. It has to be said that a powerful contributory factor was the sheer deadliness of Johnston's successor as Boden Professor of Sanskrit, T Burrow. He seemed to me to be like the worst type of Mods don (classical tutor) with interest only in the language and no inclination whatever to venture into the thought behind it. The prospect of studying for an indefinite period with this man could only have been sustained by a settled conviction that it was the indispensable means to a fully accepted end.

Contributory to my decision was what I had already discovered about the current state of Oxford philosophy. It was for the most part resolutely anti-metaphysical and thus hostile to any world-view I was prepared to adopt, whatever academic path I was to tread. So here was a prior battle to be fought. It so happened that two of the people who were prepared already to fight it were among my colleagues at Christ Church, Eric Mascall and Michael Foster. They were very different temperamentally and in philosophical outlook, but united in their determination to philosophise beyond the very narrow boundaries that current orthodoxy imposed. Eric was a neothomist in the mode of Gilson and Maritain, content to develop that tradition in solitary independence of what was going on in Oxford both in philosophy and in theology. He did not, as his friend Austin Farrer later did, enter into dialogue with the philosophers, but was content to attack them through the medium of small, lively books and, more effectively, light and witty satirical verse. With his slight frame, bird-like features and high-pitched voice he was always very good company. Michael Foster, by contrast, was something of a brooding presence, whose generally sombre mood was lightened only occasionally by a reflective smile. As V A Demant said of him in his memorial address 'He had all the marks of sanctity except joy'. Deeply conscientious he would entertain no belief that he could not live and such were his standards that he could never be content with his thoughts or his actions. He was extremely kind to me and acted as a sort of mentor to me during my time at Christ Church.

He was entirely out of sympathy with the prevailing fashion in philosophy and felt himself to be and, indeed, was, out of date. Like many of the older philosophers who had started their careers in the heyday of Idealism, he had been nurtured on Hegel who was the chief target of the so-called 'Revolution in Philosophy'. But he possessed an acute philosophical mind and could be a perceptive critic of the current orthodoxy. I myself, though deeply unhappy about its anti-metaphysical tenor, was beginning to learn its language and I deeply regret that I did nothing to moderate his self-distrust. It was only later that I came to see that his chapter on 'We In Modern Philosophy' was among the most perceptive in our joint volume of 1957, *Faith and Logic*. Michael Foster was, I suspect, not at home with the two features which I have mentioned as characterising Christ Church, grandeur and friendliness. He was ascetic by nature and would not have appreciated the great occasions which so impressed me; and, although friendly to individuals, especially when they were in need, he was not in the least sociable − at least such was my impression. But I suspect that he was held in great respect and, indeed, some affection by his colleagues, who subsequently, after his tragic suicide, commemorated him by a set of scholarships open to both British and German students.

In the summer term there took place in Christ Church, on Eric Mascall's invitation, a meeting of philosophers and theologians which was to have a lasting effect upon me and, I suspect, upon the development of the philosophy of religion in the 20th century in English speaking countries. The meeting, which took place in Mascall's room in Tom Quad, was attended by, in addition to myself, Austin Farrer, Ian Crombie, Michael Foster, Dennis Nineham, R M Hare and Iris Murdoch. There was no settled plan of action. We went on to meet three times a term with members taking it in turn to read a paper on a subject of their choice. Normally the topic chosen was one which arose naturally out of the evening's discussion. The group came to be known as *The Metaphysicals*. The meetings circulated round the colleges of the members with the host providing coffee. As time went on Dick Hare and Iris Murdoch dropped out, Dick because he found himself in a permanent minority and Iris because in relation to Christianity she was, she felt, increasingly 'a fellow traveller rather than a party member'. New members took their places, including Ian Ramsey, John Lucas, Christopher Stead and Helen Oppenheimer. With Ian Crombie, John Lucas and myself providing continuity, the group went on meeting until 1984. Over the years I found this the ideal way to try out one's ideas. One could get them tested by a critical but basically sympathetic set of people and in the light of their response, decide whether to develop them further. This was particularly important when the ideas in question were out of the mainstream of 'Oxford Philosophy' as it then was.

I am inclined to think that the college system favoured the development of such a dissident group. It was difficult in Oxford to maintain the sort of dominant orthodoxy which for many years characterised the English Faculty in Cambridge. Diversity of appointing bodies militated against it, and the company of colleagues in other subjects was a protection from the unremitting pressure which might otherwise have been exercised by one's own faculty. This was, perhaps, particularly the case in Christ Church, which, besides having the atmosphere of an independent suzerainty, contained within itself a strong Christian establishment in the form of the Dean and Canons.

Not that the latter struck one as an identifiable group. The most eccentric was undoubtedly Claud Jenkins, the Regius Professor of Ecclesiastical History, about whom numerous stories circulated in the University. Most of them arose from the fact that he had been appointed before the Canons became subject to a retiring age and, as he was heard famously to announce, 'I am of a modest, but not retiring disposition'. They are well known and I shall not repeat them here. But I shall put on record a sermon of his, which I remember distinctly, as it was delivered in the Cathedral. He began somewhat as follows in his high piping voice:

'Once upon a time there was a little boy and one afternoon he was at a loss what to do. So he decided to write a story. He drew a line down the middle of the page and on one side of the line were the words of the story and on the other the pictures. There were two characters in the story, a man and a tiger. 'It was not long before our author encountered a problem which has troubled more exalted authors: how to dispose of his characters. He solved this eventually by bringing it about that the man became *incorporated in* the tiger.'

That is all I can remember of the sermon. It was striking enough, but in my case it failed in its object because I have no conception of what the story was intended to illustrate. He dined regularly in hall and it was believed that he subsisted the rest of the time on the scraps he emptied into his apron at the end of the meal and took across to his lodgings.

The only one of the canons whose subject overlapped with mine was R C Mortimer, Professor of Moral and Pastoral Theology, who was a sound, but not original, exponent of a basically Thomist moral theology. He and his family lived on the north side of Tom Quad and a familiar sight from time to time was one or two of the Mortimer children racing towards Mercury pursued by a nursemaid.

Particularly friendly among the Students were Robert Blake, later to be Provost of Queen's, Tommy Armstrong, the organist and conductor of the Bach Choir, and Steven Watson, the historian. Otherwise, as I have said, they would all engage in easy conversation in Hall or in Common Room. With one exception. Hugh Trevor-Roper seemed to avoid me and, since the pattern later repeated itself in Oriel, I came to regard it as intentional. If he found himself sitting next to me in Hall he would reply briefly to any remark of mine, but he never initiated a conversation.

It remains to be said that, when I had access to the tutors' Report Book, to write in my own reports, I looked at Trevor-Roper's and found them extremely fair and balanced.

John Lowe, the Dean, was entirely affable, but I was of no use to him when, as was his custom, he looked for bridge partners after Common Room. I had followed advice given to me on becoming a naval officer, not to know how to play bridge. I believe myself to have been present on the famous occasion when he returned by helicopter from Torquay and was greeted by an impromptu choir and orchestra playing 'Lo, He comes with clouds descending'. I have told the story so often that I cannot be sure whether I was there or not. I think I came upon it on my way back from a walk round the Meadow. The Dean had initially refused an invitation to address the conference on the ground that he had an engagement in Oxford that evening. Whereupon the organisers offered to return him to Oxford by helicopter. Word got around among the undergraduates and they duly planned this inspired reception..

There was an instance of formal entertaining which caused me some embarrassment. I found in my pigeon-hole one day an envelope addressed to Mrs B G Mitchell. It was clearly an invitation. The first question was 'should I open it?' It was not addressed to me but to my (at that point) non-existent wife. If I did not reply, the sender's conclusion would be, not that I did not have a wife, but that she was negligent and ill-mannered. So I opened it and found that it was an invitation to lunch for my wife and her husband on such and such a day. The sender was Mrs Heaton, the wife of Dr Heaton, the medical

Student and then senior among the Students. It was a thoughtful gesture, especially at a time when wives played little part in the social life of the colleges. So I replied saying that I did not as yet have a wife, but that I should be delighted to accept on my own behalf, if she was sure it would not upset her seating arrangements. I duly went and greatly enjoyed this further dimension of college hospitality.

After the harsh winter of 1946/7 which severely limited movement in Hilary Term, the summer term was bright and sunny and tempted one into the Meadow and further afield up and down the river. On these expeditions I was accompanied more often than not by a lively and entertaining companion. I had met Dawn Irvine a year or two earlier at a party at Somerville. At that time she appeared to be a particularly robust example of a Somerville blue–stocking, with her hair done up as if to attempt an air of severity. When we met again, I don't remember how, her abundant hair was unconstrained as if to match the breathless enthusiasm which was her most striking characteristic. So far as possible, every word was given a special emphasis and every thought received as a fresh discovery. The family, I discovered, were strongly Anglo-Catholic, her elder brother, Gerard Irvine, a celibate priest at a well-known London Anglo-Catholic church, St Cuthbert's, Philbeach Gardens. She shared my philosophical concerns and we discussed the associated problems on long walks along the towpath up and down the Thames. My rooms in Tom Quad were regularly decorated with cowslips and bluebells, constantly replenished on these walks. By the time term came to an end and Dawn was to go down, I began to realise that I was on the point of falling in love with her and it was not until then that I learned from friends that she was engaged to be married to Stephen Martin de Bartolomé and that the wedding would take place shortly. He was Chairman of Spear & Jackson, the leading Sheffield manufacturers of saws and garden implements and would in due course spend a year as Master Cutler. I have always wondered why she never told me that she was engaged. I can only suppose that she wanted to enjoy to the full her final days at Oxford before entering into a very different kind of environment and I fitted happily into that pattern which she had no wish to complicate.

She duly went on to get her First in Greats and I subsequently received a compensation in the form of an invitation to be one of the godfathers to her first child, which I duly accepted and thus became a recognised friend of the family. I discovered when I stayed with them for the christening at Wotton under Edge that Dawn's highly emphatic manner of speaking was characteristic of the entire family, except for the General, her father. Indeed, in order to capture their attention and enter into the conversation at all, it was necessary to create the impression, and maintain it, that what one was about to say was of peculiar importance. The habit must have a strong genetic base as it was equally prominent in her mother and, in due course, in her daughter, my godchild. On the day of the christening I was woken by a small elderly gentleman who was distributing mugs of tea to the guests from a large tray with round holes in it to carry the mugs. I took him to be an old retainer and it was not until I met him at breakfast that it appeared that he was her father the General.

My last Christ Church occasion which took place after the end of term was one of the grand ones. At that time the Christ Church Gaudy was held on the day of Encaenia and those who had received honorary degrees from the University that morning were the guests of honour. The University was still honouring war leaders and the guests included Field Marshal Lord Wavell and General Sir William Slim.

Wavell made a most entertaining speech in the course of which he recollected the occasion when he had been deputed to confer knighthoods on Slim and another general. He did not think that the order he gave them ever had been given or ever again would be given: 'Lieutenant Generals, two paces forward, march.'

Very many years later, some time, I suppose, in the 80s, I had gone to see Anne Page who was now Cathedral Secretary, having been in my day one of the college secretaries, to see if I could get some tickets for the carols on Christmas Eve. I began 'I am Basil Mitchell. You will not remember me, but I was here for a year in the 1940s.' To which she replied: 'Of course I remember you. And you had, as I remember, a very nice sister'. It was at that time many years since I had had more than one sister and I expressed my puzzlement at this. But she insisted that she remembered my sister very well as she had been in her Guide Company.

On my way down from Anne Page's office I saw an old man with a white stick proceeding slowly along the passage outside the Senior

Common Room. I recognised him as Mr Owen who used to be chief clerk in the Treasury. My first thought was not to disturb him, but then I recollected that he had been very helpful over the White Cottage and might just like to be reminded of that. So I said 'It is Mr Owen, isn't it?' And then, using the same formula, 'I am Basil Mitchell. You won't remember me, but . . .' He replied at once 'but, of course I remember you. And, as I remember, you had a very nice sister!'

I was amazed and greatly moved to find that after so many years these old servants of the college had remembered someone who had been there only for one year thirty or forty years ago. But I continued to be puzzled by their apparently firm memories of Betty who, as far as I knew, had no contact with the House. It was only later that I discovered that while I was away at sea Myrtle had worked as a typist in the Treasury at Christ Church.

Myrtle

It is among my regrets that I never got to know that 'very nice sister' at all well.

She was born in 1924 while we were in London and was four years old when my mother became bed-ridden. Betty and I were a long established unit and she must often have been lonely. Nevertheless all the indications are that she was a happy outgoing child who made friends readily, helped by her fair curly hair and bright blue eyes. Our maid, Gladys, who came from the other side of the Itchen in a poorer part of town, would take her with her on her day off. One thing I do remember is that, when we were at Archer's Mansions, she would often be found seated on the saddle of the 'stop me and buy one' ice cream vendor at the entrance to the Common. We were a little worried about this until one day when Myrtle was ill in bed, he climbed all the stairs up to our top floor flat with a bunch of flowers 'for the little girl'.

She was fifteen when the war started and was evacuated with the Convent High School to Talbotheath in Bournemouth. A year later when my mother and Betty were settled into 18 Osberton Road, Oxford, she asked if she could leave school and join them there. I was away in the southern hemisphere for most of the years 1942–3, and otherwise during my leaves my attention was concentrated on my mother and Betty who represented 'home' so far as I was concerned. It was not until the summer of 1944 that I finally took notice of Myrtle, having been gently reproached by a letter from her in which she confessed to envying Betty who had always been closer to me than she ever had. *Oxford Castle* had a ward-room Open Day in Liverpool and, as Phoebe could not leave her work at the Air Ministry, I invited Myrtle to come instead and lodged her for the night in the Adelphi Hotel. I discovered that she had become a young woman of unquestionable beauty, as was shown by the impression she made upon my colleagues. Later when I was at *King Alfred* and lodged with a cultivated middle-class family in Hove, they invited me to join them in a family party at a dance and I asked Myrtle to come as my partner. She made an immediate impression with her fresh and unaffected charm, and the son of the house, an army officer on leave, fell for her there and then.

At that time the Inayat Khan family were living in Oxford. Noorunnissa had gone into the FANY and rarely appeared. No one knew about her work for SOE. Chairunnissa, the younger daughter, was working for Norman Heatley in the Dunn School of Pathology. Vilayat, at that time in the Navy, would appear on leave and come to visit us. He was a young man of distinguished appearance and considerable charm whom Betty and I could not entirely trust because he seemed so often to be acting a part. His was, indeed, in an awkward predicament. He knew himself to be destined to inherit the position of leader of the Sufi Movement and must act appropriately. But he had been brought up in Paris and had the outlook of a sophisticated young Parisian. We had the sense that he was anxious at one and the same time to prepare himself for his appointed role and to savour as much of life as he could before submitting to its inevitable constraints. When he asked Betty to marry him, he was clearly casting her in the role of the future wife of the Sufi leader, but when, Betty having refused him, he turned his attention to Myrtle, we could no longer be sure of his intentions.

In 1945 I had a period of leave and had planned with Christopher Rieu to explore the Quantocks. We were to stay at Spaxton with my cousin Eleanor Hook (neé Loxston) who was the local schoolmistress and church organist. Before we left, my mother and Betty asked my advice. Vilayat had asked Myrtle to accompany him to London, riding pillion on his motor bicycle. Was this wise? I said that she was twenty-one and could make up her own mind. Vilayat had promised to drive with the utmost care and we were sure that he would, so we were not unduly worried when Myrtle decided to go. The morning after we arrived in Spaxton and were consulting our map of the Quantocks, a telegram arrived 'Myrtle seriously injured, come at once'. Eleanor assured Christopher that she would gladly have him if he felt he could stay for the rest of the week, but he insisted on returning with me. At Temple Meads station, Bristol, where we had to change, there was an announcement 'Would Basil Mitchell come to the Station Master's office at once'. There the Station Master, as gently as possible, broke the news that my sister had since died. When I got back to 18 Osberton Road I learnt that on the London Road near Stokenchurch the motor bike had stopped suddenly without warning and thrown Myrtle over Vilayat's head. She had died of a fractured skull. There was no reason to doubt Vilayat's insistence that he was driving carefully at a reasonable speed. What had caused the accident was that the stand which supported the bike when stationary had slipped from its casing on the rear mudguard and jammed the rear wheel.

My father, who had always been particularly attached to Myrtle, could not bring himself to identify her, so the task fell to me. Although I had seen dead bodies floating on the sea, I had never viewed the corpse of someone I knew. I was apprehensive. What struck me at once was how beautiful she was, no longer as a person but as a sculpture delicately carved in alabaster with only a purple bruise at the base of her neck to show that she had been alive.

It must have been a devastating shock for Vilayat. I have no doubt that he had taken the greatest care of her on the day, and he had himself gone to break the news to my mother, but he could not entirely escape responsibility for having neglected the maintenance of the motor-bike. At her funeral at St Michael's Summertown, he dramatised himself as the desolate lover who had, by his own fault, lost his bride-to-be, much to the distress of Betty who knew that Myrtle had other admirers to whom she was no more committed than she was to Vilayat. Inevitably the event had the effect of estranging us from Vilayat and we saw less of him. We had lost touch with him entirely when some years later I saw an advertisement for a lecture to be given by him in the Friends Meeting Room in St Giles, charge for admission two shillings and sixpence. I paid my half crown and went to the lecture in the hope of meeting him. At the end of the meeting I joined the queue of people waiting to talk to him and, when my turn came, it was plain that he barely recognised me. I said, 'Don't you remember me, Basil Mitchell?' and he replied, 'Ah yes, indeed. It brings back memories not all of them pleasant.' I tried to arrange a meeting next day, but he had to fly to New York that night. He was obviously caught up in the demanding routine of a religious leader. Betty says that, when he proposed to her, he urged as an advantage that she would have four houses, in Paris, London, The Hague and New York, a prospect that did not attract her and must have imposed an onerous burden upon him in later life.

As for Myrtle, Betty has a bust of her cast in bronze by Kurt Matsdorf which marvellously preserves her likeness, and it was he who designed her headstone in Wolvercote Cemetery. With her sunny nature and sky-blue temperament so truly expressed in the beauty of her face, it is not surprising that she was remembered for so long by those people in Christ Church. The wonder is that I seem to have forgotten her, except that they must have known her better than I did.

CHAPTER 6

Endings and beginnings

S CARCELY HAD WE MOVED INTO the White Cottage at Clifton that, on Good Friday 1947, my mother died after a brief illness. The doctors were astonished that her emaciated frame had not only allowed her to survive bedridden for twenty years, but had permitted her to display to the end such extraordinary spirit and determination. When the time came, with her surviving daughter married and her son securely embarked upon the career he wanted, it seems that she simply declined to make the effort to stay alive any longer. The debt I owe her is incalculable.

It was not surprising that at this time my personal life became increasingly centred on my relationship with Phoebe. Before the war ended two things had happened which affected her greatly. Her affair with John Boughey ended and he shortly married someone else, and her father died and this affected her more than her separation from John. She had always greatly loved and admired her father and he was, moreover, the only member of her family she felt she could confide in with any confidence. Not only did she now lose that support, but she was increasingly dependent on her mother who loved her dearly but had little understanding of her anxieties and aspirations. It soon became clear that she needed a more professional kind of help and she embarked upon a regular course of psychotherapy with Dr Lovel Barnes of St Bartholomew's Hospital. As I later discovered he attributed her basic problem to her ambivalent relationship with her family and, in particular, her mother. She wanted the security her home afforded and, indeed, needed it, but at the same time she sought desperately to establish her independence. In the light of this diagnosis her affair with John, as she later admitted, could be seen as a frantic attempt to defy her family. It also to some extent explained the weakness of my position. While her family disapproved of John, they made no secret of their approval of me, thus giving me the unenviable status of the official candidate.

By this time both Phoebe and I had returned to our intended careers. She had left the Air Ministry and resumed her art training at the Central School. I had left the Navy and had taken up a junior research fellowship at Christ Church, to be followed a year later by a Tutorial Fellowship at Keble. It was for both of us an enormous relief to be freed from our wartime roles and the stresses that went with them. But we now faced different challenges which were more severe because they touched our essential selves. I had always wanted to be a philosopher and had now to come to terms with what this actually meant in post-war Oxford. I had done little academic work since I had finished Greats and my studies in Indian philosophy were quite irrelevant to the Western analytic philosophy which was now the dominant trend. Indeed, in terms of that, those studies and the metaphysical concerns which inspired them were not regarded as philosophy at all. I faced the future with a considerable degree of self-doubt.

Phoebe's situation was even more difficult. I had at least status, but she was a student again competing with others younger than herself who lacked the inhibitions which her Oxford education had equipped her with. Now that she was free to develop her painterly gifts she could have no guarantee that they would be sufficient to justify her decision to make a living as a painter. We were both nearly thirty and aware that we had made choices which inevitably were going to determine the sort of people we would become. Hitherto there had been a palpable indeterminacy about us, but now Phoebe was a painter and Basil was a don.

This was another point at which our friendship could have dwindled away, but didn't. I had for the time being given up all thought of our relationship changing, the warning signs having been clearly displayed. But it was more than mere habit which kept us in touch in spite of this. So many things were changing that we each needed the secure friendship which the other provided. And the fact that I was for the time being, so to speak, quiescent, while most other things were in turmoil, made it easier for her to unburden herself to me unreservedly in the old diary-entry style.

In the summer of 1946 Phoebe's mother left Upshire and moved to Oxford and Phoebe herself moved into a flat at 19 de Beauvoir Court off Commercial Road in the East End. She was deeply attached to Upshire. Although on the outskirts of London it was on the edge of Epping Forest and meant for her both home and countryside. She tried resolutely to avoid the nostalgia in which her mother and the rest of the family were indulging, but there was no disguising the underlying pain:

> . . . So at present we are pretty chaotic, turning things out and sorting and throwing away and so forth and it is all very mopifying. I suppose one will be reconciled in the end. I am sure one has got to look at each change in life as the beginning of the next chapter, not the end of one, and try to keep oneself ready for enterprise. But it seems at times as if each change that comes has a contracting effect and the list of paths that lead to haunted territory mounts up and one is, as it were, on a smaller and ever more sterile island.

We had had living with us a cousin of mine called Naomi Loxston who was a trained nurse and had been glad to help look after my mother. It became increasingly apparent that Naomi was mentally ill and badly in need of specialist treatment. Phoebe undertook to arrange for her to see Lovel Barnes in order to find out what sort of treatment she ought to have and where she might have it. Naomi was a country girl and knew nothing of London and Phoebe took charge of her, spent the entire day with her and did all she could to reassure her, though she herself was by no means well at the time. The occasion prompted a long letter in which, having discussed Naomi's problems, she for the first time revealed the true state of the relations with her mother:

> I have been a good deal better since being back here on and off, but have decided not to go home this present weekend, not as a gesture but because there are indications that I'm still rather shaky and the familiar situation might prove too strong, and I might get pushed back into the status quo ante – or rather hurl myself back into it in a passion of propitiation. And my somewhat tentative mind – but still *my* mind – tells me that I mustn't do that, that people must go on, not back. But I find it harder to remember all this at home.
>
> . . . It is like walking after a long illness; one is very weak and shaky and dizzy but one is on one's own feet, and mustn't get distracted by cars and bath chairs going past much faster for the moment or by people saying one is slowing down the traffic or even by one's own stumbles. I would like to have gone home, and shall probably hate this

weekend, but I think that is the ache of exercising flabby muscles, not an indication that one is doing the wrong thing. I do hate all this.

She went on to write about our relationship more fully than ever before:

About us, I think that it will probably all settle down in time. You know, everything – i.e. life in general – seems rather as if one were looking into a pond the waters of which are growing stiller and clearer, and the reflections and the bottom of the pond more defined, but other people and factors are constantly throwing stones into it and stirring it up and then one is in a muddle for a bit. Till it settles down one can't really talk completely reliably – because one is never sure whether confusions and disturbances, cloudinesses and discomforts are of one's own making and the result of one's own policy or of external interference.

... I have felt of recent years (chiefly I think since you left the Navy, but I can't be sure quite when – I think it's been gradual) much freer in relation to you and able to see you as you are and not in the nature of a problem. The problem I may say was never such in the usual sense of the word. You were never anything but kindness and consideration itself. The problem was probably of my own making entirely, engendered of heaven knows what sense of obligation. You knew all this – whether explicitly or not – and tried to make me feel free, but I *knew* you were doing this and this too added to that sense of obligation. Can you understand? I never felt irritated or anything like that. How could I? But I felt always that you were so nice and deserved so much more (all this backed up by the family's attitude, in contrast to John, with whom I feel I took up partly out of cussedness because mother was prejudiced against him at the start) that this engendered or added to a sense of guilt and seemed to inhibit growth in one respect. Even the ever increasing knowledge of mutual compatibility and understanding added to this in a certain way because it made my reaction more inexplicable and appear the result of sheer wilful naughtiness. The more I got to know your worth the more I felt you mustn't be wasted. I don't know what the obstacle was so how could I know whether it was removable or not? Nor could I imagine what could be the removing agent. I thought perhaps the truth was something basic in me or you. Anyway I felt I had an obligation to push you off almost in proportion to wanting you and wanting the obstacle removed, because supposing we waited to see and supposing it didn't go it would have been such a waste of you; and also I dimly knew – in the way one's hunches do run ahead of one's conscious understanding – that the mere fact of waiting on an event would make it impossible for it to happen . . . I also felt it was being very bad for you to feel yourself inadequate, because your own self-confidence had been won hardly and with much trouble . . . Anyway I just couldn't help myself. I see now it was just a part of the same struggle for freedom, the fact that mother and co all thought it would such a good thing just made the guilt worse. And here comes another of those hunches. I knew I must freely give myself to whoever I did marry – neither out of a desire for freedom, or a desire for security, or even a sense of gratitude. You see, so many things seemed to be suffocating. I just wasn't worthy to think of marrying anyone let alone a good sort of person. How could I know what feelings were there or were possible in those circumstances? In the end it seemed I just could never marry.

Anyway I've felt a lot easier with you of late and have been more able to cope with and separate out external influences, up till this last explosion anyway which caught me on the wrong foot. Even so I don't see how they can permanently affect something which essentially is none of their business, provided there isn't any *intrinsic* tension.

From this time onwards there was discernible a steady but gentle current bringing us together as this letter indicates, but increasingly there were other and, in the end, stronger, currents intersecting with this one and disturbing the waters. Fairly near the surface was the intermittent tension with her family. Just as she needed the security they afforded, so she felt the attractions of marriage. But would that be compatible with the demands of life as a painter? She loved children and she knew that if she had them, she should and would put them first. She confessed to a sense of inevitability about our marrying, but whenever she tried to envisage it as a practical way of life, she could not make it real. If she married me she would be marrying a don and she did not want to be a don's wife. She had spent years trying to free herself from one sort of ordered life and was not sure that she could identify herself with another, different no doubt, but involved in a formal institutional framework. At a deeper level still there was the old conflict between the analytic and the imaginative sides of her nature. The thing that she valued most in me, which had made my friendship a permanent resource, was my ability to think things through, to clarify problems and help resolve them. It was this, after all, which made me a philosopher. She had a capacity for this herself and responded to it in others, but she lived in a milieu where it did not count for much and she became increasingly persuaded that it was ultimately inimical to her vocation as an artist. The old Platonic war between art and philosophy began to assert itself again. In all these conflicts, both external and internal, I found myself, helplessly, on the wrong side. There were from time to time explosions on her part, which I did not know how to deal with because, in a way I did not understand, my habitual quiet reasonableness was what sparked the explosion. Needless to say these explosions were short-lived and always followed by penitence:

> I seem just to make things worse by talking, but this is just to say I never meant to hurt you and hate to see you hurt and puzzled and exasperated. I know how difficult life has been for you recently. I don't forget though I don't seem able to say anything. Muddles seem to accentuate the differences between people, and lay all the emphasis on those. Don't be more resentful than you can help. I hate it all too.

As 1947 passed into 1948 there was little change, except that our lives diverged increasingly. Mine was an ordered succession of term and vacation in which my energies were absorbed in the regular patterns of teaching and administration. Hers was altogether less structured, adapted to making the most of moments of inspiration and demanding 'the constant criticisms and companionship of other artists'. Inevitably we met less frequently and, when we did, it was less easy than it had been to bring these two worlds together.

One thing had in any case become clear. She was in no doubt about her vocation as a painter and was as securely committed to that career as I was to philosophy. And it was beginning to be apparent what shape that career would have. She was able already to sell the occasional picture, but it was publishers who promised more regular commissions. She did a book jacket for a novel by Sylvia Townsend Warner and illustrations of *The Turn of the Screw* and *Gulliver's Travels* for Chatto & Windus. There was talk of illustrations for the Pelican translation of the *Odyssey*, one of her favourite themes. It was not unrealistic to expect this market to develop as she became better known.

I am rather surprised when I read the letters she wrote at this time to discover how seriously she took the possibility of our marrying. There seems to have been an unspoken assumption that she could marry me if only certain major difficulties could be overcome. The difficulties were for the most part connected with marriage itself – to anyone – rather than specifically to me. Did she then feel that the deep friendship which had already survived so many vicissitudes was in itself a firm enough basis for marriage in the absence of the strong physical bond she had had with John, or was she confident that that would come of itself if only the difficulties could be overcome?

In the summer of 1948 Phoebe proposed that we should visit Florence together. The year before we had spent a short time in Provence along with Theo Cadoux and the original idea was to repeat the threesome, but she reckoned that Theo had been something of a distraction and we should be better off without him. She was concerned how to present the change of plan to her mother – in spite of the fact that she was now over thirty – and, as she perhaps feared, this provoked a crisis. When all the arrangements had been made, her mother was highly critical of her going away with me on the grounds that it was improper and that 'it was not fair on Basil'. This ill-judged intervention did not, of course, persuade Phoebe not to persevere with the plan but it upset her precarious balance and threatened to cast a shadow over the whole venture. I think that she genuinely wanted my company, so far as possible, on the old companionable terms. It could not have escaped her notice that it would be something of a test of how we could get on together in close proximity in what was, after all, her territory, an intensive exploration of Florentine art. And who knew what might come of it? But it was to be chiefly a period of truce, an interlude in the continuing debate about our future. Although she vigorously rejected her mother's view of the matter, the fact that the journey *could* be seen in these terms as a sort of irresponsible sexual escapade made it virtually impossible for her to take it at its face value. For the first week or so she was extremely touchy and difficult and it seems that I could do nothing right. I was, as usual when this happened, simply bewildered. When she was sharp I became gloomy. I even contemplated returning home.

But after the first week things began to improve. We *did* Florence systematically, seeing everything once and making a second or third visit to the things we liked best. She was a marvellous teacher and I was a responsive pupil. The sheer splendour and variety of what confronted us concentrated our thoughts and feelings on sources of significance outside ourselves until we forgot to quarrel. She was entirely catholic in her tastes and soaked herself in the richness of these man-made surroundings as she used to do in the Oxford countryside. There was another reminder of her youth when we stood before Perugino's *Crucifixion* and looked upon the road she had followed in her dreams as a child.

Towards the end of our stay we were visiting Fiesole and Phoebe had spent the afternoon on a hillside sketching the view over Florence. It was a hot day and, when she had finished, we lay together side by side dozing in the sun. Suddenly she turned towards me and placed a hand on my thigh – a gesture which would have been quite unremarkable if we had not in the past been so reserved with one another. I responded at once and put my arms round her. I said, 'How did you know it would have that effect?' and she replied, 'Don't forget that I am not entirely without experience.'

It was time to go, but that brief exchange was enough to assure me that there were no longer barriers, of the sort I had feared, along that particular path. Indeed there seemed to be an unspoken assumption that we would explore it further. At this point, however, an element of farce entered the proceedings. That night after supper I developed a fever, presumably as the result of sun-stroke, which lingered until we were about to leave Florence.

We were to return by train to Paris and I was much exercised by the need to make sure of a seat for Phoebe as the trains were notoriously crowded and she would get tired out on a long journey. Research revealed that a fresh train started at Turin and, if we broke our journey there we could arrive on the platform early and make sure of a seat before the crowds built up. The scheme was, however, frustrated by the railway authorities, who retained the additional coaches in a siding until not long before the train arrived from Rome. By that time a far larger mass of people had assembled on the platform than could possibly hope to find seats in the train.

So I devised an alternative plan. Our only hope of getting seats depended upon our being among the first dozen or so passengers to board the train. There were doors at either end of each coach, so that when the train stopped we must be sure to be opposite one of these doors. The crowd was ten or so people deep for the whole length of the platform and, if we were embedded in it, we should not be able to move laterally towards a door. So, I reasoned, we must station ourselves behind the crowd, ready to push towards a door as soon as the train stopped. That way we ought to be among the first dozen or so to enter the train by that door. I further calculated that the Italians would in no circumstances abandon their luggage or their children and would be hampered in their efforts by these impedimenta. We would leave our cases on the platform and retrieve them later, thus enhancing our mobility.

These tactics were entirely successful. I secured a corner seat and one beside it. The only snag was that the train was so full that there could be no question of getting back onto the platform and it was only the good nature of people on the platform which enabled us to recover our cases by having them passed through the window.

After this minor triumph the rest of the journey was passed in a mood of quiet contentment which I thought anticipated the end of our troubles. For most of the time I remained awake while Phoebe dozed on my shoulder with my arm round her.

When we got home, however, there was a further element of farce. At the first opportunity I went to see her at her mother's house in Oxford, hoping that in some way our new and easier relationship might be confirmed. I found her sitting in an armchair in the garden, her face covered in spots. She grinned broadly and there was that old black glint in her eyes. Nothing was going to happen for a while yet.

In the event nothing did. In the following few months a reaction set in and relations became difficult again, although I partnered her at a dance at the Central which went well. What happened, I think, and it was something I hadn't anticipated, was that anything which brought us closer together, as the Florentine visit had done, intensified the fear, amounting almost to panic, which the prospect of marriage induced in her. I became a threat to her independence precisely to the extent that I emerged as a potential husband and she responded to the threat by associating me in her imagination with everything that threatened the way of life which she had chosen. It was made worse for her by the difficulty she was experiencing in developing her work and her career. She was making progress but only fitfully.

Things came to crisis in December just before Christmas. I can recall nothing of the entire episode, nor can I understand how it came about, but the evidence from our letters at the time is clear enough as far as it goes. It seems that we began to make love and that this was a premeditated act, presumably as a trial and that at some point she broke it off. In a subsequent letter (or draft for one) I spoke of my 'disproportionate resentment' at 'being ordered out of your bedroom' and she protested that she had enjoyed it at the time and wasn't 'shamming'.

> . . . I said to you such a lot of things which if misunderstood could cause pain. For example about love-making. It wasn't that I was 'shamming' or that I didn't enjoy it at the time, but it made me feel shy, and also a bit guilty because I didn't fully associate you as a person with the man making love to me. I felt I was reacting so to speak on a different level from you – and that therefore I was not giving you what you really wanted, the complete and undivided response of someone . . . I don't think, therefore, that for me problems can be solved in that way – it more has to be an expression of the solution of the problem.

She ended the letter in such a way that left me in no doubt that we had reached a complete impasse:

> As you know I am a person who finds it hard to express the affection and trust and respect I feel under any sense of constriction. That is why I am glad that the miasma is passing to a certain extent. Because I do truly value you, even if I cannot respond as you deserve. I feel so bad, as if you are always a bit ahead pulling, however gently or waiting, however patiently. And I cannot make the pace, though the pace is too slow for you.

There was no way forward at all. I could only retreat. The current of genuine affection which was bringing us together was now serving only to increase the force of those other currents which were tending to carry us apart. Even if I were to put my own wants aside and concentrate my efforts entirely on helping her in her present predicament, it was clear that I must first abandon completely the hope of any relationship with her other than the close but undemanding friendship which was all that she had ever really wanted from me.

There was no denying that the occasion of my final rejection was particularly painful as tending to accentuate my sense of sexual failure. But although I was bound to feel this and she would certainly have realised it – it was plain that this was not the root of the matter. As she had clearly implied, this would have been all right if the other difficulties could have been resolved.

The next day I too drafted a letter (though I do not know if it was sent):

> The position is *so* complicated for you and I am hard put to it to know whether to stick to my hunch that we do belong together or to go by the more obvious signs. You see, I think you have already said 'no' in very plain language, although consideration for me and affection have so far prevented you saying it in words. If this is true – and I wish to heaven it weren't – it is folly for me not to heed it and no help to you. I learnt some time ago that there is no such thing as unrequited love. I can't frame the words to say how I love you, unless they are words you want to hear – and they aren't.

It was, perhaps, strange in the circumstances that she had entertained the possibility of our marrying for so long and even now did not say a definite 'no'. It would have consoled me a little if I could have believed that it was marriage as such and not marriage to me that drove her into panic. It is true that she came increasingly to think that she had to make a choice between two ways of life and one of the two was marriage, but when all allowance has been made for the distortion of her image of Basil under the pressure of events, I think in retrospect that there were things about *me* which she found threatening. Inevitably I stood for an ordered life in an institutional setting, summed up in her agonised cry to Jean Fuller, 'I don't want to be a don's wife'; and with this went an ingrained habit on my part of trying to get a coherent view of things, and a reluctance to leave matters unexplained. Here she was wrong, I think, about our not overlapping. These attitudes were not absent from her own make-up – indeed she had a profound respect for them, but she had come to feel that she must suppress them, for the time being at least, so as to give full rein to her creative imagination, which flourished in the somewhat chaotic conditions of her life with her artist friends. She had talked of her current state of mind as 'precarious' and, as I can now see, she was engaged in a desperate struggle to achieve an integrated personality in which her varied gifts could flourish in genuine independence of her powerful family. I had always wanted to help her in this, but instead of becoming someone whom she could trust unreservedly and who would help her to function securely as one person, I found myself, against my will, enlisted on one side only of her spiritual struggle, and that the losing one.

So I took the only course open to me and abandoned the appeals which were causing her such distress. It meant giving up the hope which had sustained me, off and on, for the last ten years. Not only could I do Phoebe no good by holding on, but I was permanently inhibiting the growth of any other relationship which might be open to me.

Never the less she wanted the friendship to continue in some form. She wrote:

> But you know, the slow imperceptible reduction of a close friendship may be worse than a break. Still I think I could 'take' that risk if you would like to go on. You wouldn't notice the reduction you see.

But there was no doubt that the old close friendship in the form that had sustained us both over the last ten years was now at an end and she ended her letter with a moving envoi.

> If we don't meet much now, and I suppose we won't, it has been worth it, hasn't it? I hope for you it will be a jumping off ground and not a mill-stone. I can't say in a letter all I want to say, but I hope and believe life will give you of its best, because you give it so much of yours. Don't worry about Monday's tearfulness – probably due to convalescence. Thank God you don't go about putting construction on things.
>
> Well, God bless you, my dear Basil, et nunc et semper. With love from Phoebe.

CHAPTER 7

Marriage

A T THE BEGINNING OF THE WEEK in which my mother died, although I did not know it at the time, a new era in my life began. I had arranged to go with Liselott to a performance of the St Matthew Passion in the Sheldonian on Palm Sunday and had no means of getting into Oxford. I asked the doctor who was attending my mother if there was anyone in Deddington likely to be going in by car. He said that Mrs Collin at the Corner House might well be going and he would ask her if I could have a lift. Mrs Collin said 'of course' and I duly presented myself at her rather grand house at one end of the main square. When we got back after the performance she invited me to stay for supper when I met her son Rob and his wife, Orma, who occupied a flat in an older part of the building. It was a lively party and the first of many. Mrs Collin was a widow. Although, as I later learnt, she had lived a somewhat bohemian existence in the south of France with her husband, a highly talented painter who had died prematurely, she had now settled down to the life of a distinctly grand lady in Deddington. If I say that her house was furnished in impeccable taste, it suggests that it conformed to some settled norm. In fact it was highly individual, marked by touches of bold colour, in which interesting objects of varied provenance consorted happily together with her husband's paintings, which were accorded chief prominence. Mrs Collin herself was small and precise in her movements. She suffered from severe congenital deafness which had worsened with age and which she had devised a strategy to deal with. Instead of withdrawing, as she might have done, she invariably led the conversation so that she knew what people were talking about. In this way she could, with the aid of lip-reading, keep in touch with it, although she never sought to dominate it.

There was a lovely garden at the back of the house and, across the road, a park-like area, which included a grass tennis court and, in addition to it, an extensive vegetable garden.

During that summer I was often in the company of Rob and

Orma, who were lively and intelligent and both of them by temperament active and energetic. The whole experience was as if designed to console me after my mother's death and the change in my relationship with Phoebe.

Meanwhile I was still living at Clifton in the White Cottage, which I continued to rent from Christ Church. Betty had to return to Iserlohn in Westphalia where George was Chaplain, and I needed to find some way of occupying the house, given that I should be spending the weekdays in Oxford. I could, of course, have given up the cottage and taken rooms in Oxford, but I was fond of the place and now had an interest in remaining close to Deddington. An ideal solution was found. In answer to an advertisement an RAF officer and his wife applied on the understanding that they would have the place rent free so long as they would look after me at weekends and in the vacations.

The arrangement worked amazingly well. Derek Lewis was an energetic, not to say boisterous, individual, and Gwen, his wife, lively and outgoing. They had a vigorous social life, based on the RAF establishment at Brize Norton where Derek worked. The two children, a girl and a boy, had the run of the large garden and could attend the local school. I had a room to myself as a study and was never interrupted except for a cup of tea or coffee. Apart from that I was just a slightly odd member of their family.

I was now, in effect, living two separate lives, one in college getting accustomed to the routines of academic life and discovering affinities in the University; the other at Clifton and, increasingly, at Deddington also. It was not until later in the summer that I met Margy, the fourth member of the Collin family. Up till then she had been living in Holland Park, while studying music at Trinity College. Getting to know her did not have to be a separate venture on my part. On her visits to Deddington she was inevitably drawn in to the activities of Rob and Orma and, in due course, Gwen and Derek. We played tennis together and the six of us went to dances at Brize Norton. In fact I cannot remember when I first met Margy. She was just part of a setup that I had come to enjoy and feel at home with. If I try to single anything out as particularly significant it would be the dances. Margy had a favourite evening dress of bottle green with a velvet edging. It sat low on her shoulders which had a Victorian slope to them and she melted into my arms, as if that were her natural place. I seem to remember that as time went on I wanted that closeness to happen more often. I felt increasingly at home with her.

Margy, it transpired, had started the war in the Land Army, which did lasting damage to her wrists and then, after a year at Bletchley, went into the ATS in a detachment which was among the first to cross the Rhine into Germany at the end of the war. She was a self-confessed 'bloody-minded corporal' and her gestures and sometimes her language jarred with the image of her as gentle and submissive which I had begun to cultivate. There is one occasion that I still remember in which she took pains to demonstrate this side of her character. I had invited a girl down for the weekend, having been distinctly taken with her, when introduced to her by Christopher and Christabel. She was a refugee, Martina Schulhof by name, who was studying with Christabel at RADA. She was, I think, of a genuinely sweet disposition with a natural grace which had been perfected by RADA. All her movements were graceful in a manner that appeared, and indeed I think was, entirely unselfconscious. I doubt if, at that stage of my life, I would have allowed myself to be aware of it, but I think that I was setting up a sort of judgement of Paris between these two girls, each of whom I was then capable of falling in love with without yet committing myself to either. Whether Margy realised what was going on, I don't know, but in any case she made it very clear that she was not entering into the competition. While Martina was floating around scarcely touching the ground, Margy was clumping about and jerking her thumb in a gesture I particularly disliked, as if to tell me that if I was thinking of loving her it must be for herself alone and not for any surface embellishments.

At this time I very much wanted to settle down and be married and, inevitably, I found myself considering the girls I knew in this connection. Liselott, whom I was always rather fond of, had fallen into the background as a charming friend with whom I met occasionally. Martina also I had invited to the Christ Church Summer Ball, but although charming as ever, she somehow lacked substance. Indeed my girl friends at this time must have found me very unsatisfactory. I rather naïvely thought that unless I was serious about them, I must not make love to them or use the word 'love' at all, but otherwise do all I could to charm them and entertain them. Since I was, I suppose, reasonably good looking and ready in speech, they must have found this distinctly frustrating. And in retrospect I regret it myself. It should have been possible to find some language and mode of behaviour which was expressive of affection and sexual attraction, but was not misleading in the way I feared. I deprived myself of a lot of fun and my girlfriends too.

There was one thing which undoubtedly played a part in inclining me to fall in love with Margy, and that was the suspicion that she was falling in love with me; and after years of unrequited love, this counted for something. On one occasion I confessed to Gwen Lewis that I feared I was leading Margy on, to which she replied that, if anything, it was the other way round, and I found this distinctly reassuring. As the spring of 1949 turned into summer I was more and more as a matter of course going straight to Deddington. I remember a marvellous day in May when I took the train to Heyford and walked along the towpath of the canal through fields bright with buttercups and hawthorn to find Margy sitting at the piano playing Couperin. Coming, more prosaically on the bus, I often found her thus at the piano in a favourite dress of hers, white with horizontal grey stripes. It would have been totally out of character for her to deliberately pose herself, but the effect was the same as if she had.

In the long vacation of that year we were regularly in each other's company and I felt the time had come for decision. I took her for a walk in the fields near Deddington with the intention of proposing to her. It was a most unromantic occasion. Margy remembers that I withdrew behind a bush several times to pee and when I finally said, 'Will you marry me?' she said 'Of course.' It was 10 August 1949. Although we were now firmly committed we decided not to tell anyone, not even her mother, for two months. Margy did not want to give her mother too long to plan the wedding and 'make a thing about it'. And in fact both of us could not help having some misgivings. She, of course, knew about my long association with Phoebe and wondered if I could really be happy with someone who had no claims to be an intellectual, and the Phoebe experience had left me with some doubts about my capacities as a lover. In any case, I was over thirty and she was close to it and we were both beyond the age when we could take it for granted that our present feelings would last forever.

Ma, as she was always known, was delighted at the news, if also a little hurt that we hadn't told her earlier. It became apparent, however, as Margy had feared, that the wedding would be an occasion of controversy in which she found herself in a minority against her mother and me. Ma was by nature generous and liked putting on a good show. I had always enjoyed ceremony and, with my family's histrionic bent, was not averse to public performances. Margy hated show of any kind, especially one in which her mother was entitled to play a dominant part. She had numerous relatives, especially on her mother's Dutch side, with whom she identified much less than with her father's Sunderland family. She couldn't object to their being invited, if I was having a lot of my friends from Oxford and elsewhere. Once, not long before the wedding, at her insistence, we took a day off and had lunch together in Stow-on-the-Wold, to make sure we were still the people we thought we were.

The wedding took place in the church at Deddington on 18 March 1950. I had been told by Harry Carpenter, then Warden of Keble, whom I had asked to take part, that we couldn't have a wedding in Lent, but it had to be before Easter to give time for a honeymoon in the Easter vacation. So, as a compromise, he proposed the Saturday before Refreshment Sunday in the middle of Lent. In the event it was a splendid occasion. Margy was insistent that she was too old to wear white and had a dress of a mellow golden colour.

She had at first wanted no bridesmaids but a good friend of Ma's had two little girls who had been bridesmaids before and now wanted to be regarded as professionals. Once their claims were accepted, Penny Lewis and my niece, Mary, selected themselves. Christopher Rieu was my best man. One particular blessing was vouchsafed to Margy. By right she should have been 'given away' by the head of the family, Ma's elder brother, Adrian Stoop. He was a celebrated Rugger player, Oxford, Harlequins and England, hailed often as 'the father of modern Rugby', and in Margy's opinion a terrible bore. To her relief and to Ma's disgust, he refused her invitation because it was the Calcutta Cup match that afternoon, and 'he made it a principle never to miss an international'. His place was taken by Tim Stoop who was the next brother down.

Ma thoughtfully sent a half bottle of champagne for me on the morning of the wedding but my father drank it. Margy shared hers with her oldest friend, Philippa Barton.

I had arranged for a bus to collect my Oxford friends and return them later in the evening. This provoked some delightful letters, notably one from Kay Farrer in which she contrasted the sober atmosphere of the journey out, when many of the guests did not know one another, with the merry and expansive mood of the return journey.

The honeymoon was to be spent entirely in Margy's territory at Cagnes-sur-Mer on the coast between Antibes and Nice where her parents had lived before the war and she and Rob were brought up. On the eve of war, Ma had let their house, the Villa St Anne, to an elderly French lady who was the widow of an American diplomat, Mme Heilmann de Roque. Unfortunately she seemed determined to live forever and, with the help of skilful lawyers, had refused to surrender the house. There was, however, at the bottom of the garden a small 'dower house' which Ma had hoped to retain for visiting family and friends, but Mme Heilmann insisted was needed to house her clothes. This, however, in an uncharacteristic gesture of charity, she permitted us to use on our honeymoon.

Our plan was to spend the wedding night at the White Cliffs Hotel in Dover and then, on arrival in Calais, to proceed on the *train bleu* to the Côte d'Azur. It was a superb way to travel, in a 2-berth cabin and easy access to a restaurant car with splendid meals. I remember trundling slowly round the Paris periphèrique, the wheels being tapped in the middle of the night at Dijon and dawn breaking over Avignon.

The 'dower house' was delightful, a perfect place for a honeymoon. It had a kitchen, a salon and one large bedroom with a window on to the terraced garden. One passed from one room to another through arches. In contrast with my ill-fated attempt to make love to Phoebe of which there is documentary evidence, but which I have forgotten completely, I have a clear and vivid recollection of that first night in Cagnes. It was moonlight and there was a tree with oranges on it which was clearly delineated as in a Florentine painting. Knowing that there was to be an indefinite succession of nights and no pressure to succeed this time, we did triumphantly 'consummate the marriage' and I remember the sense, not only that this was good, but that we really were indissolubly united.

We spent the following nights and days exploring our bodies and the country round about Cagnes, the one activity contributing to the enjoyment of the other. Margy loved the place and there were still people there who remembered her as a child. The high point was reached when we were invited to supper by Mme Nicolai who still ran the shop where Margy remembers that her husband, now deceased, who was an enormous man, used to raise her with one hand to get some delicacy off the top shelf. I was struck by the extraordinary dignity with which this peasant woman carried herself and helped us to '*soupe à ma pauvre mère*' and other carefully prepared dishes.

We had only one tiff. On a walk in a glade of poplars and jonquils near Biot we were conversing and I happened to remark 'I say something and I don't get any come-back'. It ought not to have been said but it was true and stirred Margy's deepest fears. When the break with Phoebe came I knew, and had reckoned with this, that I would never again experience with anyone else the quick understanding and immediate response that I had had with her. With Margy I would share many things but not this. She reacted to things immediately without the medium of reflection and her responses were to be found in action, not in words. She was, and remains, for one so intelligent, surprisingly inarticulate. Not that she didn't talk, and talk well, but she didn't naturally express her deepest thoughts in talk. It was thoughtless of me to allow a moment's irritation to disturb the confidence she was newly acquiring. Phoebe had always been a clear swiftly running stream fed by deep springs which were utterly translucent. Margy, by contrast, was a deep pool which did not want to be seen into. I knew this and most of the time took comfort from it, but on this occasion I forgot myself, and I still deeply regret it.

CHAPTER 8

Countrylife in Oxfordshire

WE STARTED OUR MARRIED LIFE in the White Cottage, Clifton, Deddington, and remained there for eighteen months, and began our family there. It became evident early on that Margy was pregnant, to our great delight. That we wanted children was never in question. Margy's only deliberation was as to how many: certainly more than two and possibly no fewer than four. This was because she wanted enough children to ensure that none of them had to endure the pressure that could be exerted by a parent of strong personality. She had been one of only two and felt that her mother had exerted such pressure upon her and her brother, Rob, with the result that she had never felt that she came up to expectation.

Margy had spent much of her childhood in Cagnes between Antibes and Nice where her parents had lived from 1924 onwards. Her father, Charles Frederick Collin was an accomplished artist who was born in Sunderland, son of the proprietor of a small iron foundry. When at Armstrong College he was awarded a Prix de Rome travelling scholarship, which he spent travelling with a friend and a donkey in Italy.

Her mother, Cornelie Dura Stoop, came from a very different family. The Stoops were a leading mercantile family in Dordrecht. Her father moved to England, made his fortune in the Stock Exchange and settled in a large house, West Hall, in Byfleet, Surrey. Cora, as she was known, was, rather surprisingly at that time, allowed to become an art student and was studying under Tudor Hart when she met Collin and married him. She was herself a talented painter but she gave up her painting in order to devote herself to furthering her husband's career.

As a result, Collin never had to earn his living by his pictures and his total output remains within the family. He struck out on his own by working in tempera in the manner of painters in the 14th century. Margy was sent to a series of small girls schools in England, in which, as she later considered, there was insufficient discipline in academic work which left her unable to gain entrance to Oxford. However, she always excelled in games and gymnastics.

She was, as I was to discover, very practical and down to earth, but at the same time profoundly musical and artistic, a combination which made her a natural home-maker. She was totally indifferent to fashion but had infallible judgement when it came to putting together items of furniture, colour schemes, pictures and the entire home environment. She had also inherited from her mother a gift for finding people to help run the house, and keeping them up to the mark while securing their lasting friendship. She always reckoned that she had greater affinity with her father's North Country side of the family than with her mother's Dutch ancestry. One consequence of this – though she would deny it – is that she always took care to see that her husband was properly fed.

She was distinctly intelligent, but quite uninterested in theory. When it came to relationships with people she made up for this by a quick intuitive grasp of what in a given situation an individual needed.

In spite of her all-round competence, the stressful relationship with her mother left her feeling somewhat inadequate, with the consequence that while she supported me most effectively in my academic endeavours, she needed the assurance of my ongoing love for the confidence she needed to give me that support.

At the White Cottage we were entirely dependent on the car and one of my clearest memories of that time is being collected from Banbury station by Margy in the blue 1938 Hillman Minx which she had been given by her mother. She was and always has been a highly competent driver. But the time had obviously come for me to learn to drive. Unlike her I was never quick to pick up practical skills and it took me some time to master this one. We both realised that I must in no circumstance take lessons from her if our marriage was to be secure, so I went to a driving school in Oxford and passed my test at the second attempt. The exasperating thing was that I failed the first time on the theory in spite of the fact that I had learnt the Highway Code almost by heart. I was caught out on stopping distances which I had totally overlooked because they were to be found on the back cover of the handbook where, as an academic, it had never occurred to me to look.

As it happened, the first time I ever drove at night was in February 1951 when Margy felt her pains coming on. I drove her in a patchy fog into the Banbury Road, Oxford, where her nursing home was. Nothing happened immediately and next day I took her to the cinema to see Jacques Tati in *Jour de Fête* and this had the desired effect. Nell was born on 14 February.

Three permanent features of our later life originated in Clifton. In Term time I had to spend all day in Oxford, leaving Margy alone for hours at a time. We decided to get a dog to keep her company. Wendy Broome, who was a tenant of Ma's, gave us a puppy which, she said, was a cockador but she looked a pure black Labrador. We called her Dido. I also decided to take Wednesday afternoon and evening off. On Wednesdays every other week there were College Meetings, and this meant going straight home afterwards, having no tutorials that evening.

Bosanquet had described the White Cottage to me initially as a very 'odd' house and indeed it was. It had been converted from a local ironstone cottage by Lord and Lady Denbigh before the war. It was then twice its present size, half of it having been burnt down during the war. It was roofed in Norfolk reed thatch and had two very steep gables on either side of the front door which reached down to within a foot of the ground. It was said locally that Lord Denbigh was a nice old gentleman but that Lady Denbigh was no lady. Against the advice of their builders she had insisted on running a flue from the boiler up through the thatch. There had been no occasion to light the boiler until the war but then, with evacuees living in it, the boiler was lit and what the builder had feared happened; the thatch caught fire and one half of the house was saved by a strong wind blowing away from it. Other oddities were that there was an extension at one end which Lady Denbigh, a Roman Catholic, had added for use as a chapel and we stored our junk in; and there was a cellar full of water which needed an hour or so with a hand pump every week to prevent it overflowing into the house. It had two large, light and airy rooms on the ground and first floor overlooking the large garden and beyond it down to the River Cherwell and the railway to Islip and Oxford. Other peculiarities were the bathroom with the largest washbasin we had ever seen and a bath with a small wash basin built into it. The hot water ran out after only one bath, so we got used to making do with the one bath full for both of us, a habit which we continued thereafter in our other houses which did not have this particular problem.

One morning I had decided to stain the attic floor, so I had not shaved and was dressed in my oldest clothes. Margy had gone up to Deddington to shop and left the breakfast things stacked in the sink for later attention. Scarcely had I begun work when the bell rang – an unusual occurrence in our lost off location. I went downstairs and opened the door and there on the doorstep was an individual I barely recognised and grouped behind him in a loose semi-circle an assembly of people, both men and women whom I could not at first identify, but were not complete strangers. 'I am the clerk of works at Christ Church,' said the man, 'and this is the Governing Body of Christ Church on their annual progress through their estates.' He went on to explain that they were visiting the farms on either side of us which were Christ Church property when they saw the White Cottage and, learning that it was also Christ Church property, expressed a wish to view it. Would I mind if they looked round? Although I was totally unprepared for such a visitation I had no alternative but to invite them in. I hastily apologised for my appearance and explained that I had taken the morning off to stain the attic floor. 'What are you using?' asked Mrs Chaundy, the wife of the maths don. 'Some stuff called Darkalene,' I replied. 'Oh,' she said, 'you shouldn't use that. It's terrible stuff.' Fortunately the clerk of works came to my rescue and said, 'It will do for that, it is only a rough deal floor, not like the beautiful elm flooring in this room.'

As they looked around I noticed the eyes of the women swivelling towards the dishes stacked in the sink and explained that my wife was shopping in Deddington. When they had seen enough of the house, they trooped into the garden and, as we explored it, I could see Margy, back from Deddington, flitting anxiously from room to room, having no idea who these people were. She did not look as if she wanted to meet them and, as I could not remember them all individually, I could only have said, 'My wife – the Governing Body of Christ Church', which would have made her feel she ought to do something about entertaining them. And in any case they were just about to go. As they filed out, Dundas said, 'You rent this place from us, don't you?' I said 'yes' and he added 'We could throw you out, if we wanted to?' 'Yes', I replied, 'but I very much hope you won't!'

We continued to look after the garden and I am sure that I fulfilled my contract with Christ Church to leave it better than I had found it. Never having been interested in gardening before, I became a gardener of necessity and came to love it. We were helped by Bill who early in the war had been a fellow cowman with Margy and, in spite of his emaciated condition, got through an enormous amount of work. One of the advantages of Clifton was that we enjoyed the social life of Deddington. Much of this revolved round Ma, who in spite of her deafness was an inspired hostess. Among the more memorable occasions were parties devoted to charades. Ma had assembled in a splendid chest in her entrance hall a wardrobe of dressing up materials and these and other more improbable items from the kitchen were put to imaginative use. The most uniformly successful game was 'Adverbs' in which all present were divided into two teams. One had to think of a word and illustrate it in one or more scenes. The other had to guess the word. Part of the fun of this game was that the most unlikely people turned out to be good at it, as if the occasion elicited normally entirely latent capacities. Christmas celebrations were particularly splendid at Deddington, when Ma would serve mulled claret (which I was privileged to brew) and in the course of the evening the Bell Ringers would come in and perform on their hand-bells.

Deddington gave Margy, too, the opportunity to practise her music. Among the residents, in the oldest house in the village, were Admiral Berthon and his family. The Admiral was a skilled woodworker and both wife and daughter were musicians. Margy used to join them in baroque trios playing her recorder with their piano and violin. Mrs Berthon was a delightful woman, so that Margy was only amused and not offended when she expressed herself as delighted that her eldest daughter had become engaged to a naval lieutenant. 'You see, we're terribly pleased because, living as we do near Oxford, she might have married a don!'

I myself seem to remember the time at Clifton as a pleasant interlude in, or perhaps I should say, prelude to, our married life. For it was obvious that we could not remain for long at the White Cottage. It was too far, 17 miles, from Oxford and life would become impossible for Margy as the children grew older and I grew busier. We needed to be nearer Oxford. We agreed that we still wanted to be in the country and we drew a circle round Oxford of ten miles diameter within which we would search.

As it happened we had no need to search, because Ma was at the same time looking for a house for her old friend, Mary Maitland, and in the course of this, came upon a house which she and Mary both thought was unsuitable for her because of her age, but might well be suitable for us. It was at Wootton near Woodstock, which we had already visited as the home of my colleague at Keble, Maurice Hugh-Jones. It must have been late October that we saw the house and it cannot have been at its best, but we took to it at once. It was originally three cottages which had been converted into a single dwelling by the architect, F R S Yorke, of the well-known firm of Yorke, Rosenberg and Mardall, architects of the John Radcliffe Hospital. The garden ran down to the River Glyme just below the bridge at the bottom of the village, and the house backed into a steep bank. A row of six Lombardy poplars bordered the stream. It was called 'Bridge House'. It had only one serious disadvantage in that it faced north and got almost no sunlight in winter. This was partly compensated for by the fact that it got a great deal of sunlight in summer. The sun rising in the North East rose at midday high above the bank behind us and set in the North West, bathing our garden in sunlight all day. It appealed to us at once as a splendid place to bring up children in. There was nothing to show the age of the cottages, but the deeds indicated that they had been built by one Thomas Sotham, who died in 1790, and some of the other cottages in West End had inscriptions dated 1750.

We decided for it with very little hesitation and Ma bought it for us for £5,000 with characteristic generosity. Thus Bridge House, Wootton, became our family home for all of forty-one years.

When we moved into Bridge House in November 1951 there was no main drainage and no mains water. The bathroom and lavatory were on the first floor to allow enough fall for a septic tank in the garden. Kitchen waste was discharged into a soak-away. Our water was pumped up from the river having passed through a filter of sand and gravel. It was judged to be chemically pure but not bacteriologically pure. The local doctors reckoned that for a year or two people who drank it might have occasional colly-wobbles, but would then get used to it and suffer no further ill effects. We as a family never had any problems with it and Margy maintains that it was tastier than the mains water we eventually got. The river just below the bridge and immediately opposite the house was comparatively shallow, although, at two to three feet, deeper than it later was when it had been dredged by the Thames Conservancy. It was not safe for very small children, so we had a light fence erected a few feet from the edge, which must have been there for five or six years until our youngest, Clare was old enough to be presumed safe. Nevertheless she did fall in once, when to our great surprise, Matthew without hesitation pulled her out. When we moved to Bridge House we had, of course, Nell with us, aged nine months, and Dido only a little older. The front door led into a large living room with a door which led into a small dining room and equally small kitchen and scullery. From the living room there was a rather awkward wooden staircase, which led up to the first floor on which were two bedrooms and the bathroom. There were two small attic bedrooms each of which had its own staircase. It became immediately obvious that there was nowhere indoors for the children to play so we got Yorke to design us a large playroom to go above the kitchen and dining room below.

At the western end of the house, over the garage and overlooking the road to Woodstock which ran along the valley in a westward direction, was a large room which selected itself as my study. It was approached by a steep ladder on the lines of a ship's companionway and with a door at the bottom was virtually child-proof. In front of the house was a low terrace on the garden side of which roses were planted and at the end of it our predecessor, Mrs Podger, had constructed a flower bed which ran at right angles to it down into the lawn.

It was obvious at a glance that the garden was exposed to flooding and indeed it was flooded regularly every winter during our time there. The waters rose very nearly up to the front door, but never actually came into the house. We could only assume that whoever built the cottages in the 18th century had a very accurate idea of the limits of the flood plain. When we first got the house there was only a wooden fence to separate the garden from the water meadows beyond, but almost at once we had a stone wall built to close off the view and give shape to the garden. It was, we thought, very attractive and I was somewhat taken aback when we invited the County Horticultural Adviser to advise us about some apple trees, which Mrs Podger had planted on the bank beyond the house. She stopped at the front gate and surveyed the scene with a plainly appreciative smile. She said, 'you know, this a perfect textbook example of a waterlogged frost-pocket.'

At nine months Nell had developed enough to become interesting and from then on it was astonishing how rapidly the changes occurred as she became a unique person. It was extraordinary how this individual for whom we were plainly responsible now had a personality which was growing at a rate and in a manner over which we had no control. Or rather the alarming thing was that we obviously did have some control, but very little idea how to exercise it to the best advantage.

I had not realised in advance what difference fatherhood would make. It is clearly a relational characteristic and yet from the beginning I felt it had changed me substantially. On the evening of the day Nell was born I dined in Keble, feeling in this way oddly different and dimly aware of undefined responsibilities. Bill Deakin, of Yugoslav fame and then Fellow of Wadham, was dining that night, and reassured me by saying that babies were amazingly tough and could survive almost any treatment.

Our second child, Matthew, was born in February 1953, and we were looking for a female godparent. The thought occurred to me that we might ask Phoebe. She loved children and was good with them and I thought that, when he got older, she would be the sort of person he might well feel able to turn to for advice when out of tune with his parents. If she agreed it would give her an attachment to our family of a real but indeterminate kind which she could make what she wanted of. She did agree after some qualms of conscience about assent to all the articles of the Creed.

She stayed the night of the christening which was in May and we mooted the possibility of her coming to stay for a week or so later in the summer. Towards the end of June I received an ecstatic postcard:

Just a line to tell you that the 'Last Supper' has been bought by an American parson! I thought you would like to know. I have simmered down now into a sober realisation that it was gigantic luck, but for a bit I felt as we did at Romsey after the Greats news! The difference is that purchase is no criterion of merit. On the other hand it does mean that someone wanted it enough to pay quite a lot of money for it and I like that thought. . . . Are you going to be away for August or might I come and stay some time?

She came for a week at the beginning of August and it was a very happy time. She and Margy got on well. They had painting and music in common and shared a characteristic which I have always lacked, a certain no-nonsense earthiness. Phoebe, as always, expanded in the countryside and spent hours playing with Nell who, aged two and a half, was at her prime.

I had a distinct sense that life was opening out for Phoebe once more and that she was beginning to draw upon all her resources in a more unified way than at any time since her Oxford days. This process was assisted by a new psychiatrist, Noel Harris, whom she found much more sensitive and perceptive than Lovel Barnes. It would mean more expense, if she were to have regular sessions, but:

I think I will try to afford it, don't you? It seems a rare opportunity. In a way I feel better already for knowing that someone of that standing feels sufficiently interested to make the offer. Perhaps doors will open and blank walls break up.

While with us at Wootton she had handed me a poem on the theme of the *Odyssey* which she wanted my opinion of. I wrote at some length about it and sent it back with some photographs we had taken of her with Matthew. There had been some talk of her coming back in September, but she was going for a cruise in the Thames estuary with Arthur Reeves, with whom she was having a rather uneasy relationship owing to a disparity in age, in a boat he had made himself. On her return from Wootton she wrote to thank me for my criticisms and discussed them in detail. The *Odyssey* had always haunted her and I was particularly struck by the way she had caught the sailor's longing for the land:

This is the hour of home when a man's hearth speaks to him
With unambiguous summons, wherever he may be
In his own fields or half the world away.
I have heard it lying in mid ocean,

In the calm following a storm,
The foursquare raft my world, and myself crucified upon it,
Worn out with seasickness, and the monotony
Of the round horizon. I have watched the sun's rim
Flatten against the world's edge, and drop over . . .

This letter was the last I was to receive from her and it strangely brought us full circle. She had told me while at Wootton that there was a possibility of John coming back into her life again. I had said nothing at the time but afterwards began to feel that this had been a mistake. Although I had been powerless to intervene when she first encountered John, I could not remain silent if there was the slightest risk of that episode being repeated. So I warned her against him.

So, as it happened, her last words to me were on that subject:

I am writing against time so will not write more now. Of course I didn't take umbrage about John. You are in any case privileged to say anything about anything. I was glad of your comments. I can't see any future to it either.

At the beginning of September Margy and I went away to France on holiday and it was not until the middle of the month that we returned to her mother's house at Deddington. There were letters from Phoebe's mother and elder brother telling me that Phoebe had died at sea and that the funeral had already taken place at Upshire.

Jean Fuller wrote to me later in the month to tell me as much as she could find out about the accident:

At 10.00am on Monday Sept 7th the *Enis* was seen by the skipper of a sand barge stuck on Buxey Sands (about six miles from Clacton) but still floating, bottom held but top part above water. He went all round it in his boat and shouted but no one answered. It was plain that she had been abandoned. He went back and informed authorities. At 2.00pm the lifeboat people were there, but confirmed there was no one aboard. The dinghy was gone as well as the occupants. Examining the yacht they found the bottom badly holed, which could not have been done by the sands, and they supposed she must have hit something, perhaps a submerged wreck, before coming to be on the sands. She was only in about 9 feet of water when first seen and, when the tide went down, was almost completely high and dry. The lifeboat authorities maintained that if she had earlier struck a wreck sticking up from the bottom, that also could not have been very far out. The weather was absolutely calm, no wind or rough sea, and, if the occupants had stayed on board, they could have waded ashore later. People at Whitstable had seen two men and a girl aboard when she put in for repairs on Sunday. There was an all-out search for them, aircraft covering this area as well as sea and land searchers. On Tuesday Phoebe's body was washed up in the foreshore at Maldon. She was wearing a white duffle coat, jeans and a life jacket. Still no dinghy.

The dinghy was never found. The bodies of Arthur Reeves and Basil Peak were found a week later further up the coast. It appears that when the boat was holed, Arthur had wisely anchored her on the sandbank to prevent her sinking. It remains a mystery why they had taken to the dinghy on a falling tide when they could have waded ashore a few hours later. One further mystery remains. The lifeboat men found one of the dinghy's oars still on board.

Phoebe's family asked me to see if some of her work could be preserved in Oxford. I was able to arrange for this. The Ashmolean Museum has two sets of book illustrations: for *Gulliver's Travels* and *The Turn of the Screw*; and St Hugh's College have hung in their Senior Common Room a set of illustrations for Milton's *Comus*.

Some forty years later I was asked by an American philosopher, Kelly James Clark to contribute to a book he was editing entitled *Philosophers Who Believe*. He wanted me to 'come clean' about my personal life and its influence upon my spiritual development. I was reluctant at first to do this but eventually agreed. I endeavoured to sum up the effect upon me of that protracted, eventually frustrated, but deeply enriching relationship:

It had become apparent that, however intractable the problems we encountered as a man and a woman of only partly overlapping vocations, involved in the complications of a specific social situation, we had nevertheless been enabled to see each other clearly and respond to each other's aspirations with a certain kind of disinterested love. I had found that, above all, I wanted her to resolve her tensions, fulfil her varied capacities as a human being, if possible with, if necessary without, my own participation. And this flourishing was not simply a satisfactory accommodation between her conflicting desires, but of her becoming fully what she was meant to be. And it had become clear that this was also her wish for me, whatever role I might subsequently play in her life.

Looking back on this time after those forty years, I went on to write that after my marriage:

> I did not have to exert all my energies to occupy a role in someone else's life that I could not adequately fill, and perhaps at the time no one could have. Instead I enjoyed the trust and support of a wife whose talents and temperament were complementary to my own and whose commitment to the marriage was never in doubt. There was in short nothing now in my situation except my own limitations to prevent me making of my life what I wanted to make of it.

It was at a very early stage that we discovered that Wootton was a very friendly village. Shortly after we arrived the bell rang and from an upstairs window I saw a young middle-aged woman with a tam o'shanter hat. When Margy opened, she said 'My name is Mary Parsons. My husband has been in hospital and I think he needs cheering up. Can you come to a party at Lower Dornford Farm?' And so we met the Parsons family and were at once introduced to people who had deep roots in Wootton and the country round. Mary, as so often happens with farmers' wives, was a good deal more cultivated than her husband, but both were transparently good people, on whom we knew at once that one could rely absolutely. Michael was a big man, whose favourite topic of conversation, aside from farming, was the Battle of Jutland of which he had an encyclopaedic knowledge. Mary was a devout churchwoman, although her devoutness did not extend to the Mothers' Union ('I don't like to take my Christianity with cups of tea').

The friends we met next were incomers like ourselves but by now thoroughly established. Bruce and Margaret Campbell lived at Hordley, a fifteenth century farmhouse, a mile or so down river from us. Bruce was a well-known ornithologist, who broadcast frequently from BBC Bristol and Margaret was active in committees around the country. She was best known as Chairman of the Oxfordshire Community Council which kept a watchful eye on the county's medical and social services. And, of course, we already knew Maurice Hugh-Jones, my Keble colleague, and his formidable wife, Dora, who was a senior probation officer in Oxford.

I should find it difficult now to give a snapshot of the village when we moved into it in 1951. It was, of course, in a state of transition and my memories are chiefly of changes that were taking place. As a result of one of these I became Chairman of the Parish Council. Village people were reluctant to 'put themselves forward' and expose themselves to criticism from their neighbours. As an incomer I had no such inhibitions. I was witness to another change which worried me. The cottagers were moving into the new council houses at Milford Place and the cottages were becoming derelict. This was understandable as the cottages had to rely on wells or standpipes for water and lacked separate bathrooms, whereas the new council estate had water laid on and sewage arrangements of its own. This change coincided with another as the men were urged by their wives to seek work in the motor factories in Oxford. I was worried by the dereliction of the cottages and even suggested to the surveyor to the Chipping Norton Rural District Council that, instead of building new council houses, the local authority should purchase the cottages and rehabilitate them. 'Don't you worry', he said, 'people will soon move in and do them up themselves'. Which, of course, they did, with the effect eventually that a large part of the old village became inhabited by incomers. Not all of it, though, because some of the 'old village', seeing what could be done with the cottages, restored them themselves and continued to live in them. All these developments contributed to an upsurge of confidence in the old villagers which eventually resulted in me and my like being voted off the Parish Council and replaced by some of their own, a state of affairs which has continued to this day.

Another change which was going on in these early years was that our own family was increasing at roughly two year intervals until eventually we had the four children that Margy had always intended. Matthew was born on 13 February 1953, almost exactly two years after Nell, Kate in December 1954 and Clare in September 1957. So when I think of them now, I always see all four of them, playing naked on the lawn in summer sunshine, in and out of the river. (This somewhat shocked the villagers who had a full view of the garden as they passed over the bridge: though not as shocked as they had been, so it was said, by Thelma Yorke who used to sunbathe in the nude, albeit protected by a screen.)

From an early stage we were drawn into the activities of the village. Supreme among these was the Wootton Annual Flower and Vegetable Show, held in the grounds of the old rectory, now called 'Wootton Place', at the beginning of September on the Saturday before the Church Patronal Festival of the Nativity of the Virgin Mary. At the first show we attended, Nell was awarded First Prize in the Baby Show. At the second, Margy got second prize for a blue embroidered table cloth. At the third, Matthew gained second prize in the Baby Show and shortly afterwards I myself got First Prize in the Men's Ankle Competition. Thereafter I regularly secured First Prize in the Flower Arrangement Class until the corrupting influence of Constance Spry introduced a tinge of professionalism into the event. It appeared that there were now rules and I never knew what they were!

Old photographs of the Flower Show showed a large marquee on the lawn thronged with people and the Rector with a party of gentry having tea under a veranda in front of the Rectory. This class division still persisted in the programme which divided the entries into 'Cottagers' and 'Open', the former confined to those who did not employ a gardener. We were compelled to enter for the 'Open' class, as we had a man in one morning a week to help with the garden.

At the time we arrived there was still a good deal of ill-feeling about the sale of the Rectory. Canon Marriott had been Rector for forty-five years from 1900 to 1945. He was an old-fashioned 'squarson', a landed gentleman in his own right and farmed in a small way. He expected and received deference from the villagers. Children were expected to go to Sunday School and many of the women were employed as servants in the Rectory. Marriott made himself responsible for the upkeep of the church and the churchyard. When he died the Diocese decided to sell the very large 18th-century rectory and its extensive gardens and it was bought by his daughter, Mrs Clutterbuck, for £3,000, which was a ridiculously small amount, given that Bridge House had cost us £5,000. Not surprisingly the village was aghast and the finger was pointed at Sir Charles Ponsonby, who as churchwarden was suspected of engineering the deal. We never ourselves got to the bottom of this, although Maurice Hugh-Jones intimated to me that the Marriotts had earlier purchased a piece of land which controlled entry to the house from the village and which, remaining in their hands, considerably reduced the market value of the property.

However this might be, there is no doubt that Marriott's long incumbency had made things very difficult for his successors. They had, initially, nowhere in the village to live. Although the villagers had been restive under the dominance of Marriott, he had shaped their expectations of what a Rector should be like, expectations which could not be satisfied by his modest successors. The people were totally unused to making any contribution to the upkeep of the church. More seriously still, having lived under a sort of theocracy, they were glad not to have to go to church again and only a faithful few continued to do so. In addition, the Rector's responsibilities were increased by his ministry being extended to the estate villages of Glympton and Kiddington, higher up the river Glyme.

H A T Bennett left very soon after we arrived and I remember that Matthew was christened in May 1953 by a very old retired priest, who we were afraid would drop him as he was a very substantial baby. Margy's brother, Rob, was one godfather and Ian Crombie another, and Phoebe had consented to be godmother.

Soon afterwards Struan Robertson was appointed Rector. He was a large vigorous man with a healthy tan who, it was said, had suffered badly under the Japanese. It was for this reason that he had been sent to a small country parish. He was a splendid man, if deeply affected by his experiences, and at one stage was suspected of removing sums from the church collection. In consequence I was appointed Treasurer of the PCC because it was thought that I should be able tactfully to look after the church's money without suggesting that he was in any way suspected. I doubt if he ever did remove anything and, if he did, it would only have been temporary, but in any case we remained on very good terms. He preached vigorous sermons, one of which was among the best I have heard in Wootton church. It was on the Good Samaritan and he brought the story vividly to life by likening the road down to Jericho from Jerusalem to the steep descent down to Milford Bridge over the Dorn.

Meanwhile Nell was rapidly developing the command of language which was to be her hallmark in later life. I was fascinated by the rapidity with which she learned to talk. Although she would not use an expression until she was sure she had got it right, she would employ a figure of speech before she could possibly have heard it, for instance the subjunctive: 'if I were to do that . . .' Puzzlement about this led me to half anticipate Chomsky's theory of 'universal grammar'.

When she was four it was time to think about her schooling. The obvious place for a bright girl was the Oxford Girls' High School and we had learnt that if a girl could gain entry to the infant school, she could continue for her entire school career, bypassing the normal entrance exam at eleven. So we entered her for the 4+ exam. This meant taking her in for an interview and various tests which took a whole morning. When Margy collected her, as she remembers, Nell's eyes were 'like poached eggs', and she reported with Nell-like precision: 'some of the time I cried, but most of the time I just moaned'. Later in the day, the school rang up and said 'We didn't feel that Nell did herself justice this morning, Could you bring her in tomorrow morning when we do the boys?' Margy at this critical moment resorted to bribery, a promised ice cream, I think it was. This and the fact that Margy was allowed to sit in the garden worked, and Nell was duly admitted. She stayed in the High School for a record fourteen years.

From then on I took Nell, and in due time the other children, into school in the mornings and went on to a civilised breakfast in Keble. There was less traffic than now, but it was aggravated by the habit of British Rail closing the level crossing before the Pear Tree at 8.50 each morning for a train carrying iron ore from South Wales, thus ensuring that there would be a queue all the way down the Woodstock Road. Relief from this was owed to Dr Beeching whose report abolished that particular line and the level crossing with it. The queue down the Woodstock Road created a moral problem which never ceased to exercise me. There would always be cars waiting to enter the main stream from the side roads. If in a moment of generosity I allowed one in the grateful driver would, in turn, let another car in at the next intersection, so that by the time one had reached the bottom of the Woodstock Road, there were six or seven more cars ahead of one than there would otherwise have been. And one had to bear in mind that the sacrifice one had voluntarily accepted, was involuntarily shared by the drivers behind one. I came to the conclusion that the harm that would have been incurred by drivers totally unable to get into the main stream was far greater than any suffered by the delay to those already in it.

One of the reasons for Nell's initial failure at the 4+ examination was that she was not used to the company of children other than her siblings. This was remedied when the Stott's came to the village in 1958. To begin with they lived in a house in West End halfway up the steep hill which led out of the village to Woodstock. They had two children, Martin and Frances, a little younger than Nell and Matthew. They would come along the bottom road to play with our children accompanied only by their yellow Labrador, Candy, there being then very little traffic. After some months they bought the cottages on the hill at the top of the path to Hordley which led past the back of Bridge House. These two cottages were, like most in the village, extremely primitive. Mr and Mrs Moss, who lived in one of them, used to have to collect their water from the river at the bottom of the valley. The Stott's modernised the two cottages and added a wing at a right angle to them. House and garden commanded a view across the valley and they purchased the field down to the river, so that there would never be any risk of the view being obstructed. Over the years they created an enchanting garden taking full advantage of the sloping site and the resources of local stone which lay all about.

We were now their closest neighbours at the foot of the path which they would take into the village. On the other side from us it was bordered by what once may have been a quarry with pine trees growing from the top of it. Hence for our children it was going 'up the rocks' and for theirs 'down the rocks'.

Frank and Clare Stott were a complete contrast. Frank was a boffin of the highest rank, whose speciality was the application of physics to medicine, largely through the invention of apparatus. His best known achievement was the construction of the oxygen apparatus for the ascent of Everest in 1953. He was a small, quiet man. Clare Stott was a nurse (a 'nightingale', of which she was very proud) currently college nurse at Merton. She was lively, energetic and sociable. She was very Irish, 'bog Irish' as she insisted. She was a lapsed Catholic, but her Catholic formation was very evident. The cause of her lapsing was, it appeared, the introduction of the English Mass. 'It didn't seem to mean anything any longer', she said in a splendid Irishism, 'now that you could understand it.'

Our life was enriched further by the arrival of Robin and Dorothy McInnes at the Mill House on the other side of the bridge. Yorke had finally left the Mill House for North Leigh where he was beginning the restoration of another derelict property. At this point his wife left him, having had enough of living in houses which were in the process of being restored until they were finally liveable in, at which point her husband moved to another property to begin the process all over again.

Robin McInnes was Medical Superintendent of the Warneford Hospital, the leading mental hospital in Oxford. As such, before the creation of a Chair in Psychiatry, he was the leading psychiatrist in the place. He was to be a great help to me in my increasing involvement with mental health problems in the University. Dorothy, who still revisited annually her roots in Orkney, was a gentle but very shrewd and perceptive individual, who was an accomplished painter who exhibited regularly with the Bury Knowle Art Group in Headington, but showed her originality more particularly in the design of decorative tiles.

With these accessions the social life of Wootton became even more agreeable and at this time and for the whole of our time there, there was a round of drinks parties to which 'old village' and incomers were equally invited. Mary Parsons' initial invitation was the first of many. It does seem to have been the case that Wootton was particularly successful in integrating incomers. This was helped by the fact that few of them were 'second-homers'. They lived in the village and wanted to be part of it. And what they wanted to be part of was an authentic North Oxfordshire village. It was true that it was largely a dormitory village. Most of the incomers worked in Oxford, but this in itself was not a divisive factor because so too did most of the indigenous population. Nevertheless the central village institutions, the Church, the pubs and the Flower Show were enabled to survive and even to flourish through the support of some at least of the incomers and their expertise. The Flower Show was a case in point. For the first twenty years of our residence in Wootton the chairman was Cyril Brown and the secretary Harold Cleaver. Cyril Brown farmed at Manor Farm, situated on the north western edge of the village and Harold Cleaver at Home Farm, just over the river from us. They were both immediately recognisable as old-style

Oxfordshire farmers and meetings proceeded at a suitably pastoral pace. Men and women were automatically segregated so that the men could concentrate on such matters as vegetables and the men's bowling and the women on flowers and cakes and home-made wines and, of course, teas. The men's bowling was for a pig and Maurice Hugh-Jones remembered that in the 1930s Edwin Ponsonby would attend the meeting and to all appearance go to sleep until there was mention of men's bowling, at which point he would show why he was there and announce 'I shall, of course, be happy to donate a pig'.

At the annual general meeting there were, of course, two sets of minutes, one of the last ordinary meeting and one of the last AGM. On one occasion Harold Cleaver read the minutes of the last AGM, as always painfully slowly, and when at last he came to the end he discovered that they were the minutes of the last AGM but one and had to begin all over again. The Flower Show was one of the oldest in the county, having been founded in 1877, and it was as if nothing had changed in all those years. Then in 1972 both Cyril Brown and Harold Cleaver died and the Show was not held out of respect for the two men who for so many years had been identified with it. It might well have died at that point, but the next year saw it revived under a new chairman and a new secretary, both of whom were incomers.

The chief agent in the recreation of the Flower Show was Mike Hallam who was first secretary and then chairman of the Show and over the years has so identified himself with the village as to become the local historian. He tells me that Cyril Brown was a member of the committee from 1932 and, incredibly, Harold Cleaver from 1919. He and his successor have ensured that the Flower Show has continued to flourish and has been kept technologically up to date, while losing nothing of its local colour.

Another village institution we became acquainted with at the very beginning of our life in Wootton was Tina Cleaver, the village postwoman. She was a splendid figure of a woman who rode a bicycle more slowly than seemed humanly possible. Her round started at West End and ended at Lower Dornford where Mary Parsons provided the last and most substantial of the refreshments which punctuated her journey. Given that her progress round the village was slow Tina saw it as part of her job to expedite communication so far as possible. We were fortunately fairly early in her progress and I remember two occasions of her doing this. On one occasion she arrived at Bridge House and asked if she could use the telephone. She had a postcard for Mary Parsons from her daughter Caroline who was away on holiday. Mary would be anxious for news of her and she wanted to read it for her over the phone. Another was when a group of men were working on the bridge. 'Bill,' said Tina to one of them, 'I have a telegram for you. Shall I open it and read it to you?' These practices would not have been approved by Frank Dallard, the postmaster, who also ran the shop, but Tina was at odds with Dallard, who was in any case a difficult character. He was a sort of Malvolio: unsure of his status in the village, he held himself aloof from everyone and plainly resented Tina's easy popularity.

It became evident to me early on that I had married a North Country housewife with a Dutch flair for interior decoration. Bridge House was a distinctly difficult house to run and the rooms awkward to furnish and to decorate. Margy was helped by the circumstance that most of the older generation of women in the village had in their younger days been employed in the Rectory where high standards had been insisted on by the Marriotts. Margy's final solution to the problems presented by Bridge House was to employ two 'treasures', Mrs Buswell to be in charge of the ground floor and Mrs Harper of the upper floors. Both were near neighbours and glad of employment close to home. Of the two, Mrs Buswell was the more distinctive. She had an enormous goitre which did not appear to worry her at all and had a daughter ('our Ettie') and granddaughter ('our Rachel') who were almost indistinguishable and shared their mother's/ grandmother's goodnaturedness. Mrs Buswell belonged to a long established Wootton family and managed to be on good terms with everyone in the village – a notable achievement.

The house being thus provided for it remained to find help with the children, and here too an ideal solution presented itself. We were put in touch with an agency in Lucerne which arranged for girls to spend a year with suitable families in England to learn the language. They were not strictly 'au pair' but came on a work permit which allowed them to share in the housework. There was no difficulty in arranging for English classes in Oxford, but I came to enjoy discovering or inventing rules for correct English speech and I like to think that I was their main teacher.

They were all very well brought up – more strictly than most English girls at that time – and we only once in a long succession had any problem, and that was with the one we became most attached to and who kept in touch with us later. Their presence enabled us to have two holidays a year, one with the children and one without. In the children's earlier years we took our holiday with the children in the Cornish port of Fowey where we were made to feel at home by an old friend of Margy's, Betty King, whose father was the local doctor and who herself had taught in a local primary school. Dr King's surgery was on the edge of the harbour and he and Betty had a boat moored there which we were free to use. (It was when rowing this boat across the harbour that, as recounted in 'The War Years' I encountered Chief Petty Officer John Ham, previously of HMS *Oxford Castle*, latterly boatman to the Customs and Excise).

Apart from the local connection, Fowey was a splendid place for a family holiday. There were two excellent beaches for swimming and sunbathing, Readymoney and Polridmouth, a number of coastal walks and, apart from its tourist attractions, Fowey was a lively working port with ships up to 5,000 tons serving the China Clay industry. This meant that, even in bad weather, there was always something of interest to watch.

On the strength of my naval connections Dr King got me made a member of the Royal Fowey Yacht Club. As an 'out of port' member it did not cost me much and I gave it up after a few years when it became clear that my vague dream of having a yacht of my own was not going to be realised. My only achievement during Regatta week nevertheless was not to be despised. We had been to the Boat Show to find a craft suitable to navigate the river Glyme and capable of being transported to the sea-side. The answer was a Klepper canoe. With a hull of rubberised canvas supported by a wooden framework it was stoutly constructed. Designed to be paddled by two persons, it could accommodate two children as passengers. Among the regular events in Regatta Week was 'First Up On The Tide'. At low tide the little port of Lerryn, on a tributary of the Fowey River, was high and dry and the object of the competition was to be first to reach Lerryn on the incoming tide. The competing craft had to carry at least four people, but otherwise nothing was specified as to the type of craft it should be. So Betty King and I entered the Klepper with

Nell and Matthew as passengers. The shallow draft of the Klepper enabled us to get ahead of the fleet from the start and the struggle was going to be to maintain our lead until the finish. This proved more difficult than we had anticipated. We were followed closely by four lusty young men who had adopted a radically different solution to the problem set by the race. Their craft was a stout wooden boat which they propelled as if it were a punt by standing up in it and urging it forward by main force. In this way they could make some progress over the river bottom without having to rely entirely on the incoming tide, as we had to do. So far as comparative strength was concerned it was plain that Betty and I were no match for these young competitors. Moreover if they caught up with us, their wooden vessel would severely damage our canoe. Fortunately for us, as time went on, the tide came in more quickly and fast enough to take us clear to the finish.

As this story indicates, the success of our family holidays in Fowey owed a lot to Betty King. She found a succession of agreeable houses for us to rent and introduced us to people and places of interest. She was never at a loss for conversation and when introduced to someone new she would set out to discover who it might be that this person knew who also knew someone known to someone who knew Betty! It always amazed us how few moves Betty needed to complete this game. A corollary of this was that she remembered everyone she had ever met, and moreover anyone who that individual had ever mentioned; so that many years later Betty would ask 'how is that woman getting on who your friend . . . talked about and who was about to start a business', and so on. And we would not have the faintest idea who either of these individuals might be. She was extremely knowledgeable about the history and pre-history of Cornwall and was always prepared into advanced old age to drive hazardously along narrow high-banked Cornish lanes to attend meetings on these subjects.

The sad thing was that Betty had a great deal of intellectual energy but none of the mental discipline that she needed to develop it. Her mother took the old-fashioned view that a gentlewoman did not require a job or training to prepare her for one and it was not until she was middle-aged that Betty herself decided to train as a primary school teacher and then to practise as one. But her interests were far wider than that required and she was left with a hunger for information and virtually no sense of relevance. But our Fowey holidays owed a great deal to her.

Meanwhile our children were steadily growing up. Nell was flourishing at the High School and Matthew achieved the distinction of becoming the last boy in the Junior School when it became girls only. Kate and Clare went in turns to the Crescent School and Matthew became a 'baby dragon'. This meant that our family was represented at different times on both sides of the annual football match between the Crescent and the baby dragons. As it happened we were never on the winning side. The game was played with two balls to make it easier for all the players to have contact with a ball. That the purpose of the game was to score goals was rarely appreciated by more than one player in each game and the side which had such a player won. On the occasions when Kate and Clare played for the Crescent, the dragons had such a player and duly won. When Matthew played for the dragons it was the other way round and the Crescent won.

Within the family it soon became evident that the one who lost out was Matthew. Not only was he the only boy but he was number two and suffered from Nell's assumption of superiority. Nell was extremely competent and had the advantage not only of two years in age but of the fact that girls grow up quicker. We sometimes wished that he would exploit his only advantage of greater physical strength, but he was a good-natured child and refrained from hitting her. Nell was always extraordinarily reasonable. When asked to do something that she was disinclined to do, she would ask for a reason and when she was told why it was necessary or desirable to do that particular thing she would more often than not say, 'yes, I see', and do it. Matthew, by contrast, was totally unimpressed by reasons. He could not see that an act's being reasonable had any relevance to his doing it. Matthew was always especially fond of Kate who was less than two years younger and was small for her age and a particularly enchanting child. She was the occasion of the family's only victory at the Dragon School Sports. Entered for the Little Visitors' race, on account of her diminutive size, and in spite of Margy's warning, 'I shouldn't do that if I were you,' she was given a generous start with the result that at the start she shot off and was at the finishing line before most of the others had started.

Kate was also the occasion of a vivid spiritual experience on my part. I was working in my study writing a review of C A Campbell's *On Selfhood and Godhood*, when I was aware of someone very slowly climbing up the ladder which I had thought was childproof. I held my breath until Kate was safely at the top of it, and, after such an effort, decided not to take her down again. Instead I found some transparencies and a viewer, placed her in an armchair and showed her how to look at the pictures. I then returned to my work and forgot all about her. Eventually I came to with alarm and remembered about Kate. I looked round and there she was fast asleep with the transparencies scattered around her, and lying in the chair beside her *On Selfhood and Godhood* and *Finite and Infinite*. I had at that moment a vivid awareness of this small fragile creature being held in life by her Creator. In order to preserve that moment I went and fetched my camera and took a photograph which I still possess (*see illustration no. 20*).

When they were small, we would both read to them at bedtime and do our best to sing to them. Margy remembered a lot of nursery rhymes, but all I could manage was the The Berkshire Tragedy and On Ilkley Moor Baht'at. It was only later that I learned that they found both of these rather alarming. At one stage Kate added interest to being kissed goodnight by stipulating the colour of the kiss, so we had to provide blue kisses, red kisses, and even black kisses according to her fancy.

Nell's reasonableness did not always extend to consistency in choice of clothes. Margy was exasperated when, having involved Nell in the choice of some article of clothing, she found that, once purchased, she refused to wear it. So she devised a pro forma which ran: 'I [Nell] like this [pair of shoes] and will wear them', which Nell was required to fill in and sign at the time of purchase. We were amused to return from a brief excursion during which we had left Nell, then aged twelve, in charge to come upon a number of such forms, duly completed: I [Kate/Clare] like [baked beans] and will eat [them].

During all this time when the children were young the family still contained Dido and it became evident that, having been got in order to provide company for Margy, she now played an important role as a member of the family, lower in the hierarchy than the children, but to be treated with a degree of consideration not less than they themselves deserved. Like all Labradors, she assumed her position in the family quite naturally. On one occasion this proved an embarrassment. One Sunday morning in summer we were all in church and were beginning the final hymn, when I noticed Dido hesitating in the church door. Rather than attempt to shoo her off, which I thought would attract attention, I decided to invite her into our pew which was just opposite the door. She came in quietly as I had anticipated, but I had left out of account her tail. No sooner was she in our pew and reunited with the family than her tail wagged furiously, thump, thump against the front and back of the pew causing the members of the congregation to look round to see what was causing this commotion. Since Dido was entirely out of sight they could see nothing but the six members of the Mitchell family singing lustily and doing their best to look entirely disengaged from the rumpus.

There was no means of keeping a dog in our garden, so Dido could not be prevented from wandering round the village, and it was impossible to control her diet. One kindly village woman said to Margy, 'I always gives her a choccy biscuit and, if I haven't got any of them, I butter a piece of bread and put some jam on it.' Margy said it was very kind of her, but couldn't she look beyond those pleading eyes and notice the expanding tummy.

If Dido belonged to anyone it was to the parents and it was not long before the children each wanted a cat. Our dogs were always, following Dido, given classical names, but cats were named after their colour – Smoky, Misty, Murky. The first and most notable of these was Smoky. He was a large grey cat – British blue, I think it was, correctly speaking. He hunted voraciously and his most spectacular victim was a fully grown stoat which we found one morning on the kitchen floor. A stoat would be more than a match for any but a very robust cat.

Smoky and Dido between them regularly presented me with a moral problem. Dido was also interested in mice and when Smoky caught one, Dido, wherever in the garden she was, seemed to sense that this had happened. Smoky's undoing was that he could not resist playing with the mouse before consuming it and this gave Dido time to discover its whereabouts and swallow it. I was sometimes in a position to prevent this. Did I have a duty to do so? On the one hand

Dido was plainly stealing Smoky's mouse. On the other from the mouse's point of view it was preferable to be swallowed instantaneously by Dido than to be played with and then eaten by Smoky. Eventually I decided that it was none of my business and let nature take its course.

Such was our domestic life at Wootton while the children were growing up. It was a happy time. I was working very hard with a heavier tutorial burden than most of my colleagues. Margy was working hard too, but whereas I enjoyed my life at Wootton as a respite from my academic life, for Margy the domestic life was the only one she had. Whether she felt it at the time I doubt, but in retrospect she certainly resents her exclusion from the social elements of academic life. Whereas I dined not infrequently, she, as a wife, was not entitled to dine in college, except on carefully rationed occasions. I might invite a woman as my guest, but not my wife. If I wanted to dine Margy I must persuade a colleague to invite her. The rationale for this was set out by Hugh Trevor-Roper later at Oriel. There was, he maintained no element of anti-feminism in it. The principle was simply that we did not allow as guests the members of any class whose members were likely to be invited too often. When there was a college feast it was, as a concession, customary to invite the fellows' wives to a meal of their own in the Warden's Lodging, although this practice was open to the suspicion that it was designed to enable the Fellows to be driven home by their wives. The only time when this principle was not observed was the year in which I was Senior Proctor (1956–7). Then I was often invited to celebrations in other colleges together with my wife. Margy's enjoyment of university as distinct from College Feasts was diminished when she was told by Mrs Williams (the wife of Bill Williams, the Warden of Rhodes House) that when the Vice-Chancellor was a bachelor (as Alec Smith was) the Senior Proctor's wife took precedence as First Lady in the University.

Margy could not complain that, in marrying her, I had deprived her of a career to which she was strongly attracted. She had a degree in music, but the only job that was possibly on offer at the time of our marriage was as a member of the WRAC band.

There was one respect in which I am afraid that I was at fault. I would sometimes come home after a day spent on tutorials, college or faculty meetings, etc., and when she asked me to 'tell my day' I would say 'Oh no, I have been talking all day'! Fairly early on I felt that I ought to involve her in my academic work and tried on her a lecture on 'Kant's Categorical Imperative'. The result, for the first time in her life, was a serious migraine; and migraines from then on became a regular occurrence, although fortunately never so severe as to be totally disabling.

I think I must be by nature monogamous for, although I was by no means indifferent to sex and always enjoyed the company of women, I never felt tempted to look elsewhere for sexual satisfaction. Hence I was never aware at all, nor even suspected, that some of my colleagues were as promiscuous as their biographies reveal them to have been. I counted Iris Murdoch as a friend and was attracted to her as a person and as a thinker but I never thought of her as a possible sex object. It is true that, having learnt later how many partners she had I do feel a slight resentment that she never attempted to seduce me. In retrospect there was only one occasion when she might have pondered it. After a meeting of the Metaphysicals, which usually finished at about ten, she suggested that we go out for a drink together. We went to a pub and had a beer and then I said that I had to get out to Wootton and that was that. Either, as is more probable, the thought never occurred to her, or she decided that I was not seducible or worth seducing. Nevertheless I treasure a note from her when I sent her half a chapter on the *Sovereignty of Good* and she replied 'A word from you always means a lot to me.' But perhaps she said that to everyone.

Life in Wootton: The Church

In a 'village appraisal' carried out in 1994/5 on the basis of questionnaires it was concluded that 'very roughly for one third of the population religious observance is a regular part of their lives, for another third it serves for the expression of public or private grief or the celebration of key moments in life, and for the remaining third it is of no personal significance.'

During our time in Wootton church attendance depended very much on the personality and outlook of the incumbent. This was dramatically indicated toward the end of our residence when attendance first sank to the lowest ever recorded under a Rector who reduced his commitment to the village to the minimum possible and then soared to hitherto unbelievable heights under a Rector who believed that his mission extended to the entire population. Jo Biddlestone, the former, once confessed that he was 'more at home with things than with people'. His role was limited to conducting services and these were kept as short and simple as possible. I was churchwarden at the time and regularly read the lessons. When I suggested that we ought to increase the number of readers his reply was 'It isn't necessary', and in general his motto was 'Nothing is possible unless it's necessary'. Things came to a head when my youngest daughter Clare wanted to be married in the church where she had been christened. She and her bridegroom, Hugh Richards, wanted to make the occasion a truly Christian celebration of their union. To this end they took trouble about the choice of hymns and Clare wanted a musical friend of hers to sing a solo. Biddlestone said firmly that this was not necessary and insisted on choosing the hymns himself. The chief matter of dispute concerned Clare's wish that the marriage should be conducted by my brother-in-law George Stokes, who had married me and Margy and Clare's sister, Kate. George was at the time Vicar of Sonning-on-Thames after a career as army chaplain, which ended with his enjoying the splendiferous title of 'Temporary Assistant Chaplain-general Libya/Tripolitania'. He was a very experienced priest who had a gift for making a congregation feel fully part of the proceedings. Biddlestone agreed to his taking part in the service, but it became apparent that he took this to mean that he could only pronounce the words that constituted the marriage. Another bone of contention was the signing of the register. At Kate's wedding this had been done in full view of the congregation in the chancel, but when Clare suggested this, Biddlestone insisted that it was not possible and that it should take place in the vestry at the West end of the church from which the bride and groom could not process out of the church in view of the congregation. We invited Biddlestone and his wife to meet George and his wife, my sister, at lunch, so that they could have a friendly informal discussion of the service. Biddlestone came and maintained an obstinate silence throughout. It became clear to me that if Biddlestone had his way, my daughter's wedding would be ruined, and I was not prepared to allow this. Since there was no doubt that the Rector was entitled to decide how things were to be done in his church, the only alternative was to hold the wedding in a neighbouring church after obtaining a special licence, so I went to see the Vicar of Combe who agreed to George's conducting the wedding in his church. When I went to see Biddlestone to tell him about the arrangement, he said 'You are blackmailing me.' I replied 'I am not blackmailing you. I am simply telling you what will happen if you continue to obstruct my daughter's wishes for her wedding.' Biddlestone then said that he could not prevent his churchwarden's daughter being married in the church where she was christened, so he would let George Stokes conduct the entire service and he himself would not be there.

The marriage took place on the 12 September 1981 and was a most happy occasion. It happened to be Flower Show day and I was President, a purely formal role which required me to make a speech after the prize-giving. We had learnt that our neighbours in West End, Mr and Mrs Branchflower had also been married on Flower Show day fifty years earlier in 1931. So Clare in her bridal dress, the bride of 1981, presented the bride of 1931 with a bouquet to celebrate the happy coincidence.

It is hard in retrospect to blame Biddlestone for his unreasonable conduct. He should never have been ordained. During his time the organ was restored and the pipes needed decorating. This he did himself, an indication of what he should have been. On his retirement, Wootton was temporarily joined to Woodstock and the Rector of Woodstock arranged that his curate, Leonard Doolan, should be responsible for Wootton, Glympton and Kiddington. This was a great blessing and was in the circumstances received by us as a miracle as Doolan set himself with great energy to revitalise the parish. Having read classics at St Andrews and theology at Ripon College, Cuddesdon, he was well qualified and he had an additional qualification which was shared by his wife. His father owned a hotel in Ayrshire and he had experience of catering on a large scale. So had his wife who was an expert cook. With these assets Doolan had no doubt that, as Rector, he had responsibility for the whole village and not only those who were regular churchgoers. Early on in his time as Rector he remarked to me that he had changed his mind about Establishment, which gave him the right to knock on every door in the village, although, of course, the occupiers did not have to open to him.

He became convinced that it was not a coincidence that the traditional date of the Flower Show was the same as that of the church patronal festival, so that he could celebrate the latter with a lunch in the marquee which would remain empty in the grounds of Wootton place until the following Monday. So he and his wife Lynn prepared a lunch in the marquee after the service for the patronal festival. Similarly he took every opportunity to link church festivities with village celebrations open to all. It was a deliberately old-fashioned approach. People were treated as church members unless they contracted out.

At the same time he offered the services of the church to any who might need them. When Clare lost her second child, Harriet, in a cot death at the age of five weeks, he took pains to make the funeral service as comforting to the grieving parents as he could, involving them fully in the preparation of it. A while later, when I showed him my contribution to *Philosophers Who Believe* and confessed to him that I had been deeply affected by the experience of re-visiting Phoebe's life and death, he offered to conduct a brief memorial service for her in the church, since, having missed her funeral, I had had no opportunity to commend her soul to God. The effect of this expansive ministry was astonishing. Church attendance which had declined to thirteen in the time of Biddelstone rose to seventy-five on a number of occasions.

In spite of Doolan's attempt to bring them together, the Flower Show remained independent of the Church, but there were two other occasions which were organised by church members for the benefit of the church and which were felt to be village occasions to which many people contributed who were not regular church attenders. One was the Church Sale held in the Village Hall in December, at which the efforts of church members were regularly supplemented by other village people, and Flower Festivals, which were held every other year, at which gardens were opened and flower arrangements erected in the church by the entire village. Although these events were organised by the church and proceeds went to church funds, no one would think of them as purely a church occasion. Only those who were vehemently opposed to the church would refuse to take part and it seems that there were very few such people.

A dispute occurred in the 1980s which affected the church financially. In Biddlestone's time a retired policeman had been appointed Verger on the agreement that he occupied a cottage opposite the church rent-free, which was made possible by the fact that the Church rented the cottage from a village charity at a comparatively low rent. For some years the scheme worked very well. The Verger mowed the lawn in front of the church and he and his wife prepared the church for services and looked after the crosses and communion vessels. As rents rose throughout the country, the charity, the Parrot and Lee Trust under a new and efficient chairman, John Harwood, who was chief executive of Oxfordshire County Council, undertook a review of the rents of their various village properties. In the course of this review they discovered that the Church rented the Verger's cottage at a preferential rate. As a charity they reckoned that they had a duty to raise the maximum possible sum from their properties and therefore must charge the Church a commercial rate. I argued as one of the Churchwardens that it was likely that the founders of the charity, both previous rectors, had intended to give the Church a preferential rate for the Verger's cottage opposite the church. It was known that the cottage had been occupied by a Mrs Lloyd who acted as Verger from 1900 and she certainly could not have afforded very much in rent. Unfortunately I could not produce any written evidence for this opinion and the charity decided against it. The most they could do was raise the rent in stages. The point would come when the Church could not afford it and notice had to be given to the Verger, thus ending a tradition which had lasted at least from the beginning of the century. It was very much resented by the Verger who had made some improvements to the house which he had assumed would be his home until he retired. He was unlikely to find anywhere else that he could afford in Wootton. Fortunately he qualified for some affordable housing which the District Council was in the process of building.

This happened while Robert Farman was Rector and greatly distressed him. Sadly, as otherwise he and his wife Roberta, soon to be ordained herself, were devotedly maintaining the church's life.

Life in Wootton: Wildlife

It would be impossible to write about life at Bridge House, Wootton without mention of the wildlife. Neither Margy nor I reckoned to be knowledgeable about wild life, but we liked to know what other creatures shared the garden with us and in this we were greatly helped by Bruce Campbell, our local ornithologist. Whenever he came into the garden he drew our attention to a nest which we had not noticed and he patiently took pains to answer our queries. There was one occasion when we thought we heard a nightingale in our meadow, but when he listened to it he identified it for us as a sedge warbler. Even he, however, was defeated by marsh tits and willow tits, which were frequently to be seen outside the kitchen window. They could only, he told us, be distinguished by their song. Sometimes, when sitting in my study, overlooking a large viburnum bush, I would see a flight of long-tailed tits drifting past and one year there was one of their nests in a hawthorn bush outside the kitchen door at the other end of the house, beautifully shaped and well out of the way of our cats.

Somewhere downstream from us there was a kingfisher's nest and we were regularly visited by one or two kingfishers. We did not own the bit of land on the other side of the river, but we always tidied it up, being careful to leave one or two dead willow branches for the kingfishers to perch upon. One morning I was looking out of the kitchen window across the river when I thought I saw something moving up and down near the water's edge which I could not identify. I got my binoculars and it turned out to be a common snipe probing the mud with its long beak. I raised my binoculars a bit and there, just a foot or so above it perched on a small willow branch was a kingfisher. I should like Bruce to have seen the two together.

We always treasured two stories about Bruce. He used to broadcast on a naturalist's programme from BBC Bristol and on one occasion while he was doing this a hoopoe, a rare visitor, was sighted in a valley near Hordley just below the house where the Campbells lived. It was sighted not by the celebrated ornithologist but by Dorothy McInnes, wife of our resident psychiatrist. The other event was distinctly touching. One of Bruce's tasks was to keep a count of swans in Oxfordshire and it always seemed appropriate to us that our local swans, always known to us as George and Maria, used to nest just below Hordley Farm House, where Bruce and Margaret lived for many years from where they would regularly visit us. The time came, however, when the Campbells had to leave Hordley and they built themselves a small house at the west end of the village overlooking a bend in the river Glyme. In the spring of that year for the first time the swans moved their nest from Hordley to that very bend. It was evident to us, as to the rest of the village, that they were following Bruce, particularly as they stayed there in subsequent years.

Our position just below the bridge on the River Glyme clearly meant that we were familiar with fish and other water creatures. There were always trout just below the bridge and on one occasion we learnt just how many there were and how many other fish. The Duke decided to 'electric-fish' our stretch of the river and they found eight trout, two pike and three eels. We knew about the pike but we had never seen the eels.

We had two encounters with stoats, both in their way equally remarkable. There was the one already mentined found dead on the kitchen floor. I took it in to the University Museum to see if they would like to stuff it and they did. The other was more dramatic. I heard a scuffling on the river below the bridge and saw two moorhens shepherding a stoat down-river: whenever the stoat tried to dart to one side or the other, one of the moorhen shooed it back into midstream and continued in this fashion until a hundred yards or so below our territory when it was allowed to escape onto the land. One wouldn't expect a cat to be a match for a stoat, let alone moorhens to be able to see one off.

On one occasion I was sitting reading by the water's edge, when a family of weasels paraded just next to me. An adult weasel – I assumed the mother – lined up a row of young weasels and swam with them one by one to the other side and then took them all off inland. Bruce found this sufficiently interesting to insist on my writing it up for *The Countryman* which he edited.

We learned early on that Wootton was famous for crayfish, until the native species were driven out by American invaders. The children adopted the local custom to catch crayfish by stretching netting across a wire ring with a long piece of string attached to it, placing a stinking piece of meat in the middle of it and throwing the whole thing into the river. After an interval the knack is to yank it out quickly while, hopefully, the crayfish are clinging to it. The son of our neighbours, Martin Stott, became expert enough at this to sell crayfish regularly to a local restaurant.

The part played by crayfish in the local consciousness is illustrated by the account given by Liz Parsons of school prayers at Begbroke Convent School. Her mother, Mary Parsons, a staunch church-woman, felt she ought to find out if the nuns at Begbroke made any attempt to indoctrinate the children. Liz explained. 'We start school with prayers every morning. Reverend Mother recites something and we all say "crayfish" then she says something else and we say "crayfish" again.'

Mary Parsons concluded that, if conversion was intended, it was not very effective.

We had a resident toad and a resident hedgehog, but most conspicuous were molehills, though we rarely saw the moles. They represented a constant challenge. If we wanted to have a lawn at all, it was necessary to control the moles. Ideally one would avoid trapping them and simply find some means of driving them away. I tried one promising method by attaching a rubber tube to the exhaust of the motor mower and inserting it into a hole. It was worth doing simply for the aesthetic effect of hundreds of puffs of blue-grey smoke appearing all over the lawn. But it did not deter the moles. I tried placing poison pellets in the runs, but they had no effect either. Eventually and reluctantly I decided that there was no alternative to the traditional metal traps. The problem was then where to put the trap. Instructions told one to put the trap into the main run. One was also told to wear gloves, the moles being very sensitive to smell, and pour water over the trap once it was in place.

I did all these things without success, until our part-time gardener Mr Grant came in. Mr Grant was a shepherd from the neighbour-hood of Aberdeen who had come south many years ago and was now retired in the village. 'I'll hae hun,' he exclaimed at once and went some distance away. He did not wear gloves, nor did he pour water on the trap, but twenty minutes later there was a mole in the trap.

After that lesson I became quite good at catching moles, but I discovered that the best plan was to seek a compromise. So long as the resident mole was content to enjoy the very extensive accommodation available under our lawn with only minimal extra molehills I would leave him be and be content with brushing the soil away. A further reason for this was that if I removed one mole, its place would always be taken by another mole, which might not be better.

We saw water voles but were disappointed not to see otters. The first year we were in Bridge House we had the otter hunt come through our garden on their way upriver, but they must have drawn a blank as they never came again. The closest I came to seeing an otter was in our first winter (1951) when in the meadow below Hordley I saw what were clearly the tracks of an otter in the snow.

Although it did not happen actually within our territory one other episode was remarkable. I was walking our two Labradors, Psyche a large yellow one and Xanthe a smaller black one (whose name was given on the 'lucus a non lucendo' principle), when they went through a hedge into an adjoining field. Suddenly I heard a shrill yelping and through the hedge came Psyche with a full-grown hare in her mouth. I was extremely worried; what was I to do with an injured hare? I called Psyche to me and ordered her to sit and then drop it. Psyche obeyed and the hare immediately ran off at full speed with no sign of discomfort. I was astonished at this, but even more astonished at Pysche's having caught the hare at all. A Labrador could not possibly catch a hare in full flight. I can only assume that Xanthe disturbed the hare at rest and Psyche intercepted it before it really got into its stride. Psyche was a splendid beast and an important ritual for the whole family was bathing her. For this we had a tin bath on the river bank which we filled with water and a shampoo which I used for my psoriasis. A secondary effect of this was that the fleas would line up on her nose in an endeavour to escape. For this occasion the children would undress and rinse Psyche by pushing her into the river and keeping her there as long as necessary. From there she would joyfully emerge and shake herself vigorously in the neighbourhood of any fully dressed adult.

CHAPTER 9

Our double life

FOR TEN YEARS LIFE at Wootton was an idyll. It was a marvellous place for children to grow up and there was no difficulty in commuting to Oxford as I could easily avoid rush hour traffic. The difficulties began when the children started to go to school. It affected me minimally. I could take them in the morning and drop them off at or near their various schools and then have a leisurely breakfast in Keble. The difficulties affected Margy who had to collect them later in the day, especially as they came out at different times. This problem was mitigated by the Hares who lived in St Margaret's Road and had a splendid woman, called Heiney, who would look after their own and other children until they could be collected. But in addition there were games and dancing classes, not to mention the Dragon School which had its own idiosyncratic programme.

Margy finally protested that with four children at school in Oxford and a household to run, life at Wootton was becoming quite impossible and we must sell up and move into Oxford. When spring came round again, the prospect of leaving Bridge House became intolerable to contemplate and I sought desperately for some alternative. The obvious solution was to buy a house in Oxford and keep Bridge House as a country cottage but this would be wasteful and in any case, we couldn't afford it. So another possibility began to develop in my mind. Would it be practicable to buy a house in Oxford and live there in the Michaelmas and Hilary Terms, while moving to Wootton in the Trinity Term and the two vacations before and after it. This would give us the summer in Wootton and the winter in Oxford. The answer was that it would be possible, but only if we were able to let the houses when we were not occupying them. So I went to the University's Accommodation Office and asked them if they thought that American academic visitors, who normally came for a year, would be interested in renting our houses on the basis that they would start in Wootton and swap with us after spending two terms there and move into Oxford. I also went to James

Styles and Whitlock to ask if they would be prepared to handle the making of contracts and the collection of rents.

I received encouragement from both agencies and it remained to find a suitable house in Oxford. We were determined to get somewhere within walking distance of the schools. There would be no point in relocating if Margy still had to collect the children by car. With enormous good fortune we found a house for sale by auction in Charlbury Road. This was an ideal location, as it was within a few hundred yards of the Dragon School and at the other end of the road was the Girls' High School. The Crescent School where Clare and Kate started off was in Norham Gardens, and Wychwood School, where Kate ended up, in Bardwell Road, were all within easy walking distance.

Number 6, Charlbury Road, was a splendid house. It was pure 'Wimbledon Transitional' in Osbert Lancaster's masterly classification of English architectural styles. Built in 1906 (I believe for David Ross, Provost of Oriel and eminent moral philosopher) it had pebble-dash, half-timbering, stained glass and a large conservatory at the rear. The interior was grand with the rooms grouped round a spacious well with staircases mounting up to a ceiling three storeys up. It was as if designed for an Aldwych farce. It had a dining room and a drawing room overlooking the conservatory and the garden, and a large kitchen with a back door into the garden. There was to be found in it a large kitchen table which went with the house. Its plain deal surface bore incisions which were said to have been made by a former resident, A D Haigh, author of *The Attic Theatre* in the course of making models of an ancient Greek theatre.

Unlike Bridge House it was ideally suited to a large family. With seven bedrooms we had one spare which was eventually occupied by a friend of Clare's from the High School, Audrey Lasky, whose parents lived in Dorset. Audrey was large and good-natured and at 5'11" the tallest in the family. With Audrey we had five children enabling us to rival other large families in the neighbourhood, the Warnocks in the next street with five children and the Lloyds opposite with seven. (The size of academic families at this time fully bore out the findings of my research with the Wrens of HMS *King Alfred*.)

The task of setting up the new scheme was going to be awkward in any case, but two events complicated it considerably. The first was that I received an invitation to go to Princeton as a Visiting Professor in the Department of Religion for the Fall of 1963. This meant that we had to find tenants for both the houses at rather short notice. This we managed to do, but it meant that the scheme as planned could not begin until the autumn of 1964.

Nevertheless in order to be able to let 6 Charlbury Road we had to furnish it and this precipitated several months of intensive attendance at auctions in Oxford and the neighbourhood. Fortunately it was a period when people were leaving large houses for smaller ones and were getting rid of large pieces of furniture which one was able to buy comparatively cheaply. Margy became a regular patron of Messrs Brooks monthly sales until she finally achieved a peculiar sort of recognition. There was a woman who was almost always present who was known simply as 'Mrs G.' At the end of each sale the auctioneer would turn to her and say 'Mrs G, can I interest you in any of the items that are left?' Margy was delighted when on one occasion he turned to her and said 'How about you Mrs M?' At a sale in Witney she managed to equip Matthew's bedroom with a set of solid Victorian pieces which had evidently come from a country rectory. They had stood and could stand any amount of hard treatment.

When we returned from North America before Christmas it was evident that we should have to install central heating, but H&E Engineers could not undertake it until the spring. In the meanwhile we should have to make do with electric convection heaters. This was when the second event overtook us. That winter was the coldest on record, exceeding even 1946/7 in the length of time the temperature remained under zero. We had a convection heater in the hall, which managed to raise the temperature to a maximum of 36°. As it happened, with improvident generosity, I had invited one of my pupils, an Indian undergraduate called Jai Kala, to spend Christmas with us. I was profuse in my apologies, but he calmly replied 'Don't worry, my home is in the foothills of the Himalayas.'

Still worse was the plight of our tenants at Wootton. The pipes bringing water to the house had frozen solid and they were compelled to collect water in buckets from the river, which being swift-flowing had not frozen. Their situation was all the more grievous in that they had just returned to England from East Africa.

We did our best to relieve them. My physicist colleague at Keble, Dennis Shaw, came out to Wootton with me with a powerful battery and managed to unfreeze the water pipe within our own curtilage, but the local authority absolutely refused to allow us to extend the process for the comparatively short distance to the main.

Meanwhile Margy suffered most. The children were warm enough at school and I had no problem in College, but she was compelled to stay in the kitchen which was the only room that could be kept adequately heated. At Keble at that time the undergraduates' studies had electric fires, but the bedrooms were not heated and an American pupil of mine, Alex Wilde, complained bitterly. He was very tall and felt the cold badly. He had asked Davidge for extra bedclothes but he had been unable to provide any. Fortunately we had bought more than we needed and I had stored these in my college bedroom. I told Alex Wilde that I might be able to help him and when I opened the bedroom door and he saw piles of blankets, his eyes lit up as upon an Aladdin's cave. He helped himself and when next week I asked him how he was getting on he said that with a track suit and a pair of thick woollen stockings, together with a balaclava helmet and the College blankets supplemented by my own he was managing to keep reasonably warm.

Meanwhile on Port Meadow the children skated with friends on borrowed skates; and two of my brightest pupils, Christopher Clapham and Michael Rayner, walked to Islip and back on the River Cherwell discussing the essay topic for the coming week. With the onset of climate change it is unlikely that this venture will ever be repeated.

So we did not settle into our regular routine until the autumn of 1964. Each house was fully equipped with towels, bedclothes and everything domestic that the incoming family would need, so we did not have to transport these every six months. But we did have to pack the clothes all of us would need, not to mention the animals and their accessories, and also reserves of food.

The animals were in themselves quite a problem. At their maximum they comprised: the two Labradors, Psyche and Xanthe; three cats, Smokey the large British blue, which is to say grey, Misty and Murky; and two rabbits, one white and one brown, both laboratory bred. The cats had to go at the same time as the children, who were needed to keep them under some kind of control. Psyche, who was an extremely intelligent dog, posed something of a problem because as soon as she sensed what was afoot, she curled herself up below the front passenger's seat from which she refused to budge. She was not going to be left behind.

I remember that on the first occasion that we transported the rabbits to 6 Charlbury Road, I left them to run free in the garden as they did at Wootton and our neighbour warned us that we ought to cage them as a precaution against their predatory cat. Nevertheless I did let them loose, but kept a careful eye on them. In due course the neighbour's cat did indeed appear and made preparations for attack. Snowy at first did not notice, but when he did, he simply lollopped up to the cat and gave it a friendly butt. Whereupon the cat, disconcerted by this un-rabbit-like behaviour, took refuge in a neighbouring tree. Whether it was that Snowy was on friendly terms with our own cats, or whether, being bred in a laboratory, he had never learned to run away from cats, I was never able to decide.

The arrangement was designed to benefit us. We had two vacations and only one term in Wootton, so that the driving was much reduced and took place at the most favourable time of the year. But it turned out to be good for the tenants too in one important respect. When they moved into Wootton in early autumn they were immediately involved, if they were so inclined, in the social life of the village. They were known as 'the new Mitchells', and people would inquire of one another 'Have you met the new Mitchells yet?' Had they moved first into North Oxford, their welcome would have been nothing like as rapid. As it was by the time they moved into Oxford in the spring they had made their Oxford contacts. In addition we made it clear that we positively welcomed children, since our houses were geared to them, and we deliberately pitched the rent below what was commercially obtainable.

As time went on we had no need to seek out tenants. People heard about us by word of mouth and we were letting our houses to friends of friends. It is not surprising, therefore, that it was only in the early days that we had problems. The first problem we might have anticipated. We had an American evangelist who was said to be Billy Graham's left hand man. He was known as 'the singing evangelist' and was all of 6'9" tall. When they first visited Bridge House we pointed out that in most of the house he would have difficulty in standing up, but he expressed himself delighted with it and refused to be deterred. His wife was a real Southern belle, carefully made up in a manner that seemed to us a little incongruous for an evangelical wife. They were accompanied by his father, who was also a retired evangelist. They were a charming family, but had the calamitous effect of losing for us two of the three cleaners whom Margy had so carefully cultivated. At Wootton they taped up the windows with the consequence that Mrs Harper on the upstairs floors could not open the windows and shake out her mop but had to go downstairs and out of the front door in order to do so. This prompted her to resign. In Charlbury Road Margy was training up a younger, livelier woman who was distinctly promising, but she also resigned when the older evangelist insisted that she spent regular periods on her knees in prayer.

The other problem was of a different order. As I have already explained, our neighbours in Wootton were normally extremely hospitable and liked to be told in advance who the next 'New Mitchells' were, where they came from and what they did. Our nearest neighbours, across the bridge, at the Gloving House, were John and Peggy Pitt, and when I told them that our latest tenant was an American forester, named Briscoe, they were aghast. It appeared that some years ago John Pitt, now a Lecturer at the Forestry Department in Oxford, had been doing research in the upper reaches of the Amazon when they were asked to entertain an American forester who was interested in their work. He was there for an extended period and their visitor did nothing but complain and criticise despite all their efforts to interest and entertain him. When finally the day came for him to depart, they said to one another as his boat rounded the first bend, 'Thank God we shall never see that man again!' The Briscoes were a strange family and did not venture much outside the house, so that they were in the event no threat to the Pitts.

One of the advantages of 6 Charlbury Road was that I could walk into College and back again. We were there for enough of spring and autumn to be able to enjoy the changing seasons and appreciate the variety of planting at different times. As one approached the main gate on Parks Road one had a splendid view of Keble Chapel which steadily revealed its magnificent proportions.

In the Parks dogs were allowed to run freely, and I was able to benefit from the care I had taken at Wootton to train them properly. This I had done in true academic fashion by buying a book on how to train a puppy and doing what it said. As always happens with books of instructions, reality did not always conform to what was said. Thus one was told to put a rope round the dog's neck and give it a tug at the same time calling 'Come Psyche' until it got used to coming. Then it tells you to remove the rope and then, the book said, the dog will come when called. But, of course, it didn't. The book did not tell you what to do in that case. What it did say in another chapter was that in no circumstances should you continue to call the dog when it was not coming. This seemed to leave me no alternative but to pursue the dog in a determined fashion until it gave up and allowed the rope to be refitted. It was clear that in open country this could go on indefinitely, so I had taken Psyche (and later Xanthe) up to Ma's courtyard where space was limited and, when she did not come, I pursued her in grim silence round the yard until after two and a half circuits she gave in, lay down and allowed me to replace the rope. After two repeats of this procedure, she decided it was better just to come when called.

In the Parks Psyche would go off and run round and round with other dogs and it gave me great pleasure to see her come when called when most other dogs did not.

On one occasion I could not refrain myself from officiously intervening in the care of another dog. The wife of the Vice-Principal of St Stephen's House was pushing a pram while her young Dalmatian was playing at some distance with other dogs. She kept on calling for her dog, who took no notice whatever. 'Forgive me interrupting,' I said, 'but I am afraid you are just making matters worse. By calling the dog when it's not coming, you are setting up a correlation in its mind between your calling and its not coming, whereas the opposite is what you want to do. You cannot expect a dog to come when called unless you train it to do so.' With intolerable presumption I went on to say, 'All you need to do is get a book on training a puppy and do what it says.' She replied, 'We did try. We got two books from the library on how to train a puppy, and it ate both of them!'

Xanthe later on turned out to be an expert swimmer and she provided a public exhibition at the Rainbow bridge where the river bank is quite high. I would place her some distance from the bank and then go onto the bridge and throw her ring into the middle of the river, whereupon she would take a flying leap into the river and in a few strong strokes retrieve it and scramble up the bank for a repeat performance.

When in the mid–nineteen seventies the children grew up and left home and we had no need of such a large house, we had to decide whether to return full time to Wootton or to find a smaller house in Oxford and continue our dual residence. We found that we were continuing to enjoy the advantages of summer in Wootton and winter in Oxford and, as there was no shortage of would-be tenants, we looked for a smaller house. It had to be within easy walking distance of the centre, so we searched south Oxford, St Clements and Jericho. Finally we purchased 26 Walton Street which was handy from a number of points of view. It was opposite Little Clarendon Street, a lively shopping area, and close to Oxford University Press, the Radcliffe Infirmary and the University Offices in Wellington Square. From our bedroom window we could see the Vice-Chancellor's office and the V–C himself seated at his desk ('slumped' as Geoffrey Warnock suggested, when I mentioned this to him). All these considerations would recommend it to our academic tenants and make it easy to sell when the time came. I had fun designing a small garden with two garages fronting on to Walton Lane. These were designed by the architect Joyce Lowrie, conveniently living next door.

Number 26 was at the northern end of row of brick terrace houses which began at Worcester College. Together with the whole area known as Jericho they were built originally to house employees of the Oxford University Press. By great good fortune they escaped the fate of a similar area, St Ebbes, which had been cleared for modern development in the 1930s. Instead they were steadily gentrified and with their modest elegance and central location were largely occupied by academics and similar people.

We discovered, however, early on a considerable drawback. One of our first tenants in the new house was an academic from Louisville, Kentucky, whose wife, it transpired, was allergic to house dust. In an early Victorian property, carpeted throughout, it was impossible to guarantee freedom from dust and we offered to release them from the contract. They refused the offer, however, because in all other respects they liked the house, and wished to stay on. This was a pity, because worse, very much worse, was to happen later. Early in the Michaelmas term they noticed faint scrabbling noises under the kitchen floor. We called in the City Council's environmental health department to investigate and paid for our tenants to stay in a hotel while they did so.

Their report was devastating. I was in College that morning and was kept in touch by telephone. I was rung up at intervals: they had found seven dead rats, fifteen dead rats, thirty-one dead rats, eventually forty-five dead rats under the floorboards. Richard Tur, our Law Fellow at Oriel, remembers to this day how the alarming news came in by stages during that extraordinary morning, I having consulted him as to what my legal position might be vis-à-vis our tenants. Eventually it transpired that when we had converted a ground floor cupboard into a lavatory, the builders had neglected to insert a valve to prevent rats from the main Victorian sewer entering the house, which they had been doing freely since we first moved in. We repaid our tenants the rent from the time they moved in and, once again, offered them the option of cancelling their contract. Astonishingly they declined.

CHAPTER 10

The Keble years

F ROM OUR FAMILY LIFE in the country it remains to go back to my
academic life in Oxford. After a year at Christ Church I applied
for a more permanent philosophy fellowship at Keble. I was duly
dined at Keble and very agreeably entertained (there were no formal
interviews in those days). And then there was a long silence broken
only by a curious interlude. I received an invitation from Donald
MacKinnon to dine with him in Balliol, where he was a lecturer. I
could not make out quite why I had received this invitation. It was
presumably not to tell me how things were going at Keble since this
was confidential and, in any case, as the retiring incumbent he would
not be playing any part in the election. It was not until after dinner
when we were drinking beer in the garden that MacKinnon began
to explain. 'I feel bound to tell you,' he announced with considerable
emphasis and some suggestion of inner struggle, 'that the Fellows of
Keble are having great difficulty in reaching a decision.' And he went
on to explain that there were two serious candidates, one of whom
was myself and the other one was an old Keble man and a former
pupil of his 'whom,' he felt bound to admit, 'he strongly favoured
himself.' As he continued to labour this point and seemed extremely
anxious that I should appreciate fully the Fellows' predicament, I
asked myself why he was telling me all this as if there was something
I could do to resolve the problems. So I said, 'I wonder if it would
help the situation if I were to withdraw my candidature?' 'Oh, no,'
he said, plainly horrified. 'You mustn't do that.' So my evening ended
and from that day to this I have never understood what MacKinnon
was up to on that occasion. I can only presume that he was in fact
exerting some influence on the election, however improperly, and his
conscience told him at least to make better acquaintance with the
candidate whose election he was doing his best to prevent. But in
that case why the confession?

Before term started I received from MacKinnon a sheaf of notes
on the pupils I was to inherit from him. They were almost

indecipherable but what I was able to read was enough to convey to me that there was not one of my new pupils but presented a psychological problem of great complexity. Since I had done no work on western philosophy, with the exception of Plato's *Republic*, since Greats, I was in any case seriously lacking in confidence about what I was to teach them and could well do without further complications.

Fortunately by the end of the first term they were reassuringly normal, except for one individual who presented no problem. He was quite happily dotty and reasonably able and destined for a secure life in holy orders. It looked for a short while as if the mantle of MacKinnon who was famously eccentric was going to descend upon me. Peter Russell whom I had known at Queen's told me one day that he had had some pupils to tea and one of them asked him whether he knew the philosopher at Keble. When he said 'Yes', they went on to enlarge upon his eccentricity. 'He conducts tutorials from under the table, climbs up the curtains and throws live coals from the fireplace into the quad,' they told him. 'You surprise me.' Peter said he replied (rather disloyally as I thought), 'I should say he was a rather straightforward, plain sort of person, not to say ordinary'.

There is no denying that I should like to have gone to one of the older established colleges and found it hard to get used to the polychromatic brick work of Keble. 'THE PROPORTIONS ARE EXCELLENT,' said Phoebe in a congratulatory postcard and I had to make do with that. But I now realise that I was in fact extremely fortunate. Keble fellowships were still subject to a religious test: candidates were required to be communicant members of the Church of England. It is highly unlikely that in the philosophical atmosphere of the time I should have been elected at most other colleges and, in the event, although I had no Anglo-Catholic connections, I found it easy to identify with 'the principles for which' the College was founded.

At the time when I was elected the College was not a full college of the University. It was in a category of its own as a 'New Foundation'. It had been founded in 1870 as a deliberate reaction against the secularising tendencies of the age, to be what the University had always been but was ceasing to be, a purely Anglican institution, delivering an education based upon the principles of the Church of England as understood by John Keble and the other

founders of the Oxford Movement and exemplified in the person of
Keble himself. To ensure the continuance of this Anglican identity
the government of the College was to be in the hands of a Council
presided over by a senior Anglican figure, who at that time was Lord
Quickswood, the former Sir Hugh Cecil. The tutors were originally
appointed by this body and employed by it. Only the Warden and
Bursar were members of both bodies.

Early in my time the process was completed of abolishing the
Council and vesting the government of the College entirely in the
Warden and Fellows. At the same time the religious test was
abandoned except in the case of the Warden who was still to be a
clergyman of the Church of England. Already in the 1930s the tutors
had become Fellows with sole responsibility for electing their
successors.

In retrospect it is hard to see how the original intention of the
Founders could have been maintained in a culture which was
increasingly liberal. The Oxford norm of self-governing colleges was
bound in the end to exert decisive pressure, but it is worth
considering whether, given that norm, Keble could have remained
in some genuine sense an Anglican college. It could be argued that it
still is, to the extent that it is dominated by an Anglican chapel and
is required by statute to have an Anglican chaplain. This is true also
of most of the other colleges with the exception of some recently
founded and, indeed, of the University itself, in that it has a number
of divinity chairs whose occupants have to be ordained clergy of the
Church of England or a church in communion with the Church of
England. In view of this it would be hard to maintain that most of
the colleges or the University itself are purely secular institutions. So
my own view is that, even in the present situation in which the
Warden no longer has to be in holy orders, the College can remain
true to its founders' intentions so long as there is a strong Anglican
presence and the College continues to provide regular teaching in
theology.

In another important respect the College has undoubtedly maintained the principles of its founders and in so doing has indeed itself
pioneered what has become the Oxford norm. Although strongly
conservative in their determination to preserve the concept of an
Anglican university, they also broke with tradition in their desire to

widen entry and establish a pattern of living that all could afford. The rooms were of uniform size and the substitution of corridors in place of staircases may have been intended to reduce the segregation that staircases could encourage.

When I first became a fellow there were only thirteen of us on the Governing Body and we could easily be accommodated round the table in the Senior Common Room. Our strongest suit was Modern History in which there were two Fellows – J E A Joliffe, a distinguished Medieval historian who suffered from ill health and appeared only occasionally at College Meetings when he would sit away from the table in an armchair as if to dissociate himself with whatever decisions we might make. A G Dickens was a brisk and vigorous individual who would leave us shortly for a brilliant career as a historian of the Reformation at King's College London.

I found myself responsible for philosophy in Greats (Philosophy and Ancient History) and PPE (Philosophy, Politics and Economics), and later PPP (Philosophy, Psychology and Physiology) when that was established. My closest colleagues were Spencer Barrett, the Classics don and Maurice Hugh-Jones, the Economist. Spencer Barrett and I were together responsible for the Mods and Greats men as we had no ancient historian. Barrett was a devout atheist who for that reason had spent many years as a lecturer because he was not qualified to be a Fellow. This could not fail to be taken as a slight by a very fine scholar who was later in the running for the Regius Chair of Greek and would shortly be elected a Fellow of the British Academy. Spencer Barrett had spent the war in Oxford as a member of the Geographical Survey Unit which pieced together holiday photographs and other incidental bits of information to build an accurate picture of the French coast and other areas in which an invasion might be undertaken. His meticulous scholarship and conscientious attention to detail were ideally adapted to this task, and when it came to drafting the new constitution, he could always be relied upon for the correct placing of an apostrophe and the right choice of a colon or a semi-colon.

One benefit I derived from the fact that my Greats men had undergone his tuition before they came on to me was that they had learned to write clear and precise prose – an essential qualification for the study of philosophy.

The only occasion when we actually had to collaborate closely was in the conduct of the annual scholarship examinations in December. On this depended the supply of able pupils for the next three or four years, and it was a serious business. There were in all three scholarship groups and Keble suffered from the handicap that on the entry form the colleges in the group were listed in order of seniority of foundation: Balliol, Magdalen, St Johns, Wadham, Pembroke and Keble. Balliol always had more applicants than they could find awards for; Magdalen and St Johns were self-sufficient – their awards matched their supply of able applicants. So Wadham, Pembroke and Keble competed for the best of the Balliol surplus. The scripts would in the first instance be marked by the college of first choice and the scripts and marks were set out in a lecture room in Balliol where they were open to inspection by the examiners in all the colleges. Each college gave an indication which candidates they thought of taking for scholarships and exhibitions. So Spencer and I would go along and see which candidates with a suggestion of alpha were likely to come our way. Spencer was not prepared to trust the marking of his colleagues in the other colleges but would carefully re-mark the scripts if they looked at all possible. On this now entirely reliable evidence we would take our own decisions, having as a rule interviewed everyone who put Keble on his list.

In this unequal struggle we had only one weapon. A scholarship trumped an exhibition and either trumped the offer of a place. So if Wadham – and it usually was Wadham – had any able candidate they could not find awards for and would like to give a place to we could secure him by offering him an award. It would sometimes not be until the final meeting that all the decisions were sorted out.

The whole process would take a week at the end of the Michaelmas Term when we were all pretty tired anyway. Was it worth it or was the expenditure of time and effort on the part of leading academics an enormous waste? We thought it was worth it as it would determine who we would be teaching during the next four years, and our collective efforts would decide the composition of the College. And there can be no doubt that it maximised the chances of good candidates being accepted somewhere.

Spencer Barrett and I were not always looking for the same qualities and the ones he was looking for were the more easily recognised. With Greats philosophy in mind I was on the lookout for imagination and conceptual clarity and for this I relied on the general papers and, more than Spencer needed to do, on the interview. Usually his criteria and mine coincided, but from time to time they did not and he would defer to me if I thought I detected Greats potential in a candidate he thought less well of. Sometimes my judgement was at fault. On one occasion a candidate was asked what he thought about the play by Aeschylus he had been reading, the *Prometheus Vinctus, Prometheus Bound*. He said he thought it 'a rather static sort of play' which indeed it was as the hero spent the whole action of the play bound in chains. I wanted to turn down someone who displayed such a lack of originality or imagination, but Spencer insisted that his classical papers merited an award. So we accepted him and he duly got a First both in Mods and in Greats.

There were no regular occasions when I was so closely associated with Maurice Hugh-Jones, my PPE colleague, but we were, of course, teaching our pupils contemporaneously, with Maurice doing whatever organisation was needed. He was more of an economic historian than a theoretical economist. His chief interest was in social and economic developments in the United States. He had made a special study of the Tennessee Valley Authority and written a biography of Woodrow Wilson. He was a kindly and affable colleague although somewhat inclined to be peppery and fussy. Towards the end of his time with us I thought he reminded me of Parkinson's description of the man who never gets the top job or who comes to it too late and 'who denied the opportunity to make important decisions comes to regard as important the decisions he is able to make'. But it was he who introduced us to Wootton and when he eventually retired there from his professorship at Keele I got to know him very well and became very fond of him. With the possible exception of Dennis Nineham he had the largest fund of good stories of anyone I have ever met, and if one ever told him one he could always cap it with a better. His asides at College meetings were frequent and always *ben trovato*, although I can now only remember one. The Warden was reading out a list of candidates we had accepted from the Entrance examinations. One was from the Royal Liberty School, Romford, whose headmaster, Newth, was an old

Keble man. 'Pallas', read the Warden. 'Freshly sprung from the head of Newth', said Hugh-Jones in a stage whisper.

Maurice Hugh-Jones took a great deal of trouble over his pupils and was affectionately remembered by them, often for years afterwards. Indeed I believe that this degree of pastoral concern was common to all of us. I was particularly shocked, therefore, when comparatively early in my time at Keble, one of our pupils committed suicide. He was quite an unremarkable man who had not stood out in any way. It was on a morning when I had three tutorials in a row from ten till one. Around eleven o'clock when I was just finishing off with my first pupil and the second was waiting, he looked in and asked if he could see me. I asked if it was urgent and he said 'no', so I asked him to come back at one o'clock. By then the news came that he had thrown himself on the railway line in front of a train at about midday.

Nothing at all emerged subsequently to explain his tragic action. I searched my memory earnestly to see if, when he looked in to see me, he had shown any sign of disturbance, and I could remember none, although, of course, I couldn't help reflecting that, if only I had seen him there and then I could have probably prevented it happening. When later on I served on a University committee on mental health, we received notice of a piece of research in the US, in which the researchers had listed American universities in order of accepted prestige and plotted against them the incidence of suicide. It was evident that the greater the prestige, the greater the number of suicides. What did not appear was whether the cause was the greater pressure that vulnerable students encountered or whether the selection process somehow favoured people who were particularly susceptible.

In the College at that time two men stood out as bearing the greatest burdens and exercising the greatest influence. They were Parkes and Davidge – and it's significant that they continued to address one another as 'Davidge' and 'Parkes' when the rest of us had begun to use Christian names as a matter of course. George Parkes was a bluff Yorkshireman from my old college, Queen's, and proud of his North Country connections. He was a chemist and our sole scientist. As such he was responsible for all the scientists in the College. Of course he could not teach all of them, so he had to farm them out while remaining their 'College Tutor'. He was a keen musician and used to play the organ every Sunday at Hampton Poyle church near Islip. Hence he was tutorially responsible for all the musicians in college, a considerable task since the college had a strong musical tradition.

As we had no music fellow the Organ Scholar was in charge of the chapel music and had something of the status of professional organist at other colleges. Past Keble organ scholars were a distinguished lot, including Meredith Davies, Tommy Armstrong and Joseph Cooper. Joseph Cooper became well known as the inventor of the television programme *Face the Music*. It is generally not known that his own contribution to each programme, the hidden melody, originated in Keble. I was told by someone, I think it would have been Parkes, that the then Classics don, A S Owen (always known as Crab Owen) used to lie in wait for the Organ Scholar after Evensong and identify the composer of the voluntary he had just played. On one occasion Cooper improvised a fugue on the theme of the popular song 'Oh, I am so happy, so happy' in the manner of J S Bach. On descending from the organ loft he encountered a rather puzzled Crab Owen, who was not to be caught out. 'Rather early Bach, I think, Joe, rather early Bach', was his comment.

Parkes was a well-rounded man, as far as could possibly be conceived from the stereotype of the narrow scientist. He used to claim that he was the only truly educated scientist in Oxford since he had taken Greek in 'divvers' and he was proud to have been the last Senior Proctor to have read the Latin Litany in person. Parkes was Senior Tutor and Secretary of the Senior Tutors' Committee, then one of the most powerful bodies in the University. In addition to all this he was for many years Secretary to the Curators of the University Parks. So far as I could tell, Parkes was totally lacking in any self-conceit or personal ambition and, although he was busier than any of us, he had the remarkable capacity to be fully at the disposal of whomever at the time he was talking to. It must have been years since he did any serious research in Chemistry and so by modern standards he was an anomaly, but he was for many years an indispensable 'tower of strength'.

The other major figure was the Bursar and Law Tutor, Vere Davidge. He would not have minded being called an anomaly;

indeed he declared his intentions of founding a 'society for the perpetuation of anomalies'. He managed to combine the job of Estate Bursar and Domestic Bursar with the life of a country gentleman on an estate at Little Houghton near Northampton where he would hunt regularly with the Oakley. He could not have done this without the bursary clerk, Charlie Bourne, who managed the college's finances and oversaw the running of the college with imperturbable efficiency. When he eventually retired, it required two people to replace him. Indeed one of Davidge's strengths was his gift for choosing subordinates and inspiring their loyalty, so that all the key positions were well filled. Nurser the Head Porter was an ex Sergeant Major of imposing presence, who had no difficulty in exercising authority over undergraduates when, but only when, it was necessary. It must sometimes have been necessary when Rice-Oxley was Dean. He was a most gentle and amiable figure and the story circulated of an occasion when Nurser went to quieten a noisy party. He advanced into the room and said in a loud voice, 'the Dean sends his compliments', but then he noticed Rice-Oxley sitting in the waste paper basket and, without a moment's hesitation, declared 'the Dean withdraws his compliments' and retreated. We had one of the best chefs in Oxford – food and drink being among the things that Davidge cared about. Smith, the Common Room butler, was an unimpressive little man who looked to everything, especially guest nights, with great efficiency. Once in my time he was lured away by better pay to wait upon the directors of Pressed Steel, but within a few months was back again. 'I didn't like the way they did things. I just had to slam the food down in front of them'.

Davidge as Law Tutor was, of course, responsible for our lawyers. He was aware of his limitations as an academic lawyer and used to make up for this by hiring 'weekenders' to teach his brighter pupils. These were often young men who were glad to supplement their earnings at the bar in this way.

Another key interest of Davidge was rowing. His son, Christopher, while at Trinity stroked the Oxford crew in two memorable races in one of which they won by a canvas and in the other lost by a canvas. Christopher was to become one of the 'Greats' of British rowing. Davidge himself had rowed for Pembroke and in a trial eight which made him a member of the Leander Club and entitled him to wear the pink cap, scarf and socks on his annual visits to Henley. He was in his element on such festive occasions and he created one such once a week at his Thursday guest night. The dinner itself was excellent and well known in Oxford for its opulence which accorded very little with the 'sober living and high culture of the mind' intended by the Founders. But it was not until the guests proceeded to Common Room that Davidge came into his own, for this was when the port began to circulate. Davidge would gather his own guest and a few others with their hosts at his end of the table and under the influence of the port would engage them in a peculiar sort of badinage which, as the night wore on, could verge on the offensive. On one occasion I had as my guest a distinguished psychiatrist, Dr Robin McInnes, Medical Superintendent of the Warneford Hospital. Davidge couldn't resist the opportunity to make fun of 'shrinks' and 'trick-cyclists' and I thought that he crossed the divide into sheer rudeness. I apologised afterwards to McInnes, who was plainly used to such nonsense and told me not to worry about it. But next morning I still felt that Davidge had gone too far and that this sort of thing was doing his reputation no good and spoiling for the college guests what should have been an enjoyable occasion. So I summoned up my courage and went to see Davidge. Rather to my surprise he was deeply apologetic and insisted on writing to McInnes. I said that this was not necessary, but he did write, as Robin McInnes told me, a charming letter of apology.

There was one occasion when, in my hearing, Davidge was worsted in one of these exchanges. Hugh-Jones had brought in as a guest a neighbour of his at Wootton, Captain Podger, a large, imposing man with a monocle. Seeing that he was a naval man and presumably much travelled, Davidge asked him which ports he had visited and, as this went on, a pattern developed. Wherever Podger had been Davidge had also been, only ten years earlier. Eventually they got to Istanbul. 'Istanbul,' said Davidge, 'Istanbul! Would that have been the place I knew as Constantinople?' 'No, sir,' said the Captain, 'you knew it as Byzantium.'

Davidge as host could manage things to his liking, although even in Keble his colleagues insisted on migrating to the Smoking Room after an hour or so, leaving him with his cronies still circulating the port at one end of the Common Room table. But at other colleges Davidge had no option but to conform. At Oriel I was told of an

occasion when Davidge was dining there and was distinctly disconcerted when the Fellows strictly on the hour got up to go into the
Smoking Room. Davidge said, 'Well at least I can take the port with
me'. He seized the decanter and marched with it to the Smoking
Room where Phillips, the Common Room Butler and himself a
considerable personality, was holding the door open. As he went
through Davidge turned to him and said, 'I hope I am not infringing
upon your perquisites!' 'That's all right, sir,' said Phillips unperturbed,
'I always make a practice of taking a glass or two when I am decanting
it.'

Davidge was always very good with the college servants, a
considerate and friendly employer. In his world everyone knew his
place and was entitled to the respect it merited.

It is hard to describe Davidge without caricaturing him. In a sense
he always caricatured himself. But as one got to know him one
discovered that he was a surprisingly sensitive man not only as things
touched himself but also in relation to other people, as the episode
with Robin McInnes illustrated. This side of him became more
apparent to me much later when he had retired. In drawing up the
new constitution in the early 1950s he had determined the retirement
age of Fellows at 67 but with a reservation that, in the case of a
Fellow occupying the position of Bursar, the Governing Body could
at its discretion continue the Fellowship until the age of 70. No one
paid particular attention to this at the time but as Davidge's 67th
birthday approached it became clear that his seventieth birthday
would coincide with the college's Centenary and he dearly wanted
to be in charge of the celebrations. The Governing Body had to
decide the question just after I left and with some reluctance the
Fellows declined to continue his tenure. The need to put the college
into the hands of qualified professionals was, they felt, overriding. A
year or two later I called on Davidge at Little Houghton and over the
sherry (it was too early in the day for port) he said, 'I don't mind
telling you, Basil, that I was very much hurt when my colleagues
decided not to renew my Fellowship. But I can see now that they
were absolutely right, not only for the college, but also for me. I am
enjoying immensely my life here in retirement.'

One of the peripheral tasks which Davidge undertook at Keble was
that of chairing the Advowsons Committee. The college had

accumulated over the years some fifty livings, more than any other college and every year there would be vacancies to be filled. They had been left to the college by devout Anglo-Catholics who wanted to be sure that their parishes would remain secure in the right tradition of churchmanship. For this reason there had before my time been co-opted onto the Committee an old member of the college, one Canon Bisdee, who had somehow acquired an encyclopaedic knowledge of Anglo-Catholic churches throughout the country. At an appropriate moment in the proceedings Davidge would say, 'Now, about the important matter of candle-power. Bisdee, how would you rate this particular parish?' Without hesitation, Bisdee would reply, 'I would put it somewhere between the Church of the Ascension, Lavender Hill and St John the Divine, Balham.'

One principle that Davidge adhered to consistently was to frustrate the intentions of the bishop. Bishops always had their own candidate whom they proposed to the college with varying degrees of tact, and these candidates were subjects of suspicion to Davidge. Not entirely without reason. Bishops had at heart the wider interests of the Church and from time to time these would dictate that an individual who was difficult, or in some other way problematic, must be placed in a parish where he could do least harm. The college, on the other hand, as patron, was concerned only with the best interests of the parish. This was not to say that the bishop's nominee was never accepted, but only after his credentials had been examined with especial care. This was a matter which needed to be handled with great delicacy, not least because at that time so many of the bishops were Keble men.

The business which occupied the attention of the college meetings in my earliest years was the Constitution. The general outlines had been agreed in advance by the Council, but it was left to the Fellows to specify them in a legal document. Besides the interventions of Barrett to correct the punctuation and Hugh-Jones' irreverent asides I can remember only one feature of these discussions. The Warden, Harry Carpenter, wanted to include a number of by-laws. 'We want,' he said, 'to leave our successors in no possible doubt as to what we intend.' At the other end of the table Davidge rejected this proposition outright. 'On the contrary,' he said, 'we want to give our successors the greatest possible freedom to do as they may think fit in the circumstances of their time.' And he quoted a saying of Churchill that, 'a constitution should be brief and obscure'. I confess, I have never read the Constitution and I do not know whose opinion prevailed, but I suspect that it was that of Davidge.

Harry Carpenter was to leave in 1954 to become a much respected Bishop of Oxford. He had been Warden since 1939 at which time he was Chaplain. He and the college endured the war-time years of austerity and he was not the man to lead the college decisively out of them. He had many admirable qualities, dignity, good judgement, considerateness and high principle, but his chief virtue was one which, while it befitted him as a man, unsuited him to be specifically Warden of Keble at that time. He was a notably humble man, unwilling to make claims for himself or for the college. And this may have accentuated one thing about the college which as yet I have not mentioned. We did not, collectively, regard ourselves as the equal of other colleges and accepted too readily that we were second class, if not second rate. This did not mean that we lowered our standards; we just did not really expect to satisfy them. Even Davidge's flamboyance could not disguise the fact that he was engaged in making ends meet, thrifty house-keeping in which the poverty of our resources was taken for granted. There was as yet no serious attempt to expand these resources. It is true that a consequence of this was that we all worked very hard and were determined that our pupils should realise the full extent of their potentialities. We saw to it that anyone capable of a First got a First, although we were reconciled to the fact that we should get fewer Firsts than other colleges. I, for example, was the sole philosophy tutor at a time when most colleges had two, one primarily for Greats, one for PPE. I did my best to make the most of any advantages there might be in this situation, two in particular. I had so many pupils that, if I was to limit my teaching to fourteen or fifteen hours a week, I must take them all in pairs. Although I started this from necessity I came to think it as in all but a few cases, desirable. The pair were encouraged to go on discussing the week's problem outside the tutorial and really able pupils sparked one another off. Hence it was often the case that Firsts came in pairs. Then I was obviously better at some subjects than others. Owing to my incapacity for mathematics I was useless at mathematical logic and needed to export people for the Logic paper. In return I could import pupils for Plato and Moral Philosophy. I had regular exchanges with

David Mitchell at Worcester and Iris Murdoch at St Anne's. I became so convinced of the benefits of such exchanges that when later as a professor I had to supervise graduate students I made a point of sending them to someone else for one or two terms, preferably someone whose views they were criticising. As we lacked Tutorial Fellows in key subjects we had to have a number of stipendiary lecturers or their equivalents. Our ancient historians for many years went to 'Tom Brown' Stevens (C E Stevens) at Magdalen who was a brilliant and highly entertaining teacher. And for politics we had Michael Foot who later became well known as the historian of SOE, who identified himself very fully with Keble and in 1953 took a party of Keble undergraduates to help repair the shore defences in the disastrous floods of that year in East Anglia.

Perhaps partly because of these arrangements my impression is that Keble undergraduates were more active in the life of the University than those of other colleges. Many of them at the time were, of course, returning warriors and almost all had done national service of some kind. The result was a very lively and variegated community – nowadays it would be called 'vibrant'. They were, for the most part, disciplined and hard working and delighted not only to be able, but to be required to engage in serious intellectual activity. It was an exciting as well as exacting time to be a tutor, especially for one as ill-equipped as I was. Fortunately my experience at King Alfred had given me a capacity to disguise my ignorance and speculate freely on the basis of very little knowledge, and I came to believe that, if and when I became a good philosopher, I should be able to become a good teacher of the subject.

One was never taught how to conduct a tutorial (though nowadays I dare say one is). All I had to go on was my own experience at the receiving end with Woozley and Hampshire. I remembered how I had prospered less with Woozley's purely critical approach than with Hampshire's taking a clear line himself and thus presenting me with one possible way of organising the material. So I started the term with a rough idea of what position the pupils would reach by the end of it and each tutorial was to fit into that scheme. I took good care not to impose my view of the matter and to encourage the pupil to develop a line of his own, but he would always know where I stood. In the early days my own view would be a plausible one, much

influenced by what my colleagues were thinking. Later on it would
be the view I myself had come to take. Some tutors were getting
their pupils to send in their essays in advance, but I preferred to have
them read aloud in the traditional way, partly, I must admit, to save
time. This enabled me to interrupt and ask for clarification and to get
the discussion running.

I had always found it difficult as an undergraduate to start each
week from cold on an entirely fresh topic, so in the course of one
tutorial I would move on to the subject of the next. I agreed with
what was later to be the complaint of the Franks Commission that
undergraduates were being required to write too many essays, so I
took advantage of their coming in pairs to reduce the load. One of
them only was to write a full essay; the other to do the reading and
make notes for an essay.

I remember two tutorials in particular form this early period. One
was with a girl from Northern Ireland and pupil of Iris Murdoch's. I
was at the time giving the 'bread and butter' lectures on Plato's
Republic, and her first essay was virtually a paraphrase of my lecture
on the topic. I took her to task as gently as I could and insisted that
her essay was to express her opinion not mine. She protested the
difficulty of writing an essay for the very individual whose lectures
on the subject she was attending. I said that she was, of course,
perfectly free to quote what I had said, but not as if they were her
own original thoughts. Next time before she started her essay, she
looked up smiling shyly and said, 'before I begin I want to explain
that when I say "it is said that" I mean you.'

The other was with a very lively pupil who had no difficulty in
developing and defending ideas of his own. On this particular
occasion Bryan Magee was challenging my own assertion that
thought had always to be expressed in language, a common enough
proposition at the time and one which I was not entirely sure that I
shared. As a counter-example he instanced the claims of music. I
countered as best I could and reminded Bryan how very bad most
composers were in describing what they meant in their music.
'Precisely so,' said Bryan, 'because they have said it already as clearly
as it could be said in the music.'

Bryan Magee was already making a name for himself as President
of the Union and I remember in my final termly report upon him

saying that he seemed set for a career in high-level journalism. In this I failed to do justice to his extraordinary versatility. After a spell as a Labour Member of Parliament, he achieved a distinction as a music critic, and wrote two acclaimed books on Wagner. He was a skilful television interviewer, particularly in the series he undertook under the title 'Men of Ideas'. In these he interviewed leading academic philosophers and enabled them to express their views in a manner intelligible to the average educated viewer. It was widely felt, indeed, that he was often able to summarise their views more clearly and accessibly than they could themselves. He combined all this with a life-long passion for philosophy which found eloquent expression in his book *Confessions of a Philosopher*.

At this time I was fortunate in being asked to teach a succession of able students from the Jesuit house, Campion Hall; two of whom, Ted Yarnold and Gerry Hughes, became in due course Masters of Campion Hall. Father Vincent Turner, the Senior Tutor of the Hall, thought that it would be good for those who were reading Greats as part of their long training to be taught by someone who was not a Jesuit, and asked me to do it. Being well versed in scholastic philosophy most of them made the transition to modern analytic philosophy effortlessly and effectively and they were a delight to teach.

In 1954 Harry Carpenter left to become Bishop of Oxford and we elected as his successor Eric Abbott. As soon as he arrived he made it clear that he would have nothing to do with any suggestion that the college was in any way second-rate. He intended to alter the image of the college and thereby the college itself. It started with the Warden's Lodgings. Harry Carpenter had never felt he could make demands on the college for himself and his wife. Throughout his time the Warden's Lodgings were cold and dreary and inhospitable. It would be wrong to give the impression that the Carpenters themselves were lacking in hospitality. Urith was lively and outgoing. Margy and I remember vividly when we were invited to tea after our engagement was announced. We were given a warm welcome by the Carpenters but what made the occasion memorable was the interruption halfway through of Humphrey, then aged three. He burst into the room uttering loud cries. 'Say Good Afternoon to Miss Collin and Mr Mitchell', said Urith. Humphrey, taken aback, paused for a moment and then declared 'I can't, I can't. I'm too sa-a-ad', and then rushed from the room, still roaring. This dramatic entry was matched fifteen years later when Humphrey, then an undergraduate, marched at the head of a drunken rout after a bump supper playing his tuba, thus preventing a riot. It is said that Carpenter had accepted a cut in salary during the war and had never asked for it to be rescinded. Abbott insisted on complete redecoration and some structural adaptations to make it more liveable in. As a result the public rooms were rendered light and welcoming and the splendour of Butterfield's proportions became apparent. He also had the place properly heated. When much later we visited the Carpenters, now retired, in their new little modern house in Cirencester, they confessed that for the first time in their married life they were really warm. Where Carpenter was withdrawn and ascetic, Abbott was confident and ceremonious. He liked to make a good show and clearly believed that outward show would eventually be matched by inner confidence.

One of the first things he got us to do on the Governing Body was bring our stipends up to the Oxford norm. We were not in any way to think of ourselves as inferior. And, very importantly for the college, he quickly brought Davidge onto his side. He approved of the college's reputation for generous hospitality, and moreover he shared Davidge's enthusiasm for rowing. He had coxed a trial eight at Cambridge and was also entitled to war the Leander pink. Davidge had always wanted to make Keble a rowing college, with little encouragement from his colleagues. Abbott was prepared to countenance a policy of attracting good oarsmen so long as it was not at the expense of academically gifted candidates. In practice this meant that they must be in addition to Davidge's normal quota and read either law or for a pass degree. Indefensible in abstract principle as this might have been it was acceptable in practice at a time when we never had to turn away good candidates. And it made some sort of sense for the college's long term academic prospects, as the case of St Edmund Hall illustrated. In the inter-college rivalry it was good for a lesser college to be known for something and it was noticeable over the years that Teddy Hall's academic standard rose. Having become known as a college for athletes, athletes applied in large numbers and some of these were academically able. These the college would accept whilst turning down others less gifted academically of the sort they once would have accepted.

As the college boat rose through the 1st division in Eights we had a series of bump suppers and Abbott showed a remarkable talent for oratory on these occasions. Most speakers just accepted that they would be subject to noisy interruptions in the course of every sentence and took no trouble in preparation. Abbott, in consequence of his own experience at Jesus, Cambridge, a rowing college par excellence, had perfected a style of oratory to suit the occasion. The speech was carefully constructed in units of two or three words, each of these elements inviting a loud response of acceptance or, more often, rejection. The following element would then negate this, showing the recent response to have been totally mistaken. In this way he would tease his hearers in a semi-humorous manner which in their drunken state they did not quite know how to handle; but they always ended by cheering generously the skilful way they had been outwitted. The same command of language enabled him to produce sermons which were exquisitely formed works of art.

When after four years at Keble he was invited to become Dean of Westminster I did my best to dissuade him. I drove him to Henley one day during the Regatta. It was the only time I had seen him without a dog-collar, which made way for his pink Leander tie on that one occasion in the year. On the way back, in the relaxed atmosphere of our return journey, I endeavoured to make the case for Keble as a growing institution in which he could still exercise a vital influence as against Westminster which he would indeed grace by his presence but whose role in Church and nation was firmly established. We became so deeply engaged in debate that we ran out of petrol, but fortunately within two hundred yards of a petrol station. He stated what was indeed the truth, that *au fond* he was an ecclesiastic rather than an academic and this was the deciding factor. So far as one could tell he was thoroughly at home at Westminster. He enjoyed the great ceremonial occasions which attached to the office and discharged his role with easy dignity and charm. In addition he was able to extend his role as spiritual director more widely than had been possible at Keble. He had plainly made the right choice.

There was so much artifice in his make-up that it was not until towards the end of his time with us that I decided that he really was

a good man. I found it hard to believe that anyone so smooth could
be a good man, but in the end I was convinced that he was. But there
can be no doubt whatever that he was a good man for Keble and set
the college on a path of development which was noticeable by the
time I left in 1967 and has continued at an accelerated pace ever
since.

During this period we were able to make some very good
appointments. Rice-Oxley retired and was replaced by John Carey in
the first stages of a distinguished career which was to culminate in his
tenure of the Merton Professorship of English Literature. Denys Potts
was our first ever Modern Linguist and soon established his reputation
as a student of the French Enlightenment and D'Alemnbert in
particular. Dennis Shaw was appointed to succeed George Parkes as
our sole scientist. His activities outside the college were almost as
extensive as Parkes', but he was also a well known research physicist.
He was able to add to our strength in science by enlisting the services
of Hans von Engel, an Austrian refugee physicist whose academic
distinction was matched by the distinction of his appearance. Shaw
could not, of course, fulfil Parkes' role as a college man par
excellence, but Parkes' mantle in this respect was to descend in due
course on another newly elected Fellow, Douglas Price, a Tudor
historian who replaced Dickens. Price, as a bachelor, lived in college
and became a familiar and friendly presence at Tenmantale (a society
for historians), the Mitre Club (for theologians and churchy people
generally) and other more occasional gatherings.

Of particular interest to myself was the election of a new Chaplain
and tutor in Theology. Charles Stuart had been a lively and
approachable pastoral chaplain but he had as yet no claim to serious
academic standing – Christopher Stead by contrast came to us from
King's College, Cambridge, with an already impressive record as a
patristic scholar with an especial interest in the philosophical aspects
of the Fathers and, indeed, in philosophy generally. He was able to
boast of having attended Wittgenstein's classes, a record matched in
Oxford only by Iris Murdoch and Elizabeth Anscombe. His support
and friendship was of enormous benefit to me and did much to
encourage my growing interest in the philosophy of religion. He
immediately joined the Metaphysicals and duly contributed to *Faith
and Logic* in 1957. One of the enduring effects of 'the principles for

which' was that Keble continued to get good applicants to read Theology and Christopher Stead ensured that the college remained strong in the subject.

It was a college thus strengthened which faced the problem of electing a new Warden. We were not likely to find someone with Eric Abbott's capacity for discreet but effective advertisement. To my mind what mattered was to confirm Keble's standing in the University by appointing someone of acknowledged personal and academic distinction. In my view there was only one such man in sight and that was Austin Farrer. There was one, personal, reason why I wanted him to be given a post proportionate to abilities. He had just suffered the disappointment of being passed over for the Regius Chair of Divinity, which everyone in Oxford thought was his for the taking. The successful candidate was Henry Chadwick and none could dispute his worth, but I felt that Austin deserved more than to live out his days as Chaplain of Trinity, dearly as he loved the job. When I had written to him after that election, he admitted his disappointment but said that he had forfeited the appointment by his 'exegetical extravagances'.

So I had set my heart on having Austin Farrer as Warden of Keble. The problem was how to persuade my colleagues, only one of whom, Stead, knew him at all. His brilliance was generally acknowledged, but what reason was there for supposing that he would have any interest in or capacity for administration? Such information as had been obtained from Trinity did not serve to allay these anxieties. It was said that during meetings of the Governing Body it was his habit to read *The Times*. I had, of course, no hard evidence to go on. I simply said that he was a notably honest and conscientious man and would not accept the job unless he felt satisfied he could do it.

In the event he was duly elected and, so far as I can remember, there were no other strong candidates. My own uncertainties were not overcome until the first college meeting at which he presided. It was an informal meeting regularly held on the Friday morning before Full Term at which the College List was gone over to make sure there were no problems concerning those about to come up. In addition to this it was customary to raise any matters which could not wait until the first formal meeting on the following Wednesday afternoon. It was a fairly relaxed occasion on which Abbott was in the habit of providing sherry, a custom which I suggested to Austin that he should follow.

We had gone through the list without problems and Austin peered round the room asking if there were any other matters which needed to be raised. 'Yes, Warden, I'm afraid there is,' said Parkes, and then went on to explain that a disagreement had arisen between himself and the Chaplain as to who should occupy the Sub-Warden's stall in Chapel. Rice-Oxley as Sub-Warden used not to attend Chapel and so it had become customary for the Chaplain to occupy it as it was opposite the Warden's and convenient for his coming and going in the service. When Parkes and Stead had set out their competing claims, Austin said, 'Perhaps someone would be good enough to tell me how matters of this sort are settled in the college.' 'Well, Warden,' said Parkes, 'as I understand it, it is at your entire discretion.' 'Very well,' said Austin, 'as soon as I have acquired sufficient discretion I will decide it.' From that moment on I knew it would be alright. And he turned out to be an excellent administrator, whose only fault, perhaps, was that he reached decisions too rapidly or, at least, before his colleagues had caught up with him. He seemed always to be several moves ahead of the rest of us. His conduct of college business was not exactly frivolous, but suggested plainly that the matters we discussed were not always the most important things in life. This disposed of one of my worries – that he would not have enough time to get on with his own writing.

It was obviously necessary that he should get on well with Davidge and in fact he warmed to him as belonging to the same species as Landon, the Law don at Trinity whom he had also liked. Davidge in his turn liked Austin, while being a bit wary of him as someone rather too clever for the job.

In 1957 Warden Smith of New College, then Vice-Chancellor, initiated the 'Oxford Historic Buildings Appeal' to undertake work which was long overdue on the fabric of University and college buildings. It was the stonework of the older buildings which most needed replacement or restoration, but Keble had its own problems with, especially, gargoyles, which the Victorians had sought to strengthen with iron rods. These in the course of time rusted and began to eat away the stone itself. The Appeal document defined 'historic buildings' as 'buildings erected before 1800 together with notable exceptions of later date'. So it was open to Keble to apply and I was asked to prepare our case. I argued that the wording implied that there would in fact be some 'notable exceptions' and that, if so, Keble's case was pre-eminent. The only possible rivals, I maintained, were the University Museum by Woodward and the Ashmolean Museum by Cockerell. In comparison with these Keble stood out in virtue of its sheer scale and of the fact that it was the acknowledged masterpiece of an outstanding architect. To obtain support for this case I wrote to four leading architectural historians and asked them to give their opinion on the historic and architectural importance of the buildings of Keble. They were Albert Richardson, Kenneth Clark, H S Goodhart-Rendel and John Betjeman, only the last of these being an acknowledged champion of Victorian Gothic. All four replied at once saying that they had no doubt whatever of the historic and architectural importance of the buildings and one, I think it was Richardson, added that in his experience, when architects from overseas came to Oxford, the one place in particular they wanted to visit was Keble.

In the event we did not get a grant, although it was indicated that we might receive one later. The news came to the Fellows by way of a poem from the Warden which was posted on the notice board in the Senior Common Room. It compared the committee's 'No' with the famous 'Non' of de Gaulle regarding the British entry into the Common Market. The Appeal was the first instance since the war in which Oxford had sought to get financial support from outside on a substantial scale and in due course the colleges, including Keble, followed suit.

But it had another more immediate effect in Keble. I think most of us had continued to feel somewhat defensive about Butterfield's design and now we could face down our critics in the knowledge that they had failed to catch up with the best architectural opinion. The proportions, as Phoebe had said, were indeed excellent, especially in the relation between the Chapel and the long range of the Hall and Library, emphasised by the sunken quadrangle. The secret lay in the balance of asymmetrical masses. The polychromatic brickwork also I could see to have been artfully contrived in such a way that the total effect would have been weakened without it. This becomes most apparent in conditions of strong sunlight and intense blue sky, as if Butterfield had in mind Mediterranean conditions not often seen in Oxford.

In 1956 I became Senior Proctor and as such was a member of Hebdomadal Council and numerous other University committees. It gave me an insight into how the central administration of the University worked and brought me into contact with innumerable people in other colleges whom I should not otherwise have met. My colleague was Michael Brock, a modern historian who would later become Warden of Nuffield and editor of the nineteenth-century volume of the History of the University. He was a man of enormous energy and almost fanatical attention to detail. As we met daily throughout the year, dressed alike and shared numerous ceremonial occasions, it was essential that we should get on together and we did.

The year was marked by four outstanding occasions. There were official visits from Bulganin and Kruschev and by ex-President Truman, who received an Honorary Degree. Smith as Vice-Chancellor received the two Russians on the steps of the Clarendon Building where they were greeted by a group of undergraduates singing 'Poor Old Joe'. I do not think anyone undertook to explain the reference. The Truman visit was a delightful occasion marked by the unsophisticated pleasure the Trumans took in the whole thing. It was notable also by Elizabeth Anscombe's dignified protest on account of Truman's having authorised the dropping of the atom bomb. I am afraid that the chief concern of the Proctors was that she should be properly dressed and not in the shapeless trousers she usually wore. The other occasions were Suez and the Hungarian Revolution, both of which sparked off large undergraduate demonstrations. In the absence of a Students' Union, Michael and I saw the officers of the main political clubs and explained to them what our policy would be. We entirely endorsed their right to demonstrate so long as they were orderly and no damage was done. They accepted our policy as their successors of ten years later would certainly not have done.

There was one other incident which involved the college and caused me some embarrassment. An undergraduate of Keble who was also a pupil of mine was sent down by the college for repeated offences against college discipline. It was rumoured that he intended to organise a funeral procession, in which he was to be ensconced in a coffin, to the station. We as Proctors were determined to prevent this, and in a final interview with him as his tutor, I warned him against it and received an assurance that no such thing was intended. Nevertheless the Marshal was suspicious and he persuaded me to go down to the station with himself and his bulldogs to make sure he actually left on the train he had promised to go on. There was no sign of him or his friends on the platform when we arrived, but, as the train drew in, a coffin was carried out from a waiting room with him in it and he duly emerged and boarded the train. There was no doubt that he had outwitted me without violating my instructions as there had been no procession. I felt foolish and was made to feel even more foolish when I discovered that there was a press photographer in the crowd who had obtained some unobstructed views of myself and my party, all of us in our formal uniforms which could be made to look entirely ridiculous in that particular setting. The University, as always, was getting some hostile publicity at the time and I did not want to add to this. I hastily rang the editor of the *Oxford Mail* and asked his advice. He said he knew the man, who was a freelance photographer who had been sent to Oxford by one of the tabloids to get spicier stories than those supplied by the rather staid *Oxford Times* reporter who usually gathered Oxford news for the London press. He said that there was no way of stopping publication of the pictures, unless I was prepared to take the man into my confidence and tell him the whole background of the case. He duly came to see me in the Proctors' Office. He said that the undergraduate had invited him to a party in his rooms in Blackhall Road where he had plied him with drink and explained how he was being sent down for a comparatively minor offence. He portrayed the college officers as extremely high-handed and unwilling to give him any chance to exculpate himself. I said I could understand how he, the photographer, had found this story easy to accept and, if I could speak off the record, I would fill in the background for him. I then said that the offence was the last in a series of misconduct; that colleges were extremely reluctant to send anyone down and that he had seen his tutor, the Dean and the Warden before the College as such had taken the final decision. He said that he for his part had formed an unfavourable impression of the man, but had no means of checking his assertions and was unwilling to pass over a good story. He was glad to be given some insight into how University discipline worked.

The one thing which I could not do was ask him not to publish the photographs, or indeed, make any request to him at all. For the next week or two the Marshal kept an eye on the popular papers but to my intense relief no photographs appeared.

Like many ex-Proctors, when my time of office came to an end and I returned to the routines of college life, I became restless and unsatisfied at no longer knowing what was going on. There were two areas in particular in which I wanted to have my say. Both concerned the shape of the University; the first its actual physical setting – the roads debate still rumbled on and certain high buildings, completed and projected, threatened the Oxford Skyline; the other concerned the constitution of the University and its robustly democratic character which had been criticised in an *obiter dictum* in the Robbins Report. So in 1958 I stood for Hebdomadal Council and was duly elected – the first ever Keble man, I believe, to have been elected that that body.

I remained on Council for the next six years during which the two problems that had concerned me were both resolved. The threat to the Oxford skyline was removed by the City. In my endeavours to get the University to act I went to see the City Architect and learned from him that he was preparing proposals to introduce a height limit of sixty feet on all buildings within a central zone. To decide the limits of this zone he had had photographs taken from the main viewpoints around Oxford, Elsfield, Boars Hill and Wytham Woods. So the University was saved from itself.

The pressure to build high buildings came from the scientists who had a reasonable case. The existing science area was severely limited in space and unless a new science area was developed elsewhere, to build high seemed the only answer. Moreover it was widely recognised that, if the University was to maintain its reputation it had to increase its science base, which in any case could achieve funding more readily than the humanities could do. The issue came to a head with the appointment of a new professor of Zoology, John Pringle. Like all newly appointed science professors he wanted to bring his research team with him and this demanded a new building. The Sites and Buildings Committee of Council proposed a tower to be erected in an allegedly neglected corner of the University Parks, and all of us had christened it 'Pringle's Pagoda'. This was an inflammatory proposal and brought out all the latent tensions in the University. Not only did it horrify those like myself, who were opposed to high buildings as such, it outraged many otherwise uncommitted who regarded the Parks as inviolable. And here also there was an arts and science component. It was arts dons who were able to observe the traditional University day in which the afternoons were devoted to exercise and who particularly enjoyed walking in the Parks and whose pupils could afford time off to play games in the Parks while the scientists were busy maximising the use of their apparatus in the laboratories. The dispute about Pringle's Pagoda provoked two massive debates in Congregation, in one of which I led for the opposition, ably supported by Kenneth Wheare, who vacated his Chair in order to participate. Pringle's Pagoda was decisively rejected in June 1962.

This outcome showed that the two issues about the shape of the University, the aesthetic one and the constitutional one were more closely connected than at first appeared. For a proposal which had been declared by an authoritative committee and a majority on Council to be in the interest of the University and, arguably of the nation, had been defeated by a coalition of amateurs, predominantly arts men based in the colleges. This was just the sort of thing which served to intensify press criticism of the governance of the University. There were even threats of parliamentary action.

In the face of these criticisms it became apparent to some of us that we could not simply go on as before and hope to ride the expected storm. I seem to remember discussing the matter with Alan Bullock who eventually proposed the setting up of the Franks Commission. Its impressive Report based on detailed research represented a thorough vindication of the essential features of the collegiate University and the tutorial system. It tidied up the role of Congregation but did not noticeably diminish its powers.

It had seemed to me as the result of my proctorial experience that the University's relations with the press needed to be handled professionally and I successfully proposed the appointment of an Information Officer.

By 1964 I had achieved sufficient seniority on Council to be in the running for the Chairmanship of one or other of the major committees and I could see that this could greatly increase my administrative load. I suppose I must have shown some signs of stress, for Austin made an opportunity to raise the issue. He said something like this: 'There are some people, Basil, who are able to handle three major preoccupations at the same time, but I do not think you are one of them'. And he pointed out that I was trying to sustain three commitments: teaching, administration and philosophy. I needed to decide which of them I was prepared to sacrifice. Once the question was posed, the answer was obvious. Teaching was my main job and I thoroughly enjoyed it. I was beginning to make some serious contributions to philosophy and it was important that I prepared something for publication. So I resigned from Council and ensured a right-minded successor by engineering the election of my proctorial colleague, Michael Brock.

One of the problems which had surfaced during my time on Council was to have a significant impact on Keble. This was the problem of 'non-dons', the large number of highly qualified scientists pursuing research in the laboratories without College Fellowships. This was a legitimate cause for complaint in a collegiate University and Council decided to put pressure on colleges to offer Fellowships to, at any rate, the most deserving of those people. It was a splendid opportunity for the college to remedy the lack of balance on Governing Body and at the same time increase the total numbers of Fellows at comparatively little expense, as the scientists were already being paid by the University. Most colleges already had enough Fellows and were reluctant to take in many more, so Keble had a clear run.

This was undoubtedly a decisive moment in the development of the college. There had been some anxieties as to how well these men would adjust to college life. In the event they all became excellent college tutors and made possible a salutary change of emphasis in its recruitment policy. It made sense for Keble to exploit its geographical proximity to the science area and, because scientists get a higher percentage of Firsts in Schools, it helped our academic record.

Meanwhile my own situation was much improved by the appointment of two new Fellows, a tutor in Economics and a second philosopher. Neither of them was appointed by the normal method of advertisement and short-listing. Adrian Darby was to prove an asset to the College on account of financial expertise and associations as well as for his role as tutor in Economics. He must have been a godsend to Davidge for this reason as well as being acceptable to him for having an estate in Worcestershire and a wife who was the daughter of the then Prime Minister, Sir Alec Douglas-Hume. He was moreover a man of great personal charm and vivacity. He brought with him a friend, Jim Griffin, who was a quiet, cultivated, Anglophile American and an able philosopher who ended his career in the White's Chair of Moral Philosophy.

These changes meant that I had a period of great contentment in which my teaching load was reduced by a congenial colleague and I was able to get to work on my first book. The Metaphysicals were flourishing and with Austin and Christopher Stead and me there was significant Keble involvement. One further delight was the Holy Lunch, which was one of a number of circulating luncheon groups in Oxford. We had lunch every Monday, each of the eight members providing the meal once a term in rotation in their college. We were expected to arrive punctually at 1 o'clock and said Sext together before lunch (leading one of my daughters to announce that 'on Mondays Daddy has sex before lunch'). We finished strictly at 2 o'clock, so that any member on Council could get to it in time. The basis of membership was four clerical and four lay members. When I was invited to join (I think in 1957) I was told by Bobby Milburn, then Dean of Worcester College and later Dean of Worcester Cathedral, that the lunch was to be 'agreeable but not apolaustic'. Within this formula the competition was to produce a simple but interesting meal (except in the time of Sandy Ogston at Trinity who was somewhat puritanical in such matters).

In the mid-nineteen-sixties I began to feel twinges of conscience. I had spent the whole of my academic life in Oxford which I was finding increasingly agreeable. I began to wonder whether I ought not to consider moving elsewhere. My involvement in constitutional matters in Oxford might make me a useful contributor to one of the new universities that were being set up at the time. Oxford dons had done much to help them start up. I was attracted especially to York where Eric James, ex High Master of Manchester Grammar School and an old Queen's man, was endeavouring to set up a collegiate university on the Oxford pattern.

Margy and I decided that I should apply and we did serious investigations into problems of housing and schooling in York. In the event I did not get the job which went to J L Mackie, Professor of Philosophy at the University of Sydney. It was a surprise appointment but an undeniably strong one. I was not greatly disappointed. My feeling was that I ought to put myself in the position of possibly leaving Oxford and let God decide whether I stayed or went. And in this case there was a curious sequel. Mackie left after a year or two for a Fellowship at University College, Oxford, and he was replaced at York by Ronald Atkinson, one of my early PPE Firsts at Keble. By an odd coincidence the then Senior Lecturer and later Reader was another of my Keble pupils, a First in Greats, Roland Hall. So I was able to reflect that I was present at York by proxy.

There were two other overtures at about this time. It was suggested to me, I cannot remember by whom, that I might like to be considered for the Principalship of Westfield College, London. It was a college, small by London standards, of about 800 students which, situated in Hampstead, was away from central London and had an uncertain future. There was talk of plans to amalgamate with Queen Mary College. I was attracted by the prospect of reviving the college and taking advantage of its small size by encouraging a genuinely collegiate atmosphere. The situation was agreeable and there should be no problem about finding suitable schools. When I was inter-viewed I was given to understand that there remained at that stage only two candidates of whom I was one. In the course of the interview I was asked if I minded the fact that philosophy was not one of the subjects taught in the college. I replied that I should be reluctant to give up philosophy teaching altogether, but that it was the sort of subject that consorted well with other subjects and that I could put on general lectures which would aim to relate philosophy to other items in the curriculum. I was told very firmly that the students were used to concentrating hard on their given subjects and would not readily interest themselves in such a venture. On the way home I became increasingly dispirited about this disclosure about the ethos of the college and found that I did not now want to spend much of my time in negotiations about the future status of the college. Accordingly I wrote next day to the Chairman of the College Council and withdrew my application.

The other possible opening came by way of an enquiry from Steven Watson, the new Principal of St Andrews as to whether I would be interested in succeeding my old tutor, Tony Woozley, as Professor of Moral Philosophy there on his departure to the University of Virginia. He indicated that an application from me would be taken very seriously. Margy and I had visited there when I was External Examiner for Woozley and found it, of course, most attractive. I was naturally pleased by this approach and could not turn it down out of hand.

Meanwhile there was a dramatic change in the Oxford situation. Ian Ramsey had looked to be a fixture in the Nolloth chair and was generally agreed to have made a success of it. His predecessor, Grensted, had been a psychologist rather than a philosopher and Ramsey with his eccentric but vigorous brand of empiricism had brought the Chair back into the place in the field of philosophy which it had occupied under its first holder, C C J Webb. With his enormous and, as later became apparent, excessive addiction to hard work, he had also done much outside Oxford to bring the Church into touch with the professions, especially that of medicine. Nevertheless it was a total surprise to everyone at Oxford when it was announced that he was to be the next Bishop of Durham, not least because his diminutive size was so markedly out of proportion to that most massively splendid of cathedrals. It was, however, an inspired appointment and Ian Ramsey in his sadly short time at Durham managed to both win the confidence of the Durham miners with his unpretentious friendliness and to become an influence for enlightened change in the Church at large.

I had become immensely interested in the philosophy of religion and had just published my first book (other than *Faith and Logic*), *Law, Morality and Religion in Secular Society*. It was an attempt to mediate, even adjudicate, between the legal philosophies of H L A Hart and Patrick Devlin. It was a competent piece of work and, I still think, made an original and substantial contribution to that particular debate, but it could not be thought to challenge comparison with the works of other established figures in the Philosophy of Religion. But, given the interest I had shown in other possible jobs, it was impossible for me not to consider applying for the vacant Nolloth chair.

There was a problem, however, in finding suitable referees. Price, who had always given me his support, declined on the grounds that

he was committed to another candidate (who, I have since discovered, was John Hick). My other possible referee, Austin Farrer,
was a member of the Electoral Board. It would be absurd and, indeed,
of doubtful propriety, to ask him to act as referee for one of the
candidates. So I went to see Kenneth Wheare, the Vice-Chancellor,
who was *ex officio* Chairman of the Electors, explained my predicament and said that if it should happen that the Electors were disposed
to choose me, they might regard me as available. In due course I
received a letter telling me that I had been elected. It was evident that
in electing me they had relied on promise which they thought they
had detected. I reflected that this was the second time in my career
that I had been appointed to a job for which I was inadequately
prepared and was apprehensive as to the outcome.

At the same time I was absolutely delighted. It was as if the
restlessness of the last few years and non-success of other applications
had been working up to this moment in a providential manner.

On the downside it meant leaving Keble, which had for twenty
years been my academic home – longer than I was to spend at any
other college, and which has remained very close to my heart. I have
often reflected since that the striking developments of the last thirty
or so years, the greatly increased Fellowship, the new buildings, the
increase in endowment, which have removed it from the category of
'poor college', have all occurred since I left – to the extent that I have
been tempted to regard it as a case of negative causality, all this being
caused precisely by my no longer being a Fellow of the college. But,
apart from the outrageously self-centred character of this hypothesis,
it is plain in retrospect that the seeds of these later developments were
already to be found in the successive periods that I have been
describing.

CHAPTER 11

Oriel

M Y ELEVATION TO A CHAIR had the consequence that I must change my college. In Oxford as distinct from Cambridge each professorship is allocated permanently to a particular college with the result that if elected to a chair one automatically becomes a Fellow of the college to which that chair is attached. In Cambridge, by contrast, a newly appointed professor has to find a college prepared to accept him. This means, of course, that if he is already a fellow of a Cambridge college he does not have to leave it. It is widely believed in Oxford that, as a consequence of this arrangement, there exists in Cambridge a limbo of professors whom no college has been willing to accept.

My chair, the Nolloth Professorship of the Philosophy of the Christian Religion, is attached to Oriel and so it was to Oriel that I had to migrate. In some ways the change was considerable – from a relatively modern college to an ancient one; from a large one to a small one; from well north of the High to just south of it. But in other respects the move from Keble to Oriel was like going home. Keble was founded to be a memorial to John Keble and the Oxford Movement, and Keble and the other originators of the Oxford Movement had been Fellows of Oriel. So when I left the cavernous hall of Keble to dine in the more domestic hall of Oriel I was surrounded by portraits of the same persons as at Keble – Newman, Pusey and, of course, Keble himself.

However, the transition from the status of a college tutor to that of a professor was altogether more disconcerting and the oddity of the experience was assisted by the circumstance that in my first year at Oriel I occupied no less than three rooms. The first was a large barn-like room on the second floor of the Rhodes building overlooking the third quad. Very sparsely furnished, it made me feel scarcely part of the college at all. Altogether I felt as if I was in an academic vacuum. I no longer had undergraduate pupils to see and to organise for the term. I had only the one graduate student, John

Brennan, who was far enough advanced to need no regular supervision. The University statutes were of minimal assistance. They mainly required a professor to deliver twenty-four lectures or classes during the academic year. Ian Ramsey, my predecessor, was not available for consultation, having left the college a year before to become Bishop of Durham.

I cannot remember my second room at all. The third was agreeable enough but is hard to reconstruct in my memory since it has ceased to exist, having been incorporated in the splendid new Senior Common Room donated to the College by Sir Weldon Dalrymple Champneys.

Eventually I was given the set of rooms that I was to occupy for the whole of the rest of my time in Oriel. They were ideal, situated on the second floor of the staircase between the first and the second quads. This position gave them a view to the south over the first quad and to the north over the second quad. I could see the entrance to the Hall and the Chapel through one window and to the Senior Common Room through the other. Thus I could appreciate, and explain to guests, how the staircase system worked. Because all the rooms were grouped on staircases, their occupants, whether dons or undergraduates, had to go down into the quad on their way to anywhere else, and this maximised the chances of people meeting one another. This became particularly noticeable when finals were in progress. Candidates with the latest exam papers in their hands would encounter their tutors in the quad and together they would go through the papers and see what they jointly thought of them, it being the case that neither of them had known in advance what the questions would be.

I found in due course that, being used to the two flights of stairs several times a day, I could mount them very rapidly, while my much younger graduate students would arrive at my room breathing heavily.

So here I was right in the heart of the College, illustrating Oriel's boast that it was 'good to professors'. Some colleges did not even give rooms to professors at all. Nevertheless it could never be forgotten that on admission as a Fellow a newly elected professor, whatever his seniority in his Faculty, was the junior Fellow in the college and thereafter ranked in seniority according to the date of his admission.

Hence it became his duty on certain occasions in Common Room to hand round the coffee. I thoroughly approved of this, but there were more serious disadvantages of one's comparative lack of seniority. Rooms, for example, and even more seriously parking spaces. Given his relatively advanced age on admission a professorial Fellow could never expect to graduate to the very best rooms in college; and it was not until the final year before retirement that I became entitled to a half share in a parking place. Before I retired I tried to persuade the college to allocate a suitable room of the middling sort to each professor to which he would go automatically on appointment, as had become the case, by way of long custom, with the Regius Chair of Modern History. But I failed to persuade my colleagues.

One signal advantage from my point of view of migration to Oriel was that another professorship attached to the college was in the Faculty of Theology, the Oriel and Laing Chair of the Interpretation of Holy Scripture. Hedley Sparks was not only a very meticulous Old Testament scholar but also an extremely adroit academic politician, who in his earlier career at Birmingham University had almost single-handedly frustrated an attempt by Marxists to determine University appointments and was a helpful adviser to me when a year after my appointment I was prematurely made Chairman of the Theology Faculty. There was also the Chaplain, Canon F W Dillistone, sometime Dean of Liverpool and a liberal theologian of note, always known affectionately as 'Dilly'.

As a counterpoise to all these the Philosophy Fellow, Richard Robinson, on the point of retirement, was a devout atheist, who in a book *An Atheist's Values* set out his creed with characteristic clarity and incisiveness. His Ancient History colleague, Peter Brunt, told me this story about him. They had a Greats pupil who came to Brunt and asked his advice about the Civil Service interview which he was about to undergo. 'It's no good asking me,' said Brunt, 'I have no experience of it, ask Richard – he has sat on the interviewing panel.' So the man went off to see Richard Robinson. When he next saw the man, Brunt asked him what Richard had said. The man said that Richard had given him two pieces of advice. One was 'Don't throw yourself about as you usually do'. The other was, 'Try and look as if you were enjoying it.' Here Richard raised his hand, 'Yes,' he said,

'Life is a grim business, but if you want to get into the Civil Service, you must look as if you were enjoying it.'

Some Fellows of Oriel I had already met. Arthur Crow was a long time Chairman of the Senior Tutors Committee whom I had met when I was Senior Proctor on University business; and Christopher Seton-Watson had been a colleague on a University Committee on Student Mental Health. But it was none of these who was responsible for my initial welcome to the college. Before the beginning of term I received an invitation to dine from Dr W E Parry, Mathematician and Fellow-Librarian, who was to become a life-time friend. So all in all I was made to feel entirely at home in Oriel, although, inevitably, I lacked the close contact with undergraduates which are needed for complete identification. This has become apparent to me in retirement when I regularly return to Keble for old-member gaudies where I meet my old pupils, now themselves retired, whereas I have no such ties with Oriel.

One exception to the general friendliness, as before at Christ Church, was Hugh Trevor-Roper, now Regius Professor and Fellow of Oriel. Some years earlier, after Rob Mortimer had left Christ Church to be Bishop of Exeter, he invited me to give a series of three lectures to his clergy school. He had also, as I did not know, invited Trevor-Roper to address the school. My wife and I arrived in mid-afternoon and were shown into the library, there to await tea. Shortly afterwards Trevor-Roper was ushered in to join us. It soon became apparent that he would answer a remark from me but not from my wife, Margy. Margy was not someone prepared to put up with this and, as soon as the pattern was established, she got up, went to a bookshelf, took down a book and began to read it. Trevor-Roper then got up, also took down a book and started to read it. Left thus high and dry, I had no alternative but to follow their example. When our hostess came in to invite us in to tea, she found the three of us reading our books in a temperature well below zero.

One of the first things I had to do on arrival in Oriel was to go and see the chef. I was still a member of the circulating Oxford lunch group 'the Holy Lunch', whose members took it in turn to provide lunch in his or her college. Upon changing colleges to Oriel, I felt that I should consult the chef there and brief him on the requirements for the once-a-term 'agreeable but not apolaustic' luncheons. When

I met the chef at Oriel he told me that he already knew what I wanted to see him about. The chef at Keble had come round to see him and told him about the lunch and at the same time listed my favourite dishes. I was greatly touched by this revelation of inter-college co-operation at a level which we for the most part took entirely for granted.

Our chef, Norman Clark, was excellent and, moreover, his wife managed the kitchen very efficiently. They were both strict Baptists and were entirely free from the corruption with suppliers which was a permanent temptation for college chefs. A day came when Clark announced to the Domestic Bursar that, much to his regret, he felt obliged to hand in his notice. He insisted that he had no complaints about his treatment by the college. On the contrary he was most reluctant to leave. What prompted his decision was the education of their children. Even the strict Baptists in Oxford were less strict than those he remembered in Scotland. He and a colleague, also a strict Baptist, had therefore decided to set up a hotel near Aberdeen which was now thriving owing to the proximity of the oil rigs. The Bursar did his best to dissuade him, but he remained adamant. Still retaining some hope that he would return, the Bursar promoted the under chef to replace him on a temporary basis. Next summer Hugh Browne decided to take a holiday in Scotland during which he would pay a friendly call on Clark's hotel, suspecting that it might not be flourishing. This proved indeed to be the case. Clark's principles required that the hotel should be a temperance hotel. Clark had served alcoholic liquor with meals at Oriel, but they were not his responsibility and lay on the Fellows' consciences and not his own. But this policy proved a deterrent to prospective clients from the oil rigs, for whom excellent cuisine was not enough. As the Bursar had hoped, Clark returned to Oriel and resumed his position to the delight of everyone, not least the under chef, who had disliked the increased responsibility.

I had only been in Oriel a short while when a more serious crisis exploded across the western world – the students' revolt. Its manifestations in Oxford were comparatively muted. In Britain only the LSE was seriously disrupted. Oxford was different from other universities, except Cambridge, in that it was ruled by the academics themselves and not by a 'faceless' administration and power was dispersed among some twenty-eight colleges each with its own Governing Body. Hence when a body of students occupied the Delegate's Room in the Clarendon Building, where the Hebdomadal Council regularly met, it did little actually to inconvenience the Fellows of colleges who could even rejoice at the cessation of communication from the central bodies of the University. It occurred to me at the time that if the revolting students really wanted to disrupt the University, they should have occupied the Bodleian and its dependent libraries which would really have upset senior members and could, moreover, be plausibly represented as simply a somewhat excessive devotion to their academic studies.

But, of course, what they intended was a dramatic challenge to the authority of the University and for this purpose the Delegate's Room was an appropriate choice. By the greatest good fortune the Vice-Chancellor at the time was Alan Bullock, a distinguished Modern Historian, author of a book on Hitler and Stalin and a bluff Yorkshireman who had retained his north country accent. He could be relied upon to keep his nerve and was impossible to represent as the face of unfeeling authority. I do not remember how the central dispute was finally resolved or whether there exists a record of the encounter comparable to the close analytical documentation of the troubles at LSE, but, to my mind, the most significant move was when the Vice-Chancellor's wife, Nibby Bullock and the wife of a previous Vice-Chancellor (Joan Wheare) took sandwiches into the students who were encamped in the Delegate's Room, thus introducing a benign personal element into the proceedings.

In Oriel the revolt followed the central pattern. A party of undergraduates invaded the Senior Common Room while we were engaged in a College meeting. The Provost, Kenneth Turpin, responded immediately by gathering up his papers and leading us out of the room to continue our business elsewhere. In a move which some of us considered unwise he subsequently demanded a written apology from the culprits on pain of being sent down. What then happened was significant. They consulted their tutors. Since I had no undergraduate pupils I was not immediately involved; but two graduate students whom I did not know came to see me and asked my advice. They were concerned above all to explain to me that they had followed their consciences in doing what they did: how then

21. *In the river with Nell and Matthew*

22. *Equipoise: Kate and Clare in the garden*

23. The Fellows of Keble in 1952

24. The Proctors (Michael Brock and I) call upon the Mayor, Councillor on MA Lower in 1956

25. Being presented by Maurice Wiles for the degree of DD

26. With Matthew BA after the Degree ceremony

27. *In the Encaenia Procession with Arthur Peacocke*

28. *Four of my Oxford D.Phils including from left to right Steve Holtzer, Chuck Hugher and Rob Prevost at Rob's Wedding*

29. Eric and Victoria Robinson with Margy at Encombe, Dorset

30. Nell, Matthew, Kate and Clare

31. Grandchildren – Josephine Dand and Isabel Richards having a tutorial with Peter Millican and John Lucas

32. Mme Gorre doing her washing in the river Dronne, seen from our terrace

33. Margy with Mme Fochetti and a basket full of cèpes

34. Birthday Lunch at the Grand Hotel, with the entire family

35. *With family on our terrace at La Varenne at 90th Birthday*

36. *The Pelisson Brothers and their wives in front of the Grand Hotel after the Birthday Lunch*

could they now apologise? I said that it was not what they thought at the time that mattered but what they thought now. Did they *now* think that they were justified as members of the college in defying the legitimate authority of the Provost and Fellows? They replied that, having thought it over, they would not now have acted as they did. I said that in that case they could properly apologise, since to apologise was to unsay what could not be undone, and this they could do without casting any doubt on the purity of their motives at the time. In the event they all signed a statement, prepared by the Law tutor, which the Provost was prepared to accept as constituting an apology.

So ended the Student Revolt in one of the colleges and much the same happened in the others. The question remains what caused the revolt and what effects did it have. My impression is that very few of the student leaders shared the philosophical anarchism which inspired their counterparts in the United States and mainland Europe. What they did share and what led a sizeable proportion of undergraduates to support them was a generalised anti-institutionalism which remains wide-spread today in the country at large.

The effect of this could be seen in the life of University and college societies. Pre-revolution these were organised on a recognised pattern. There would be a Chairman, a Secretary and a Treasurer and there would be College Representatives. Members would pay a small termly subscription and the society would be registered with the Proctors who had an over-all responsibility for their good conduct. After the revolution they decreased in number and those that remained became more difficult to organise. I became aware of this change in the *Socratic Club*, whose founding president was C S Lewis, whom I had succeeded on his appointment to a Chair in Cambridge. It flourished exceedingly and for two decades was by far the liveliest philosophical society in Oxford. We had three meetings a term and had no difficulty in getting distinguished speakers from inside and outside the University. There were minimal minutes taken by the Secretary which recorded the name and provenance of the speaker or speakers and the names and colleges of all who attended. The names of speakers included Bernard Williams, Isaiah Berlin, Gilbert Ryle, Elizabeth Anscome, J R Lucas . . . And amongst the student members were many who attained distinction as philosophers in later life. In the 1970s the Society suffered a severe decline as it became increasingly difficult to find students prepared to sustain the minimal organisation required. The overall numbers of societies registered with the Proctors declined markedly.

A further outcome of the revolt was a thorough overhaul of University discipline which up to this point had been unashamedly paternalistic. Decisions were left largely to the discretion of the Proctors and of the Deans in colleges and the decision to send students down lay with the Vice-Chancellor and Proctors and the Governing Body in Colleges. There was a minimum of legal procedure. Although student demand undoubtedly precipitated change, developments in legal philosophy, supported by liberal opinion among senior members, made change inevitable.

Meanwhile I was gathering a collection of graduate students for whose supervision I was responsible. My room was ideal for this purpose, being large enough for a class of up to a dozen people consisting of all my graduates taken together and on a sufficiently domestic scale for them to feel at home when coming to me one by one. I had always adhered to the tradition that a Fellow's room should be more like a sitting room than like an office and I always felt uncomfortable when an American referred to my 'office'.

As numbers in the college gradually increased it became essential to maximise the available accommodation and, throughout Oxford, provision for conferences became an important element in college finances. Thus the college embarked on a comprehensive redevelopment of what was called 'the island site' which comprised the area bounded by Oriel Square, Oriel Street and the High Street. The fourth side of the square, King Edward Street, formed the western boundary of the area, but could not be developed because it was leased profitably to solicitors, estate agents, etc. The obvious Oxford solution was to construct a quadrangle, but this was ruled out, apart from the unavailability of King Edward Street, by the existence of a Tudor tennis court in the middle of the site. It was listed and could not be demolished in spite of the fact that a larger and more complete Tudor tennis court was to be found adjoining University College less that a quarter of a mile away, where the University's Real Tennis Club had its headquarters. The college appointed an architect, Geoffrey Beard, and set up a committee consisting of the Bursar,

Hugh Browne, a retired Brigadier, Royal Engineers' Jeremy Catto, a medieval historian, and Graham Vincent-Smith, a mathematician, ably supported by Richard Ward, master builder and college Clerk of Works. The solution was to strengthen the foundations of the tennis court and to construct upon it a second storey in brick to provide graduate accommodation. The result is quite unlike a quadrangle and more like a winding medieval street. The space bounded by the tennis court was used for an up to date lecture hall and a large ante-room, the whole serving as accommodation for medium-sized conferences. A year after this part of the project was completed the architect sacked himself, protesting that the College Committee could rehabilitate the old houses in Oriel Street without assistance from him. He was right. This project proved a triumphant success. With the greatest ingenuity the team managed to take rooms of various sizes and ages and turn them into modern apartments each with lavatory and a shower. To the outside observer nothing would seem more absurd and more typical of Oxford than to make a small team of academics responsible for such a practical concern plainly in need of professional oversight. But as it happened every member of the team supplied an essential component of the task. The mathematician could look at a space, turn it round in his imagination and work out how it could be modified for its new uses. The historian knew the history of the buildings and could judge which features should be retained as of abiding historical interest. It would not be unusual, for example, to find a Victorian fireplace on top of a classical one, itself on top of an Elizabethan one. Which to retain? The combined expertise of the builder, heir to generations of Oxford builders, and the military engineer, as well as that of the historian was needed in particular to deal with Tackley Hall on the corner of Oriel Street and the High Street which had once been a medieval hall of the sort that housed students in the earliest days of the University.

One of the greatest achievements of Oxford colleges in the post-war period was the way in which new buildings were inserted into the historic centre of the city in such a way that they provided the accommodation needed and, for the most part, were distinctively modern, but did not spoil the setting into which they were inserted. The curious thing about this Oriel development was that it was entirely concealed from the road. The development gave me an opportunity to make my own modest contribution to the fabric of the college. One day at lunch I heard the Bursar remarking to a colleague that we were £40,000 short of what was required for the refurbishment of one of the houses in Oriel Street. It so happened that Margy and I had at that time been reviewing our finances. As a result of Ma's generosity we found that we had more money than we reckoned we needed. The children were at a stage when they could do with some financial help and I was anxious to do what I could to help my colleges. So, having worked out what we thought we needed ourselves for the remainder of our lives, we decided that we were in a position to give away £100,000. So we divided this sum between us. Margy gave her half to the children and I was left with £50,000 for the colleges. Thus I was in a position to offer the Bursar the sum he required, and the remaining £10,000 I gave to Keble.

The development team discovered that when they had executed their plan there was going to be a distinctly oddly shaped space for which they needed to find a use, and with typical ingenuity they managed to turn it into a seminar room, to be called the 'Basil Mitchell' Room. I believe it is in regular use although it is situated up an awkward staircase which I still have difficulty in discovering. I am glad to have been commemorated in this way, because I never occupied a position in the College which entitled me to be represented among the many drawings and etchings in the Small Common Room.

However I was to be represented in that room at second hand, so to speak. For one individual who was clearly destined to find his place in that room was Reggie Burton, the classics tutor and for many years Steward of Common Room. Much of the credit for the harmony that prevailed in the Common Room during my time was due to him. He was one of those classical dons who were totally at home in the classical world of Greece and Rome and who explored its language and literature as a matter of course in the pursuit of learning. It would not have occurred to him to think of his academic activity as constituting 'research.' He was a true representative of *Literae Humaniores*. It was felt, quite properly, that there should be some representation of him in the Small Common Room. A committee was set up to choose a suitable artist and one was selected. When the drawing was produced it was beautifully executed but to general alarm bore no resemblance to Reggie. Should we ask this artist to do another drawing or look for another one? At this juncture I mentioned my daughter, Clare, who at the age of eighteen was about to go to Bristol University to read French and History of Art. Within the family she had displayed a gift for catching a likeness. It would do no harm to let her have a go; and it was duly agreed to give her the commission on the understanding that, if she failed she would be paid a small sum for her time, and, if she succeeded, she should get what we had agreed to pay the professional. In the event she produced a drawing which everyone, including Reggie himself, agreed to be remarkably like him; and that drawing now hangs in the Small Senior Common Room where I can point it out to visitors and say proudly that my daughter had done it.

At about this time Kenneth Turpin retired from the Provostship and proceedings began to find a successor. This took me entirely by surprise. I had not realised that Turpin was about to go and I had given no thought to the question of his successor. Early in the Hilary Term of 1980 two of my colleagues, Bill Parry and Derek Morris, asked me if I was prepared to stand. I was surprised but gratified and readily agreed. As the term wore on I warmed to the idea. I dreamed of myself addressing an old members' Gaudy or a bump supper or receiving the Queen on a Royal visit. I anticipated no difficulty in chairing the College Meeting, having become by now an experienced chairman. I would enjoy doing what I could to enable the constituent elements in the college to work together in a harmonious way. As a result of my year as Senior Proctor and my six years on Council I knew how the Government of the University worked and was familiar with most of the people who were influential in it. So I came to think that, in spite of the fact that this had been sprung on me, I was quite a respectable candidate. There was one respect in which I knew I was seriously deficient. I had no interest or experience in finance and had no idea how to go about raising large sums of money for the college, and this then and later was one of the main functions of the Head of a House. One far from negligible circumstance was that Margy hated the idea of her being installed in the Lodgings and required to entertain as First Lady in the college. I was prepared to discount this objection, since I knew she would in fact do it very well and, moreover, would be in her element in transforming the Lodgings which had become dreary and lifeless under the Turpins.

The matter was decided at the final College Meeting of the term after which I learned that I had accumulated quite a respectable vote but not enough to secure my election. Margy was enormously relieved and I was disappointed but not desperately so. In the event we elected someone from outside the college, Sir Michael Swann, recently retired from the Chairmanship of the BBC. After a year in office he resigned from the post, confessing that he had under-estimated how much work it entailed. In the ensuing election the college's choice was simplified by the emergence of a candidate whose credentials were unchallengeable. Sir Zelman Cowen had recently retired as Governor-General of Australia and earlier in his career had been Fellow and Tutor in Law at Oriel. For the rest of my time at Oriel he presided over the college with complete success, ably seconded by his wife Anna.

If anything the Provostship election had made me feel even more at home in Oriel. I had by now accumulated eight doctoral candidates and the 'domestic class' had become well established. As well as the two university classes, one with John Lucas, the other with Maurice Wiles, I had a class for undergraduates in which I was assisted by David Brown who, after a period in Cambridge where he had taken his doctorate with Elizabeth Anscombe as his supervisor, had returned to Oriel as Chaplain and Fellow and Tutor in Theology. This class was intended to help undergraduates with the 'bridge paper' in the new Honour School, and David more than compensated for my comparative ignorance of Theology. David's presence in the college together with that of Ernest Nicholson, recently elected Oriel Professor, established Oriel as the natural first choice of people wishing to read the new School. Since the college now had some graduate accommodation I felt able for the first time to steer my graduates in its direction.

During my final years in Oriel, the college was chiefly concerned with the question of the admission of women. It was widely felt both in the University and in the country at large that the imbalance between men and women in the University needed to be redressed. It was well below the national average (although, significantly, the proportion of women dons was higher). Apart from the creation of new women's colleges, which was unrealistic, the only way of achieving this was to admit women to the existing all-men colleges. Although the general principle of sexual equality was undoubtedly the preponderant motive, it soon became apparent to the existing colleges that they would benefit academically by the admission of women, since a large number of able women had not as yet been able to gain admission to the University and the women's colleges were always high up in the Norrington Table, based on the results of the Final Schools. It was plainly a matter which affected the entire University and needed regulation by inter-college agreement, but the advantages to first-comers were so obvious that a number of colleges jumped the gun and announced that they were going to alter their statutes by abolishing the clause that 'No woman shall be a member of the college.'

In the event the most that could be achieved by common consent was that the change should take place at the same time in all the colleges. At no point, so far as I know, was there serious consideration of what the shape of the University should be. Little concern was shown for the interests of the women's colleges. They were remarkable institutions which on their foundation were pioneers of women's education and, in spite of having always to make do with limited financial resources, had developed an ethos of high scholarship and cultivation. It was arguable that they made a unique contribution to the overall character of the University which ought not to be wantonly destroyed. My feeling at the time was that the best solution would have been to retain the five women-only colleges, to keep five of the men's colleges as men-only colleges, and to have the remainder go mixed. But none of this was discussed. The women's colleges had either to join the rush to go mixed or hold out as single sex colleges under conditions of considerable handicap. St Hilda's alone decided on the latter course and remained a women-only college, convinced that there were virtues in a single-sex institution, different from but not inferior to those that were mixed. That this judgement was correct is indicated by the continued success of women-only colleges in the United States such as Mount Holyoke, Wellesley and Bryn Mawr, and this in a culture in which co-education is much more firmly established as the norm than it is in this country.

Oriel's decision to remain a men-only college was widely regarded outside the college as a product of sheer conservatism, not to say anti-feminism, but it was entirely defensible in terms of the above discussion and as a means of supporting the decision of St Hilda's. Both colleges had to hope that there were enough men and women who would prefer a single sex college to give them a selective advantage in the search for able students.

In the end after ten years it became apparent that this was not the case and the decision was taken to join the remainder of what had been men-only colleges in admitting women. I remember my last act in the college at my last College Meeting as being to propose that the change be made, and it was duly passed by well over the two thirds majority required.

So ended my time in Oriel and my tenure of the Nolloth Chair. The college had not only provided a supportive environment for my academic work but had also allowed me to play a full part as a Fellow of the college and member of the Governing Body. For this I remain deeply grateful.

CHAPTER 12

My philosophical development

W HEN I FIRST TOOK UP MY FELLOWSHIP at Keble in 1947 I was woefully ill-prepared. Since I graduated in 1939 I had spent most of the time in the Navy and what little philosophy I had done was in relation to my Indian studies and had little to do with what I was now required to teach. Moreover I had to come to terms with the so-called 'revolution in philosophy' which had its origins in Logical Positivism and had the effect of severely restricting the topics that were considered properly philosophical. Although there were differences between its practitioners, and perhaps only A J Ayer himself for a few years remained a strict Logical Positivist, they were agreed in regarding metaphysics and theology as meaningless or, at least, beyond the scope of rational discussion.

Although there were a number of respected philosophers in Oxford who continued to philosophise in the old way, ignoring these restrictions, they were able to exercise only a declining influence and were not representative of the 'Oxford Philosophy' which for some twenty or thirty years had a world-wide reputation. It might have been thought that in this revolutionary situation there would have been a good deal of personal friction, but in my experience this was not the case. One reason for this was that as philosophers we did not meet very often. The social unit was the College Senior Common Room and the people one met there were one's colleagues in other subjects. One met one's philosophical colleagues twice a term at meetings of the Philosophy Sub-Faculty which were drearily prosaic and quite spectacularly poorly organised – I always found it hard to decide between two possible candidates for the most chaotic meetings in my experience, the committee of the Wootton Annual Flower Show and the meetings of the Oxford University Sub-Faculty of Philosophy, where it was not unknown to accept a proposal first and then discuss it afterwards.

There were also three times a term meetings of the *Philosophical Society* which in the absence of a Faculty Centre were held in colleges by rotation. These were rarely the scene of debates about fundamentals except when visitors from outside were invited to speak. These occasions, it has to be admitted, were sometimes the scenes of gladiatorial combats. I can remember only two. One was when Bland Blanshard, a highly respected philosopher from Yale, was cruelly demolished by Gilbert Ryle; the other when Gabriel Marcel addressed the Society and Iris Murdoch replied. The only person who emerged with any credit on that occasion was Iris who managed to mediate between the parties with a paper of admirable subtlety. To no effect. My Oxford colleagues obstinately refused to make any attempt to understand Marcel and he, poor man, proved quite unable to get the measure of their questions. As Christopher Stead and I walked back to Keble, we were overtaken by Paul Grice who was consumed with fury that such a charlatan had been invited to address the Society.

My impression is that when it was a case of one of my colleagues replying to another, it was generally not in order to challenge his main thesis but to seek clarification of some minor point. The consequence is that I retain no memory of anything said at such a meeting except for a single devastating *obiter* from J L Austin. Patrick Nowell-Smith had read a paper on Universals and in reply Stephen Toulmin had gone on at unreasonable length to the effect that Plato's theory of Forms was a natural, if mistaken, attempt to solve the problem. At a convenient pause, Austin, who was stretched out on the floor and leaning on one elbow, cut across the discussion and said, 'I quite see that we all have to make mistakes; what I don't see is that all the mistakes have to made.' Toulmin was effectively stopped in his tracks.

The intensely critical atmosphere of the time led people to develop defensive strategies. One of these was to fail to understand the questioner, and ask him to state his question more clearly, thus insinuating that you had detected ambiguities in his formulation that he had failed to notice. I remember Henry Price remarking about the *Philosophical Society* that 'the air is full of inhibitions.' Hence there was a story circulating in Oxford at the time about an American who had spent a period in Oxford. When, back home, someone asked a friend whether the experience had changed him, the reply was 'He's just fine. Only he's gotten so he can't understand'.

An extreme case of philosophical inhibition occurred when I was examining in Greats. We had a candidate who in his written papers showed indications of first class ability but not clearly enough to dispense with a viva. It proved impossible to get him to answer any questions. In philosophy he simply spluttered and made gestures of incomprehension. Finally we gave up. As he had good marks in Ancient History, the historians took over the questioning and at once his tongue was loosed and he answered freely and got his First that way.

The generally non-confrontational character of proceedings in the *Philosophical Society* bore witness to a genuine esprit de corps among the Oxford philosophers. Partly, of course, this was owing to their sharing a social milieu in which their children went to the same schools and brought them together on non-academic occasions. But it is my impression that they felt themselves to be engaged in a common enterprise of clearing up philosophy and rebuilding it anew on sounder foundations. In this enterprise all were assumed to be engaged and, where individuals engaged in this task disagreed, it could be assumed that it was in the interests of greater clarity and rigour. Indeed if philosophy were thought of as excluding those issues which had historically been the great occasions of controversy it followed that no fundamental disagreements would remain. An amusing illustration of this situation arose during the period in which I examined Greats in 1953–5. The convention was that every paper was marked by two examiners, but for some time it had been the custom that the Logic paper was marked by all three philosophy examiners. This was because it had been found that it was in this paper that the examiners differed most. Indeed it was still the custom at that time for the Ancient Historians to pay the Philosophers half a crown for every script in Logic on which they all gave the same mark. The payments ceased during my time because the practice had become too expensive as the three examiners agreed too often. The Revolution in philosophy had finally triumphed.

It was perhaps this assumption of basic agreement which occasioned the curious linguistic convention observed by philosophers at that time, whereby the pronoun 'this' was universally employed at the expense of 'that'. 'This,' a philosopher would say to his colleagues, 'is very interesting.' And he would expect them to gather round the specimen thesis as being worthy of close analysis. 'That' would have indicated some subject comparatively remote from the proper interests of philosophers.

The official meetings of philosophers being so unfruitful, it is not surprising that the real work was done in smaller groups of like-minded people. One of these had begun before the war and consisted of A J Ayer, Isaiah Berlin, Stuart Hampshire, J L Austin, Donald MacNabb, A D Woozley and Donald MacKinnon. Another, composed of younger people such as Peter Strawson, Geoffrey and Mary Warnock, Jim Urmson, David Pears and Patrick Gardiner, was to be heard in discussion on the BBC's newly introduced Third Programme and it was this group which was seen to form the nucleus of what the world knew as Oxford Philosophy. The tone of these discussions was civilised and urbane, marked by intense concentration on the chosen topics which remained circumscribed by the omission of substantial questions of value.

A pupil of mine, Ogilvie Buchan, who had just taken a First in Philosophy, Politics and Economics, was studying for a while in Paris from where he was able to take a detached view of current British philosophy and compare it with that in France. What struck him about the former was the absence of discussion of questions of value. Whereas in post-war France thoughtful people were bombarded with moral issues because of the divisions created by the ambiguities of French politics during the occupation, the British enjoyed comparatively stable political circumstances. The French experience of sharp ideological conflict encouraged the existentialist contention that morality was a field of incommensurable decisions open only to displays of fierce rhetoric. The British meanwhile, who were not troubled by questions of morality, could acquiesce in the notion that the analysis of 'good' is a proper task of philosophy, whereas the question of what things are good does not admit of philosophical treatment.

It was here, in relation to morality, that the post-positivist limitation of meaningful discourse to science and common sense came under the greatest strain. Theology and metaphysics could plausibly be relegated to a sphere of personal decision, but morality could not readily be disposed of in this way. It cried out for philosophical treatment. This was provided in the first instance by R M Hare. Dissatisfied by the prevailing post-positivist attempts to analyse moral judgments in terms of expressions of emotion or of 'attitude' he was determined to remain within that tradition while at the same time vindicating moral reasoning as a valid undertaking. His solution was to characterise moral judgments as expressing 'impera- tives', which could be justified by a type of reasoning based upon Kant's categorical imperatives. Sketched at first in *The Language of Morals*, it was further developed into a formidable system in *Freedom and Reason*, which thereafter became the standard work in Moral Philosophy with which any proposed alternative must reckon.

This was the point at which I myself began to attempt some contribution. I was required in my capacity as a 'CUF Lecturer' to give two series of lectures or classes every year, and the advantage of classes was that they required less previous preparation than lectures, and I had very little time to write lectures. Even in spite of my taking pupils in pairs I had fifteen hours of tutorial teaching a week and these too at that early stage required preparation. So I was glad to share a class with Iris Murdoch and Philippa Foot. Iris I knew from the Metaphysicals and Philippa was the wife of our Politics Lecturer at Keble, Michael Foot. I cannot remember the title we gave to the Class, but we had a common interest in enlarging the sphere of moral philosophy and establishing the objectivity of moral judgements, which to our minds Hare did not adequately acknowledge. Iris was on her way to developing the broad Platonism of *The Sovereignty of Good*, and Philippa was feeling her way towards the full-blooded naturalism of her later work *Natural Goodness*. My own interest was in extending the range of moral concepts in such a way as to allow for the influence upon ethics of the other forbidden subjects, metaphysics and theology. I suspect that at that stage I was less clear than the other two were as to where I was going.

My recollection is that we spent a good deal of time in the study of 'mixed words'. One of the weaknesses, as it seemed to us, of the current fashion of distinguishing between evaluative and descriptive uses of words was that it led philosophers to suppose that one could take an entirely general evaluative word like 'good' and apply it to whatever set of descriptive facts one liked. But this took no account of the many words of moral commendation or condemnation which could not be prised apart, so to speak, from a comparatively narrow range of descriptive terms. Thus to call a man a coward did not allow one to say, by way of explication, that he habitually stood fast against the enemy or refused to betray his friends. Nor could one call him a coward and at the same time commend him on this account. Hare had, of course, anticipated this line of criticism by providing a criterion for the genuinely evaluative use of a word and dismissing other uses as 'inverted comma' expressions. By proceeding the way we did we were following the pattern of argument then being developed by J L Austin and carefully studying the use of words as actually employed in every day speech. We were examining the use of moral language and uncovering features of it which, in our view, were incompatible with the abstract theory that Hare and others were developing. It then became possible to apply this method to, e.g. religious language, which provided the title to Ian Ramsey's book *Religious Language*.

My own introduction to this sort of linguistic philosophy came by way of a card which I received from Austin at the beginning of my first term. It announced that the Saturday morning meetings this term would be held in the Common Room dining room at Christ Church and that the subject for the term would be 'Marks, Symbols and Signs'. I vividly remember that first meeting. I arrived in that room, which of course I knew well from my Christ Church days, to find an assemblage of my philosophical colleagues seated round a green baize table on which were displayed an assortment of maps, charts, railway timetables and the like. Proceedings started with Austin pointing to a chart in front of him and asking Jim Urmson 'What would you say to me if I asked you "are there any symbols on that chart?"'. Urmson hesitated for a while and then said, 'But I don't think you *would* ask me "are there any symbols on that chart?".'

I cannot now remember how the discussion developed on that occasion, but it does illustrate the care that was taken to study words in their full context and the suspicion that attached to any usage that could not easily be given an appropriate context.

Austin's method did not, it seemed, yield any positive conclusions. Its destructive effects became apparent in his series of lectures published as *Sense and Sensibilia*. These were enormously entertaining and their tendency was to demolish the sense datum theory which the Logical Positivists had inherited from British empiricism as refined by Bertrand Russell and C D Broad.

The ordinary language investigated by Austin and his followers was not extended to moral or religious language, although it could well have been. I doubt if Austin himself would have subscribed to the dogma that morality and religion were not susceptible of rational debate. I did not know him well but he was always friendly and the only time in my presence that he ventured onto the subject of religion, he said 'I should like to believe that my sins are forgiven but I don't have any reasons to think they are.'

An early paper which I contributed to the Joint Session of the Aristotelian Society, entitled 'Varieties of Imperative', showed clear Austinian influence.

Although most 'Oxford philosophers' continued to subscribe to the positivist claim that the domain of Fact was coincident with that of natural science, they did not for the most part interest themselves in science as a subject for philosophical analysis. Indeed they were open to the charge levelled against them at the time by Bertrand Russell and later by Bryan Magee that they were ignorant of science, having been educated, almost all of them, in the Greek and Latin classics. The Metaphysicals were better placed in this respect than the majority, since Eric Mascall was a Cambridge mathematician and John Lucas had a scientific as well as a classical formation. I myself was particularly impressed by John Lucas's article *The Lesbian Rule*, published in 1955 which had been anticipated by the distinction suggested to me earlier by Ian Crombie between 'canonical and non-canonical' reasoning. This was in the course of conversation at a conference run by the Student Christian Movement at Swanwick in 1950. Ian and I had been invited to run a study group on Philosophy and Theology at this conference which was chaired by Alasdair MacIntyre, then an extremely precocious undergraduate at Queen Mary College, London. Alasdair with typical bravura was combining Logical Positivism in philosophy with Barthianism in theology. As a philosopher, he said, 'Theology is nonsense'; as a theologian he replied 'Of course, intelligible only to faith'. Ian and I pressed him to admit the need for some analogy with everyday speech if theological language was to be intelligible even to faith. 'Otherwise,' I can remember Ian saying, 'we could as well say "God is our aunt" as "God is our father".' He, Alasdair, was not then persuaded, but it is a matter for rejoicing that after a brilliant career in which he has occupied a succession of incompatible positions, he has found himself able to make a series of original contributions to a basically Thomistic philosophy.

So far there had been no published work on the problems posed for theology by analytical philosophy. Philosophers were too busy on other and more interesting topics. When the silence was broken it was not in one or other of the recognised periodicals but in one of those transient publications which have always been a feature of the Oxford scene. It was called *University* and was edited by David Edwards who then, as throughout his career, had a journalist's nose for important issues which had not yet been publicly acknowledged. In the first of, I think, two numbers, it contained an article by Anthony Flew presenting a vigorous statement of the verificationist case against theistic beliefs. Flew argued that such beliefs were inevitably subject to 'death by a thousand qualifications'.

It was a splendid piece of controversial writing and provoked several replies in the next number. When, a year or two later, Flew and MacIntyre produced their *New Essays in Philosophical Theology*, they selected two of these to form an introductory dialogue together with Flew's original piece under the heading 'Theology and Falsification.' One of them was by Richard Hare and the other by myself. This little dialogue was destined to be repeatedly anthologised with the result that my name is known to many people who never had occasion to read anything else that I have written since. It was called 'The Parable of the Stranger' and was intended to illustrate how the Christian story was capable of being defended against criticism based on human experience, but not in such a way that it could be definitively proved or falsified. As a parable it was required to satisfy the requirements of the genre: it must be convincing as a story in itself; and it must succeed in illuminating the subject it was designed to illustrate. As a story it did seem to catch people's imagination and to that extent can be pronounced a success. But, inevitably perhaps, in interpretation it suffered from a certain ambiguity, and when, later on, people have confidently proffered competing interpretations I have found myself unable to rule between them.

The second piece from Dick Hare had no such ambiguities. It displayed the clarity and precision that characterised all his writing.

In it Hare introduced the concept of a 'blik', which proved a convenient label for a distinctive approach to the philosophy of religion in subsequent discussion. This approach involved rebutting the verificationist critique and any other attempt to undermine the factual claims of theism by maintaining that religious statements did not assert such claims at all, but rather expressed a certain attitude to life with its associated pattern of activity. This approach was later to be developed by R B Braithwaite and, more subtly, by Wittgenstein. D Z Phillips presented a version of it in a B.Litt thesis at Oxford, subsequently published as *The Concept of Prayer* and continued to refine it with characteristic panache in his later works. Although I believe it to be fundamentally mistaken, I find that when presented with lively imagination, as it is by Phillips, it affords occasional insights which might not otherwise have been available.

Meanwhile the Metaphysicals were joined by Ian Ramsey, newly appointed to the Nolloth Chair. He arrived in Oxford from Cambridge with a metaphysical scheme of his own fully complete and equipped with its own technical vocabulary. Finding that none of us could understand it, he abandoned it for the vigorous theological empiricism which inspired his first book *Religious Language*. Faced by the problem of finding an empirical reference for religious language, Ramsey focused upon those moments in ordinary human discourse when one becomes aware of a further dimension, when, as he liked to say, the light dawns, the bell rings, the penny drops.

These disclosure experiences were readily recognisable and not only in the lives of religious believers. Indeed they frequently lead people to dissatisfaction with a flat materialistic account of the world and human life and tempt them to a search for the spiritual. But they do not in themselves indicate how they are to be interpreted and how a particular interpretation is to be vindicated against others.

It was these questions which preoccupied the Metaphysicals at the time. We found we could not separate the question of the intelligibility of religious statements, as posed in the falsifiability debate, from the question of the sort of reasoning involved in the assertion of religious claims. When, in the mid 1950s we came to feel that some public statement was called for, if only of a preliminary kind, and I was asked to edit it, I did not invite Ian Ramsey to contribute because at that stage he did not seem to me to exhibit the degree of clarity and rigour which we needed to display if our book was to be taken seriously by philosophers.

By this time two of our main concerns were being assisted by developments in other branches of philosophy. In Logic, W V Quine in his *From a Logical Point of View* had weakened the force of Hume's distinction, memorably expressed by Hume himself: 'If we take in our hands any volume of Divinity or school Metaphysics for instance; let us ask: does it contain any abstract reasoning concerning quantity or numbers? No. Does it contain any experimental reasoning concerning matter or fact or existence? No. Commit it then to the flames for it can contain nothing but sophistry and illusion.'

In its modern form as the analytic/synthetic distinction it had been wielded confidently by Flew and others. All sentences were either analytic or synthetic. The former were true in virtue of the definition of the terms involved. They contributed nothing to our understanding of the world. The latter were vulnerable to the falsifiability test. Quine argued that the distinction was of limited applicability; it was valid only within a given conceptual scheme and could not be involved in decision between conceptual schemes.

In Philosophy of History, William H Dray in *Laws and Explanation in History* argued convincingly that historical judgments could not be interpreted in terms of the Popper/Hempel analyses of scientific theories, that is to say in terms of general explanations of human behaviour as proffered by psychologists or sociologists. There was an irreducible need for historical judgment.

The case was to be further strengthened by Thomas Kuhn in his *The Structure of Scientific Revolutions* (1962). If Kuhn was right, the falsifiability test was applicable only to what he called 'normal science' where there was agreement as to what criteria were applicable in the testing of theories. In scientific revolutions where what was in question was the adequacy of the current 'paradigm' these criteria were no longer applicable. Kuhn was ambivalent on the question whether decisions between paradigms were rational, but it seemed to me that his overall argument required that they should be.

In 1957 when *Faith and Logic* came out, Kuhn's thesis had yet to be published. In my own contribution on 'The Grace of God' I endeavoured to provide a specimen of the sort of reasoning which could be employed to sustain a particular application of a Christian concept, which was open to criticism in the light of experience but could be defended against the criticisms. This allowed for Ramsey's appeal to disclosure situations but suggested a conceptual framework which made them intelligible and capable of being argued for and against.

The culmination of the process of reflection that I have been describing was *The Justification of Religious Belief*, published in 1972. John Hick had asked me to contribute a book on religious language to a series he was editing, but I found I had nothing interesting to say on that subject. An American pupil of mine, Gordon Bjork, gave me a copy of Kuhn's book and I read it with mounting excitement and saw at once how it provided the coping stone to the structure which, with the help of the Metaphysicals, I had been gradually assembling during the 1950s.

What struck me was that the dispute between theists and atheists resembles the choice between 'paradigms' in science as set out by Kuhn. Proof and strict probability operate within 'normal science' but not between paradigms. Influenced by this I argued that 'in fields other than Theology we commonly, and justifiably, make use of arguments other than those of proof or strict probability; and that, typically, theological arguments are of this kind.'

Before this, however, I had developed another interest, in jurisprudence. Quite how this came about I cannot remember, but quite early on I found myself thinking about the definition of *mens rea*, criminal responsibility, the necessary condition of an individual being liable to punishment for breaking a law. I had thought at first that it must involve moral responsibility, but Herbert Hart persuaded me that all that was required was that the accused knew what the law required and was physically and intellectually capable of understanding it. Hart was at this stage and later extremely helpful. I found myself increasingly interested in the debate between himself and Lord Devlin on the topic of Law and Morals. When I was asked to give the Cadbury Lectures at Birmingham by Ninian Smart, I chose this subject rather because I thought it was manageable and I wanted to get to the bottom of it than because I had already got something definite to say about it.

It was extremely presumptuous of me with no legal background to embark upon the subject, but I was helped by two circumstances.

One was that my legal colleague at Keble, David Williams, was interested in it and told me what I must read, and the other was that Herbert Hart agreed to read the first draft of the book and sent me no less than nine handwritten pages of critical comment. I have always regarded this as an outstanding example of the disinterested concern which leading scholars are prepared to show to the work of younger colleagues even when, as in my case, they could not be numbered among their disciples. The resulting book, *Law, Morality and Religion in a Secular Society*, enabled me to bring together a number of themes which had been exercising me for some time. One was that morality could not be understood independently of the overall world-view in which it was set. One's views on virtues and vices were inevitably affected by one's conception of the nature of human beings and the world in which they lived. This meant that one central thesis of Hart and, as it also appeared, of P F Strawson, that one could distinguish between a public morality which was rational and universally applicable and an array of private moralities which were valid only to those who subscribed to them, was untenable. On this was founded a variety of liberalism which is now taken for granted in most of our political discussion. Law, it is argued, may be used only to impose the public morality in order to prevent tangible harm to individuals. It must be disinfected of any religious influence, which *ex hypothesi* derives from a purely private conviction devoid of public rationality.

Devlin, I felt sure, had sensed that this liberal thesis would not do but failed to identify the particular feature of human society which it failed to acknowledge. The dichotomy of public and private took no account of the role of institutions in society. Human welfare is very largely dependent on institutions like the family and property which enable individuals to develop and express their personalities in a satisfying manner. I had been impressed by this in the Navy in which the firm but humane discipline had derived from the need to maintain fighting efficiency in the conditions of life at sea, which included a certain kind of courtesy made possible and necessary by the close confinement of a limited number of people mutually dependent against 'the raging of the sea and the violence of the enemy'. It occurred to me that the role of institutions was illustrated by the case of universities.

The university itself involved a complicated network of responsibilities and obligations which contributed to its overall purpose as a place of 'religion, education and learning'. Teachers were committed to the dual task of extending knowledge and teaching students to understand their subjects and develop the habits of mind necessary to thinking in the manner these subjects required, and more generally to be respectful of the views of others and critical of their own. These general requirements were compatible with widely differing patterns of university organisation. I remember an occasion when, after a lecture tour in Holland, I had invited a party of students from Leiden to spend a week in Oxford during Term in which various friends and colleagues would come and lecture or conduct tutorials with them. I began the week by explaining to them how Oxford was organised, the college system, the tutorial system, how teaching and examining were separated and so on. Expecting, as an Oxonian does, a degree of appreciation in my audience, I was disconcerted to find that my description aroused a mounting horror. 'What about *academische freiheit?*' they exclaimed. It was to them an essential principle of university education that the student should be free to decide what he studied, where he studied and with whom he studied. The Oxford system violated all three requirements. The student had to decide before entrance what he wished to study and then stick to it. He had to be admitted to a college and could not change it later and, once admitted, he found himself assigned to whoever was the tutor in that subject at his college.

All this appeared to my Dutch students to be a denial of what was for them the basic principle of university education. That the freedom they stood for was a good I could not deny. But it was incompatible with other goods which the Oxford system permitted and encouraged; the experience of life in close communities of teachers and taught; the responsibility accepted by teachers for assigned individuals whom they taught or whose teaching they arranged. Examiners were able more easily to be impartial in that they did not examine their own pupils. The greater freedom between pupils and their tutor which followed from their tutor not also being their examiners. You did not have to impress your tutor.

My thoughts on this subject had been concentrated by the setting up of the *Franks Commission* in 1964. The University then, as always, was under political pressures to change its system of governance in order to conform more closely to the national norm. The Commission was headed by Oliver Franks, whose career as a don and a civil servant had established him as the greatest administrator of the time. I decided to make a submission to the Commission and duly found myself invited to be interviewed.

My argument was that it was a fundamental mistake on the part of critics of Oxford to approach the University with a general conception of what a university should be like, based as it inevitably was on whatever was the pattern elsewhere. In reforming an historical institution one should by all means examine its weaknesses but also look for its strengths and see to what extent its weaknesses could be remedied without detriment to its strengths. You had to study the spirit of the particular institution.

I maintained that, if you approached Oxford and Cambridge with this question in mind you would be bound to identify their characteristic strengths as lying in the college system and the tutorial system, the two being intrinsically bound together. The Governing Body of the College was for the most part constituted by the Fellows and Tutors who had the responsibility for the teaching and general welfare of the students, whom by virtue of the tutorial system, they knew. From the point of view of the individual academic one of the advantages of the system was that he or she had considerable freedom as to what they studied or how, as has been illustrated by the failure of 'The Revolution Philosophy' to establish an unquestioned orthodoxy in the post-war years. A nice illustration of this, indeed an encouragement to one's following one's own line, was a letter I received from Gilbert Ryle saying how much he had enjoyed *Law, Morality and Religion in a Secular Society*.

No one doubted that the government of the day had the right and duty to exert ultimate control over the universities, if only to make sure the country's money was well used. But this must not take the form of imposing on all universities a single pattern deriving from some one existing model, least of all one based on some extra-university pattern, such as line-management in industry. The Franks Commission in its impressive Report finally endorsed the College System and the tutorial system, with the recommendation, in the case of the latter, that the number of tutorials should be reduced. This recommendation, for various reasons, has not been followed out, and is reiterated in the 'Green Paper' on the governance of the University. At the end of my interview, which was conducted almost entirely by Franks himself, I took leave to remind him gratefully of the only other occasion he had interviewed me for entry to Queen's in 1935.

I had an amusing experience of how even comparatively minor, even ornamental features of university life might incur controversy. I was dining in hall with a lively young teacher of philosophy from a top American university, and I asked her if she was enjoying the experience. She said she was, but would prefer it if the faculty and students all ate together. She objected to 'High Table' at which we were sitting. I asked her how they ordered things in her university. She explained that there was a university refectory at which both faculty and students were expected to eat. I said that I had myself as visitor eaten in their refectory and been impressed with the standard of fare, but that I had been interested to observe that very few faculty members were eating there. She admitted, a little shame-facedly, that most of her colleagues either went home for their meal or ate a 'brown-bag' confection in the privacy of their offices. Seizing my advantage I said that it was entirely natural that older men and women would have different interests and tastes in food from the young and that the young should not want to share in the tastes and conversation of their elders, not to mention that the elders liked to linger over their food, while the younger wanted to get out quickly. The Oxford system catered for both while also achieving the symbolic advantage of the members of the College eating together.

The relevance of these examples in relation to Hart and Devlin is that institutions like the Navy and universities, while subject to the law of the country, nevertheless need their own arrangements which are peculiar to them and derive from their character as the institution they are and require certain virtues of their members. Any academic institution demands a certain sort of integrity and regards cheating and plagiarism as vices. And these arrangements at the end of the day need the backing of the law.

It was shortly after the publication of this book that I received my surprise appointment to the Nolloth Chair. This required me to leave Keble and migrate to Oriel to which the chair was attached. It meant also an entirely new set of teaching responsibilities. I should no longer be responsible for the tutorial teaching of the undergraduates of my own college, but would have to supervise graduate students in my subject from whichever college they came.

As I have already said, the change in college was in many respects a considerable one. It meant moving from a large college to a comparatively small one, from a comparatively modern one to an ancient one, from some way north of the High Street to a position just south of it, the main consequence of which was that I once again moved into the same soundscape as I had occupied as an undergraduate in Queen's and later at Christ Church. The hours were punctuated not by the rather tinny bell of the clock tower at Keble, but by the sonorous sequence of Merton, St Mary's and Great Tom. In a curious way this helped to make me feel at home.

As seems to have been the case at every fresh stage in my career I was intensely conscious of my incapacity for the job. I knew nothing of theology and my explorations into the philosophy of religion, although continuous, had been peripheral to my official duties. This meant that many of the graduate students I was to supervise would know more about the subject than I did (which I came to believe was not altogether a bad thing).

I was a little worried as to whether the change would effect my status as a philosopher, but was reassured at this point when I received a card from Ryle which said 'Congratulations to you and to us'.

Meanwhile I had been developing the ideas that I had begun to explore with Philippa Foot and Iris Murdoch on the relation between morality and religion. I was invited to give the Gifford Lectures at Glasgow University and these were published as '*Morality: Religious and Secular*'. In these I maintained that morality should be thought of as essentially concerned with the fulfilment of people's needs as individuals and as members of society – with the necessary conditions of human wellbeing. There is some disagreement as to what these needs are; for while some human needs are so obvious and exigent that it is virtually impossible to overlook them, others are open to dispute among adherents of different world-views.

Thus Christianity has its own characteristic conception of human needs. The needs of men are those of a creature whom God loves, has created, redeemed and destined for eternal life and who, therefore, has unconditional value.

In Glasgow while giving the lectures I was generously entertained and was subsequently enabled to enjoy the splendid celebrations in 1977 of the refoundation of the university, at which I was privileged to receive the honorary degree of Doctor of Divinity.

Mention of the book *Morality: Religious and Secular* enables me to give a further illustration of the courtesy extended by Oxford philosophers to those with whom they disagreed. Shortly after its publication I received a charming letter from Peter Strawson, then without doubt the leading Oxford philosopher, which ran: 'Dear Basil, May I say how much I enjoyed your book on Morality. It was so much more *interesting* than most of the aridities produced on this subject.' Then he went on: 'Not that I agreed (you wouldn't expect me to) with every word,' and ended with a quotation from Voltaire.

Graduate students: A new challenge

So I had to think out *ab initio* how I was going to meet the needs of my graduate students. It struck me that the chief disability of graduate students in Oxford was isolation, so I tried over the years to mitigate this. In addition to any formal university classes there might be, I held every fortnight what I called 'my domestic class' which consisted of all the graduates I was currently supervising together with a few interested hangers on. The one rule for the class was that no paper was to be written specifically for the class. It was to be an opportunity to present half-baked papers that were intended for a formal university class or for publication. I had learned myself from experience in the Metaphysicals what a blessing it is to be able to present work at an early stage to a group that is both sympathetic and critical.

The latent purpose of the domestic class was to enable the graduates to get to know one another in the hope that they would meet outside the class and discuss with one another. My wife and I needed to decide how to entertain them. We tried sherry parties, but these were not a success. The traditional time clashed with university classes and for the married students, it was not worth looking for a baby-sitter just for a sherry party. It had to be an evening meal. So we went for a series of supper parties and these were an instant success. The number to be invited followed from a simple set of principles. Graduates would not want just to meet other graduates, so we must invite at least one senior couple. But they would not care for an occasion which was palpably designed to enable the Mitchells to work off their graduates. So there must be at least two senior couples. Hence the formula:

2 Mitchells
2 graduate couples
2 senior couples
10 altogether at least, but we generally had 14–16.

These were among the most enjoyable occasions we can both remember.

So far as formal supervision was concerned I decided to adapt my undergraduate pattern. I got my graduates to come once a fortnight and read me a paper on a subject of their choosing. In the later stages it would be a draft chapter for the thesis. Earlier on it would be on any subject in the area in which the graduate was looking for a thesis topic.

Most supervisors, I think, preferred to have essays typed and sent in in advance. I liked to have them read to me, partly, I must confess, to save time, but also to enable me to interrupt and seek clarification as one did in an undergraduate tutorial. I liked, too, to be able to comment on their English style. Here, I think, I differed from many of my philosophical colleagues who believed on principle that it was none of their business to correct their graduates' English: they were concerned only with their philosophy. I took the view that clear and concise English was an essential element in good philosophy. Especially with American students, I found that they expressed themselves well in oral discussion, but had not learnt, because they were not required to, how to express themselves on paper. So I would endeavour to urge on them certain principles: never to use a long word when a short one would do; never to use a long sentence when a short one would do; never to say in a paragraph what could be said in a sentence.

My first ever graduate student was John Brennan, an American Roman Catholic priest. He had a tragically short career, in the course of which be became laicised in order to marry, and after an all too brief married life died in a fire in their cottage in Islip. His D.Phil thesis was rejected, mistakenly in my view, but published later under the title *The Open Texture of Moral Concepts* and was well received. He came to see me shortly after its publication just after I had finished a session with a newly arrived American student. I turned to him and said, 'I am afraid I cannot refrain from correcting the English of American students on my first few sessions with them.' And then I remembered that he too was American and added, 'But I have just been reading your book and that is extremely well written.' John grinned broadly and said, 'Perhaps you don't remember what happened when I came to see you for the first time.'

I always thought it important that the individual should choose a thesis topic upon which he or she could say something genuinely original, even if the selection process were to take all of the first year. My notion was that the Doctoral thesis should be their first book rather than simply a propaedeutic exercise. And I always bore in mind that the art of teaching, at every level, consists in the proper balancing of encouragement and criticism. So the early days were spent in convincing the student that he or she really had it in them to produce something worthwhile. Once this had been achieved it was time to ensure that what was produced was of the required standard. To this end, and aware of my own limitations, I would endeavour to make sure that each of them was for a period supervised by someone else, preferably someone whose work they were criticising.

I was extremely fortunate in that my graduate students came to me by way of two channels, one philosophical and one theological. As my chair was formally situated in the Theology Faculty, I was naturally given the last word on who should be admitted for the Philosophy of Religion. The Chair was not similarly situated in the sub-Faculty of Philosophy, but I was personally a member of it, and the relevant philosophy committee readily allowed me the last word on the philosophy applicants. So I was happily able to choose the candidates from both channels and I think this made for a good balance between them.

It remained to complete the formal provision of lectures or classes for graduates doing work on the borders between philosophy and theology. The pattern which eventually developed was of two graduate classes, one in the philosophy of religion and one on the relations between philosophy and theology. For most of my time the first of these was conducted by John Lucas and myself and the second by myself and Maurice Wiles. To these we were always glad to welcome visiting philosophers and theologians and we would pull in Oxford colleagues when the topic called for specialised knowledge. In some such classes the protagonists would present papers throughout the term, but we preferred to lead off at the first two meetings and invite members of the class to be responsible for the remainder. John and I were in fundamental agreement on most issues and for us the excitement of the class lay in trying to refine the conceptions we started with and weave together the comments and criticisms which the class produced into an altogether more substantial and satisfying thesis. With Maurice and me the situation was different. It was Maurice who put forward positive proposals for the interpretation of Christian doctrine and I, affecting an ignorance which was often all too genuine, who endeavoured to persuade him to qualify it or withdraw it. These were very friendly encounters in which I did learn a lot and Maurice, I think, did come to appreciate better the strengths and weaknesses of his own position. He complained ruefully on one occasion that I had put his own position so well that he was genuinely puzzled as to why I didn't accept it.

At this time Philosophy of Religion appeared as a separate paper only in the Honour School of Theology, where it could be offered as a special subject. It seemed increasingly unsatisfactory to me that no provision was made for it in any of the philosophy syllabuses. Early in the 1970s an opportunity occurred to remedy this. Council had decided that the range of subjects offered at Oxford needed to be extended, especially as we were in competition with the Cambridge Tripos system. It suggested, therefore, that the various faculties might like to submit proposals for joint honour schools with other faculties. This idea was particularly attractive to the Philosophy sub-Faculty, since at Oxford philosophy had always been combined with another subject, as with Ancient History in *Literae Humaniores* and Politics and Economics in PPE. This made sense since it was difficult for a student to spend all day philosophising and the other subjects provided something to philosophise about.

But not surprisingly the philosophers were not so keen about an alliance with Theology. A J Ayer in particular made no pretence about his opposition to an Honour School of Philosophy and Theology. His real objection, as everyone knew, was that theology was nonsense, but he was reluctant to base his opposition on this and instead argued that all of us philosophers wanted the ablest pupils we could get and no able philosopher would be interested in theology.

It fell to me to put the case for the new school. I had long ago added to *Microcosmographica Academica* a further principle of academic politics: if you are trying to get a proposal through an academic body you should use the weakest arguments that are capable of carrying the day. In no circumstance should you use the strongest possible arguments. These will simply challenge all present to look for holes in them. On this occasion I think I pointed out that all the greatest philosophers into the present century had concerned themselves with questions of a broadly theological kind. I then took advantage of someone having said that there would be problems in examining and took some time elaborating how this might be done. John Lucas has always maintained that my tactic was simply to bore the audience into submission but this is entirely to misunderstand my approach, although it may in fact have had this effect.

In the event the proposal was carried, Ayer, I seem to remember, absenting himself from the meeting at which the decision was made. There is, as it happens, a very satisfactory sequel to this story. When the new school was first examined in 1972 there were seven candidates in all, including one David Brown from Oriel. The number being so small, the papers had to be marked by examiners in other schools of which philosophy formed a part. David Brown was awarded a First and, moreover, shared the Henry Wilde Prize, which went to the best performance in philosophy in the University. Freddy Ayer's argument could not have been answered more conclusively, and so I have always said that, when I die, David Brown's name will be found engraved upon my heart.

The job of designing and regulating the new Honour School was given to a committee drawn from the faculties of philosophy and theology with myself as Chairman. In two ways I think I exercised my own influence upon it. One is that I wanted the philosophy of religion to be a 'bridge paper', which had no parallel in the other joint schools. It would, in effect, be a paper on the philosophy of theology, in which the work done in theology would be subject to a philosophical overview. The parallel in Greats would have been a paper on the philosophy of history. The other was that I very much wanted it to be on the model of Greats rather than of PPE, with a clear structure of main papers and few special subjects. The reasons for this were educational:

1. with a few main papers which were taken by everyone, there was maximum opportunity for students to discuss with one another. In studying for the school they would be undergoing a common experience.
2. with a limited number of core papers a single tutor could teach the students for two years and get to know them well. A proliferation of special subjects meant that students were sent out and these benefits were lost.

I doubt very much whether this line can be held. The pressures towards specialisation are too strong, in particular the fact that dons themselves, under pressure to increase their 'research' output have an obvious motive to limit their teaching so far as possible to the subjects of their research.

One innovation remains controversial. We included among the theology papers a paper on 'Morals'. This paper was devoted to practical ethics in relation to which religious considerations were controversially involved, such as sexual, medical and industrial ethics. The intention was to enable the students to concentrate on the actual problems which arose in practice when ethical principles and concepts were involved and in this way to clarify them and work out how theological notions bore upon them. The introduction of this subject reflected the fact that some members of the committee were actively involved in issues of this kind on behalf of the Board for Social Responsibility of the Church of England, viz Dick Hare, Peter Baelz and myself. We had experienced personally how the attempt to grapple with these issues had tested our theological resources to the limit.

The introduction of this new Honour School did a lot to improve the standing of the Nolloth Chair. From being something of an anomaly as a philosophy chair in a theology faculty, it became the natural bridge between philosophy and theology in a partnership to which each faculty was formally committed. This was something I had always tried to make it.

An interesting consequence of the introduction of the new School was that a philosophy or religion paper was now available which attracted the attention of undergraduates reading other schools. It was not long before the Philosophy sub-Faculty found itself considering a request from PPE candidates that philosophy of religion should be included in its range of special subjects. I found myself somewhat divided in my mind on this proposal. On the one hand I was against the proliferation of special subjects in general; on the other, if there were to be more of them, I naturally favoured this one. The debate was drawn to a close by a typically fair-minded judgment from Jonathan Cohen. 'We may not be specially keen on teaching this subject,' he said, 'but we cannot ignore the fact that the undergraduates want it.' And that settled the matter.

J R Lucas

During most of my tenure of the Nolloth Chair I was greatly assisted by John Lucas, who became both a personal friend and a professional ally. As soon as he returned to Oxford from Cambridge, where he had been a junior fellow at Corpus, and became philosophy tutor at Merton, he was an active member of the Metaphysicals where we rapidly discovered an affinity, and this in two ways. We agreed in our basic attitude to theology; that divine revelation as found in scripture and tradition needed to be interpreted in such a way as to be compatible with knowledge otherwise derived. And, equally important, we had a similar way of thinking – what I like to call an 'epidiascopic' sort of mind as distinct from a 'searchlight' mind. Rather than proceeding step by step from a set of ideas already clearly formulated we would start with an as yet inchoate vision of an entire topic and endeavor to arrive at a logically coherent account of it. This habit of mind favoured discussion and John and I would regularly take walks together and discover that some set of ideas would get clarified between us in a way that, it seemed, neither of us could have achieved by our separate endeavours. We liked to walk every Monday afternoon in Christ Church Meadow and from time to time would take longer walks in Wytham Woods, for which John had a pass. Although we spent a good deal of the time talking philosophy, we were not insensitive to the beauty of our surroundings. We particularly enjoyed the dog roses in the Meadow in June and the bluebells in Wytham Woods in May. Nor did the view of Oxford from the Broad Walk fail to move me. It is not quite as grand as the view from the Backs at Cambridge, but it is in its own way quite entrancing, especially when in the spring and autumn the sun is low and the stone reflects it. I remember on one occasion, as we viewed both Merton tower and Magdalen tower, that I said I found it difficult to decide which was the more beautiful, and John, as a Fellow of Merton replied 'I find that I look upon Merton as a wife and Magdalen as a mistress'. On our longer walks in Wytham Woods, out of bluebell season, the interest was to view deer. On one occasion we extended this walk into Wytham village itself and we exchanged confidences which helped us to make sense of our earlier lives.

Our academic alliance went back to the publication in 1955 of John Lucas's article entitled 'The Lesbian Rule', originally given as a paper to the Philosophical Society, in which he explains the sorts of reasoning which could not be analysed as the following of rules, but which could nevertheless be judged right or wrong. This was so close to my own concerns, less fully worked out, that I immediately recognised an affinity, which was enhanced by the publication of *Faith and Logic* in 1957 which I edited and to which John contributed a chapter on 'The Soul', in which he subjected to criticism the then fashionable thesis of Ryle's *Concept of Mind*.

Although both of us were concerned to defend the intelligibility of religious discourse against philosophical criticism we were neither of us specialists in the philosophy of religion. John's primary interest was in the philosophy of science and mine in moral philosophy. But this meant that our interests were complementary and, if both converged on the philosophy of religion, the philosophy of science had perhaps the greater relevance. For it was generally assumed at that time that scientific discourse was the standard case of intelligible utterance in comparison with which religious speech was defective. To assess the validity of this line of argument demanded a familiarity with scientific thinking which few Oxford philosophers possessed, and which I certainly did not, but which John did. It was when I took up my chair in the philosophy of religion that I particularly felt the need of support and John generously provided it. We together ran a graduate class on the philosophy of religion which benefited from our combined philosophical interests. I also was helped by the fact that John was appreciatively better at thinking on his feet. When a fresh awkward question arose, as they were liable to do in a group of brightly intelligent graduate students, I would find that I needed time for reflection whereas he would be ready there and then with a range of possible answers.

The same valuable assistance was afforded me in my chairmanship of the Socratic Club, particularly in its later days after the 'student revolution' when it required a good deal of effort on the part of both of us to keep it going. John's greatest contribution to the Socratic Club was his willingness to repeat with Elizabeth Anscombe the famous debate she had had with C S Lewis on his book *Miracles*. In this repeat discussion John succeeded in showing that Lewis's original thesis, when defended by an experienced analytical philosopher, was a good deal more defensible than Lewis was able to show at the time.

John was something of an Oxford personality, partly because he was well over six foot, as Austin Farrer used to say 'plainly visible to the naked eye'. He was from time to time invited to speak at the Oxford Union, being used to the sort of discourse that was customary there, and he became a regular contributor to the Oxford Magazine on matters of University governance in defence of the tutorial system and the autonomy of colleges.

When deep in retirement we decided to co-author a book on Plato's *Republic*. We had both conducted tutorials on it, John for the whole of his career, I while I was still teaching undergraduates. In addition I had for a number of years given 'bread and butter' lectures on the *Republic*. The enterprise was based on the conviction that the *Republic* was not an object only of antiquarian interest but was worth engaging with as a work of enduring significance. Hence we entitled it *Engaging with Plato's Republic*. We read leading books on the subject and some key articles but did not attempt to tackle all the periodical literature, because we were primarily concerned with the book's impact upon the average educated reader. It was our failure to assimilate the vast periodical literature that proved our undoing when we offered the book to the Oxford and Cambridge University Presses, both of which turned us down. When we read their very thorough reports we became aware that in the course of our careers a change had occurred which we had not recognised, as a consequence of which one was not expected to comment on Plato unless one was an accepted specialist in ancient philosophy. For us

Plato's *Republic* was a work which was an essential element in the study of philosophy, which any philosopher was expected to have a thoughtful response to.

The attempt to produce a joint work of this kind raised amusing problems: should we produce individual chapters under our own names; or should we present the work throughout as a product of the joint authors? The difficulty of the first solution was that by the time each chapter had been exhaustively commented upon by each of us, it was no longer the work of one author. The difficulty of the second solution was that our styles were very different. We finally decided on joint authorship throughout, content that readers who knew us well would be able to detect which part of each chapter was attributable to John and which to me.

While working on this book I was naturally reminded of the time when I gave the *Republic* lectures and of one incident in particular which called to mind Freud's *Psychopathology of Everyday Life*. I always liked to write out my lectures to make sure that I made no mistakes. But occasionally I would think of something extra and introduce it there and then. On one occasion I had said, 'What I have just said reminds me of two other points. Let me recapitulate – I was saying such and such, when I thought of two additional points. The first of these was . . . and the second was – the second was –. I am afraid I have forgotten what the second was.' There was a slight titter at this and I continued my prepared lecture. Some time later I remembered the second point, so I said, 'I have now remembered the second point. To recapitulate, I was saying such and such when I thought of two further points. The first was . . .; and the second was – I am afraid I have forgotten the second point again.' This brought the house down and I had difficulty in continuing the lecture. This incident had a sequel. The same evening I was presiding at a meeting of the Socratic Club at which Gilbert Ryle was reading a paper. I began by saying 'there is no need to introduce Professor Ryle to an Oxford audience, and I don't want to take up time because of the intriguing title of Professor Ryle's paper. So without further ado I will ask Professor Ryle to give us his paper on –, his paper on –' Ryle looked up with a grin on his face and supplied the title of his paper which was *Forgetting the difference between right and wrong*. 'Anyone who was at my lecture that morning would know why I could not remember the word "forgetting".'

CHAPTER 13

Activities inside Oxford

S O FAR MY NARRATIVE HAS MOVED in a forward direction tracing my
arrival at a particular academic position. From now on it will
move sideways into activities which were not required by that
position but followed naturally from it.

When I resigned from Hebdomadal Council in 1968 I managed to
remain on the Committee on Elevations and Choice of Architects,
and in this capacity was party to a significant and enjoyable
undertaking, the restoration of the Sheldonian Theatre. The most
intriguing matter which came our way was the future of the
'Emperors' Heads' in the forecourt of the Sheldonian. The existing
heads, which had replaced the originals in the Victorian period, were
now so decrepit that they were a danger to the public, and the
question was 'replace them with what?' Some felt that since no one
knew why they were there or how the title 'Emperors' Heads' had
been attached to them, the sensible thing was to start afresh and look
for some suitable ornaments such as, for example, pineapples. But the
predominant view was that since the Loggan print, contemporary
with Wren, showed clearly heads like the existing ones, these must
be carefully copied. It was left to the Committee to see to this.
Accordingly we appointed a local sculptor, Michael Black, and he
addressed the work with enthusiasm. It was discovered that the
existing heads were of two distinct models, so Black undertook in the
first instance to produce two model heads by way of samples.

In due course he let us know that two model heads were ready for
our inspection in his workshop by the river and before we inspected
them he gave us a fascinating account of how he had gone about the
commission. He had first examined carefully a set of blown-up
photographs of the heads in the Loggan print and these had presented
him with a problem. It was apparent that the 'emperors' were
wearing chaplets round their heads, but what plants were these
chaplets made of? He thought they were ivy, but in that case, what
kind of ivy? With commendable assiduity he went to the Botanic

Gardens and consulted the curator. He said 'We have a wall covered with nothing but ivies', so they went to look at it with Black taking his blown-up photos of the heads. Black found one variety which looked to him right and the curator said: 'That suits. That particular ivy was planted in 1637'. So Black felt justified in copying that ivy on the heads which he then showed us.

When I look at the 'Emperors' Heads' now I get particular pleasure from the thought that so much diligent research had gone into the production of these archetypal Oxford figures.

The Committee was also requested to choose between two alternative schemes for the internal decoration of the theatre, one of which was an attractive modern one and the other the one favoured by Wren himself. We chose the latter, which has lasted well. One thing which gave me additional pleasure was that the architect responsible for the restoration of the Sheldonian was Arthur Llewellyn Smith, Phoebe's elder brother, who himself had got a First in Greats at New College.

In the middle of my proctorial year I was approached by Nicolas Zernov who said, 'Basil, there is something I very much want you to do for me.' Nicolas was University lecturer in Eastern Orthodox culture and a member of the Keble Common Room. He was a man of unbounded enthusiasm who did not allow his Russian exuberance to be tempered by English reticence. Knowing this I said simply, 'No, the answer, Nicolas, is no.' 'But, Basil,' he said, 'surely I may be allowed to say what it is that I want you to do.' I could not deny this reasonable plea and so he told me about the House of St Gregory and St Macrina that he was set on founding and that he wanted me to be the first Chairman of it. I knew at once that I should not be able to refuse him, especially since, when he explained it, it was obviously an inspired idea. It was designed as a meeting place between Eastern and Western Christians. He had purchased a large house in North Oxford on the junction between Canterbury and Banbury Roads and in addition to spacious public rooms there were enough bedrooms to accommodate visitors from abroad, some of whom could be semi-permanent.

The project was helped by the existence in Oxford already of distinguished scholars who were orthodox, including Kallistos Ware and Dimitri Obolensky. It became a centre for all parts of the

Orthodox church, especially Russian and Greek and I believe Nicolas wanted a non-orthodox chairman for two reasons. One was to have a chairman who did not represent one branch of orthodoxy as distinct from another; another to show that it did indeed represent both Eastern and Western Christians.

My task as Chairman was made all the easier by the fact that Nicolas's charisma was supported by the business sense and practical energy of his wife Milissa. She was an outstandingly handsome woman with penetrating eyes and, whenever she needed it, a radiant smile which could be relied upon to dissolve opposition. (I remember that, at a later stage, when the small orthodox church was being constructed in the garden, the architect said to me that Milissa could be so difficult that he would sometimes decide that next time he saw her he would resign the job but that his determination would melt away when he was confronted with that radiant smile.) It took me a little while to get to know everyone, and in this as in everything else I was helped by the secretary, Helen Brock, who was expert in translating Russian extravagance into English prose.

Nicolas Zernov's lack of inhibitions no matter who he was talking to was nicely illustrated one lunch time at Keble when he remarked to me 'I dined in New College the other night and met a most interesting man whose name was Isaiah Berlin. We discussed his religious opinions.' Shortly afterwards he invited Berlin to dine in Keble and as we made our way up the long staircase into hall I found myself next to him. 'I see you are dining with Nicolas Zernov,' I said. 'I hope you have your soul adequately protected.' 'That's alright. That's alright,' said Isaiah, 'My soul's very opaque; very opaque.'

Nicolas's approach was not going to work in this instance but it was evidently his view that since what mattered supremely in life was the truth of Christianity, every occasion must be taken to discuss the matter. I remember on one occasion being invited to tea by the Zernovs and, when I entered the room, I found a small circular table surrounded by six chairs. In the middle of the table was a cake carefully cut into six pieces. Nicolas started proceedings by giving each of us a piece of cake and saying 'I would like to ask each of you in turn how you conceive of the soul.' I was greatly embarrassed, but I have to confess that, thus challenged, I found myself discoursing more effectively on the soul than on any other occasion.

Nicolas's tendency to make every occasion an opportunity for discussions of a religious topic was illustrated when the House was entertaining a distinguished French philosopher – I think it was Berdyaev – and we had been invited to an informal party to meet him. We found the room lined with chairs on which we duly sat. Nicolas then said, 'Friends, the first question is what shall we discuss?' As we had not been expecting to discuss anything no suggestion was forthcoming, so Nicolas said, 'I suggest that we discuss 'la chrétienté et l'esprit Russe.' And the distinguished visitor had no choice but to lead off on this subject.

The House of St Gregory and St Macrina continues to flourish and has become an accepted part of the Oxford scene. It still bears the imprint of its founder of whom Isaiah Berlin once remarked to me 'Nicolas Zernov is a typical Russian type, that of the Holy Rogue'. If 'rogue' is taken in one of its possible senses of 'adventurer' this is true. He knew what he wanted and allowed no constraints to stand in his way. I am glad to have made some contribution to the development of the House but do not reckon to have done very much.

Not long after I resigned from St Gregory and St Macrina I was asked to assume another chairmanship. In 1976 an extremely attractive young clergyman from Cuddesdon, Christopher Lewis, along with a colleague, called upon me to ask if I would consent to become chairman of an institution which they wanted to set up in association with Cuddesdon. It would be entitled 'The Oxford Institute for Church and Society.' In its training for the ministry Ripon College Cuddesdon attached importance to acquainting young clergy with the secular world and this was a development of this idea. Individuals with the required talent and experience were to be encouraged to undertake research on a limited scale into aspects of society in the neighbourhood of Oxford. These should be published locally and made available to Cuddesdon and any other bodies that might be interested. When I asked 'why me?', not being a sociologist, they said that they wanted someone with a genuine interest in the relation between church and society. Moreover, they assured me, I should have very little to do, since they personally as Directors would do all the necessary work.

Not long afterwards, of course, they both moved on from Cuddesdon and it fell to me to find a new director with the help of

Ripon College and we appointed Alastair Redfern. Apart from helping to form the careers of two distinguished ecclesiastics, (Christopher Lewis is now Dean of Christ Church and Alastair Redfern Bishop of Derby) it did instigate some useful pieces of research. There was obviously a limit to the amount of useful local research that could be done and the Institute ceased to exist after 30 years.

Another chairmanship I took on proved to be a mistake. This was that of the Oxford house of the Richmond Fellowship in Davenant Road. I had asked Robin McInnes to join me in the expectation that his experience as a psychiatrist would be needed, but it turned out that policy was determined entirely by the headquarters in London and the local committee had no serious work to do. I had had no hesitation in taking the job when invited because I entirely approved of the underlying principle, that people who were mentally ill often needed a 'halfway house' between mental hospital and life in the outside world.

The final chairmanship I undertook was of an altogether different character in that I myself had a great deal to do with the setting up of the institution in question. The Ian Ramsey Centre was set up on the 22 February 1985 in St Cross College with myself as Chairman and Arthur Peacocke as Director. There is no doubt whatever that Arthur was the dominant figure, not least because he was prepared to give up his post as Dean of Clare College, Cambridge, in order to become the first Director of this experimental institution. He was ideally suited to the position. While a practising biochemist, first at Birmingham, then at Oxford, he had taken a diploma in theology and a bachelor of divinity degree and became aware in his theological studies how little attention was paid by theologians to the problems raised by the sciences for traditional theology. Although, if he had remained a scientist, he might well have become an FRS, he decided that he must concentrate on these problems from the theological side and became convinced that this could only be done effectively if there were regular contacts between theologians and scientists. So he became ordained himself and founded the Science and Religion Forum.

He was also involved in discussions in a body called the 'University Teachers' Group' which had been set up after the War as a kind of senior counterpart to the Student Christian Movement about the possibility of establishing in a university an institute of contemporary thought and religion. Ian Ramsey embodied these proposals in a University Sermon on the 14 June 1964 with the title 'A New Prospect in Theological Studies', which was published in *Theology* in December, 1964.

During the 1960s there was general agreement that there should be such an institute, but proposals at Birmingham and King's College, London came to nothing and there were no immediate prospects at Oxford. It was not until the early 1970s and the untimely death in 1972 of Ian Ramsey, then Bishop of Durham, that the idea was revived as a way of commemorating his widely influential inter-disciplinary work.

It so happened that there were a number of us in the theology faculty at Oxford who warmly supported the idea, including Maurice Wiles, the Regius Professor of Divinity, Peter Baelz, the Regius Professor of Moral and Pastoral Theology and myself, Nolloth Professor of the Philosophy of the Christian Religion and Ian Ramsey's successor in that post. During the 1970s those of us in Oxford who were intent on bringing the Centre into existence were facing something of a dilemma. We could not take advantage of any opening that emerged unless we had a definite scheme fairly thoroughly worked out, but we couldn't provide such a scheme unless we had reasonable assurance of support and consents from the University and the individuals in it, without whom it could not be made to work. With this in mind I went to see Alan Bullock, then Vice-Chancellor, whom I knew from my days on Council and who warmly approved of the scheme.

From 1980 onwards discussions were proceeding between Pusey House and the recently founded St Cross College about the possibility of Pusey House making over part of its buildings in St Giles to the College, which then might be prepared to provide a home for the Centre. In the event St Cross were very happy to welcome the creation of a Ramsey Centre in the College, making the Director a Fellow and agreeing to the Centre's use of its seminar rooms and other facilities. Meanwhile in my rooms in Oriel in November 1983 the informal committee which had been operating up to that point constituted itself as a Steering Committee. This Steering Committee met again in December at St Cross College. It then constituted itself as the Management Committee of the Ian Ramsey Centre. This then proceeded to its first meeting at which it appointed Dr A R Peacocke as its first Director for five years from 1st January 1985.

The Centre now existed and was committed to commencing operations in 1985. The whole thing represented a remarkable act of faith on the part of Arthur, who had resigned from a secure and distinctly prestigious position in Cambridge to take up an entirely speculative job in Oxford. With characteristic energy and efficiency he and Rosemary found and moved into a splendid house in St John Street, a stone's throw away from Pusey House, and he secured and furnished two rooms in Pusey House, one for himself and one for a secretary.

It remained to do two things before the Centre could get going. One was to raise enough money to last out the first five years. The other was to bring the Centre to the awareness of people who mattered both inside and outside the University. In all this I was no mere figurehead. I had been in Oxford continuously longer than any of the other people involved in the project – I was, in fact, due to retire in 1984 – and knew personally most of the people we might need to approach

This was true even in respect of the fundraising. It was suggested to me by John Dancy, who was on the Council of St Luke's, Exeter, that we might approach the various church college trusts which had been set up on the demise of the church colleges. I had been on the Council of one of them, Culham College, and was familiar with their situation and I had known John Dancy himself when he had been Master of Marlborough, where my son Matthew was at school. Moreover we heard that the Archbishop of Canterbury was in the habit of suggesting every year to these Trusts a charity which they might support. I had known Robert Runcie while he was at Cuddesdon and we accordingly wrote to him and he duly gave his support in this way. Also it did seem desirable that we should find some support from within Oxford and I went to see Robert Blake whom I knew from Christ Church days and who was Chairman of the Rhodes Trust which eventually gave us a grant.

We needed the agreement of the University if we were to be fundraising for an institution within the University and this we received from Hebdomadal Council together with consent for the University to hold funds on behalf of the Centre. To explain the proposal to him I had a meeting with Geoffrey Warnock, whose wife, Mary Warnock, had given us her support. It remained to indicate the level of support across the faculties and we drew up a list of 'associates', which included members of different faculties.

As soon as the Centre was opened on 1 January 1985, Arthur Peacocke and I planned an Inaugural Event for 22 February. It began with open lectures in the Taylorian Institute by the Archbishop of York, Dr John Habgood, on 'Bioethics in Theory and Practice' and Sir John Walton, Warden of Green College and President of the Royal Society of Medicine, on 'Challenge and Responsibility in Clinical Medicine'. These were followed by an Inauguration Dinner in the Sangman Hall of St Cross College, which was attended by guests including Mrs Margaret Ramsey and her two sons, the Vice-Chancellor, the Master of St Cross, the Principal of Pusey House, as well as representatives of the Press and of the supporting Trusts. It fell to me to propose the toast of the guests of honour, Mrs Ramsey and her two sons, Paul and Vivian, and to explain how the co-operation of various individuals inspired by Ian Ramsey's vision had culminated in the birth of the Centre. Arthur then outlined plans for the future and introduced Lord Bullock, Master of St Catherine's and former Vice-Chancellor, who as a distinguished modern historian had encouraged us at an early stage. He made it clear why he had given the project his support. He spoke of 'the great geological fault in western culture', viz the difficulty of rendering compatible the view of the world seen by scientists and that derived from Religion and the arts and the humanities. And he ended by expressing his hope that the Centre would help to bridge this divide and proposing a toast to the Director and other members of the Centre's management.

On the same day there appeared in *The Oxford Times* on the centre page a very sympathetic article along with photographs of Arthur Peacocke and myself together with Ian Ramsey, Lady Warnock and Sir John Walton.

I remained as Chairman for the first five years while Arthur Peacocke was still Director and our original funding still lasted. At the end of that period we could not expect our original backers to continue to finance us, since their motive had been to bring the

Centre into being. Arthur's hope had been that once the Centre had demonstrated its worth, sources of government funding would be available, but this proved to be unduly optimistic. However, the Centre was asked to co-operate in a project for which funds were available, the Oxford Skills Project, which was concerned with developing a course for medical students in ethics, law and communication skills. At this point Caroline Miles succeeded Arthur Peacocke as Director and I resigned the Chairmanship in favour of Kenneth Wilson who was President of Westminster College. I was seventy-two in 1989 and, having retired from my university post, felt that I had exhausted my usefulness.

This initial period, however, provides the best indication of what the Centre was able to do. We started off by setting up two working parties, one on 'Values, Conflict and the Environment' and the other on 'Quality of Life and the Practice of Medicine'. I was Chairman of the latter, and was assisted eventually in the editing of it by Michael Banner who had been one of my latest graduate students. It occurred to us that, if we were going to consider some problem in medical ethics, it might be sensible to gather together a representative group of doctors and ask them what ethical problem they would most want to investigate. With surprising unanimity they suggested 'the quality of life'. They had found that the quality of life was a concept they frequently appealed to without being at all clear what it meant and how it was relevant to their medical practice. So we decided to concentrate on 'Quality of Life and the Practice of Medicine.'

It fell to me to chair this one and it turned out to be quite an exacting task. Those of us who were not medically qualified had to learn to understand the experiences and problems of those who were and they, of course, had to understand those of medical practitioners in other disciplines than their own: in particular those who worked in hospices represented a type of medical practice which was almost entirely new.

The medical members of the group encountered for the first time from philosophers and theologians types of reasoning with which they were unfamiliar. One member, indeed, Professor G Adams, a retired professor of Geriatrics, resigned from the group because his own experience, apart from medical practice, was of medical working parties which sought to compare the effectiveness of alternative medicines or clinical methods. Their reports would proceed by recognised methods and yield precise conclusions. Professor Adams felt that what we were doing was reaching no definite conclusions and followed no precise methods of reasoning.

In my preface to the published version of our Report 'Quality of Life and the Practice of Medicine', I endeavoured to anticipate such misgivings. I wrote:

> In the course of this exercise which, in the event, spread over several years, it became increasingly clear to the members of the Working Party (not least to its chairman) that there is no substitute for the informed and experienced judgment of those (both medical and lay) who have to make the decisions. Nevertheless we came to feel that the sustained attempt to clarify the concepts and elicit the principles involved in these decisions can reinforce this faculty of judgment. The process is more akin to getting a large scene into clear focus than to following an argument step by step. For this reason the report does not issue a set of recommendations, or even a body of conclusions that can be readily summarised. We hope, however, that those who, in any capacity, are confronted with the problems with which it deals, will find them illuminated by it.

This is not the occasion to attempt a full account of the development of the Ian Ramsey Centre since I retired from the chairmanship of it, except to mention that it has been enthusiastically promoted by Margaret Yee, who was one of my latest graduates. The most significant event has been the willingness of the Templeton Fund to ask the Centre to be responsible for the European dimension of its American operations in the field of Science and Religion. An appreciation of the part played by the Centre in his life's work must have played a part in the award of the Templeton Prize to Arthur Peacocke in 2001.

I think I can say that the Centre's record in its first five years during which it was adequately funded shows that the aims and purposes of such a centre are worth pursuing and that the pursuit of them is practicable in Oxford.

CHAPTER 14

Activities outside Oxford

My NOLLOTH CHAIR PREDECESSOR, Ian Ramsey, was extremely active in the service of the wider Church even before he went to Durham, and then his activity, if possible, increased. He was spoken of as a future Archbishop of Canterbury, but eventually the strain of overwork proved too much and he died prematurely after only four years in office. By then he left behind an enormous legacy of achievement. His great strength lay in his ability to discern problems which were of national concern and which the Church needed to address. He was able to assemble experts in various fields together with philosophers and theologians, and encourage them to a frank exchange of views from which, miraculously, he would elicit an agreed Report, which was largely written by himself. He knew me well from the *Metaphysicals* and for many years I found myself part of a nucleus of philosophers and theologians who were retained in a succession of 'working parties' as they were called. The first of these, more elaborate than the others, was the Commission on Religious Education, which produced the *Durham Report* in 1970. This was very highly organised and each of the members not only took part in plenary sessions of the Commission but was also allocated to a series of sections. I was appointed Chairman of the section on *Religion and Morality*. The Commission enjoyed the support, financial and administrative, of the National Society. The ground was fully prepared by questionnaires sent to various bodies, such as the Methodist Education Committee and the British Humanist Association, so that their views could be taken into consideration and the Commission's Report thereby made more relevant and representative.

The Report remains a very impressive piece of work and has a claim to be the most thorough study of the problems of religious education produced in the United Kingdom in the twentieth century. My contribution as a philosopher consisted in an attempt to sort out a distinction, which emerged early in the discussions, between 'indoctrination' and an 'open' approach to religious education. As a philosopher I was distrustful of sharp antitheses and I suspected that this was a false antithesis. I endeavoured to clarify my position in a paper on 'Indoctrination' which was published as an appendix to the Report. My argument was that 'indoctrination' was a pejorative expression which meant teaching something in such a way as to imprint it on the mind of the recipient and render it difficult or impossible for him or her to abandon it or criticise it later. To teach something in an 'open' way, by contrast, was to leave it as an entirely open question whether what was being taught was true or not. Given this dichotomy it was tempting to conclude that, since 'indoctrination' was evidently wrong, the only right way to proceed was in the open manner which, it was assumed, was the sole alternative. If religious educators, to be truly educational, must refrain from assuming the truth of any one religious tradition, it followed that they must confine themselves to a comparative study of religions, while taking care not to recommend any of them.

Traditionally in Britain, religious educators had been Christian and the question was whether this tradition could be maintained without its falling under the ban on indoctrination. In terms of my analysis this was plainly possible. One could teach Christianity as true without being indoctrinatory so long as one was fair to other religions and philosophies, and exposed the Christian tradition to criticism, and refrained from submitting children to excessive intellectual and emotional pressure.

The significance of this debate emerged clearly in the section I was chairing on religion and morality. Was morality to be taught in an entirely 'open' way with the teacher setting out alternative answers to moral questions and refusing to adjudicate between them? In paragraph 158 of the Report (p80) we declared that 'openness did not preclude the taking of a definite position: hence "openness" does not require us to proceed as if operating in a cultural vacuum – it cannot mean "not having any presuppositions, not accepting anything which one cannot here and now justify to any reasonable man, not being prepared to accept anything on authority". It must mean "not being doctrinaire, encouraging people to think for themselves, being ready to consider arguments against one's own position". As such it is compatible with having and with communicating a definite position which one is prepared to defend.'

One consequence of my involvement in the *Durham Report* was that I was invited to join the steering committee of the Bloxham Project. This was concerned with religious education in boarding schools, most of which, of course, were independent. The project was financed by Robert Wills, whose family already made generous contributions to charity through the Dulverton Trust. Most independent schools were religious foundations and were furnished with chaplains and conspicuous chapels. They were anxious to remain true to their Christian traditions but also to make allowances for the increasing secularisation of society. They welcomed the contribution which the Bloxham Project made to the review of their problems through the activities of a series of able directors. The Project had an annual conference at Bloxham School at which progress was monitored and policy debated.

One school which became particularly closely involved with the Project was Bryanston. There a lively member of the teaching staff, John Mott, in liaison with the Headmaster and the chaplain, introduced what they called 'Bryanston Humanities' as an alternative to Chapel on Sunday mornings. This arrangement offered one solution to the problem that faced all such schools, whether to make attendance at chapel voluntary. Boys at Bryanston could avoid Chapel, but only if they opted to attend a lecture and discussion which concentrated their attention on competing world-views. John Mott, in due course, left Bryanston and succeeded Alec Knight as Director of the Bloxham Project in which capacity he was able to make his Bryanston experience available to other schools. I was myself in due course invited to speak at 'Bryanston Humanities' and used the occasion to discuss varieties of reasoning, from pure logic and mathematics, scientific theorising, historical reasoning and reasoning in relation to world-views. In this way I invited my audience to compare the different disciplines they were studying as exercises of reasoning of related kinds. Thus I tried to assist in something which John Mott was always trying to effect, the involvement in religious education of members of the teaching staff other than the chaplain or RE specialist.

I enjoyed these school visits very much. From the standpoint of the students they were, at least, a change. Here was someone from outside the school, whom they didn't have to impress and who was under an obligation to take what they said seriously. I have the impression that these sixth formers were livelier and more uninhibited than undergraduates, even though the Head or some member of staff was usually present. I once remarked on this to the Headmistress of the school in which my elder daughter teaches and she rather nullified my observation by saying that her sixth form teachers often expressed their envy of kindergarten teachers because of the greater spontaneity of their pupils.

One occasion I remember with great pleasure was a visit to Cranborne Chase School for Girls (now alas defunct) at which the very lively Headmistress, Betty Galton, had asked me to give two lectures on Ethics on a Friday evening, one before dinner and one after. I thought that this was working the girls rather hard at the end of the week and myself too. I was invited to stay the night, but expected to leave soon after breakfast. But the Head had other ideas: would I be so kind as to have a discussion of ethical problems after breakfast on the basis that attendance would be entirely voluntary and no member of staff would be present. I could scarcely refuse and when the girls assembled it seemed that the entire sixth form had volunteered. The discussion was lively and entirely uninhibited. It ranged widely over abortion, contraception, euthanasia, marriage and cohabitation; no matter of controversy was missing. I was exhausted but the girls appeared to be ready to go on for ever. I think it was I who finally called a halt. After a cup of coffee and as I was preparing to leave, the Head thanked me warmly for what had obviously been a successful session and then said apologetically, 'I know we have already worked you very hard, but do you mind staying for lunch and just hanging around in the lecture room for a while in case any girl wants to consult you privately.' I was distinctly alarmed about this, fearing that I might be asked personal questions which it was quite outside my competence to answer.

But I did as I was asked and before long a girl did approach me. She wanted to ask me a question about Christian belief. I was relieved at this. Here was something about which I might be able to help. So I said, 'Is there a good walk about here, where we can talk?' (as I imagine, I should not be allowed to do now). So we went for a walk in the grounds and I prepared to rehearse the arguments for and against Christian belief. 'That's not my problem,' she said straightaway. 'I am a committed Christian, wholly convinced by the case for Christianity. My difficulty is that, though intellectually convinced, I cannot make it *mean* as much to me as it ought to do.' I thought it might help her a bit if she were to realise that her predicament was not confined to herself. And I told her about Newman's distinction between noumenal and real assent. She evidently had noumenal assent, but had not yet attained to real assent. She agreed that this was a good way of describing her problem, but it didn't help her to deal with it. At this point in the conversation I explained that I was not a spiritual director, but a philosopher of religion and the only thing I could do was to mention the advice of another Christian thinker, Pascal, in such a situation, which was 'masses and holy water'. She should continue in the practice of her religion and the faith that she should try to develop was the faith that God would respond to her approaches to him and in time give substance to her faith. She was an intelligent and sensitive young woman and I have often wondered what became of her.

These school visits were, I think, of value to me as a University teacher. With undergraduates one can to some extent get away with the shorthand of technical vocabulary, but with school audiences one has to explain things in language intelligible to them. Indeed the experience helped to convince me that the art of teaching remains the same at all levels. It consists in the right mixture of encouragement and criticism. This varies from person to person. This came home to me on another school visit, to Aylesbury Grammar School. After my lecture the Headmaster took me out to lunch and, in the course of conversation, remarked on the appointment, recently announced, of Mary Warnock to the headship of Oxford High School for Girls. We both approved of it, but then he said, 'All the same, it's a pity they couldn't have found someone from within the teaching profession'. I reacted against this and said, 'But don't you think that University teachers belong to the teaching profession?' Mary Warnock, of course, was highly successful as Headmistress as I knew well from the reports of my daughter, Nell. She was a member of a form which contained a group of highly intelligent girls who at one stage were insufficiently stretched and sat light to school discipline. One instance of their boisterousness I feel bound to recount, because I had a first-hand account of it.

I had two pupils at Keble who were Senior Students reading PPE in two years. One was an all American College football player, the other a Canadian basketball player. The two of them were punting up the Cherwell opposite the Dragon School playing fields, when the pole stuck in the mud and they had no alternative but to abandon it. Before they were able to take to their paddles and retrieve the pole, a chunky schoolgirl leapt into the river, seized the pole and refused to give it up until the young men answered some questions. 'Are you undergraduates?' 'Yes.' 'What College are you at?' 'Keble.' 'What are you reading?' 'PPE.' 'Who is your tutor?' 'Mr Mitchell.' 'Ah yes,' said one of the girls, 'Nell's father.' The next question was on philosophy, 'What did they think of W V Quine?' My pupils had not yet started logic and knew nothing of Quine. 'What,' said one of the girls 'you know nothing of Quine, perhaps the leading mathematical logician in the world!' Not surprisingly my pupils had enough of this and wrested back the pole by main force before proceeding on their way. When they next came to a tutorial they were still in shock when they told me about their experience. I questioned them closely in pursuit of the girls' identities and they had heard the girls addressing one another. They remembered the names of Mary, Julia, Bridget and Allegra, revealing that all but one were philosophers' daughters. When the two men came to visit me years later, separately, I asked them if they remembered the incident and both independently shuddered and said they would never forget it. And later still when I told the story to Dick Hare he was inclined to doubt it, but he asked Bridget and she confirmed it.

But even this uninhibited set of girls were impressed by Mary Warnock. As Nell explained, they did not want to be thought fools by her.

After the Bloxham Report and still chaired by Ian Ramsey, were a series of 'working parties' on questions of social ethics set up under the aegis of the General Synod's Board of Social Responsibility. The topics chosen reflected the Church's view that its established position in the country gave it a responsibility to prepare a considered judgement on matters of ethical significance, which might become the subjects of legislation. This would give the Bishops in the House of Lords something to go on, if and when these matters were debated in the House. The constitutional position was such that, although the

Church did not have a prescriptive right to determine the content of legislation, it did have the right and the duty to present a distinctively Christian viewpoint. The Reports I myself contributed to were on Abortion, Euthanasia and Homosexuality. The one which I myself think was the best was the one on Euthanasia, entitled *On Dying Well*. Its success was very largely due to our having Cicely Saunders as our medical specialist. Cicely Saunders (later Dame Cicely Saunders) was at that time Director of St Christopher's Hospice at Sydenham which was to become the prototype of similar hospices world-wide. Her remarkable career started when she was a nurse at St Thomas's Hospital. She became aware, early on, that doctors, whose professional ethos was bound up with curing diseases and keeping their patients alive, were uneasy in the face of death, which for them represented defeat. They tended, therefore, to lose interest in the dying. Cicely early on in her career realised that it was important to give proper medical attention to the dying. A spell at St Joseph's Hospice as part of her training showed her something of what could be done by devoted care, but one thing was missing – specialist medical attention to the needs of the dying, the relief of pain and helping the dying to live as fully as their condition allowed. Single-mindedly she prepared herself to undertake this task. She became qualified as a medical social worker and then she became medically qualified and specialised in the relief of pain and what has become known as 'palliative medicine'.

At the time of our Working Party she had set up St Christopher's and its fame was beginning to spread, but the hospice movement had not yet extended over the whole country and over the world. Our friend and neighbour at Wootton, Clare Stott, remembers her when they were both in training at St Thomas's. She was tall and awkward and conspicuous because of her red hair. She did not seem cut out for a career in nursing.

I remember that we had one of our sessions at St Christopher's. It was a hot summer's day and by the time we finished at around tea-time I was very tired after a concentrated day's work, and I had a long journey back to Oxford. After tea, Cecily asked us if anyone would like to see over the hospice. My immediate thought was 'Oh no, I can't face seeing a whole lot of dying people!' I was so ashamed of this reaction that I said 'Yes please' and joined a group who accepted her invitation. Before we went in, Cicely explained to us two conventions which we needed to know. One was that, if people did not want to be talked to, they would keep their eyes closed; anyone with eyes open would be happy to engage in conversation. The other was that people who were dying were not screened off. Thus prepared we went in and I knew at once that my fears had been groundless. The sun was streaming in and the place was full of flowers, not cut flowers but potted plants which individuals were encouraged to care for. The atmosphere was one of joyous tranquillity. In a corner of the room a woman was obviously dying and a young nurse was kneeling beside her bed holding one of her hands and apparently quite unaware of the small huddle of visitors. I spoke to one woman who said she had multiple sclerosis. She told me that when she first got the disease she used to come in for a period of respite care and, when she had seen people in the state she was in now, she felt she would never be able to stand it, but now that she was in that condition, she felt that her life was still worth living.

If this Report was one of our best, and I think it was, it was undoubtedly due to Cicely's participation.

The first Working Party that, under Ian Ramsey's chairmanship, I took part in produced a Report entitled *Personality and Science*. It was a one-off under the aegis of the Ciba Foundation. It was the first of a series in that it involved three philosophers who were to form a nucleus of the specifically Church related working parties, Ian Ramsey, R M Hare and myself. Dick Hare and I differed substantially in our approaches to moral philosophy and it took all of Ian Ramsey's chairmanly skills to accommodate both of us. Hare was at the time undoubtedly the leading moral philosopher in the country and wherever in the world analytical philosophy preponderated. His presence in the group guaranteed that the discussions did not lack analytical rigour. After lunch when coffee was on offer Dick would refuse it because he said it made his temper unduly sharp. He was notorious for his reluctance to relinquish an opinion once he had formulated it and the determination with which he would elaborate it to meet objections. It was not to be expected that he and I would agree in the formulation of a problem or the solution of it, but if we could both be persuaded to accede to a conclusion of the whole group, that would be reasonable guarantee of its soundness.

The nature of our fundamental disagreement became apparent in the cause of the 'Personality and Science' discussions. In those discussions there was much debate about the justifiability of medical interventions which fundamentally affected an individual's personality. Some of us had expressed this in terms of the invasion of a person's inner citadel. Hare objected to this and insisted that the language was misleading and that the point could be better put in terms of damaging the person's interests.

I endeavoured to find an example which would clarify the difference between us: 'Can we take the example of a hypothetical non-addictive drug which permanently makes the taker more contented with life and less capable of using his talents. Suppose someone wished to take the drug would it be acting in his interest for another person to offer it to him?' 'Yes, but if the drug were distributed widely it would prove to be against the general interest. The case against such drugs is that they harm society.'

In consequence of these activities I found myself in 1977 a member of the Church of England's Doctrine Commission. The existence of this body seems to be generally unknown to the world at large and many Anglicans seem not to be aware of it. It is appointed by the Archbishops to formulate the doctrines of the Church in relation to contemporary knowledge, or that is what it comes to, although it does not receive clear instructions to this effect. If its Report receives the imprimatur of the General Synod, it has to that extent a degree of authority. It is often said that the Church of England, as distinct from the Roman Catholic Church, has no recognised authority, but this is not entirely true. The views of the Archbishops and the Bishops collectively have considerable weight and so do decisions of the General Synod. It should not be difficult for a diligent enquirer to discover where the opinion of the Church preponderantly lies, but none of these has the binding authority of the *magisterium* of the Roman Catholic Church. The Doctrine Commission is part of the genuine but diffused authority of the Church of England and in its deliberations is aware of its duty to be representative.

The Report of the previous Commission had proved controversial and had not been accepted by the General Synod. So instead of setting down to write a report on a particular point of doctrine, the new Commission undertook to review the place of doctrine in the

Church. This was done by the way of a series of individual essays published under the title *Believing in the Church*. The ambiguity was intentional: believing, in the Church; and believing in the Church. Although published as individual essays, they added up to a coherent position, as shown by a summary written later by Anthony Harvey and entitled *Believing and Belonging*.

My own contribution addressed two related problems about the unity of doctrine; how could the same doctrine be maintained by the Church over time; and how could the doctrine as held by an individual believer be said to be the doctrine as held by the Church. These problems, as it seemed to me, were fundamental to the role of a Doctrine Commission in the Church of England. The Report of our predecessors (*Christian Believing*, SPCK 1976) had been rejected as excessively liberal. Its authors had been too ready to abandon or radically revise Christian doctrines as traditionally received. But, surely they were not mistaken in attempting to interpret traditional doctrines in such a way that they were compatible with truths known today, but not known to the scriptural writers and the Fathers of the Church. My piece was an attempt to show that this aim was intelligible and coherent. However, if this was the task of a Doctrine Commission it was also one imposed upon individual members of the Church, who in being prepared to think about these things themselves could make their own contribution to the Church's ministry while adhering to the tradition as so far formed. It was largely experience on the Doctrine Commission that prompted the writing of my later book, *Faith and Criticism*. There I argued that the familiar dichotomy, dear to journalists, between Liberals and Conservatives in the Church was misleading. There was a plainly recognisable division between those who insisted on the literal interpretation of scripture as the basis of Christian faith and those who believed that Scripture needed to be interpreted and developed in the light of Christian experience and knowledge, derived from whatever source, of the nature of the world and the course of human history. The former party are fundamentalists, the latter, if you like, liberals. But within the latter group are conservatives and progressives, according as they reach conservative or progressive conclusions. There is, perhaps, a further distinction within the 'progressives.' There may be some who are prepared to depart from scripture and tradition altogether in deference to secular thought and in their case it is open to question whether they are Christians at all. One of my happiest memories of involvement in theological controversy was in 1978. In 1977 a book had been published, entitled *The Myth of God Incarnate*, which was edited by John Hick. It was a 'liberal' manifesto, as that word has come to be understood. Its authors argued that the doctrine of the incarnation, as traditionally understood, is unintelligible or, at any rate highly paradoxical: that its spiritual or moral value can be given as good or even better expression by viewing it as myth rather than literal truth; and that it is not to be found in the New Testament.

It was followed shortly by *The Truth of God Incarnate*, edited by Michael Green.

In a splendid example of an irenic temper it was decided to hold a conference in Birmingham at which both sides would be represented with a view to achieving agreement, if possible, but at least greater understanding of each other's positions. To my great delight I was asked to chair the conference – a tribute I hope to my philosophical impartiality rather than to my theological ignorance.

At the end of the conference which was conducted with remarkable honesty and good feeling, I had to decide how to conclude it. I decided that I must try to summarise the week's discussion and indicate the nature of the agreements and disagreements that it had revealed. It was a challenging assignment. I had to stay up most of the night to complete my paper and throughout my career I had been very much a lark and not an owl. In spite of this handicap, I managed to finish my summing up, which I still feel was one of the best pieces I have ever written, and it duly appeared in the report of the Conference, entitled *Incarnation and Myth*. Michael Goulder, who edited the volume, wrote in his introduction: 'Several possible points could be foreseen. First the whole thing was set up in unhappy similarity to a seven-a-side rugby match, with Professor Mitchell to blow the whistle, and there might be strong feelings and a bad atmosphere. On the other hand university good manners and a supply of the best university wine might result in a failure to come to grips with the hard issues. The fact that neither of these things occurred was due in considerable degree to the Chairman's skill. The meetings were extremely friendly throughout, but strong things were said, and there was some cut and much thrust.'

I myself said in my summing-up: 'there is, for the most part, a welcome absence of the sort of mutual incomprehension which so often bedevils philosophical and theological debates. Both parties recognise the force and relevance of the arguments that the other addresses.' One of the benefits I enjoyed as a result of this experience was a concentrated education in contemporary theology of a kind that it would have been difficult and time-consuming to acquire in any other way. I was also struck by the extent that the issues at stake were philosophical ones and this strengthened my conviction that philosophy should form part of a theological education.

It may be questioned whether I was wise to engage in so many of these 'outside activities'. They took up a great deal of my time and I suppose that the various chapters and drafts that I wrote or the lectures that I gave would have made up at least a couple of books. But I think it was worth doing for a variety of reasons:

1. From a purely personal standpoint they benefited my work as Nolloth Professor. The contacts with schools helped me simply as a teacher and the various commissions and working parties contributed greatly to my theological education, far more than listening to lectures and reading books alone could do. Although lacking the specific training of an academic theologian I did benefit from close association with people who had it and gained some understanding of how they thought.

2. More generally, I believe that it is incumbent upon academics in return for the privileges they enjoy, to make their expertise available to the outside world. In particular I think it is important for philosophers to do so. They do have a capacity to clarify concepts and arguments which is widely applicable, and to do so impartially. And I have always insisted that impartiality does not imply neutrality. It does not mean not reaching firm conclusions, but being fair to opponents and giving full weight to their arguments. If it were not so we should indeed be in a desperate situation. We should have to choose between firm convictions and fairness in debate.

CHAPTER 15

North America

Princeton 1963

IN 1963 I WAS INVITED to Princeton as a visiting Professor in the Department of Religion for the Fall Semester. This provided an opportunity not to be missed to visit Margy's brother Rob and his wife Orma, who were living at Hudson on the Ottawa River near Montreal. With the long vacation ahead of us there was no hurry at all so, following the example of Ian Ramsey, we elected to go by sea taking half of the passenger places available in the SS *Cairngowan* due to sail in early July from Grangemouth to Montreal. After enduring four days of haar (coastal fog) in Edinburgh we embarked on the *Cairngowan* and I sailed for the second time under the Forth Bridge en route for the North Atlantic. The weather was disappointingly stormy and we arrived off Belle Isle among ice floes in freezing temperatures. Then in twenty-four hours occurred the greatest increase in temperature I have ever experienced and we were in the bay of St Lawrence in the nineties. We discharged cargo at Baie-Comeau where to our amazement the dockyard workers looked unmistakably French, although we were hard put to it to identify what it was about them that revealed this.

By the time we had continued by way of Quebec to Montreal we had given the children a history lesson which explained to them how it was that this part of Canada was still predominantly French.

Not so Hudson, which was an entirely Anglophone community within commuting distance of Montreal on the Ottawa River. In high summer it was an outdoor life with Rob and Orma and their family, Jane, Sarah and Charles, in and out of the water or on it, excelling in every kind of outdoor sport. (As we were to discover later it was not that much different in winter, although the outdoor activities were different, skating, skiing, etc.) Unknown to us Rob and Orma had prepared a special experience for us: a triangular cruise up the Ottawa River to Ottawa, from there along the Rideau Canal to Kingston and then down the St Lawrence to Montreal and back to Hudson again. It was a week to each leg with Rob and me as permanent crew and the rest joining us in relays. They had hired a comfortable sloop-rigged yacht, *Custard*, which awaited us in midstream.

Each leg of the cruise had its alarms. On the Ottawa River all went quietly until we reached Ottawa itself. As we entered the pool below Ottawa, between it and Hull we were beset by a sudden squall which threatened to blow *Custard* on to a lee shore on the Ottawa side. Rob made for the Hull side and sent me forward to make the ship fast to one of the numerous logs which lay dozens deep on the Hull side. To do this I had to balance on the logs in the driving rain and clamber back on board again. Never particularly agile I could easily have slipped between two of the logs and found myself unable to surface again. Friends of ours, natives of Ottawa, have assured me that even if I avoided drowning, the pollution in that pool was such that I was unlikely to survive prolonged immersion in it.

Having survived this peril we had then to negotiate the ascending series of locks which took us up into the centre of Ottawa and the level of the Rideau Canal. The Rideau Canal itself was a stupendous piece of engineering which cost thousands of lives and ruined its brilliant engineer. We learnt that it had been constructed, at a time of tension with the United States, to enable the British navy to avoid a risky passage down the St Lawrence by providing a safe alternative route from Kingston to Ottawa. By the time the canal was completed, the tension had abated and the triumphant engineer had to spend the rest of his life trying to get payment from the British Government.

The Rideau Canal is now used only for recreational traffic and is quite enchanting. It links a series of natural lakes, which it is a delight to explore at leisure. Unfortunately most of the traffic consisted of what Matthew, aged ten, called 'carboats' and one of these, proceeding at speed, caused a wash which rocked *Custard* so vehemently as she lay at anchor that her mainmast was snapped. So we had to proceed with a jury rig until we could get it fixed at Kingston.

The last leg of the cruise down the St Lawrence Seaway was the most challenging. The chief traffic consisted of huge lakers laden with timber which had to be steered clear of and there were two enormous locks which had been designed to accommodate the lakers. If a small yacht got in behind one of these it was exposed to the turbulence of its propellers as the big ship went out; if we went in first we had to get out very quickly as soon as the lock gates were opened and then get out of the way very quickly. After escaping from one of these locks, Rob and I were relaxing over a can of beer when we ran aground where we were exposed to the wash of the laker as she gathered speed. Having got off the shoal by the use of a kedge anchor we were enjoying the freedom of running downstream before the wind with a spinnaker billowing out ahead of us when Sarah, aged fifteen, slipped and fell overboard. Fortunately she was an expert swimmer and was in no danger but to get the spinnaker down and turn into the wind and stream so as to recover lost ground and pick her up was an awkward operation which tested even Rob's sailing skill. What impressed me most in the whole episode was Sarah's response as she finally scrambled on board. 'Sorry, Dad,' she said.

By the time we headed south to Princeton in September we had already got used to English spoken with a Canadian accent. Across the border it was very little different, but in due course we discovered that it was important to learn to discern the difference. Few things annoy Canadians more than being taken for Americans. I eventually concluded that the pronunciation of one word was diagnostic. Canadians pronounce the word 'about' as 'abote', so that in the presence of a North American one must wait until he or she had occasion to use that word before committing oneself as to their nationality.

We had, of course, to obtain a car and were in doubt as to whether to hire a car or to buy one was the wiser course, when a neighbour of Rob's with characteristic generosity solved the problem for us. He was about to sell a large Ford car, complete with trailer and he insisted on postponing the sale for a few months during which we could take the car into the US and bring it back again in time for Christmas.

So we set out, ourselves and the four children, together with all our baggage in the trailer. The Thomases had advised us to keep off the roads over the Labour Day weekend, so we took refuge in an attractive country hotel in Piermont, New Hampshire, where we spend the time playing tracking in the woods which surrounded the town, our first introduction to the secondary woodland which extends over most of New England.

It was after this leisurely journey that we at last arrived in Princeton to be greeted by George and Dorothy Thomas who were to be our hosts. George Thomas had recently founded the Department of Religion at Princeton and a year or two earlier had visited Oxford where I had introduced him to the Metaphysicals. He had written a book on moral philosophy which had not anticipated 'the revolution' in philosophy but which displayed a thorough knowledge of the history of the subject. His wife Dorothy was a charming person, who was a product of Mount Holyoke College and could only be termed a 'lady', because of her easy assumption of responsibilities without the least assumption of superiority. Both the Thomases were devoted parishioners of Trinity Episcopal church to which they introduced us as a matter of course.

At that time, not long after the war, when the British for the first time were beginning to visit the USA in increasing numbers, the papers at home were full of warnings to English people to remember that America was very different from England and we must not make the mistake of underestimating this difference. Having prepared ourselves for this, we were surprised on arriving in Princeton to discover in most respects how like Oxford it was. Indeed many of the people we had expected to meet were actually in Oxford. In some respects, indeed, Princeton was more fully a university town. Architecturally it was more uniform, in an extremely attractive style dating from the 18th century with wooden houses painted white with green windows. This style had not altered significantly since Georgian times with the result that we found it difficult to date any given house. This provided a pleasing background to the collegiate gothic of most of the university campus. Moreover, the main street, Nassau Street, which ran parallel to the campus had not (or had not been allowed?) to suffer the same fate as Cornmarket and been monopolised by impersonal department stores. Instead there was a variety of individual shops kept in relation to one another by uniform shop fronts.

An exception to the attractive style of most of Princeton houses was the street in which we were to live, Bank Street, a row of rather dingy houses of painted grey wood off Nassau Street. Matthew, when he saw it, burst into tears and said he could not bear to live in such an ugly place. In fact it was a house normally occupied by a faculty member at the time on sabbatical and extremely convenient for the Department and, of course, for the shops. Our next door neighbour was a young mathematician and his family, whose children were the same age as ours.

This central position was extremely convenient for the children's schools. In this respect their experience varied. Nell, having come from the Oxford High School, found herself effortlessly ahead of her classmates and did not conceal her scorn at the laxity of marking, especially when she got 120% for an essay on Leonardo da Vinci. Kate found herself endlessly repeating arithmetic she had already done and was never, however much repeated, going to do well. Clare was not really required to do anything and thoroughly enjoyed a term's undemanding play.

The one who came off badly was Matthew. At the age of ten he encountered boys at an age when they were least prepared to accept anyone at all different from what they were used to. So, what with his English accent and short trousers he was inevitably bullied. Poor Matthew suffered in another way. On condition for releasing him the Dragon School had insisted that I make sure that he maintain his Latin, so every week we did a dozen or so sentences. I found this more difficult than I had bargained for. Each time I asked him to translate a sentence he would make a mistake. When I then said to him, 'What is wrong with that sentence?' he would at once point it out and I would then get him to write the correct answer down. Since he could always spot the mistake, I couldn't see why he couldn't get it right in the first instance and this I endeavoured to bring about – without success. Thinking that his concentration lapsed between sentences, I tried distracting him. 'Matthew,' I would say, 'go into the kitchen and kiss Mummy and come back again' or 'go and hug Nell and come back again', until protests from the rest of the family compelled me to stop. We made one sad discovery about Matthew's school. It had a black headmaster as a matter of racial principle. But he was somewhat ineffective, so people got used to going straight to his deputy who was a very competent white woman. The general feeling was that this was not a very good way of overcoming racial inequality.

One marked difference from Oxford was that the campus was dry. So whereas in Oxford visitors would be welcomed to a sherry party or a dinner with wine, we were invited to a reception in which there was a long table at one end of which sat a dignified matron wearing a hat and dispensing coffee and at the other end another dignified matron wearing a hat and dispensing tea.

My sole academic duty was to hold a class for graduate students on Moral Philosophy and this I very much enjoyed. The students were bright and I could map out a coherent programme while giving individuals free rein to develop their own ideas. I remember only one difficulty. There was one rather uncultivated member of the class who kept on trying to monopolise the discussion to such an extent that I had to exercise some restraint over him. Half way through the term he came up to me and said, 'I don't know whether you are aware of it, but you keep on preventing me having my full say. You probably don't know our system, but one of the main objects of a class like this is to enable students to impress the professor, so that he will give them a good grade at the end of term.' I tried to explain to him that I was only restraining him so that others could have a fair share, but he seemed still to feel that he was being unfairly treated.

We wondered how to entertain 'my' graduates and, with our limited resources, decided to invite them in turn to a typical English tea in Bank Street. Meanwhile Margy was invited by Dorothy Thomas to join a group of young family wives and, when they introduced themselves, was a bit embarrassed to discover that, along with one older woman, she was the only one without a college degree – until, that is, she learned what subjects they had degrees in, such as flower arranging. I thought she could have mentioned her music diploma from Trinity, which would have been strictly comparable.

It is said that everyone remembers where they were at the time of President Kennedy's assassination, and I have a clear recollection of coming out of a departmental meeting in the Firestone Library to find a crowd of people in consternation at the shooting in Dallas of Kennedy. Margy had already heard the news when I got back to Bank Street and we stayed glued to the radio listening to the successive bulletins until he died. I was to have given a lecture at Union Theological Seminary, New York, on the day of Kennedy's funeral, but it was cancelled and we were invited by an elderly couple opposite us in Bank Street to watch the funeral on television as we did not have one. In its simplicity it was every bit as moving as Churchill's very splendid funeral had been in England, and each event had the effect of unifying a nation.

Princeton was well provided with open spaces in which we and the family could take exercise. There was a well-wooded park in which with the children we played 'Lurky', which Matthew had learnt at the Dragon; and Margy and I were able to take splendid walks in the grounds of The Institute for Advanced Studies. At that time in the Fall trees overhanging the little river were in a range of splendid colours, displaying in microcosm the splendours of New England. We had these walks very much to ourselves, sharing them only with people earnestly jogging, who to our surprise we often overtook. All this was helped by the weather which was uniformly calm and sunny. I am tempted to say that Princeton, like Oxford, was at its best in the autumn, when the declining sun is reflected in the one case off the stonework and in the other off the white painted houses, had I not on a later visit seen Princeton in the spring, when it is garlanded with flowering trees and shrubs, in particular dogwood.

Princeton itself was so entrancing that we did not venture very much outside. On one occasion we took the car to a beauty spot within a day's drive and the clutch fell out just as we reached it. When we had it replaced we felt we had done something to recompense the kind Canadian who had lent it to us. On another occasion we were all taken to the coast by the parents, the Loves, of Nell's best friend at school. But our longest and most enjoyable trip was to Hamilton in New York State to which we were invited for Thanksgiving by a couple we had met in Oxford. This was our first experience of this charming festival which, though it has an obvious religious significance, does not have to have one and, rather surprisingly, does not seem to be commercialised, but retains its simple, domestic character. The first snow fell just as we arrived in Hamilton in anticipation of the holiday we would spend in Canada before our return to the UK.

Hamilton, as we were to discover thirteen years later, was a delightful small town on the edge of which is an attractive Liberal Arts College, Colgate University, where I was to be a Visiting Professor in 1976, and this was our first very enjoyable introduction to it.

For the whole family this stay in Princeton was a most enjoyable introduction to America. Princeton University now has a formal relationship with Oxford, but, at this time, the informal links were strong and, in addition there were certain academic resemblances. In particular Princeton prided itself on its 'preceptorial system' which bore obvious resemblance to Oxford's 'tutorial system' in that the students in a given year were divided into 'precepts' of around six individuals who were taught together. Indeed, while I was there, I was asked to give a talk on the tutorial system, so that comparison could be made. Princeton was, perhaps, unique among American universities in taking its undergraduate education seriously. My chief academic contacts, apart from George Thomas, were Mal Diamond and Paul Ramsey. Mal was an inspiring teacher, whose lectures were enthusiastically attended. To my surprise he spoke with a broad Bronx accent which reminded one irresistibly of a Hollywood villain. It struck me as a striking indication of American democracy that such an individual could be found in the faculty of one of the most prestigious of American universities. He was an engagingly lively companion. A greater long term influence, however, was Paul Ramsey. He was a quiet, somewhat reserved man, whose influence was exercised chiefly by his books. My subsequent interest in medical ethics was very largely owing to him, a subject in which he was a pioneer.

At the end of our time at Princeton, we returned to spend a fortnight with Rob and Orma at Hudson, which was by now under a deep carpet of snow. Rob and Orma and their children, Jane, Sarah and Charles, were thoroughly at home in skates and skis and Margy and our children were determined in the time available to copy them. I, however, not being quick at picking up new skills, reckoned that two weeks was not long enough for me to learn to ski, but quite long enough for me to break a leg, so I did not venture to join them.

Colgate University, Hamilton, New York, 1976

Our next visit to the USA was in the bicentenary year, 1976, when I was invited to spend a term as Visiting Professor at Colgate University in Hamilton, New York, where our host was Bob Smith who had just spent a time in Oxford.

Once again we had the whole of the Long Vacation before term started at Colgate, so it was an opportunity to see more of the country. In particular Margy was anxious to revisit Carmel in California where her father had died and, if possible, see Winifred Howe who had taught her the piano and whose friendship had kept her going during the long period when her father's illness had absorbed all her mother's attention. This meant that we should have to drive right across the continent in order to get to Hamilton. With good fortune Margy was able to contact Winifred Howe who invited us to stay with her in her delightful house in Carmel Valley. When there, our most urgent task was to buy a car, not too expensive but robust enough to take us safely across the country. Winifred knew nothing about motor vehicles but recommended a salesman in Monterey 'who has been there twenty-five years and is probably reliable'. There we bought a Mitsubishi two-seater, having been assured that it was wiser to buy a car on the west coast and sell it on the east coast than vice-versa because it would be in better condition.

All this meant that we started this American trip on Margy's territory. She had taken her first driving test in Monterey, and I have little doubt that the reunion with her old friend did much to allay the self-doubt she had felt since her time there as a sixteen year old.

So it was in good spirits that we set out on our long journey eastwards. We decided to go north into Canada before turning east and were encouraged to do this by an invitation from my old pupil, Gordon Bjork, to stay for a few days in a villa he owned on the coast of Oregon. Gordon was about to leave Linfield College, a prestigious college in Oregon, because of a dispute with the Trustees, which meant he could not accompany us. It turned out that the coast was covered with trunks of trees as a result of logging operations in the neighbourhood and covered with a heavy mist, as San Francisco often is.

After this unusual experience we continued on into Canada and up the Fraser River Valley to Jasper. What remains in the memory from that part of the journey were the sirens of the two railways, Canadian Pacific and Canadian National which rebounded off the sides of the valley throughout the nights.

From Jasper we drove to Banff on a spectacular road over the Icefields glacier. We stayed the night in a motel at the top of the glacier and found to our dismay that on account of the cold our little car would not start. Fortunately, being at the top of the glacier we were able to start it by first coasting downhill.

It was clear now that we should proceed eastwards along Highway Two which runs just south of the 39th parallel which separates Canada from the USA. To get to it from Calgary we went through the Waterton National Park, spending the night in a remarkable hotel which resembled an over-sized swiss chalet and was staffed entirely by extremely willing but not very skilful college students. The next day the Canadian Waterton Park merged into the American Glacier Park and we debouched onto Highway Two in Montana.

We had been advised to avoid the Interstate if we wanted to see the country, and we did indeed see the country on Highway Two through Montana but it was a monotonous succession of enormous fields of grain interspersed with small towns of identical appearance, which were both attractive and unattractive. Unattractive was the approach to each of them which was an untidy collection of gas stations and light industry. Attractive was the inhabited area which one reached after walking a few hundred yards from the main road with comfortable, usually wooden, houses, surrounded by spacious lawns with no hedges or fences to separate them. As it was the bicentennial year we found that most of these small places had exhibitions to celebrate their history and, since the territory was agricultural, many of the exhibits were out of date agricultural implements which Margy enjoyed recognising as identical with those she had used in the Land Army at the beginning of the War.

I remember an odd incident at one such town. We booked in at a motel and the proprietor noticed the California number plates on our car. 'You've come quite a long way', he said. 'Yes,' said I, 'and in fact we are from further away than that. We are from England.' 'Ah', said he, 'I thought I recognised the brogue'. I was somewhat shaken that my distinctly Oxford accent should be so described, but I thought it better not to correct him.

The time came as we got further east that we saw signs to Chicago and, as we dislike driving through large cities, we decided to go straight on into Western Michigan and down along the coast of Lake Michigan. This was an enchanting series of small ports, as if by the seaside. Our destination was South Bend where an old graduate of mine, Bill Frerkin, now at Notre Dame, had asked us to visit him.

When we arrived at Notre Dame it was a very hot day and, as it happened, the beginning of Term. Bill was a monk who was severely crippled and had only just managed to climb up to my room in Oriel. When he arrived at Notre Dame he noticed that injured football players were given golf buggies to get around the campus, so he put the case that handicapped students should be allowed the same privilege. The outcome was that he was able to take us round the campus in his golf buggy and freshman fathers with their cases would hail him and say, 'Say, can we hire one of those?' So we had a privileged tour of the very magnificent Notre Dame campus.

Thence we proceeded by way of the Finger Lakes to Hamilton. As we already knew, it is a most attractive town with houses in the style of Greek or Roman temples and a park-like area rising to the site of Colgate University itself. We were accommodated just below the campus in a brick house which looked as if it might have been built for the President, conveniently placed between town and gown. We shared it with the family of an Indian academic by the name of Aggarwal who was an expert on agricultural reform.

Our first reception was disappointing. Margy found the supply of utensils considerably less than was needed for even a family of two. On learning that the arrangements were in the hands of the Provost, we left a polite but firm message for him, with the result that next day the Provost himself, John Morris, called upon us with a shower of domestic utensils. It transpired that the women in the office, of their own accord, had resolved that we should not repeat the record of an English classical scholar who had just departed and had put everyone against him and against his nation by his determination to take advantage of any privilege accorded to him. As it happened we made friends with John Morris and his wife from the start. They were as Welsh as could be in every respect, including speaking the language, although totally at home in the United States, a shining example of how the melting pot could absorb people without depriving them of their native identity.

Like most academics, I had no hesitation in fulfilling my obligation to Colgate by delivering a course of lectures on morality and religion identical with those which I had just given in Glasgow as Gifford

Lectures. This would enable me to make corrections in response to criticisms from my new audience, one advantage of American audiences being that at the end of a lecture one would always have a line of people wishing to discuss what one had said, whereas in England one was rewarded only with polite applause.

My time at Colgate left me with a considerable admiration for the concept of a liberal arts college. They were institutions devoted to teaching undergraduates, it being left to faculty members as individuals to decide whether to engage in research of any kind. This meant that they took more trouble with teaching and it was common for bright students to attend such colleges as undergraduates and apply to good universities' graduate schools to complete their education. My experience at Colgate left me wondering whether in Britain it might not have been wiser to convert polytechnics into liberal arts colleges rather than into universities with all the commitment to expensive scientific research that this implied.

The individual with whom I found discussion most rewarding was something of an anomaly. Steve Wykstra was doing research on his own in philosophical theology to be with his wife who was on the faculty as a teacher of French Literature. He later got a job at Calvin College, Michigan, to which he was entirely suited and in that capacity came for a period to Oxford where he gave great assistance to John Lucas and myself in our graduate class.

While at Colgate Margy and I took full advantage of what the place had to offer outside the academic sphere. We explored the surrounding countryside and picked what wild flowers we could. It was mainly second growth woodland intersected by attractive long rides. At first we were worried by signs which read 'Keep Out' 'No Entry' until reassured by friends who said 'You don't need to take any notice of that. It's intended to keep you from hunting. It never occurs to anyone that you might want to walk!' Later it was the hunting season and we were warned to keep out of the woods at that time. When we asked a friend what we could do to protect ourselves at that season he replied, 'It is generally thought that to make yourself look as much like a stag as possible is the safest plan.' In the event we were reduced to walking on the golf course, which had its own risks. Among the attractions of the countryside were isolated farmhouses dating usually from the early nineteenth century which would originally have been farmhouses but now, with the decline of farming, were private residences. The local county council issued a guidebook which gave a history of each of them. Farming had disappeared from New York with the opening up of the Middle West, except in the valleys where there were at that time prosperous dairy farms.

Besides exploring the countryside our other outdoor activity was attending football games. We had come to understand American football at the Palmer Stadium at Princeton but it was taken less seriously there than at Colgate. Indeed Colgate was having a very successful season and there was a distinct possibility of winning all their matches. This gave the final game particular importance, the more so as it was against Rutgers, a larger institution which had moreover indicated that it was going to drop Colgate from its fixture list in the next season. So important was this game that it was to be televised and the Morris's invited the Smiths and us to watch it. Bob Smith, it transpired, was going to watch it in a state of considerable anxiety. His worry was that if Colgate achieved an unbroken record, there was a real danger that the football coaches, supported by many of the alumni, would seek to turn Colgate into a 'football college' which it had been once in the past. In such a college the football coaches would carry more weight than the faculty in matters such as admissions. This would mean that all the effort that Bob Smith and his colleagues had put into raising the academic status of Colgate would be wasted. But Bob yielded to no one in his support for the Colgate football team.

It struck me at the time, and has served as a philosophical example ever since, that Bob Smith provided a perfect illustration of Plato's doctrine of the Tripartite Soul. The rational part of Bob's soul was aware of the dangers attendant upon the Colgate victory and wanted them to lose, but the spirited part longed for them to win. In the event the outcome hung in the balance almost to the end of the game. Against all expectation Colgate were in the lead at the beginning of the 4th quarter, when they were penalised and compelled to give up territory to such an extent that Rutgers could not fail to score and win a narrow victory. After the game the rumour circulated that the referee had admitted to having made a misjudgement in awarding the penalty, which meant that in the eyes of God

Colgate had won, although they had lost in the record book. This, if true, was the ideal solution from Bob's point of view. The spirited part of his soul could be satisfied, while it was evident to his rational part that nothing but an actual unbeaten record would be enough to fuel the coaches' case.

Our chief memory of our time in the US in 1976 is of our warm reception into a close-knit community in an attractive small town in an appealing countryside, but we were also taken, I cannot remember by whom, to the centre of the bicentennial celebrations in the Capitol in Washington. There we saw Magna Carta which in an imaginative gesture had been sent from Salisbury Cathedral to bear witness to the common heritage of the two countries. While we were in the capitol there appeared a party of dignified ladies clad in dresses of red and white who were, we were told, Daughters of the Revolution. When we returned to Hamilton we were told by Bob Smith's wife that she was entitled to be one of their number, having been descended from a Signer of the Declaration of Independence but had not wanted to be part of the show.

Yale and the University of Virginia, 1986

No sooner was I retired from the Nolloth Chair than I received an invitation to deliver the Nathaniel Taylor Lectures at Yale. This, I think was at the suggestion of Gene Outka, a friend who had studied with me at Oxford several years earlier. I remember this with some embarrassment as I treated this outstanding scholar as if he was one of my graduate students and got him to read to me what were in fact chapters of his magisterial book *Agape* and proceeded to correct his English as with other Americans. Now as a professor at Yale University he was a leading American teacher of Christian Ethics.

As soon as it was known that I was to be visiting the USA in 1986 I began to receive other invitations to speak and it was clear that it was going to be very difficult for me at a distance to arrange a timetable and to see which of these invitations I could accept, so I was glad to take up the offer of Billy Abraham to do it for me. Billy had secured a D.Phil with me as supervisor at Oxford and was about to take up a post in Theology at Southern Methodist University in Dallas. He had had his thesis published under the title *Divine*

Revelation and the Limits of Historical Criticism and was about to embark upon a series of original books on the role of the Canon in Christian Doctrine.

He was a Northern Irishman of unusual energy who was going to establish for himself a deserved reputation. I cannot think that I contributed much to this, except perhaps that I helped to give him confidence as the outset of his career.

Billy with characteristic energy worked out an itinerary for me on the basis of people I said I would like to visit and people who said that they wished me to visit them, accommodating as many of the latter as he could within the limits of my stay. The result was a most enjoyable tour both on account of the people we met and of the countryside we visited.

This latter was owing to a principle we early adopted. When possible we did not fly from one assignment to another, but hired a car and drove. The initial reason for this was my discovery that American academics were not only extremely hospitable but also distinctly exacting so that although ostensibly one was invited to give a single lecture, one was expected, while on the campus, to engage in a number of informal occasions and meet other select groups with whom one was judged to have a common interest. Although this added considerably to the interest and enjoyment of the visit, it also meant that by the end of it one was in a state of exhaustion. If, then, one had only a short flight between assignments, one had not had time to recover strength. We soon discovered, however, that by taking the time to drive from one place to another, I not only revived, but we also were able to explore the countryside and, at the same time, learn something about American history. This also had the advantage of making the whole experience more of a holiday for Margy who, although she was generously entertained by our hosts, inevitably felt that she was just an appendage to me.

The Yale lectures were fixed for early April and I was fortunate to be able to spend a number of weeks before that in Princeton. This was arranged by Diogenes Allen of Princeton Theological Seminary, who had been one of the principal hosts to Austin Farrer on his American visit in 1961 and was known as a particularly sympathetic interpreter of Farrer. He not only arranged for us to stay in the Seminary, but put me up for membership of the newly founded

Centre of Theological Inquiry, which was housed in a splendid building
not far from the Seminary. Here I had a room to myself in which I
could work on my Yale lectures and where I was provided with
generous secretarial assistance. The sole obligation upon visiting
scholars was to take part in discussions in the Centre from time to
time.

The Centre was a godsend to tired academics in need of the
opportunity to get on with their own work in peace and quiet. I was
very grateful for this opportunity, although I never got reconciled to
the use of 'of' rather than 'for' in the title.

Paul Ramsey took us to Trenton in his car to catch a train to New
Haven. We were met by Dean Leander Keck and entertained to
dinner at his house. It was explained to us that the lectures were
taking place in the annual 'convention' when old students of the
School came back 'for stimulation and renewal of friendships.' It
happened that in that year the returned students were mainly black
and their main focus of interest would be the Beecher lectures, to be
given by James Forbes, Professor of Preaching at Union Theological
Seminary, though, of course, these would not clash with mine.

I was entirely free to choose the subject of my lectures and the ones
I gave formed later the first three chapters of *Faith and Criticism*. They
were concerned with the nature of reasoning in theology and the
relation of this to faith. They went reasonably well, although I have
since discovered that Yale was more interested in another topic, the
topics raised by G. Lindbeck in his book *The Nature of Doctrine*, and
I wish I had tried to link up with them.

I received a shock when I went to the first of the Beecher lectures.
I have always thought of myself as a good lecturer. Unlike some
philosophers who deliver their lectures in a dull monotone, as if they
thought that any attempt to interest their audience was an insult to
their intelligence, I have always tried to hold their attention, to
project my voice, to pause at significant moments, to introduce jokes
from time to time, and so on. At my inaugural lecture in the Schools,
for example, as the room was rather stuffy, I resolved to keep the
audience awake and to ensure this I kept an eye on Christopher Stead
who was the most accomplished dormouse of my acquaintance.
Whenever his head dropped I raised my voice or paused significantly
and in this way I kept Christopher awake until the end. But then

Ted Yarnold of Campion Hall, an old Keble pupil of mine, came up to me and apologised for having fallen asleep. Apparently he was an even better dormouse than Christopher.

But the Beecher Lecture was a display of oratory such as I have never heard the like of. Dr. James Alexander Forbes used the full range of his powerful voice. At one moment he would lower his voice to almost a whisper only to raise it to a deafening roar a moment later. And he expected and received audience participation – 'The Lord be praised' – 'Alleluia'. In comparison with this my restrained utterance must have sounded weak and bloodless. Did, I wondered, English oratory ever sound like this, perhaps in the era of Pitt and Fox, when what was said in Parliament really mattered?

After the lectures each day there was a reception and I must confess that when I saw a large bowl in the middle of the room full of pink liquid, I assumed it was rosé, only to be disappointed by a characterless soft drink. One special delight was to be taken out to dinner by Leonard Thompson now the doyen of professors of African History in the USA whom I had last met as First Lieutenant of HMS *Genista* in Cape Town. He and his wife Betty, whom my mother and sisters had met in Oxford during the war, took us to lunch at Mory's. It never ceases to amaze me how quickly one takes up with friends over never mind how long a period of years.

Yale is particularly rich in art collections, including a remarkable Museum of British Art, and these we had time to visit to our great improvement. Lansing Hicks had insisted on our borrowing a car of his and in it we drove to Litchfield, a beautiful spacious New England village with fine large houses facing onto spacious expanses of grass and tree lined roads. Though entirely different in style it had charm equal to that of a Cotswold village.

There was no question of driving from New Haven to Dallas where our next invitation was to Southern Methodist University, so we flew, and were welcomed by Billy Abraham, who had arranged a varied programme for us for the next week. One of the first items was a tour of Dallas in a tourist limo called 'Silver Cloud'. This had a running commentary on points of interest in the city, which was catholic in its choice of subjects. Thus we were shown the spot at which President Kennedy was shot and shortly afterwards a window in a large office block which was 'where JR had his office'. Perhaps most revealing was the tour of the wealthiest part of town. We were struck by the fact that the houses were not particularly magnificent; it appeared that they were not expensive because desirable, but rather desirable because expensive. We were told how much it cost to get into the golf club and how long one had to wait for entry. One thing which struck us about the centre of Dallas was the number of cars and the absence of pedestrians. Although it looked splendid from a distance, on closer inspection it appeared not to be a community at all.

This was not at all the case with the University which was full of activity, in which our hosts took pains to involve us. On 9 April someone had remembered that it was my birthday (I was 69) and after my lecture on 'Reason in Religion' we were given a dinner which was turned into a birthday party by the Ogdens, complete with a cake and candles. Schubert Ogden had recently delivered the Wilde Lectures at Oxford and he and his wife still remembered having supper with us at Bridge House. One of the guests, a lively young woman called Bonny Wheeler, was about to take a party of SMU student to Oxford in the coming year and the following day I was entertained to lunch by her in order to meet the rest of the party and tell them about Oxford. (It was she who, when dining in an Oxford college, took exception to the presence of High Table which I undertook to defend.) Then we had lunch with the philosophy majors and an ethics colloquy. All this was in the Perkins School of Theology to which Billy's chair was attached.

An alternative to Dallas was afforded us by Rob Prevost who had been one of my last graduate students. His parents lived near Fort Worth and Rob insisted on showing us that town, which he declared was the real Texas. It was recognisably part of the West, based on cattle and later meat processing – vestiges of cattle sheds, meat processing plants etc remaining. There were recently designed water gardens in the centre which helped to provide a focus for the community. To emphasise the impression of local colour, Rob and his parents took us to Joe T Garcia's Mexican restaurant, reckoned the best in the area.

It was good to see Rob Prevost in his native scene. When he first came to Oxford, large in physique and incredibly slow spoken, it took me some time to believe that he was at all intelligent. In the event, though, he was bold enough to write a thesis in which he assessed the work of both his supervisors, myself and Richard Swinburne. It was published by Oxford University Press under the title *Probability and Treistic Explanation* and is an excellent introduction to contemporary philosophy of religion. His commentary on my own work I find very perceptive and he states my own viewpoint better than I had done. It was equally a delight to find Billy Abraham evidently flourishing at SMU with a steadily developing reputation, but we could not help feeling that Dallas was not a very suitable environment for his wife, Muriel who remained deeply attached to her native Northern Ireland. Fortunately some years later they were able to buy a house in Belfast to which they could repair in vacations.

After this invigorating stay with the Abrahams in Dallas our next stop was to be Baton Rouge in Louisiana where there was to be a conference on the work of Austin Farrer organised by Professor Ed Henderson of Louisiana State University. In his biography of Farrer, Philip Curtis says of Austin's visit to the USA that such was the impression that he made that American Scholars initiated a series of conferences on his work, with which his British friends were also associated, and this was to be one of them under the title 'The Idea of Divine Action in the World'. I was very anxious to go to this, so that Billy Abraham had fitted it into my programme. This time it was possible to drive and we hired a car at Love Field Airport.

We drove to Jasper where we spent the night and then to Natchez. The latter part of the journey was through beautiful green forest scenery along single roads with wide green verges and mixed wild flowers. Once into Louisiana the verges were narrower and the forests less thick and varied. Then we were into farmland with scattered trees and regularly shaped meadows. As we sat down for a picnic we wondered where else we could be and decided that we could easily be in France. Natchez was fascinating with its houses of classical design. It had recently discovered conservation, but a lot of it was still run down. We stayed at the Ramada Inn and had our first view of the Mississipi, a most impressive view with the fascinating sight of barges pushing five or six heavily loaded ones at a time. From there we proceeded to New Orleans by way of Rosedown Plantation with its elegant ante bellum house and gardens. We were received at New Orleans by Nancy and David Perkins at the Baptist Seminary, who took us round New Orleans, which provided a marvellous antidote to Dallas, being, as it seemed to us, amazingly French on a domestic scale.

At the conference in Baton Rouge I was expected to sum up along with Ann Loades. This meant that I was bound to attend all the sessions against my normal practice of taking the afternoons off. (When I organised similar conferences in Oxford, I always left the afternoons free.) Ann Loades I knew from having been one of her PhD examiners. She was now a professor of Theology at Durham University. She was to have been a ballet dancer, but her height of six feet or so precluded it, though she regularly acted as a ballet examiner in England. Nevertheless her ballet background had given her a stately carriage. She had an encyclopaedic knowledge of modern theology which with her sympathetic temperament made her a good person to sum up the conference. She was like me in wanting to ensure that all contributions were properly acknowledged. With Ann and myself we had a representative British contingent which included David Brown, Bryan Hebblethwaite, and Richard Harries.

From Baton Rouge we flew to Memphis where we were welcomed to Rhodes University by Larry Lacy and I gave a lecture and a class. We failed to pay tribute to the King but paid our respects again to the Mississipi. From there we were taken by Lou Pojman to Oxford, Mississipi, where I was to give a lecture at the University, 'Ole Miss'. I had been one of Lou's D.Phil examiners at Oxford and he and his wife made sure that we enjoyed everything that the town and university had to offer. It was a very pleasant, unpretentious campus in a small leafy town. It was hard to believe that it had been the scene of one of the bitterest encounters in the battle for racial equality. We were housed very comfortably in a guest house which illustrated for us once again the difference between a Bread & Breakfast in the USA and Britain. In Britain hotels are expensive and B&B's provide a cheap and modest alternative. In the US hotels are cheap but uniformly and reliably boring and B&B's offer a characterful alternative such as this guest house was. My lecture on 'Faith and Reason' had an enthusiastic audience of some 200 students. What struck me at once was the number of radiantly beautiful girls who appeared to listen to my words with rapt attention. When I commented on this to Lou, he explained that what fascinated them was my English accent. As often, I was introduced to some students who were hoping to come to Oxford, UK.

After being shown William Faulkner's house situated in quiet woodland and incredibly cut off from the world, we were taken to meet the Mayor of Oxford in his downtown drugstore. He showed us with pride an (I thought) unworthy map of Oxford, England, which he had received from the eponymous Oxford. I was moved by what it evidently meant to him.

The next place which Billy Abraham had arranged for me to lecture was the University of Virginia at Charlottesville. Before that we were entertained by Bill Poteat, whom we had ourselves entertained in Wootton, at Duke University. He also showed us the University of North Carolina, Chapel Hill, both of them impressive campuses.

We hired a car and on our way to Charlottesville saw a sign to Apomattox, which somehow rang a bell with me as a place of importance in American history. So we decided to go there and found that it was the scene of the surrender of Robert E Lee to Ulysses S Grant which signalled the end of the Civil War. We saw the path down which the army of North Virginia marched to the surrender and it was altogether a most moving historic site, which represented the occasion in the same dignified manner in which it appears that the surrender itself took place, not, sadly, exhibited in the political negotiations which followed.

Our host at Charlottesville was Jamie Ferreira whom I had been able to assist in Oxford as she endeavoured to complete a book which she needed to qualify for tenure at the University of Virginia. I had met her first at Yale where she was a student of Gene Outka's and it was evident that we had interests in common. By the time of our visit to Charlottesville she had published her book and secured tenure, my only contribution to this having been to reinforce her self-confidence. Jamie added to our satisfaction in Charlottesville by inviting to dinner my old tutor, Tony Woozley, with his wife-to-be Cora Diamond, a fellow philosopher and charming individual who would make him a delightful companion. He came to my lecture on 'Reason in Religion' which can only have confirmed his fears when I was an undergraduate about 'the great rolling themes of philosophy'.

But over and above these personal experiences was the impression made upon us by the buildings of the University itself. Designed by

Jefferson himself in a classical style which bore the impress of Jefferson's own personality, they were by far the most impressive university buildings we had seen in the US, bearing comparison with those designed by Christopher Wren in Oxford and Cambridge. We had the good fortune to be wandering round them in the evening at the end of term. End of term parties gave it a festival air and showed how readily the buildings gave themselves to undergraduate use. Jamie enabled us to appreciate the genius of Jefferson further by taking us to his house, Monticello, surprisingly small, but elegant and comfortable and betraying once again the personality of its owner and builder.

From Charlottesville we headed for Washington where I was to give my next lecture at American University on 'The Enforcement of Morals'. This journey justified our policy of driving rather than flying as the mere description of our route testifies. We drove to the Blue Ridge Mountains and then along the Skyline Parkway, then down into the Shenandoah Valley after taking a brief walk along the Appalachian Trail. The weather was bright, cold and clear and the countryside at its best, in Spring. We had little excuse then on entering Washington by the Theodore Roosevelt Bridge for failing to find Rock Creek Parkway and ending up (suitably enough) behind the Jefferson Memorial. Somehow we made contact with John Shosky of the American University who took us for a drive round Washington which was as much an introduction to Washington driving as a guide to that city. He took us out to dinner at a restaurant near the White House, from which we were driven elsewhere by a bomb scare. Next day we were taken to lunch at the Cosmos Club by Os and Jenny Guinness. Os, who was working at the time at the Brookings Institute, was an old graduate student of mine, who had settled in America although looking and sounding as entirely English as if he had stepped out of the pages of P G Wodehouse. When he first came to see me in Oriel he was already an effective advocate of a Christian voice in public life and, when I asked him why he needed a doctorate, he replied that he wanted to gain a sound intellectual foundation for what he was doing. His charming wife, Jenny, he first saw on the cover of *Vogue* and the pair made a very persuasive team. It was apparent that Os was going to become an influential voice in Washington.

Before I gave my lecture that evening I was taken to see the cathedral in Washington. The building, only just completed, was a very convincing reproduction of mediaeval Gothic and, when we entered it, they were just coming to the end of evensong, singing 'The day Thou gavest, Lord, is ended'. When they processed out, the choir, followed by the Dean and Chapter, it was so strongly reminiscent of evensong in any English cathedral that, nervous as I was at the prospect of my coming lecture, I was strangely moved. The lecture was well received and followed by a friendly reception.

Os had arranged for us to stay that night at Fellowship House which dispensed Christian hospitality to visitors entirely free. After this friendly experience of Washington we walked next day through the woods to Georgetown where we met Warren Reich, editor of the *Encyclopedia of Ethics* and others who expressed an interest in the *Ramsey Centre* which we were then setting up in Oxford.

So ended the lecture tour that Billy Abraham had arranged which had been extremely happy and enjoyable both from an academic and travellers' point of view. We could not help being struck by how uniformly friendly our reception had been and I was encouraged to discover how the philosophy of religion as we were pursuing it in Oxford was flourishing all over the USA. Another thing which impressed me greatly and gave me great satisfaction was how widely the influence of Oxford had spread and contributed to this. Many of my contacts had been either Oxford pupils of mine or visitors to Oxford who continued to remember their time with us. This was the case, even though only a minority had been given paid employment through delivering named lectures or receiving visiting research Fellowships. In most cases the best we were able to do was to give them the status of Faculty Visitor which entitled entry to libraries and access to lectures. We were usually able to arrange limited dining rights at a college. But I got the impression that, apart from all this, the reputation of Oxford itself counted for a lot. The fact that I came from Oxford was in itself a passport to a warm reception. There are so many links between American universities and Oxford that there exists a genuine sense of fellowship which should not be underestimated, in particular by British Governments which, in their treatment of Oxford (and Cambridge), seem not to appreciate what a precious asset this University is to the reputation of Britain, in the USA and all over the world.

The next day we left Washington and drove through Maryland into Pennsylvania and Amish country back to Princeton. There we found spring at its height with dogwoods white and pink, jacarandas, azaleas, magnolias, and acacias.

There we found a surprising and very welcome invitation from John Morris to come and give a talk at Union College at Schenectady where he had been appointed President. Union was best known for its engineering school and its best known alumnus was Jimmy Carter. Schenectady itself was a fascinating small town divided by the statue of an Indian. Your status in society was determined by whether you lived 'above the Indian' or 'below the Indian'. Conspicuous in the town was St George's Episcopal church, build in 1750, and its equally conspicuous Rector, the Revd Darwin Kirby, in cassock and biretta proceeding from his house to the vestry smoking a Sherlock Holmes pipe, followed by a shorter priest similarly clad trailing a trolley with a black box on it (containing what?). On the Sunday we went to the Eucharist at St George's Church and the whole had a curiously timeless Anglo-Catholic character. We were taken to lunch by the Morris's to the Mohawk Club which was surprisingly elegant and luxurious for so small a town.

We were back in the 20th century after a dinner with the Morris's after my lecture when members of the Philosophy Faculty were anxiously debating what they could do about the increasing incidence of plagiarism. Most thought that steps must be taken to prevent it, but some thought that the students were entitled to take any steps that would get them the high grades they wanted.

There followed what amounted to a remote lost-island holiday made possible by an old graduate student of mine to whom I had reason to be grateful. Together with Billy Abraham, Steve Holtzer had edited a book of my essays entitled *How to Play Theological Ping-Pong* at a time when I was too busy to do it myself. After leaving Oxford Steve had found a job in the University of the Pacific, Seattle, but, having arrived in Seattle, gave up the job for a most distressing reason. Throughout his time at Oxford he had been accompanied by his wife, a very beautiful girl who helped to keep both of them by doing modelling all over Europe. While he was making arrangements for them in Seattle, she returned home to California and announced that she intended to stay there. She had stayed with him until he had achieved his doctorate, which he would not have been able to do had she left him earlier. But the result was the same: Steve gave up academic life altogether and went into commerce. He could have been forgiven if he had cut off all connection with the Oxford of painful memories, but he welcomed us to Seattle and found accommodation for us in a remarkable B&B in Seattle, situated on a bluff which looked over the harbour and Bainbridge Island. He took us up the Space Needle and drove us to Anacortes to the ferry for St Juan Island, where we were to stay with a very old friend of Margy's, Evelyn Heath. Evelyn was a GI bride and her husband, a doctor, was now the sole doctor for the St Juan Islands. To get from the house in San Juan Island to the others he had a light aircraft in which he took each of us up to view the whole panorama of the islands and the mainland of Canada.

Mac and Evelyn's house was on a stretch of coast looking across to Victoria and the Canadian mainland. Each morning we would walk down to the shore and felt unlucky if we did not see two bald eagles and a shoal of killer whales. Here for a few days we enjoyed the company of our hosts in virtually complete calm.

Last academic visit to the USA

My last academic visit to the USA in 1989 introduced me to another facet of religious life in that country. I was invited to deliver the Norton Lectures at the Southern Baptist Theological Seminary, Louisville, Kentucky. In that year I was going to be seventy-two and this was going to be a considerable undertaking. The lecture audience over all four lectures would be between 300 and 800. In addition I was to lecture at a family dinner 'on a topic of more scholarly concern' and 'we normally like to involve our guest lecturers in several dialogue conversations during the week, in particular with our graduate students and faculty.' To encourage me to accept the President told me that the lectures had been given by Arthur Peacocke recently and would later be given by Alvin Plantinga, both of whom, of course, I knew and admired.

In any case I was happy to accept this invitation, because I had developed the theme of the Yale lectures into what would become my next book, *Faith and Criticism*, and would be glad to try this out on a discriminating audience.

When we arrived in Louisville we found that the Seminary was a real powerhouse of Christian thinking with 2000 students altogether and 150 PhD students. It was as stimulating as any university campus; and also, as I discovered, under threat. The Southern Baptist convention which has general oversight of the Seminary had been undergoing a fundamentalist revolution since 1979 and their aim was to enforce this upon the Seminary, whose aim had hitherto been 'to combine the best of critical scholarship with a high view of biblical authority'. It only required, so I was told by the President, one more fundamentalist trustee to be appointed for this drastic change to be enforced.

I was further encouraged to accept by the information that Ernest Nicholson had been a visiting professor and had entertained Richard Cunningham, Professor of Christian Philosophy, to dinner at Oriel in 1980.

So it happened that my lectures on Faith and Criticism were entirely relevant to the conflict that was taking place. And the conflict seems inevitable in a revealed religion. If God reveals himself in a particular time and place and there exist documents and practices which are records of this revelation, it is necessary that these should be carefully kept and accurately interpreted. But human beings have other means of discovering truth, themselves god-given, and these newly-discovered truths need to be reconciled to the revealed ones, and the latter interpreted in such a way that this reconciliation can be achieved. Christians believe that this happens under the guidance of the Holy Spirit. It is to be expected that there will be some whose chief concern is that nothing in the original deposit of revelation is lost or distorted; and others that no freshly discovered truth is left out of account. The danger with fundamentalists is that the revelation becomes ossified; the danger with liberals is that it becomes assimilated to some contemporary fashion. To someone who was deeply interested in the character of this problem, Southern Baptist Seminary was a stimulating place to be, and I owe a special debt to Dick Cunningham.

After Louisville, we were to experience two different elements of American life. We had met in Oxford Bert Keller, a professor of Medical Ethics at one of the hospitals in Charleston, South Carolina, and his wife, Lucille, a talented amateur actress, and they invited us to stay a few days in Charleston after our time at Louisville. Charleston, like Bath, is a city of one splendid architectural style which, like Bath's, is basically classical but in which each house has on one side a handsome veranda so placed that it avoids the prevailing wind. Before our visit the Kellers warned us that a hurricane was imminent and it occurred just a week before we arrived. We could see the damage as we approached but, astonishingly, the old part of town was largely undamaged because of the design of the houses. We arrived at the Kellers in time for Halloween, which Bert had told us they took seriously. There was evident agreement with neighbours as to where the children should call and what they should expect, so that the abuses could be avoided that have spoilt the occasion in Britain. All this was explained to us and in this way we were welcomed into the family.

From this domestic celebration of Halloween to our next stop requires a somewhat roundabout story. The year before, Margy and I had spent the autumn in Hong Kong where I had been giving the Martin Lectures at the University of Hong Kong at the invitation of my old Keble pupil, Tim Moore, who was Professor of Philosophy there. At the end of term it occurred to us that this was the best opportunity we were likely to have to visit China. So we decided to spend the whole of my Martin stipend on visiting three centres – Beijing, Xian and Canton. We did this in style with a car and driver of our own and guides at each place. The hotels were designed for tourists up to international standards and in Xian, after we had seen the terracotta soldiers, we found ourselves placed at a table with two young Americans. We learned that they were Billy and Jodi Webster on their honeymoon. We had a very lively conversation and at the end of the meal we exchanged addresses and invitations to stay in the unlikely event that we found ourselves anywhere near them.

Their home address was Greenville, South Carolina, and when we knew we would be in Charleston, some 200 miles away – no great distance in American terms – we got in touch with them. Here the hurricane came to our assistance because Billy was driving into the outskirts of Charleston to deliver supplies of food to a school which had been badly damaged and could pick us up and take us back to his house in Greenville. Over dinner Billy explained to us with great enthusiasm the work he was engaged in. It was part of a social experiment known as 'workfare' designed to tackle the problem of poverty without reducing the poor to such dependence that they lost all self-respect and all sense of responsibility. His contribution to this movement was to run a chain of restaurants called 'Bo Jangles'. These were cheap fast-food outlets. Billy explained that he had to make them pay, so he was employing the least employable of the workforce, chiefly single mothers. His aim was to organise these as effective business concerns while making the conditions of work such that the employees felt themselves to be respected as persons. He produced, for example, a magazine which went to all the restaurants in the chain and kept them in touch with one another. It would sometimes feature competitions which individuals or restaurants could enter. Next morning Jodi, who was a lawyer, had to leave early for the office, and Billy took us for breakfast to one of his restaurants where it was apparent that he knew the names of the manageress and all the waitresses, as he said he aimed to do in all the chain.

This combination of business sense with a genuinely charitable impulse was typically American, we thought, and also represented a typically Southern form of charity derived from the example of those slave-owners who acknowledged a duty to care for the well-being of their slaves.

North America in 1997

All these North American visits had been characterised by a combination of hard academic work and generous hospitality and exploration of the country. In 1997 when I reached the age of 80 I could not help feeling how nice it would be if we could disjoin these elements and visit the continent without having to carry out academic duties. Margy also shared my wish to revisit American and Canadian friends. We should not be constrained by the need to join together lecturing commitments, but could work out an itinerary that was workable on its own.

But could we impose on our friends in this way? The only way to find out was to write and ask. So I wrote to each of a number of friends and said that, while the strength remained for us to do so, we should very much like to see them again and would it be possible for us to spend two nights with them on a date to be arranged on the basis that they would find somewhere for us to stay and would take us out to dinner on the first night and let us take them out to dinner on the second.

To our great delight we received affirmative responses which enabled us to draw up the following itinerary:

Itinerary: USA and Canada, 1997

Thursday 1 May	Fly to	Washington, DC
Monday 5 May	Fly to	Baton Rouge, LA
Wednesday 7 May	Fly to	Charleston, SC
Friday 9 May	Drive to	Wingate, NC
Sunday 11 May	Drive to	Williamsburg, VA
Monday 12 May	Drive to	Washington, DC
Thursday 15 May	Drive to	Lancaster, PA
Wednesday 21 May	Drive to	West Point, NY
Thursday 22 May	Drive to	New Haven, CT
Friday 23 May	Drive to	Hamilton, NY
Sunday 25 May	Drive to	Niagara Falls, Ont
Monday 26 May	Drive to	Kitchener, Ont
Thursday 29 May	Drive to	South Bend, Ind
Saturday 31 May	Drive to	Bloomington, Ind
Monday 2 June	Fly to	Seattle, WA
Friday 6 June	Fly to	Calgary, Alb
Saturday 7 June	Fly to	Saskatoon, Sask
Sunday 8 June	Go to	Winnipeg, Man
Saturday 14 June	Fly to	London, Heathrow

This time we flew into Washington and were met by Eric Robinson, an old friend whom I had first met lecturing on world affairs in HMS *King Alfred*. Since then Eric had had a varied and often tempestuous academic career. After occupying a series of positions in England which did not match his capacities, but nevertheless making some original contributions to economic history, he decided to seek his fortune in the United States, where he was appointed Professor of Economic History at Boston University. Not wanting to uproot himself from his home country with no guarantee of permanent employment he secured release from the usual requirement of a review of his appointment after a year. Nevertheless at the end of his first year he was informed that his appointment would not be renewed. Eric was not the man to accept such a setback and he took every possible legal step to get the decision reversed, including appeal to the Trustees and to the President which was eventually successful. It appeared that the cause of his unpopularity with his colleagues was that he was a notably conscientious teacher and in particular was not prepared to relax his grading to make allowance for the poor performance of many of the students. It probably did not help his cause that he was now devoting himself primarily to research into the work of John Clare, on whom he was now a world authority. As editor of the Oxford University Press edition of Clare's works, he was chiefly responsible for ensuring the recognition of Clare as a major English poet and when Clare was admitted to the Poet's Corner in Westminster Abbey, it was he who was invited to give the address.

His domestic life was not straightforward either. He married his first wife, Rosemary very young and had two daughters by her, before they were divorced. Then in the USA he met and fell deeply in love with an older woman who was already suffering from cancer. He nursed her with great devotion and wrote a moving account of their life together.

By now Eric had retired to Falls Church, Virginia, where he lived with his third wife, Victoria, who had been a student of his and was very much younger. They seemed very happy and received us very warmly.

Our next stop with Edward and Tricia Henderson at Baton Rouge was made memorable by our being shown magnificent watercolours of Louisiana wildflowers in the University Library, done for the Millenium by Margaret Stones.

Our visit to Charleston with Bert and Lucille Keller enabled us to see them and that splendid city again. In addition, they took us to Magnolia Plantation where we saw magnificent gardens and an extended swamp garden with three alligators. Elsewhere we saw the oldest live oak in North America with no sign of decay or dying back, estimated to date from about 1330.

We went next into North Carolina to stay with Rob and Kathleen Prevost where we arrived in time for Commencement at Wingate University and I had the pleasure of seeing Rob process in his Oxford D.Phil robe.

After this we were due to return to Washington but I had always wanted to visit Williamsburg and we reckoned we could do it via Raleigh and Norfolk. We were rather tired when we reached Williamsburg and I had made the mistake of taking the turning to Williamsburg centre rather than the earlier one to Williamsburg Hotels. So that at about 7.30pm we arrived in the centre of Williamsburg and could see no sign of hotels or B&Bs. As we wandered around disconsolately we noticed a man and a woman who were wearing badges. Thinking they might be officials of some kind we stopped them and said, 'can you tell us where we can find somewhere to stay?' 'Yes,' said the woman, 'stay with us' and her husband nodded agreement. We had experienced hospitality in America before, but never anything like this. It transpired that they had rented a condominium for the week of Commencement at William and Mary College where their son and daughter-in-law were taking their MAs (presented by the Chancellor, Margaret Thatcher). The next morning I thanked her warmly and murmured something about payment, but she said, 'Don't thank me, thank God.'

We walked round Colonial Williamsburg all morning and into the College of William and Mary. There in the chapel I was glad to see a monument to a 'Reverend Professor Dawson, sometime President of the College, born in Aspatria and educated at the Queen's College, Oxford.' It was good to see the North County connection maintained in the 18th century.

Back in Washington we were taken out to dinner by Os and Jenny who were now obviously deeply involved in the religious life of the capital. Os was doing what he had always intended to do: writing books of popular apologetics which avoided technical language but did not avoid intellectual difficulties.

While in Washington we stayed with Eric and Victoria Robinson. Eric took us to visit Mount Vernon, George Washington's home, which was an interesting contrast with Jefferson's home, Monticello. Whereas what struck me about Monticello was the way it reflected Jefferson's individual personality, Mount Vernon bore the stamp of an English country gentleman of the period, an impression enhanced by the care which as been taken to plant the garden with flowers which would have been at home in an English garden.

On the way to our next stop, Lancaster, Pennsylvania, we were met at Longwood Gardens luxuriously planted by the Dupont family, by Diogenes and Jane Allen who had come from Princeton for the day.

While staying with Herb and Joanne Poole near Lancaster, we had the pleasure of watching a group of Amish boys fishing on the opposite bank of the Conestoga River, a tributary of the Susquehanna, joined later by their father and sisters. The boys has long trousers and braces and straw hats and the girls white muslin caps. It all looked like a Renoir painting.

Our next visit was to the Pojmans at West Point, Lou having left Ole Miss to be Professor of Philosophy there. We were introduced to the Head of Humanities, a very courteous and cultivated man whose subject was the history of art, particularly twentieth century architecture – not what one expected to find at a military academy. We were helped to appreciate the splendour of its situation by being taken to the summit of Bear Mountain, with fantastic views of the Hudson River and the surrounding hills, but above all of the skyscrapers of Manhattan fifty miles to the south. In all the effect was quite magnificent.

The next visits were to New Haven, where we spent a pleasant evening with the Outkas, and Hamilton where we enjoyed once again the attractive small town and had diner with the Morrises and the Smiths.

Our next invitation took us into Canada where we were to visit Rod and Marilyn Sykes at Kitchener, Ontario. On the way we were able to see Niagara Falls, which were distinctly impressive but did not challenge comparison with Victoria Falls which we had visited with Matthew at the time of his wedding in Zimbabwe. Rod Sykes had been a very lively graduate student with me and had introduced the term 'soft rationalism' for my own account of theological reasoning. Although well qualified for a university post, he had devoted his considerable energies to the Methodist Ministry. Memorable in our stay with him and Marilyn were visits to a large wood carpeted with trilliums, small three-petalled lilies, and to the theatre in Stratford, Ontario where we enjoyed the musical *Camelot*.

A long drive back into the USA took us to South Bend, Indiana where we were entertained by Jean Porter and her husband, Joseph

Blenkinsop. At an earlier stage arrangements for Jean to study with me had, to my disappointment, broken down, and she had gone on to make signal contributions to virtue ethics. They took us by train into Chicago which we had not seen before. It struck us as an impressive and human city with splendid skyscrapers of varying dates and plenty of people walking in the streets.

From South Bend we drove to Indianapolis where we surrendered the car in which we had driven three thousand miles. We were met by David Smith who, with his wife Weezie, had stayed in our house in Walton Street. We stayed in their house in Bloomington and were shown around the campus with its splendid auditoria and music rooms. That evening we enjoyed watching *Yes Minister* which it was a pleasure to share with these very Anglophile American friends.

There was no question of our driving to Seattle to meet with Steve Holtzer and Margy's old friend Evelyn who was now a widow living in Bellingham. She showed us the countryside set off by marvellous cloud-effects but with no view of Mt Baker. She and her son drove us to Steve Holtzer's house in Newcastle where we met his new wife Carla. They took us to a splendid restaurant overlooking the harbour in Seattle with moored yachts in the foreground and a container ship in the harbour and beyond the skyline of downtown Seattle. Mt, Rainier, the highest mountain in the USA outside Alaska, appeared for a moment and on the way back to their house Mt. Baker could be seen at last to the North as a faint outline. This, sadly, was the last time we were to see Steve, who died from cancer some years later.

This was also our last experience of the United States, as we were to end our tour in Canada. We flew to Calgary and were met by Hugo and Jenny Meynell and taken to see Terence Penelhum and his wife. Hugo was a like-minded philosopher who had been active with me in setting up the British Society for the Philosophy of Religion. Terence Penelham had been Professor of Philosophy at the University of Calgary and had given the Wilde Lectures at Oxford and made important contributions to the philosophy of religion.

Calgary had splendid views of the Rockies. Our next stop, Saskatoon, was set in a featureless flat expanse of agricultural land. There we were met by Caroline and Gary Davis, both of whom were active in the University, Gary as an astrophysicist, Caroline as an administrator. Caroline was a very talented philosopher whose thesis was published under the title *The Evidential Force of Religious Experience* which has become something of a standard work. She has given up philosophy and takes a lively interest in wherever Gary's work takes him. The two of them took us to a Heritage Centre which celebrated Native Canadian history and culture which to a suspicious degree appears to be all sweetness and light.

Still in a flat featureless landscape we next flew to our final destination in Winnipeg where we were entertained by Murdith and Lynn McLean. Murdith was one of my earlier and most agreeable graduate students who later spent time in Oxford as one of our tenants. He was at this time Head of St John's College in the University of Winnipeg, his academic work somewhat hampered by the need to care devotedly for Lynn who had begun to suffer from the cancer from which she died some years later. While there we were introduced to Antony Waterman, a very vigorous economist, with whom I discovered two affiliations. He had been at King Edward's School, Southampton and regularly visited Oriel College in order to consult the papers of Richard Whateley, who as Fellow of the College was one of those who built its reputation in the early nineteenth century.

In spite of Lynn's illness we were warmly received by the McLeans who provided us with a warm conclusion to our North American Journey, which had shown the extent to which academic contacts had issued in genuine friendships.

CHAPTER 16

Epilogue

My ninetieth birthday and the family, 19 April 2007

M Y NINETIETH BIRTHDAY was celebrated by lunch at The Grand Hotel, Nontron, Dordogne, France, and was attended by the whole family, which consisted of Nell and her husband, Anthony Richards, and her two daughters, aged twenty and eighteen, Philippa and Josephine; Matthew who had insisted on coming from Zimbabwe; Kate and her husband, Stuart, their daughter Nikki, aged 25, and their son, Tom, aged 22; Clare and her husband, Hugh, and their son, Mark, aged 25, daughter, Isabel, aged 18, and son, James, aged 15; also my sister, Betty, aged 88, and her daughter, Libby, aged 58.

This occasion illustrated that we were a close-knit family who had no hesitation in travelling some distance for a celebration such as this.

It remains to describe their present situations and how they got there.

Nell is the head of Modern Languages at Clifton High School for Girls. I recently suggested to her that she was well qualified to be a headmistress but she said that teaching was what she enjoyed and she had no interest in administration. Her second husband, Anthony, is an interior designer, Bristolian born and bred who, after re-modelling the interior of a grand 18th-century house belonging to the University, is now working on another 18th-century building, the Clifton Club. They are both now so well settled into Bristol that neither of them would want to move. They live in a large Victorian house on the edge of the Downs with splendid large rooms which have been recast by Anthony in such a way as to take every advantage of the light which streams in through the large windows. There is room for the two girls, Philippa and Josephine, to have their own space without encroaching on the other two. It is entirely understood that Anthony is their mother's husband but not their father. Philippa has a very good voice and has sung in the Bristol Cathedral girls' choir for a number of years; she is now reading Music and Theology at Sheffield. Josephine is still at school studying science and art, and is going to Cardiff to study Architecture.

Matthew is living with his wife Rosie in Harare and enduring the hardships and uncertainties which this entails. He went to Zimbabwe to work as a forest entomologist, but this soon collapsed and he now describes himself as an expert in computer graphics. He is an excellent wildlife photographer from the largest mammals to the most microscopic insects and much of his work is for the World Wildlife Fund. Rosie is an extraordinarily energetic woman who loves roaming the hills of Zimbabwe on her own, leaving Matthew anxious about her safety. They have a house in a mainly middle-class black district in Harare with a four acre garden which Matthew has planted mainly with indigenous trees.

Kate and Stuart live in Woodstock on a housing estate about ten minutes from us. Their house is a modern one which they spend a lot of time adding to and re-building so that it reflects their own individual taste. They are both extremely practical and have friends who share their interest in improving their environment whether in Woodstock or, twice a year, in our house in La Varenne on the banks of the river Dronne. Stuart works as an electrician for a housing company, which took over the housing responsibilities of the local authority. Stuart regards his job as an extension of the social services, as the old people whose electrics he goes to attend to often need his help and advice on other matters. Although in practice this amounts to an important aspect of his work it is not officially recognised. Kate spent many years as a teaching assistant at the local primary school, where she did much more than she was paid to do and encouraged the children in their art work and in decorating the school. In addition, the two of them take it upon themselves to keep an eye on us in our old age which means not only doing odd repairs but also consulting Nell and Clare about our general well-being. They have two children, Tom who read History and Film at the University of Kingston, and Nikki who works for an estate agent.

Clare's husband, Hugh, is a director of a private equity firm, in which capacity he shares in the fortunes of the City of London. They live in a square in Islington which was designed by a distinguished architect, Edward Carpenter, as an essay on Victorian Gothic or, perhaps more accurately, Victorian Elizabethan. Carpenter, who died young, is best known for the pure gothic of Lancing College Chapel. Clare is, as a mature student, studying architecture. Hugh is an accomplished musician, a cellist of professional standard, and the two of them every year take a Palladian villa near Venice where, with a group of like-minded friends, they make music in ideal surroundings. Altogether they use their wealth well. They buy paintings in a discriminating fashion, usually by artists of the second rank, which their house displays to good effect. Hugh is interested in old clocks and every hour the house resounds with their varied strokes. But they also support a number of charities, including, in a modest way, St Mary's Church, Wootton, which they attend whenever they can. They have three children. Mark, aged 25, who after gaining a first in Engineering at Bristol has gone into an Australian bank. Isabel, aged 18, has been Head Girl at Channing School, Highgate (where, I am delighted to see, the Honours Board contains the name of Phoebe Llewellyn Smith who gained a scholarship to St Hugh's College, Oxford). Isabel is starting in October 2009 at University College, Oxford. James, aged 15, has now started at St Paul's School.

So that is our family as it is now and they are a great blessing to us in our old age. They keep in regular touch with us and with one another. It remains to say how each got to this point.

Nell

Nell, having got into the Girls' High School at the 4+ examination remained there for a record fourteen years and thoroughly enjoyed it. As I said earlier, she was from the start happy with language and seemed to be able to master complex constructions before she could possibly have heard them actually used. I remember particularly when we were staying with Margy's aunt in Middleton-in-Teesdale, we took Nell, aged 5, to Hadrian's Wall and I tried to explain to her why the Romans built it and how the various parts of it, the vallum and the fossa, actually worked. When we arrived back in Middleton, Nell came out with a tumble of words, among them all the words that I had used, although she couldn't possibly have understood them. Her academic record was continuously successful and she must have been a delight to teach. As I explained earlier, she was an astonishingly reasonable child, who always wanted a reason for being told to do anything and would do it without demur on the reason being given. She applied to read French at St Hilda's but without success as they had a particularly strong entry that year. So she went to Bristol University and began her long association with the city. She got a First in French and went on to do a doctorate in the *nouveau roman* which was well enough thought of for her to be interviewed for fellowships at Magdalen and St Hilda's. In these she was unsuccessful but she was for two years a temporary lecturer at Bristol, followed by another two years at Exeter. At this stage she decided that what she wanted to do was school teaching rather than university teaching and she got her job at Clifton High School for Girls where she has been ever since. She clearly is a good teacher and enjoys it thoroughly.

While she was at school she took up ballet and was quite good at it. She took part in a performance of Sophocles' *Antigone* at Magdalen in which she was required to dance 'the spirit of Antigone' (a character unknown to Sophocles). There she met Andrew Dand, then reading PPE at Magdalen, who was playing Antigone's lover, Haemon. They fell in love and were married at St Cross Church by a friend of ours, Adam Duff, with the reception in Oriel. She did not want, unlike her sisters, to be married by my brother-in-law, Betty's husband George Stokes, I think because she was uncertain at that stage to what extent she still adhered to the Christian faith in which she had been brought up.

Andrew Dand was a splendid man of whom we became very fond. He was in every sense a 'gentle' man who came from a large family who took to Nell very warmly. Andrew started his career with ICL, the English computer firm, but quickly became associated with the University of Bath until he and a number of his associates set up their own company, which was mainly concerned with enabling computers to communicate with one another – something which is now taken for granted.

Nell and Andrew found a delightful house in a terrace in Clifton which had splendid views over the floating harbour. Brunel's SS *Great Britain* could be seen with its masts in transit just off to the left as one looked out of their drawing room window. Margy and I had the impression that Nell was a little uncertain about having children, but in time they had two daughters, Philippa and Josephine, who could not have been more fortunate in their parents.

The conspicuous happiness of this small family was in 1993 terminated by the onset of bowel cancer in Andrew. He died in 1994. About three years before his death while Margy and I were on holiday in France, I was called to the telephone and told that Andrew wanted to speak to me. He said, 'I have a request to make of you which may surprise you, but I think will please you. I have decided to be baptised and I wonder if you would be a sponsor'. He and Nell had recently decided to have the children baptised and, on reflection, Andrew felt he should be baptised with them. It was no sudden conversion; indeed he liked to represent it as a matter of simple fairness to the children: 'I felt I shouldn't put my children through something which I wasn't prepared to go through myself.' But it was no mere formality either. I think it was an acknowledgement of what lay behind the principles which had always governed his life and the spirit in which he had lived it. It brought these things into a clearer focus.

For some months after Andrew's diagnosis there seemed to be a reasonable prospect of recovery and, while hope was still possible, Nell and Andrew bravely hoped. But in September it became clear that there was no possibility of a cure and that further treatment of an aggressive kind could do no more than extend his life by a few weeks. Andrew decided not to undertake such treatment and Nell supported him in this. They determined to do all they could in the time that remained to them to make the most of their life together for one another and for the children. It was a brave decision and one which they were able to carry through with the skilled and sensitive assistance of a medical team who at every stage did all they could to keep Andrew free from pain and in full possession of his faculties. But it was Andrew's quiet determination and Nell's unceasing and devoted care which played the main part.

Nell in her widowhood was greatly helped by the deputy head of her school, Elizabeth Anderson, and her husband who was Professor of Geography at the University, both of whom were regular worshippers at Christ Church, Clifton, where Nell and Andrew had begun to take the children and Nell continued to do so. Nell was greatly supported by these and other friends, not least Andrew's family who never ceased to look upon her as one of their number.

As soon as they were old enough Philippa and Josephine went to Clifton High, which helped to strengthen Nell's attachment to the school. So, with many friends and her very attractive house, Nell was for some years living a contented life when Anthony Richards, a widower, asked her to marry him. Anthony's wife, who was French, had worked in the University and Nell had known and liked her. His two children had grown up and were now independent. Anthony still had French in-laws with whom he wished to keep in touch and whom Nell, with her French connections, would be happy to meet. So they decided to get married and had a delightful wedding with a reception in the University house which Anthony had recently re-decorated. Since both of them were well known in Bristol, it was well attended and Nell's costume illustrated a point which I made about such a wedding in the speech I was invited to make. In a marriage between young people, I said, one looked for a process of assimilation; over time they would grow into one another. In a marriage between two mature individuals this could not be expected to happen as by then they have already developed strong personalities. What was needed was a process of negotiation, in which each made concessions to the other. This was nicely illustrated at the wedding because Anthony liked hats and Nell did not. So Nell wore a most attractive creation which is call a fascinator.

One deeply entrenched feature of Anthony's which Nell is happy to encourage, is his approbation of Nelson. Not only does he have a shelf full of books about him, but there are portraits of him and Emma in the dining room and what amounts to a small shrine in his honour that is full of representations of various kinds. No one who has spent time in the Royal Navy can fail to be moved by this, because the spirit of Nelson continues to inspire it.

Meanwhile the girls have flourished. Neither of them can remember their father, but when I see Philippa who is tall and slim, processing in the girls' choir of Bristol Cathedral, my heart stops as I recognise her movement as the image of Andrew's.

Matthew

We ought to have realised it, but did not, that Matthew's childhood was lived in the shadow of Nell. Whether or not Nell actually oppressed him, her consistently serious-minded good behaviour imposed a pattern which he, with a very different temperament, not only could not imitate, but increasingly did not want to. At the Dragon School, away from Nell, he found himself in what had every appearance of a chaotic environment, in which he made adequate academic progress and was able to develop his capacity for music by learning the trombone, while showing a distinct talent for painting.

The question then arose where he should go on to secondary school. Margy's mother offered to pay his fees at a public school and that became a realistic possibility. We were not sure, but we thought that it would be a constant battle at home to get him to do his homework and that the regular discipline of a boarding school would ensure that he stuck to his schoolwork. On the other hand he had a particular friend, Martyn Lloyd, one of the sons of our opposite neighbour in Charlbury Road, who, if he went also to Magdalen College School, would steady him and give him confidence. Eventually, however, we decided to send him to Marlborough which was not too far away and, because of its clerical connections, would not simply be a preserve of the rich. But we were told that at a boarding school everything depended on the character of a boy's housemaster. So we spent a day at Marlborough interviewing the various housemasters. The result was quite decisive. One house-master, Dennis Silk, not only impressed us, but attracted Matthew by being the only one who actually talked to him.

So Matthew went to Marlborough on the expectation that he would have a sympathetic housemaster. But our careful plans were frustrated when Dennis Silk was appointed Warden of Radley and his place was taken by a worthy enough successor who entirely lacked the antennae which Silk so obviously possessed. He was, as it seemed, a cold disciplinarian, for whom Matthew felt no personal warmth. The outcome was that Matthew did not enjoy his time at Marlborough and, far from benefiting from the regular discipline of a boarding school, rebelled against it. To our distress he never once visited the school's splendid art room where he could have developed his artistic gifts. He took to smoking, no doubt to calm his nerves, and, as this was against school rules, was in some danger of expulsion. He did, however, manage to gain entrance to the University of Southampton to read physiology and biochemistry, but he dropped out in his first year and for some time kept himself going by working on building sites in and around Oxford.

By this time Margy and I had decided to give what money we could spare to the children and Matthew was able to buy a small terrace house in Bridge Street, Osney, where he lived with a succession of girlfriends. One thing which they had in common and which cast light on a significant feature of Matthew's temperament, was that they each suffered from some sort of nervous trouble and required that Matthew should care for them tenderly.

At this point things improved dramatically for Matthew. Fed up with sporadic work on building sites, he got a job as a laboratory technician in the Forestry Department of Oxford University. There he came under the aegis of Martin Speight who was investigating the causes of Dutch Elm Disease. Here was a first-rate scientist engaged on work of evident importance who was able to kindle a similar enthusiasm in Matthew. When Matthew asked him how he could himself progress further in his pursuit of these researches, he was told that he would need a university degree if he was to go further.

At this point for the first time Matthew turned to me and asked for my help. Could I find out which colleges took people for Agriculture and Forestry? I gave him a list of colleges, one of which was Keble. So Matthew applied to Keble and was admitted as a mature student in 1979. Happily his tutor was Bob Lucas who, whenever I asked how Matthew was getting on, replied 'Matthew and I understand one another.'

Matthew eventually got a second in Agriculture and Forestry on the penultimate occasion that it was examined. While he was looking for a job John Pitt told him about an advertisement by the new government of Zimbabwe for a forester. Matthew applied and was accepted. His main task on arrival in Harare was to find out the cheapest and most effective way of controlling termites. The government was encouraging people to plant gum trees which grew quickly and provided firewood, but they were peculiarly attractive to termites. In the course of this work he became deeply interested in the life cycle of termites about which not much was known. This was work he thoroughly enjoyed but, as the economy of Zimbabwe declined, the government was forced to abandon it and Matthew undertook the same sort of work for the Tobacco Board until government policy forced this too to abandon much of its work, thus hampering one of the country's most profitable exports.

At this time, when on holiday in England, Matthew discussed with Martin Speight the possibility of doing a doctorate. Speight favoured the idea and when Matthew asked where he should do it, Speight answered, 'here, of course'. But the fees for non-members of the European Union were so steep that he was compelled to give up the idea.

Eventually as Zimbabwean government policies threatened to destroy everything but subsistence farming, there was no longer any possibility of Matthew doing the job he was now expert in and he was forced to find an alternative. So he took up computer graphics, being an expert photographer who had mastered computer skills, and he worked mainly for the World Wildlife Fund as well as for the remarkable Harare International Festival of the Arts which every April attracted a world-wide patronage.

In this he was joined by his wife, Rosie, whom he had married not long after his arrival in the country. Rosie was highly intelligent, born in Rhodesia as it then was, she had gained a degree in law at Durham University and made her living as an independent journalist. She was extremely lively and enormously energetic. She had in common with Matthew an intense attachment to the countryside of Zimbabwe and its wildlife. Indeed, she often alarmed Matthew by exploring mountainous areas on her own and ascending peaks where he did not dare to follow. She was what used to be called 'highly strung' and had a nervous breakdown which required and received the services of a skilled and sympathetic psychotherapist. So once more Matthew needed to be the careful and tender companion.

They had a delightful wedding in the garden of her mother and stepfather's house in a suburb of Harare which verged on open countryside. Our whole family were present and Rosie was not alarmed by Matthew's three sisters. I had acquired a reputation in the family for flower arranging and was duly asked by Matthew to do the flowers. I knew nothing of African flora and the best I could do was to fill vases with the splendid leaves of Canna which did not collapse until the wedding was over. We were taken by Matt and Rosie to Victoria Falls and Wanke Wildlife Park. Rosie was a sharp-eyed guide and would see animals before anyone else. Leopards are notoriously hard to discern and on one occasion Rosie saw one at a distance and insisted on moving towards it in the hope of getting it to come towards us and become more visible – a risky strategy which was entirely characteristic.

We made a number of visits to Zimbabwe and were taken to most of the wildlife areas. One in particular brought us into close contact with wild animals. It was in the valley of the Zambesi and we were allowed to camp in the open. One night we had a bull elephant near our tent and on another we found our way to the wash place blocked by an enormous hippopotamus. Matt and Rosie took care not to bring any citrus fruit which is a lure for elephants, but one night the food they had brought, though carefully packed, attracted a pack of hyaenas. We learnt next morning that Rosie, naked, had kept them off by throwing clods of earth at them.

Matthew and Rosie between them employed two members of one Ndebele family. George helped Matthew in the house and garden and Rosemary acted as secretary to Rosie. Matthew was very distressed when George died of AIDS and insisted on going to his village to attend his funeral, at which he gave an address and called George 'my brother' which moved his family deeply.

When we urged him to consider seriously leaving the country Matthew was very reluctant to do so. He had grown to love the country and the people. The most he was prepared to consider was to look for a job in some neighbouring country, preferably Botswana or Mozambique, where he could make use of his expertise in dealing with termites. But he comes back to England for three weeks or so every year to see us and his sisters, including Nell of whom he is now very fond.

Kate

Kate was an enchanting child, small for her age and extremely active. When we entered her for the Dragon School little visitors race, they gave her a start, which Margy warned them against, with the result that she reached the finishing line before the others had even started. At the time when our children were regularly going 'up the rocks' to visit the Stotts, she was warned once about the presence of a bull in the Stott's field, to which she memorably replied 'Bulls don't bite me; I bite bulls.'

She was early to attain puberty and it was obvious that she was going to be extremely attractive. Nell remarked that when they stood together on the quay at Fowey they were in a very short time surrounded by a group of boys, and when Matthew invited her with us to a dance at his house in Marlborough, by the end of the evening Kate was being taken over the hallowed lawns by the Head of the House.

With all this she was also extremely lively and bright and it was a shock to me when she failed the 11 +. I had failed to recognise that her brightness was of an entirely practical kind and not at all academic. I took her to see a woman psychologist whom I had met when on the University's committee for mental health and who earned my approval when she reported about a pupil who I thought had some psychological blockage, 'I think the trouble with your man is that he is lazy'. That a psychologist should even know this word gave me immediate confidence in her. She told me that Kate was distinctly intelligent but not at all academic, which I ought to have known.

Not surprisingly this led Kate to think that she had been a disappointment to me and led her to strike out on her own. When in Wootton she sought to attach herself to the 'old village' and used to hang about by the signpost to Rousham where the local 'talent' used to assemble. Margy was a little worried about this and when Kate, aged 13, asked her if she could go for a ride on a motor bike with a young man of 18, said 'No', whereupon Kate burst out 'Why? Don't you trust me?' Margy replied that it wasn't that she didn't trust her but thought she might find herself in a situation that she wasn't experienced enough to cope with.

In feeling anxiety about Kate's growing independence, what we did not realise was that she was a very good judge of character and the time came when she wanted to marry a young man in the village who was the youngest of a large family of character in the village, his name Stuart Davis. He had been apprenticed as an electrician and was now working in that capacity for the West Oxfordshire District Council. He was shy and retiring and it took Kate to discern his underlying strength of character and kind-heartedness. One morning in 1975 Kate in a flurry asked me to be sure to stay in because Stuart was coming to ask my permission to marry her. This was even at that time a rather old-fashioned gesture, but it was sensible of him to want to make sure that Kate's parents would accept him.

The wedding, performed by George Stokes in Wootton Church with the reception on our lawn by the river at Bridge House, was a particularly happy occasion. Not only was it a marriage between two individuals, but it was also a marriage between the old village and the new village. As it happened it coincided with the introduction of main drainage to the village, so the road out of the village was blocked just beyond Bridge House, thus emphasising our unity with the village and from a practical point of view providing free parking just outside the house.

Kate and Stuart started their married life in a modern estate in Woodstock from which they moved shortly into a rather more attractive one largely inhabited by young professional people. Over the years they steadily improved their house, often doing the work themselves. When the district council made over their housing stock to a housing association, Stuart happily joined the new employer, and continued to enjoy the social service aspect of the job.

Meanwhile Kate joined Marks and Spencer in Oxford, rising rapidly to the rank of staff supervisor, in which she was generally relied upon to deal with customers who were difficult or who had particular problems. She developed a reputation for being particularly good with people. After many years at this she was happy to move back to Woodstock as teacher's assistant in the local primary school which was only a short distance away from their house. In this capacity she became informally responsible for much of the art work in the school and took charge of the children's entry into the annual carnival. The result of her having this job was that very quickly she became very well known in Woodstock, so that we became known as Kate Davis's parents.

It had long been clear to us that Kate could have married anyone, but that her actual choice had led to a marriage of great contentment. The two of them made many friends, two couples in particular. Ken Wilkins was a self-employed builder and his wife, Anthea: Jacques Verdon, a Frenchman, was head waiter at the Sorbonne restaurant in Oxford, from where he moved to be Common Room butler at Merton. Ken, Anthea and Stuart and Kate constituted themselves a 'working party' and regularly once a year would go to our house in La Varenne and undertake necessary repairs and improvement.

When I reached the age of 75 we decided that Wootton, though
a splendid place to bring up children, was not a good place to grow
old in. So we decided to move into Woodstock where there were
good shops and regular buses to Oxford. Hugh's mother, who lived
in Woodstock, let us know that a large house in Market Street would
soon be on the market, as it owner, Elizabeth Mitchell, an artist, was
about to move closer to her daughter in Oxford. It was a rather
splendid house, listed grade II*, mainly 17th century, but with parts
a century earlier: however, it was very badly in need of repair. The
housing market was in a very depressed state, which made it
uncertain whether we should get enough from the sale of Bridge
House, Wootton, and 26 Walton Street, Oxford, to pay the purchase
price and the cost of essential repairs. In the event we just managed
to purchase the house and were fortunate to secure the services of
Richard Ward, Master Builder whom I knew as Clerk of Works at
Oriel, a third generation Oxford builder who was experienced in
caring for buildings of all periods. Early on Richard Ward said to us
'The other evening I sat in the cellar and listened to the building.' At
that point I knew that he was the man for us and he proved to be
excellent at deciding what must at all cost be preserved and what
needed to be replaced, and how to replace it in an appropriate
manner.

As we were looking round the house Margy and I went down a
short flight of steps into a room with an attractive 'Ipswich' window,
dating we later learned from 1635. 'A lovely bedroom' said Margy.
'Bedroom my foot' said I, 'this is cut out to be a study'. This time I
prevailed and the room became a delightful study with my desk in
the window overlooking Market Street and the Woodstock Arms
opposite. I have never been one of those scholars whose concentration prevents them noticing their surroundings and I enjoy watching
our Wootton friends who have come in to do their shopping.

One uncovenanted blessing of our move into Woodstock has been
that Kate and Stewart assumed responsibility for looking after us in
our old age in the most unobtrusive manner possible. This has been
helped by our joint ownership of a dog, on the basis that we look
after him during the week and Kate and Stewart walk him at the
weekends. Hector is our fourth Labrador and the first to be, initially,
a dog. I had heard, and know from experience, that bitch's urine was

bad for lawns and since only bitches were mentioned in the gardening books, assumed that dog's urine was harmless. Hector soon proved me wrong. We have two walled gardens and I, laboriously, trained Hector to pee only in our further utility garden, until my painstaking procedure was frustrated by Margy letting him out early into our nearer, ornamental garden.

Clare

Our fourth child, Clare, was the result of our experimenting with the rhythm method of birth control and it is odd to reflect that, if that had worked, she would not have been born. From the start she was a very positive individual, active, lively and confident. One of my first memories of her is on a holiday in Fowey when she moved around on all fours and announced that she was a 'Mouster.' By the time she could have explained what she meant, she had grown out of this phase. When we took her to Polridmouth she alarmed us by climbing up on rocks and hurling herself off. On one occasion as we made our way over a rocky terrain, Margy told Nell to prevent Clare clambering up rocks. 'What makes you think,' said Nell, 'that she will let me stop her?' Her early school reports revealed that although her schoolwork was patchy she never lacked confidence and the problem was to get her to be consistent. She was, however, consistently good at art and games.

Her lack of consistency in school work ruled out the Girl's High School where Nell was making steady progress. So we toured various schools, one of which was Downe House, where she caught sight of Kitty Warnock, so we sent her there, where her performance remained patchy. We thought that at this stage the High School would be good for her and she was admitted to the sixth form. There she achieved prominence as one of the two leading characters in the *Birds* of Aristophanes.

Although she was bright and lively in the High School there was no question, as there had been with Nell, of her applying to Oxford. Instead she followed Nell to Bristol to read French and the History of Art. Here the usual pattern repeated itself and at the end of her first year she passed comfortably in the History of Art but narrowly failed in French. This meant that she had to take the French again for a second year. This called for a degree of consistency, the lack of which was still her weakness and she again failed French by a still narrow margin. At this point she decided that, since history of art was her favourite subject, she had better study it where it was best taught and she applied to and was accepted by the Courtauld School of Art.

But Bristol had played its part in Clare's life. She and four friends had shared a house in their second year. Remarkably when they gave up the house, the owners found that it was in better condition than when they had taken it on. More remarkably two marriages ensued and the married couples remained firm friends for the rest of their lives. Clare's future husband, Hugh Richards, was to be her ideal partner. She was small and volatile; he was tall and steadfast. She was confident and capricious; he was cautious and in some need of re-assurance. Each supplied what the other lacked. Hugh started in Boots, then took a London MBA and joined the private equity firm, 3 I's. Their increasing prosperity enabled Clare to develop her gifts without needing to be hampered by financial considerations. It became apparent that her lack of consistency was the counterpart of a temperament that was predominantly creative. Her activity came in spurts and she could not progress with tasks for which inspiration was lacking.

By a lucky accident she found her way into television and gained employment in the experimental TVAM, where an amusing incident occurred. Compared with most of her colleagues she had a posh accent and one day a man gave up trying to ring her and got onto a neighbour. 'Can you get Clare Richards for me? I have been trying for ages and keep on getting Claridges'. Eventually Clare found her métier as an independent television producer. She teamed up with Frances Tulloch, whom I had met at St George's, Windsor, and in due course set up her own company, Pillarbox Productions, and specialised in programmes on social issues which hitherto had lacked exposure.

It always amused us that her company most of the time consisted of one person, herself, but that it could expand at her will in two stages, the first when developing a proposal, the second when actually making a programme. Among her programmes were *Tales from the Wasteland* about poverty and the Welfare State, *Who killed my baby?* about neonaticide, *Kids on the Rocks* about drug abuse by children,

Public Eye, Dyslexia and Crime which revealed that 50% of offenders have learning disabilities. In the course of making these programmes she would meet all sorts of experts, chiefly academic, whose views were relevant to these issues, but who lacked the connections with the media which were necessary to influence public opinion.

Clare and Hugh's first child was a boy called Mark. He was extremely lively and inventive as I discovered when it fell to me to play with him an elaborate game whose rules were invented by him and constantly varied without notice.

Two years later they had another child, a girl whom they named Harriet. Clare brought her down to Wootton to introduce her to us and to Kate. One afternoon the others went out and I was left alone with Harriet. In order to make proper acquaintance with my most recent grandchild I lifted her from her cot and looked intently at her. She did not smile but I had the distinct impression of being recognised. That evening Kate invited us round to her house to complete the process of induction in the family. Clare put Harriet up into Kate's bedroom to nap while we chatted quietly in the room below. After a while Clare went up to see how the baby was doing and there was an unearthly cry such as I have never heard before or since. Then Clare came down with the limp body of Harriet in her arms for all the world like Lear carrying the body of Cordelia. Her child was dead and there was nothing we could do but call the doctor to bear witness to the fact. The next thing to do was convey the news to Hugh who was at a conference in Coventry. Then we called George Stokes at Charlbury and asked him to say some prayers over the dead child. This he did and after that Kate called an ambulance and made all the arrangements for the funeral, demonstrating once more her capacity to act in a crisis, although as the tragedy occurred in her house, she felt it with a distinct acuteness. This happened before 'cot death' was widely recognised and investigated as 'sudden infant death syndrome'. Clare found that a television associate, Anne Diamond, had suffered in the same way and together they set up a charity to investigate cot death. Harriet is not forgotten. Whenever Clare and Hugh come to Woodstock they go the Wootton churchyard to visit the place where Harriet's ashes were laid and in our garden we have a *prunus cerasifera* planted in her memory. Not long afterwards Clare had another daughter who has now reached adulthood and is full of promise. It is impossible not to wonder what Harriet would have been like if she had survived.

After a successful career in television, for which she received a prize from The Royal Television Society, Clare found it more and more difficult to survive as an independent producer. The BBC and ITV were increasingly anxious to produce their own programmes in-house. In any case she came to feel that she had made all the programmes that she had to make, although there were still others she could make, and an earlier ambition began to assert itself – to become an architect. She applied to become a mature student at the Bartlett School of Architecture, attached to University College, London. She still retained her uncanny capacity to gain entry to any institution she tried for and she was duly accepted at the age of forty-seven.

Hugh, after many years with 3 I's, took the risk of starting an independent firm with three of his colleagues, which flourished and left Clare free to follow her own inclination, even though she was unlikely to actually practise as an architect. As it happened she did not need to be doing this in order to exercise her creative imagination. Their elegant house asks for appropriate decoration and for works of art to grace its walls. Its only drawback is that it is a 'ladder house' with two rooms only on each floor. With Clare needing an office for herself and the children as they grew up requiring more space to themselves, Clare and Hugh have gradually expanded into the house next door until they now occupy the whole of it. Re-designing both houses to the extent that their listed status allows has demanded all their ingenuity and imagination, as do their two sizeable gardens.

This then was the family that attended the ninetieth birthday party in France, which was also a celebration of Hugh's fiftieth birthday. That they continue to make up a family is something that Margy and I in our old age have reason to be grateful for. The task of keeping an eye on us inevitably falls mainly upon Kate and Stuart, who live only ten minutes walk away, but we are aware that they keep in regular touch with Nell and Clare who visit us from time to time to see for themselves how we are. It is our firm impression that they love one another as well as loving us, so that the family remains a genuine entity.

CHAPTER 17

Postscript

The French house

HAVING GIVEN THE HISTORY of the family as they attended the ninetieth birthday party, it remains to explain why we celebrated it at a hotel in France in a not particularly well-known town but where we ourselves were well known. To do this it is necessary to go back thirty years. In 1978 Margy's mother died, also like my own mother on Good Friday. It is Margy's belief that unable through age to be as active as she wished, she deliberately ignored advice to keep away from people with 'flu and made a point of visiting friends with the disease. She caught it and it turned to pneumonia which led to her death. Margy had always had strained relations with her mother, but I remember how she cradled her mother in her arms as she lay dying.

As a consequence of her death, the Villa St Anne in Cagnes passed to Margy and her brother Rob and they had to decide what to do with it. One possibility was to retain it and let it to tourists, but this would have required expensive alterations to meet the standards then required, in particular a swimming pool; and neither party could afford this. I would quite have liked to have them sell the main house and retain the 'dower house' where we had spent our honeymoon. But Rob and Margy were quite clear that they did not want to maintain a connection with a Cagnes that was no longer what they remembered as children. An *autoroute* had been constructed at the base of the hill which placed Cagnes on the main tourist route to the Riviera and the Haut de Cagnes would have its character irretrievably altered.

Moreover Rob's younger daughter Sarah had married a French nuclear scientist (who was eventually to become director of atomic research for the whole of France) and he wanted to buy a flat for them in Grenoble. Margy and I were quite happy to look for a *pied à terre* somewhere in France.

So the Cagnes house was sold and Margy found herself with 30,000 francs with which to buy a house in France. The first question was where in France to look for a suitable property, preferably an old building in need of conversion.

We decided to tour the suitable areas in France. We took Clare with us, then 18, as likely to be a good judge of possibilities. We started down the Rhone Valley and were much taken with the landscape of the Ardèche. Unfortunately, when we explored the picturesque villages we found that they were largely occupied by northern Europeans, especially Germans and Scandinavians. This meant that they would be expensive and, moreover we encountered hoardings 'Mort aux colonisateurs' which suggested that incomers might not be very popular.

We were much attracted by the foothills of the Pyrenees but reckoned that they were too far. Eventually we found ourselves in the Dordogne which we already knew very well and decided that this was where we should institute an intensive search. It was obvious that the region of the Dordogne river itself with it dramatic landscape and archaeological and architectural splendours would be too expensive and we therefore concentrated on 'Perigord Vert' the area north of Perigueux which had its own chief attraction in Brantôme. We stayed a night at the Grand Hotel at Nontron and made a preliminary search, which proved fruitless. But we had seen enough to persuade us to make a further intensive search in the following spring.

This we did and a local agent at Nontron told us that there was one possibility which might interest us. An English architect with a French wife had made a living out of restoring old houses and now had two houses for sale. Or rather, he wanted to sell one of these houses on the basis that he and his wife would continue to live in the other. This, the agent admitted, was not what we wanted as we preferred to do the restoration ourselves, but he thought it was worth investigating.

One house was at La Varenne on the River Dronne just outside the village of St Front La Rivière; the other was at La Bucherie about twenty minutes drive away, a village on higher ground surrounded by woodland.

When we saw the house in La Varenne we were immediately captivated. It was in the centre of a terrace and had been a farmhouse with farm buildings on either side. It was the only one of the terrace buildings which had been restored skilfully by Clifford Duke to be close to its 17th-century origins; the others had been modernised. On the first floor was a spacious salon with views over the River Dronne to the local chateau. It had a splendid stone fireplace with a classical overmantle. It was, I think, this room which finally chose the house for us. But a contributory factor was that we immediately took to the Dukes themselves, who it turned out, were greatly esteemed in the neighbourhood and would ensure that we had the goodwill of neighbours. It became clear that Margy and Madame Duke were soul-mates and I particularly enjoyed overhearing their conversation as they bartered for the items that Margy was to take over from her, each anxious not to take undue advantage of the other.

So, after looking for somewhere on a hill with distant views we ended up with a French counterpart to Bridge House, Wootton. We had to endure one disappointment. We were just below the bridge in La Varenne and the bridge was a graceful medieval one which would frame our view as we sat drinking on our terrace. But when we returned the next year the bridge had been modernised and the parapet straightened out so that we were left with only a memory of what it had been. Nevertheless our terrace had a very satisfying view, bounded by the bridge below which the river widens out to be bordered on the one side by a trim house and a small waterfall from an adjacent stream and on the other by a handsome washplace with three columns and a tiled roof, where the village ladies like to do their washing. The whole was given distinction by a stone cross which used to be on the bridge but was now re-sited alongside it. With this view Margy and I would sit and drink *Cremant de Loire* and watch the resident birds, wagtails, redstarts and swallows, while waiting for the scene to be completed by the flight of a kingfisher straight up or down the river.

We were fortunate in that the Dukes were on good terms with their neighbours and commended us to them. They were chiefly members of the Gorre family. The mother of the family, Madame Gorre was a small serene old lady whose contentment in the place was manifest when she remarked to us that it was 'un petit coin de Paradis.' As she grew older she would add to the conversation by saying from time to time 'oh la la'. Her husband, the father of the family, had been the local postman and greatly respected in the neighbourhood. On the house by the bridge with a beautifully tended garden was the eldest daughter, Paulette married to Yves de Nerf; together with their son they ran the local bar in St Front. She was evidently a woman of strong character who was dominant in the family with the result that she and her sister-in-law, Therese, a lively and intelligent woman, never spoke to one another. Therese and Margy became very good friends. She and her husband Marcel had built themselves a house on the other side of St Front.

But inestimably the most precious new acquaintances were Monsieur and Madame Fochetti. Madame Fochetti had been in the habit of acting as a sort of caretaker for the Duke's house and, with Madame Duke's recommendation, was happy to continue in the role. We have always felt that, apart from all the other advantages, our French property was worth while for our getting to know Madame Fochetti. The Fochetti's had come to La Varenne by way of Montignac from the toe of Italy where in pre-war years they had lived in abject poverty. It required intense hard work to stay alive at all especially with three children so François made his way to France to seek work. According to French law at the time it was three years before his wife and children could join him. Eventually he found work in a factory near St Front and she and the children were able to settle with him in what had been a forge in La Varenne. There they had three more children, so that when we met them, they had three Italian and three French children. She and Margy became firm friends from the start, helped by the fact that Margy could understand her better than anyone else in the neighbourhood having been brought up in a part of France where the local patois was a mixture of French and Italian. In spite of being immigrants the Fochettis were greatly respected in the vicinity. Although having to work extremely hard to boost the family finances and to bring up six children Madame Fochetti was never heard to complain and was always ready to help people in need. Margy and I were always amused when we went to pay her and she would raise her arm in a dramatic gesture and insist that she did everything 'de bon coeur'.

A splendid moment in our time at La Varenne occurred when the land opposite became vacant and, to our great delight and surprise, the Fochettis were able to buy it. For landless Italian peasants this was an undreamed of achievement. One of their first actions was to build a log hut in which they celebrated their new-found fortune by a lunch party to which we, along with all the neighbours, were invited. It was impossible not to feel that we were celebrating not only the Fochettis' good fortune, but the generosity of this French neighbourhood in accepting these strangers so unreservedly.

Our French connection was obviously part of Margy's domain, for the obvious reason that she had been brought up in France and still spoke passable French. My own French was only schoolboy French more at home in reading and writing than in speaking which was hampered in any case by my increasing deafness. But there was one circumstance in which my French was serviceable. In our first few years at La Varenne the *curé* at St Front was Père Adair, who, as his name suggests, had some Scottish ancestry and who spoke a little English. He was moreover a scholarly theologian and was glad to find an opportunity to discuss theology. On one occasion my brother-in-law, George Stokes, was staying with us and we invited Père Adair to lunch. I discovered that my theological French was just about up to it, and this along with Père Adair's English was enough for us to communicate reasonably well. Père Adair turned out to be remarkably ecumenical and was anxious to involve George Stokes in next Sunday's Mass at St Pardoux, which he did by inviting him to read the Epistle from the Authorised Version, to be followed by the same passage read by himself in French.

We learnt that his subject of research was the 'Parousia', Christ's second coming, and he kindly gave me a copy of his book. Sadly, when Père Adair retired he was replaced by a severely orthodox priest who not surprisingly being extremely busy with seven or eight parishes, did not have time for visiting Anglicans.

A pattern developed over the years: Margy and I would stay at La Varenne for three weeks in the spring and the autumn. Other members of the family would stay there for a week or more during the summer and we let the house to friends and friends of friends for a week or so at a time. We did not do it commercially, because the house, though attractive, did not meet the standards laid down for '*gites*.' We charged a nominal sum for water and electricity. We kept a blue exercise book in which people, ourselves included, were invited to leave a record of their stays. In this book we left information about walks and local places to visit, restaurants and lakes in which to swim and so on. Chiefly recommended was the Grand Hotel Pelisson at Nontron, where we ourselves and our family became well known to the two head waiters, both members of the Pelisson family.

But in the middle week of each three-week period Margy and I would make an excursion to another part of France, typical of which was a journey which we dubbed 'spiritual and spirituous'. We went first to Sancerre and explored the *caves* of the Vacheron family. Margy was delighted when Madame Vacheron asked her '*De quelle region de France venez-vous madame?*' From Sancerre with its splendid position we made our way to Chablis and the enormous cooperative '*la Chablisienne*'. From there, laden with Sancerre and Chablis, we went on to Vézelay, where a beautiful Romanesque church is situated on a commanding height from which one can see the Burgundian countryside. Although much restored by Viollet le Duc who probably saved it from total ruin, the transverse arches of the vaulting which extend the entire length of the church give it an air of utter serenity.

From there, with the spiritual side of our journey still in the ascendancy, we made our way to Autun, where the Roman influence upon Romanesque is more evident than elsewhere and the only place where the name of a superb medieval sculptor is known. On the imposing tympanum is the inscription '*Gislebertus hoc fecit*'. We had been to Autun before but had been prevented from examining the capitals by an earlier German party who made a slow and thorough progress through the church. This time we were determined to study them closely with the aid of an authoritative guide we had purchased. As we were concentrating intensely on this, two men came into the church, one of whom broke off and came over to us and said 'I see you have the first English edition of this work. I am one of the authors; can I sign it for you?' So we now have this reminder of Autun along with four reproductions of the best capitals which adorn our curving staircase at home. After Vézelay and Autun it was time to renew the spirituous element in our journey and we visited the giant cooperative '*de Lugny*', where their Montagny was an excellent buy.

Another particularly memorable excursion was to my niece and god-daughter's house in Orange where her husband Jean-Pierre

Pervès was director of the nuclear power station of Pierelatte. She introduced us to a Jesuit friend who made demands upon my theological French, and also to the newly appointed winemaker of a leading chateau in Chateauneuf du Pape. On the way to Orange we visited Albi with its museum of Toulouse Lautrec and stayed in a delightful hotel at Najac with its dramatic ruined castle at the bottom of a precipitous street. While in the neighbourhood we called in at the winery Jean Cros, whose manager was an Englishman, and bought some of their Gaillac Perlé which in its first year or so is attractively pétillant. Subsequently we used to be able to get it at a small supermarket in Brantôme where the proprietor's wife came from Gaillac, but for some reason the supply recently dried up.

Other younger members of the family swam in nearby lakes and canoed in the river and made use of the sports facilities in Nontron. They also paid regular visits to the Grand Hotel where the whole family became well known.

One remarkable and very welcome development in later years was that Kate and Stuart and their friends Ken and Anthea Wilkins constituted themselves a 'working party' and would spend a week doing any repairs or alterations they deemed necessary. As the only one with even a smattering of French, Kate was responsible for obtaining tools and materials. In this she was greatly assisted by the neighbours who admired their efforts and enjoyed their progress. Kate, a lively and attractive woman who looks half her age, had always been a born communicator and had no difficulty in indicating what she wanted or in getting it.

Thus, as we grew older, Margy and I were relieved of the burden of ensuring that our overseas property was kept in good repair.

We all of us on our visits would eat at the Grand Hotel and found ourselves welcomed by the two headwaiters, both of whom were sons of the proprietor Madame Pelisson. It was only on my ninetieth birthday party that we discovered that a third son was the chef.

It is always a special experience to dine in a French restaurant and we have often wondered why, although British cooking has improved, this is so. Our tentative explanation of this is that eating in a French restaurant is an established social ritual, of which those who serve the meal and those who consume it are jointly partaking. So to be a head waiter in a French restaurant is to occupy a respected situation in society and it is not necessary, as in Britain, to recruit immigrants. By arranging to have our joint birthday celebration in a French hotel, we knew that the occasion would be organised for our enjoyment, but with due solemnity. This was an entirely suitable culmination of my first ninety years.

Index